UNHOMELY WESTS

GENERAL EDITOR

William R. Handley
University of Southern California

SERIES EDITORS

José Aranda
Rice University

Melody Graulich
Utah State University

Thomas King
University of Guelph

Rachel Lee
University of California, Los Angeles

Nathaniel Lewis
Saint Michael's College

Stephen Tatum
University of Utah

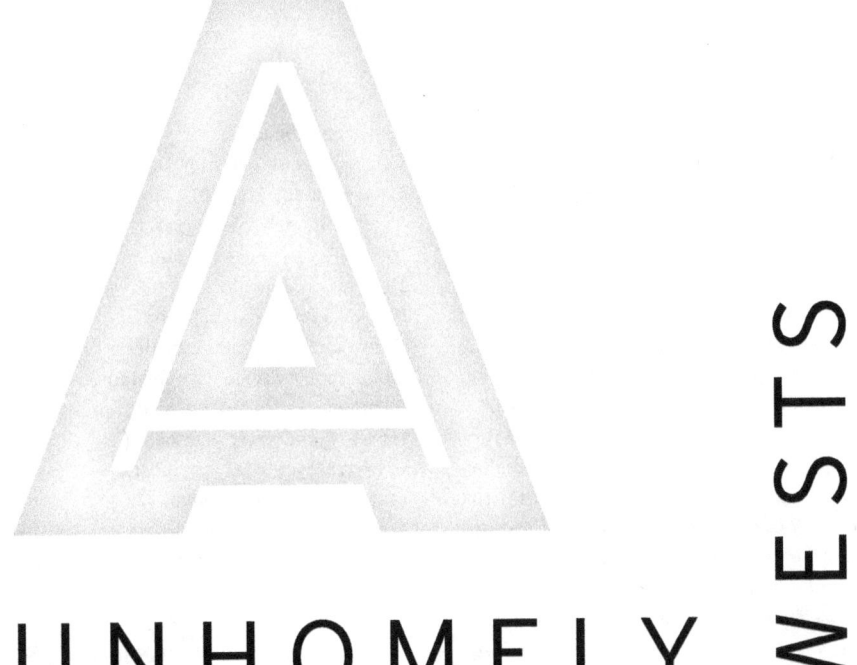

UNHOMELY WESTS

ESSAYS FROM A TO Z

STEPHEN TATUM

UNIVERSITY OF NEBRASKA PRESS   LINCOLN

© 2024 by Stephen Tatum

The essay for the letter **G** represents a revised version of "Cryptonymy, Revenants, and *All the Pretty Horses*" in *Beyond Borders: Cormac McCarthy's All the Pretty Horses*, edited by Rick Wallach (Miami: Cormac McCarthy Society, 2014), 274–97. The essay for the letter **V** is a revised version of "Melancholy Soundtracks of Vagabondage: Four Riffs" in *Under the Western Sky: Essays on the Fiction and Music of Willy Vlautin*, edited by Neil Campbell (Reno: University of Nevada Press, 2018), 60–83. Portions of the essays for the letters **J**, **R**, **U**, and **V** first appeared as "Urban New Wests" in *A History of Western American Literature*, edited by Susan Kollin (New York: Cambridge University Press, 2015), 345–61. The essays for the letters, **D**, **E**, **H**, **I**, **K**, and **S** represent revised and expanded versions of individual sections of Stephen Tatum's "Unhomely Wests: Meditations in Critical Archaeology" in *Western American Literature* 53 (Spring 2018): 31–44.

All rights reserved

The University of Nebraska Press is part of a land-grant institution with campuses and programs on the past, present, and future homelands of the Pawnee, Ponca, Otoe-Missouria, Omaha, Dakota, Lakota, Kaw, Cheyenne, and Arapaho Peoples, as well as those of the relocated Ho-Chunk, Sac and Fox, and Iowa Peoples.

Library of Congress Cataloging-in-Publication Data
Names: Tatum, Stephen, 1949– author.
Title: Unhomely Wests: essays from A to Z / Stephen Tatum.
Description: Lincoln: University of Nebraska Press, [2024] | Series: Postwestern horizons | Includes bibliographical references and index.
Identifiers: LCCN 2023034994
ISBN 9781496237187 (hardback)
ISBN 9781496238924 (paperback)
ISBN 9781496239334 (epub)
ISBN 9781496239341 (pdf)
Subjects: LCSH: West (U.S.)—In literature. | BISAC: LITERARY CRITICISM / American / Regional
Classification: LCC PS169.W4 T38 2024 | DDC 810.9/3278—dc23/eng/20240226
LC record available at https://lccn.loc.gov/2023034994

Set and designed in Minion by N. Putens.

For Kathy

Heimlich, adj.: 1. Also heimelich, heimelig, belonging to the house, not strange, familiar, tame, intimate, comfort-able, homely, etc. . . . Unheimlich, uneasy, eerie, bloodcurdling; "Seeming almost unheimlich and 'ghostly' to him." . . . "'Unheimlich' is the name for everything that ought to have remained . . . hidden and secret and has become visible," Schelling. [Throughout this paper "uncanny" is used as the English translation of "*unheimlich*," literally **"unhomely."**—Trans.]
  —SIGMUND FREUD, "The Uncanny" (1919)

Home: Women-headed households, serial monogamy, flight of men, old women alone, technology of domestic work, paid homework, reemergence of home sweat shops, home-based businesses and telecommuting, electronic cottage, urban homelessness, migration, module architecture, reinforced (simulated) nuclear family, intense domestic violence.
  —DONNA HARAWAY, "A Cyborg Manifesto" (1984)

"Safe as houses" is something closer to "the house always wins." Instead of a shared structure providing shelter, it means that the person in charge is secure; everyone else should be afraid.
  —CARMEN MARIA MACHADO, *In the Dream House* (2020)

Contents

List of Illustrations xi
Acknowledgments xiii
About this book xv

AN ALPHABET OF UNHOMELY WESTS

Alphabet/Abecedario,
    una ofrenda 1
Boredoms, generational
    and otherwise 20
Cryptography, or the architectonics
    of the crypt 34
Diapers and loading docks 48
Exposure, a poetics of 58
Freeways and highways, a
    literary collision 67
Graves and gravestones 85
Hotel life 93
Idyll of the idle 100
Junkspaces, outtakes from an
    unhomely archive 108
Kotex, Keds, ketchup, and
    dead kids 119
Lipstick traces 126
Motel noir 137

Noir motel 149
Oil rich, core samples from a
    personal ledger 161
Psychometropolis 190
Queues for the gallows, sing the
    praises of the hallowed 198
Rivers, all my tears like
    water flown 209
Scene of the crime 215
Television, the slow parade
    of fears 222
Urbicide, what the master
    plan was 232
Vagabondage, all this venturing
    in the slipstream 243
Windows 249
X-ray, let us talk crossly now 260
Yellow ribbons, yellow light 273
Zombieland 289

Notes 299
Bibliography 319
Index 331

Illustrations

1. Alice Leora Briggs, "A," from *Abecedario de Juárez*, 2010 **3**
2. Alice Leora Briggs, *Narcoinsurgencia*, 2010 **8**
3. Wenceslaus Hollar, *The Knight and Death*, from the *Dance of Death*, 1651 **10**
4. Alice Leora Briggs, *Musica (Julián Cardona)*, 2018 **13**
5. José Guadalupe Posada, *This Is About Don Quixote*, after 1891 **14**
6. Edward Hopper, *Western Motel*, 1957 **139**
7. Susie Vargas (Janet Leigh) at the Mirador Motel in *Touch of Evil*, 1958 **151**
8. Lee Robert Tatum in San Antonio, Texas, 1945 **189**
9. Alice Leora Briggs, *Pietà*, 2007 **200**
10. Anthony van Dyck, *The Lamentation over the Dead Christ*, ca. 1635 **203**
11. Man Ray, *Untitled Rayograph (Gun with Alphabet Stencils)*, 1924 **261**

Acknowledgments

First of all, I am grateful to Susan Kollin, Sylvan Goldberg, and Stephen Ruffus for their careful reading of this entire manuscript from *A* to *Z* and for their insightful critiques and suggestions for potential revisions as I prepared the final manuscript version for publication. Individual essays benefited from the collegial support and stimulating comments offered by Brett Clark, Neil Campbell, Audrey Goodman, William Handley, Forrest Robinson, Barry Weller, Krista Comer, Robert King, Nathaniel Lewis, Billy Stratton, Craig Dworkin, and Andrew Hoffmann. Special thanks to Krista Comer and José Aranda for their suggestion that I consider expanding an initial short article experiment centering on literary sketches of unhomely Wests into a set of essays that would further explore this topic and be arranged in alphabetical order from *A* to *Z*. Clark Whitehorn, my editor extraordinaire at the University of Nebraska Press, has offered companionable support from the outset of this book project and has exemplified the mind and spirit of discernment.

Financial support for this book was provided by the Department of English at the University of Utah, chaired by Scott Black. For their permission to reprint and to supply high-resolution digital images of Alice Leora Briggs's artwork, I especially thank Alice Leora Briggs and Peter S. Briggs. I also acknowledge the assistance in acquiring other images that appear in this book provided by staff members at the Art Institute of Chicago; the Yale University Art Gallery; the J. Paul Getty Museum; and the Royal Museum of Fine Arts in Antwerp, Belgium. Special thanks also to musician and novelist Willy Vlautin for permission to reproduce lyrics from his songbook for the essay in this book titled "Vagabondage."

This book is dedicated to Kathryn Kingdon Tatum—as the song goes, "You're as good as good can be."

About this book

EXTRACTS

8. Item: Something is uncanny, that is how it begins. Investigative uncovering is indeed only one aspect, aimed at the origin. Investigative edification is the other, aimed at the destination. There, the finding of something that has been, here, the creation of something new, this tense often no less labyrinthine process.
—Ernst Bloch, from "A Philosophical View of the Detective Novel" (1963)

This is my job: to report from the scene of an undead past colliding with a still-to-be-determined future.
—Billy-Ray Belcourt, *A History of My Brief Body* (2020)

How ought such a natural history of destruction to begin?
—W. G. Sebald, *On the Natural History of Destruction* (2004)

1. "Something is uncanny, that is how it begins." The twenty-six essays arranged in alphabetical order that comprise *Unhomely Wests* explore both the aesthetic forms and the contents of selected literary, visual art, cinematic, and musical representations of homelessness in the late modern and postmodern American West produced since the post-World War II era. In its dialectical interplay with the signifiers "home" and "homesteading" familiar to us from the mythic iconography and history of settler colonialism, homelessness here will be equated, on one level, with the literal condition of "houselessness," a grounded example of which we witness at the outset of Héctor Tobar's novel *The Tattooed Soldier* (1998) when one of its two main characters, a Guatemalan refugee named Antonio Bernal, is evicted along with his Mexican roommate from the apartment they shared in Los Angeles (see the "**I**dyll of the idle" essay). But in another direction, my critical exploration of various textual representations of homelessness in this book, to borrow phrasing from Homi

Bhabha writing in another context, will have "less to do with forcible eviction and more to do with the uncanny literary and social effects of enforced social accommodation, or historical migrations and cultural relocations."[1]

Thus my concern here will go beyond bearing witness to homelessness as a theme and trope deployed in my selected texts to represent existential and affective modes of being in the world by individual human subjects. As Bhabha's remarks suggest, any critical exploration of literary and cultural representations also needs to be situated in relation to "the rhythms of capitalist economic and cultural development," especially those rhythms associated with a globalizing economic and cultural world system that, to compile a short list, has accelerated uneven economic development across spatial scales; introduced new territorial divisions of labor; and continuously triggered both the spatial displacement of humans and the dispossession of nonhuman inhabitants from local places and sociocultural traditions.[2] More specifically, Bhabha also urges that any critical exploration of textual representations centering on the serial "historical migrations" and "cultural relocations" associated with capitalist development needs to focus, as *Unhomely Wests* will do, on the production of "uncanny literary and social effects" in such representations.

Now I begin these prefatory remarks to *Unhomely Wests* with this particular Bhabha quotation because it introduces in shorthand fashion one of this book's major themes and leitmotifs (the uncanny) and provides a transition into one of this book's origin stories. Not so long ago, during the research and writing phase conducted with my co-author Nathaniel Lewis for the manuscript that eventually became the book *Morta Las Vegas* (2017), I discovered the above extract from an essay on the philosophy of the detective novel written by Ernst Bloch, the German philosopher whose massive three-volume study of utopian thought, *The Principle of Hope* (1938–47), had influenced my earlier critical cultural studies of everyday life and popular culture. My interest then was (and still remains) in "the uncanny," a concept theorized by Freud in 1919, in the immediate wake of World War I, and elaborated by others since then, including Bloch, whose 1960 essay on the detective novel was influential in shaping one of our book's chapters, "The Problem of the [Uncanny] West."

In any event, the first epigraph to this book references the opening moment of Freud's classic essay on the uncanny that begins with his consideration of the etymological history of the German words *heimlich* (homely) and *unheimlich* (unhomely). Interestingly, he discovered how, over time, the connotations attached to unheimlich became synonymous with rather than opposed to the meaning of heimlich. Under certain conditions, such as a traumatic event in one's living present that triggers the return to consciousness of a repressed memory of past individual or collective historical trauma, the existential condition or physical place heretofore regarded as home or being at home in the world (with its connotations of the domestic, the familiar, the legible, the secure) suddenly becomes an unheimlich or unhomely state (with its connotations of the alien or foreign or strange; the opaque or illegible; the indeterminate and insecure). Symptomizing this transformation of the homely into the unhomely in the wake of an individual or collective trauma (or the remembrance of it) is the feeling or belief that both time and space seem out of joint—the living present moment now saturated by the spectral traces of a heretofore repressed past trauma. For the human subject, then, such an unhomely interruption of domestic everyday life's routines is both strange and estranging: everyday life seems to be severed between a before (what Bloch calls the homely "what has been") and an aftermath, which is to say the now unhomely living present defined by cognitive and affective disorientation if not also corporeal dispossession (for example: catatonia; vertigo).

Like Freud, Bloch regarded the uncanny on one level as a class of morbid anxiety, that unsettling feeling of not being centered or at home in the world resulting either from one's mental ideation and preoccupation with death or from a close physical proximity to the dead. And also, like Freud, Bloch deployed the architectural metaphor of "the home" in describing the onset of the uncanny mode as analogous to what, in the example of detective or crime fiction, we could identify as a home invasion, where a transgressive act—say a theft or murder or accidental death—blurs both the spatial and psychological boundaries demarcating insides and outsides, thus giving rise to the symptomology I note above. What mostly piqued my interest in Bloch's perspective, however, was his emphasis on how that uncanny "something" that constitutes the "it" that inaugurates the detective novel's plot actually has two referents and hence two origins. One of course is the traumatic event or crime occurring in the living present that sets in motion what Bloch calls the "tense, labyrinthine process" of investigative analysis. The second "how it begins" is the prior and heretofore unknown or forgotten traumatic event, the spectral traces of which have seeped into and shaped the living present, making it look and feel like it constitutes a harrowing double or uncanny repetition of some past (and often intergenerational family or national) trauma. In so-called traditional examples of the detective genre, the investigator's procedural methodology at some point shifts from an exemplary mode (the interviews and the collection of physical evidence) into an explanatory mode of interpretation that resolves enigmas and answers questions. So it is that an emergent, disruptive homely-becoming-unhomely plot—the word *plot* simultaneously connoting real estate and property, criminal planning, and narrative logic—in the end arrives at its restorative unhomely-becoming-homely destination, which Bloch identifies as the detective novel's "edification."

For those perhaps unfamiliar with theorizing about the uncanny, I offer this brief primer. And with these prefatory remarks I also want to underscore here how, in Bloch's developed model of the uncanny, the irruptive return and repetition in the present moment of either repressed or unacknowledged personal and collective historical trauma (genocide, for example) essentially repeats some pivotal, original misdeed from the recent or remote past—thus confirming how our world remains, at bottom, founded on disorder and disarray and destruction. In Bloch's consideration of investigative analysis as it plays out in crime stories, any hard-won achievement of law and order, much less of justice, represents a rather abnormal condition in the overall scheme of things rather than a return to any so-called normal state of affairs. So whether regarded as a phenomenological principle, as an unsettling structure of feeling, as a morbid anxiety, or as a narrative form invested in the leitmotif of the doppelganger figure and a narrative logic defined by copious repetitions and returns, in Bloch's elaboration of the uncanny/unhomely dyad, what's at stake—as Colin Harper observes—is that "we are like foundlings lost in the world, suffering from homesickness without knowing where home is."[3]

Homesickness, this word that literally reproduces the etymology for the word *nostalgia* (the Greek *nostos* [home] + *algia* [sickness]). This word connoting that perennial human desire to recover an imagined lost home, one either to be found, say, on the open range or surrounded by cottonwood trees and beside a graceful bend in a river. This same word also reflecting that perennial human desire to recover certain past moments always regarded, while under the spell of homesickness, as constituting a moment of plenitude in relation to one's fallen present moment marked by lack or scarcity and insecurity. "Without knowing where home is": Harper's concluding phrase here gestures toward the exact nature of our "suffering." That regardless of whether by "home" we mean a locatable, physical dwelling place of security or that feeling of being at home in the dwelling place afforded by our minds and bodies, all of us "lost foundlings" are fundamentally unedified about where and what a *true* home might be and feel like. And without such knowledge, let alone experience of true dwelling, how then would we be able to recognize any so-called true home even if, by chance or accident or good fortune, we found it during our life's journey? As the song goes, one doesn't realize what is lost (or what has been found) until it's already gone. Our lived experience always is mediated by our language and tools, by our desires and fears and anxieties—and by our memories, some of them undeniably traumatic. The somewhat melancholy fact, then, is that the uncanny "something" inaugurating any investigative procedure just might underscore how "edification" not only connotes the "creation of something new" (like, say, the detective's explanatory narrative attempting to provide closure). Rather, the meaning of true edification in this context perhaps instead refers to the need for a radical acceptance of our "foundling" status in this world. "Foundling" here meaning not so much a state of birth, but rather how, as Bloch's theory of the uncanny states the matter, our life's sentence is never to be fully present or at one with either this "something" or this moment of presence we desire to grasp and hold—or this person we desire to know but who eludes us from the beginning as well as at the end of the day or a life.

To summarize to this point: An emergent uncanny structure of feeling exposes how our lived present is saturated with history's apparitional revenants, their disruptive presence choreographing our everyday life existence as a being pinioned betwixt and between a perceived then and the now, as well as between the now (which includes the haunting residue of intergenerational trauma) and what is to come. As I will elaborate more fully in the following essays, the various creative artists whose texts I investigate here "uncover," to use Bloch's word, the look and feel of various modes of homelessness, in the process discovering how expressions of the hoary utopian desire for true dwelling in the world are fated to be inchoate at best; to be glimpsed at a remove or tangent; and to be inexorably twinned with all that is unhomely and estranging in our everyday lives, the ragged appearance of which is shaped by all the decisions being made about local places and regions by the invisible faces of multinational corporate power—the fabled *they* who operate in distant places. Or, as Luis Alberto Urrea ironically remarks toward the end of one chapter in his *By the Lake of Sleeping Children*, "Jump in—you own it: it's Lake Nafta" (see the "Kotex, Keds, ketchup, and dead kids" essay).[4] To paraphrase another old song lyric, that's always the way it goes, as everybody knows.

2. "There, the finding of something that has been." Homesickness, homelessness, the homely becoming unhomely dyad—such words and phrases depicting affective and material changes in the status of an alienated human subject allude to a metaphysical or transcendental homelessness.[5] Furthermore, such symptoms of the "something that has been" transforming the domestic home and neighborhood, the local town and city, and the nation into unhomely dwelling places need to be regarded as both a collective as well as an individual, a systemic as well as a singular, and a specifically historical as well as a transcendental occurrence. In the history of the U.S. West, the social, economic, and political problems posed by the specter of homeless threats to the domestic family and national order began after the Civil War with the tramp and hobo crisis, then intensified during the 1890s and later during the Great Depression as a result of periodic economic recessions that produced, especially in the agricultural sector of the wageworker's frontier, seasonal migrations of laborers in search of work. And closer to our own contemporary era, since the 1980s, a new round of homeless crises emerged, primarily spurred by two developments. One factor was the reductions in state and federal expenditures on the social welfare safety net as well as the disciplining of labor unions by political policies and corporate practices. A second factor centered on how an emergent, global finance capitalism fostered investments that promoted, at least in the Global North, selective deindustrialization (rather than upgrades in the manufacturing infrastructure), technological innovation (communication technologies, transportation logistics, and robotics), and selected projects of downtown urban renewal (new corporate offices and campuses for the advertising and marketing, banking,

and legal sectors; new architectural projects to stimulate tourism and entertainment zones; and neighborhood gentrification projects that typically lead to the loss of affordable housing units).

Certainly, the selfsame boom and bust rhythm of industrial and postindustrial capitalist development throughout the twentieth century led the late historian Mike Davis to observe, "where technology has achieved an apparent victory over the limits of nature ... the coefficient of known and, more significantly, unknown danger has increased proportionately." In short, the more things are networked, the greater the risk and impact of systemic breakdowns of such entities, for example, as transportation and electric power grids. As Davis also concludes about the new urban ecologies of the U.S. West, the century-long quest "for the bourgeois utopia of a totally calculable and safe environment has paradoxically generated radical insecurity (unheimlich)."[6] In concert with the phrase "century-long quest," the parenthetical insertion of "unheimlich" after the phrase "radical insecurity" underscores his general point that a chronic affective unhomeliness (fear, anxiety, dread, uncertainty, boredom, loss of faith in the social contract) constitutes a specific consequence of the modernizing process underway throughout the twentieth century. As his 2002 book *Dead Cities* discusses at length, the emergence of a "radical insecurity" can be traced specifically to the anxieties devolving from an abiding fear of ecological apocalypse, a fear of domestic and international terrorism, a fear of global pandemics, and a fear regarding the potential systemic collapse of our agricultural and industrial supply chains. So it is that the more things change, the more they remain the same.

On this point architectural theorist and historian Anthony Vidler would agree. For as he explains in his book *The Architectural Uncanny*, during the early years of modernity, the unheimlich ironically realized its imagistic "home" not only in the architectures of Victorian–era cities and, later, post–World War suburbanization and urbicide but also in the human psyche, as we witness through such psychological diagnostic labels as malaise, ennui, and alienation. Vidler explores the unheimlich/unhomely dyad through various spatial frames of reference that reveal the evidence of both a continuous "radical insecurity" throughout the twentieth century and also the advent of what he calls "pathological" and "paranoiac" or "panic" spaces. Thus on the scale of the individual body: the uncanny imaged as an invasion of one's body through viral contagion and of one's mind by unsettling morbid visions or an inability to distinguish dreams from real life, as if one were sleepwalking in a hypnagogic state. On the scale of the domestic interior: the uncanny imaged through both the trope of home invasion and imagery of traumatic pasts hidden in architectural forms of nested or receptacle crypt-like rooms and furnishings. On the scale of the urban: the uncanny imaged as a downtown urban "center" occupied by various Others from the margins (the homeless, refugees, immigrant service economy workers, parolees in halfway houses), their presence often juxtaposed to the new urban skyline of high-rise architectural structures and the newly branded museum district and entertainment zones. On the scale of the nation-state: the uncanny imaged through dominant class and caste fears and anxieties about domestic or foreign-based terrorist acts or by domestic borders transgressed by "alien" immigrants.[7]

As other cultural geographers and urban theorists also have observed, the restructuring of the economic, sociocultural, and political landscapes by multinational corporate capitalism is primarily driven by the hypermobility of forms of electronic or virtual capital untethered by geopolitical boundaries. This development intensifies uneven regional economic development both above and below the national scale (for example, the gap between the Global North and South; the gap between local or regional high-tech, "wired" economies and those dependent on extractive industries). And it also spawns new spatial or territorial divisions of labor and labor markets. Consider the economic restructuring of the regional landscape, for example, in the spatial divide between, on the one hand, suburban and edge city research campuses or parks where highly educated workers perform computer, biotech, and medical research and development and, on the other hand, the so-called surplus labor who staff minimum-wage service economy jobs in downtown hotels with conference centers, in corporate banking and investment and insurance offices, and in newly branded tourist entertainment and museum districts.[8] In an increasingly postindustrial economic environment in the United States dominated by continuous global flows of capital, voluntary and forced human migrations, technological innovation, and mass culture imagery, the rhythms of capitalist economic and cultural development (and, I hasten to add, culture wars) also produce, to refer again to the Homi Bhabha quote in the first paragraph of this preface, "uncanny literary and social effects." Such uncanny effects are especially evident in representations of the ways in which embodied laboring populations are voluntarily and involuntarily brought into the lower-class sectors and urban spaces of relatively wealthy societies.

Let me ground these observations by referring once again to Héctor Tobar's novel *The Tattooed Soldier*. I am thinking here about a scene in which the Guatemalan refugee Antonio Bernal returns on foot to the homeless encampment on Crown Hill in downtown Los Angeles after he had visited a soup kitchen. And on this particular return journey to Crown Hill, he recalls an early moment at the beginning of his exile in Los Angeles when he comes across a group of native Guatemalan women standing on a street corner downtown, not that far from the vacant lot on Crown Hill where the homeless encampment was located:

> They were wearing their traditional dress, embroidered huipiles and long rainbow-striped skirts. He watched them, these ancient people of the corn, as they walked through a canyon of brick tenements, their leather sandals scraping along the oil-stained sidewalk on Bixel Street. What were they doing here, in this place where not a single stalk of corn could grow? It saddened him to find so many of his countrymen transported, as if by some dark magic, to this freeway-covered plain, wandering about Los Angeles in an amnesiac daze, far from even the memory of the soil.[9]

"What were they doing here? . . . As if by some dark magic": The primary themes emerging at the center of this recognition scene center both on the existential reality of homelessness and deracination and, more specifically, on Antonio's cognitive and affective disorientation—this status manifested by the his jarring juxtapositions (ancient and modern, agricultural and urban) and his speculative turn, as the passage exhausts itself, both to the interrogative mode and the "as if" conditional mood while he strains to process what he sees before his eyes. With regard to the question he considers regarding just how these Guatemalan women ended up in Los Angeles, Antonio does not provide a definitive answer per se. Rather, their uncanny appearance in this place at this time makes everything immediately strange and estranging. So he responds to his own query first by projecting onto these women in traditional dress his own cognitive and affective displacement (their "amnesiac daze"). Secondly, his response mystifies one rational explanation about how these "ancient children of the corn" end up in this city by conjuring up a metaphor keyed to occult forces ("dark magic"). In this scene, as well as elsewhere in *The Tattooed Soldier* as its plot unfolds, we are solicited to recognize instead how both Antonio's local experiencing of homelessness and these women having experienced deracination are enmeshed within not just one but several all-pervasive crises "in which geopolitics; capitalism; climate change; and racial, ethnic, and religious divides interlock, each amplifying and accelerating the other."[10]

These are the major concerns or issues I address in the critical essays that comprise this alphabet of *Unhomely Wests*, essays that strive, as Rob Nixon defines the critical task in his *Slow Violence: Environmentalism and the Poor*, to attend "to 'the close living substance' of the local while simultaneously tracing the 'occluded relationships'—the vast transnational economic pressures, the labor and commodity dynamics—that invisibly shape the local."[11] Essays that aim both to explore both the major themes forwarded by certain literary or cinematic or visual artworks, and also, through a close reading of the granular details evident in various textual moments and sequences, how a given text produces uncanny atmospheric affects and implicitly or explicitly addresses the "occluded relationships" shaping both the external world and the world of the text. Essays that also desire to create—through their own periodic vagrancy or aleatory wandering through textual built environments—a surplus of meaning, an undigested remainder whose presence just might unsettle preconceived perspectives and trouble certain formulaic pieties pronounced by latter-day representatives still wedded to the prevailing coloniality of power. A remainder or excess of meaning that just might contest "the silence, that reserve, that instinctive looking away," that human propensity "to forget what they do not want to know, to overlook what is before their eyes."[12] And finally, a residue of meaning informed by my desire, to cite a Charles Bowden observation from his 2010 book *Dreamland: The Way Out of Juárez*, to articulate "the feel of the past, of dust and ruin and dead dreams" created by the interlocking and accelerating crises associated with homelessness and poverty, the continuous migration of refugees to the U.S.–Mexico border, and the reality of global warming.[13]

3. "Here, the creation of something new." A more immediate origin of this book's present form can be found in my article "Unhomely Wests: Meditations in Critical Archaeology," published in a 2018 number of *Western American*

Literature. This critical essay continued my critical explorations of literary and cultural productions of unheimlich/uncanny American Wests, and it turned out to be an experiment with the conventional academic critical essay form. Each of the essay's eight sections was introduced by a heading composed of a single word whose first letter was capitalized and set in bold font (for example, **O**bjects) and by a few numbered prefatory notes that ordinarily would have been placed in a standard endnote format at the end of the essay. By the time the reader reached the essay's final section, the capitalized first letter in bold font for each of the article's eight sections, when assembled in the order of their presentation from start to finish, spelled out the word "HOMELESS." In addition, this journal article did not offer a conventional argument with a single covering thesis but rather articulated a set of eight critical sketches, each one discretely focused on briefly exploring a literary textual moment exemplifying the title word of the heading (for example, Labor) framing the section. This heaping together of textual fragments loosely cohered, then, because of the armature provided by the section headings' keyword and by each of this article's sections focus on the production of uncanny literary effects.

Articulated, as in "to connect," and armature, as in "framework" or "scaffold": my diction here is purposeful, aiming to underscore two points. First, how the form of this relatively short four-thousand-word article provided the anatomical template for its eventual transformation into this book, *Unhomely Wests*, that has expanded this article's initial set of eight critical sketches into twenty-six essays, one for each letter in the English alphabet and articulated by their shared focus on selected representations of homelessness as a theme, a trope, an affliction, a threat, and a condition of disaffiliation. Second, how all the essays comprising this book's content would explore both uncanny textual architectures and aesthetics (whether on the level of the word, sentence, paragraph, singular sequence, chapter, or completed narrative) and uncanny textual representations of natural and built environments. Such as: residential rooms, homes, and apartments; a cartel "death house"; hotels and motels and commercial spaces of consumption; freeways and highways; crime scenes and morgues; cemetery graves and crypts; a concentration camp; industrial junkspaces, including landfills and loading docks and toxic lakes; roadside architectures of abandonment and ruin; homeless encampments; silent, brooding mesas and howling hot winds and fallow fields of stubble on fire.

As for the armature or framework of the twenty-six critical essays, each of them follow the same tripartite structure: an introductory section titled "Extracts" that presents a few quoted passages from various literary or theoretical texts; then the longer essay of critique, its content divided into numbered sections introduced by a phrase or clause from one of the extracts; and finally, after each essay's conclusion, a single running line of titles enclosed by brackets appears that refer the reader to other related essays in the book. While a few of the critical essays in this book develop extended critiques by attending to one or more of the prefatory textual extracts, most develop close readings of an unhomely single passage or textual sequence from an altogether different text than those quoted in the "Extracts." In general, then, my aim with each set of prefatory "Extracts" is that they will focus the reader's attention on a theme or image or critical problem suggested by the alphabetic letter's title (for example, "**B**oredom"), and simultaneously that they will offer some historical breadth or range of reference to the specific topic the critical essay that follows explores in more depth. And while the final line of various essay titles included at the end of each critical essay suggests a potential pathway for the reader to navigate their journey through *Unhomely Wests*, I also suppose that the reader will regard the list of titles as suggestive rather than prescriptive. And, hence, that the reader will wander around this alphabetic ordering of essays in errant fashion, exemplifying Roland Barthes's cinematic or theatrical directive to regard any alphabet as a call to disorder as well as order—his imperative for the reader to "*Cut! Resume the story [in still] another way.*"[14]

As for the essays themselves, twenty of them closely attend to selected literary works by various authors of fiction, creative nonfiction, and poetry; three are primarily concerned with visual artwork (sgraffito illustrations by Alice Leora Briggs; an oil painting by Edward Hopper); one examines a film noir text and another discusses the music and lyrics of novelist Willy Vlautin ("**V**agabondage"). One outlier essay presents fragments from a personal memoir ("**O**il rich"). Two of the essays in the following pages form a diptych: "Motel noir," which focuses on Edward Hopper's 1957 painting *Western Motel*, and "Noir motel," which focuses on director and screenplay writer Orson Welles's 1958 film *Touch of Evil*. Two other essays, "Lipstick traces" and "Junkspace," depart from the usual tripartite structure of the rest of the essays, the latter one posing as an incomplete, disorganized archive whose implicit aim is to work through, around, and against the knowledge production of a traditionally sanctioned archive.[15] As does the "Freeways and highways" essay, which is comprised of seventy-nine quoted passages drawn from over forty books, these numbered textual excerpts from various writers grouped into different sections with different title headings and then arranged in alphabetical sequence from A (**Audio**) to Z (**Zero degree writing**).

So on one level this literary montage of quoted passages represents an uncanny, miniaturized double of the larger alphabet of essays that constitutes this book. Considered as individual components of a larger, unhomely transportation ecology, these quoted extracts, on another level, are intended to function as historical commentary, as theoretical interpretation or judgment, as shimmering prose descriptions, and even as short fictional vignettes. In any event, this literary collision of textual fragments in the "Freeways and highways" essay, aims to foster—as does the tradition of the cento poem composed of verses from one or more writers—a different sensibility. One where the predominant language of critique cedes space to the affective atmosphere and tonality of past lifeworlds, this primarily revealed by the uncanny repetitions and rhythmic returns of words and phrases in each of the twenty-six groupings of quoted passages. The resulting soundscapes thicken language, underscoring its haptic presence as the typically melancholy recognitions in each section's entries unfold.[16]

4. "Investigative edification is the other, aimed at the destination." Each of the critical essays gathered here are occasional, free-standing essays, essentially comprising a miscellany rather than a traditional monograph advancing a central proposition. Indeed, in several of the essays the numbered, individual sections themselves can be regarded as standalone critical reflections, even as they also constitute structural components of a larger processual critique, one whose analysis characteristically develops in spiraling fashion by weaving together centripetal and centrifugal energies of critical exploration. However, this miscellaneous heaping together of various textual fragments does demonstrate a level of coherence beyond the simple fact that the essays themselves are arranged in alphabetical order and their content centers on critical explorations of the textual spaces and verbal economies of literary and cultural representations of homelessness in relation to the more general

economy of late capitalism. These essays supplement such gestures toward the potential coherence produced by a "preexisting concept or idea of order, dictating in advance" but also strive to model coherence itself as an emergent process of discovering how textual parts are articulated or made to stick together like a conglomerate, one whose subterranean affinities surface to "challenge existing notions of form and aesthetic order."[17]

In the essays that follow, one challenge to existing notions of logical consistency and systemic connections (such as those provided by transitional statements) can be found through a consideration of what I have come to regard as the dominant combinatory formula or logic utilized by several of the writers and the visual artists discussed in *Unhomely Wests* in order to create the compositionality or formal architectures of their texts. As I discuss, for example, writer Charles Bowden's discursive economy of representation in the "Lipstick traces" and "X-ray" essays, one predominant formula for organizing sentences into paragraphs, as well as chaining together paragraphs to create narrative and descriptive sequences, is this: "one image plus another."[18] This particular way of heaping together textual components or fragments jettisons graduated, incremental transitions and logical consistency in order to promote unsettling swerves from conventional grammar and usage. We witness such swerves, for example, when authors and visual artists become highly invested in assaying such rhetorical figures as, say, catachresis or mixed metaphor and parataxis or startling juxtapositions. Consider how, at the level of the sentence, a preference for a serial grammar and syntax predominates, one whose lengthy compound sentences stack phrases and clauses on top of each other at times in breathless fashion, as if to relay an uncanny vertiginous moment by troubling the conventional distinctions between clauses and sentences and sentences and paragraphs. Or consider, at the level of scenography, prose descriptions that unsettle expectations as a result of two features: contrapuntal spatialities (in the above example drawn from Héctor Tobar's novel, the paratactic syntax juxtaposes a financial district and a homeless encampment; Guatemalan "ancient people of the corn" in downtown Los Angeles) and a conjunctive temporality in which the narrative present is irradiated both by past trauma and haunted by anticipatory anxieties about the future. At the level of structural ideologies and affective structures of feeling, this prevailing "one image plus another" formula, I suggest, promotes a dialectical tension and hence disjunctive frisson rather than dualistic opposition between, say, such categories as the sacred and profane, the native and alien, or the feeling states of ecstasy and paranoia (see, for example, the "**P**sychometropolis" essay).

As we witness in the fictional works not only of Bowden and Tobar but also of Karen Tei Yamashita, Roberto Bolaño, Brett Easton Ellis, and Cormac McCarthy, the prose discourse typically will swerve abruptly between rhetorical modes and linguistic argots, all the while offering narrative speculations about being and becoming, fate and chance, fixity and flux—all this jumpy movement, all this uncanny accretion of repeated imagery and irregular yet rhythmic soundscapes, desiring—as does this errant sentence I am writing here—to reproduce the uncanny fissures in and the unraveling of the often vertiginous flow of experience as various characters prosecute, like detectives, their quests for edification. This seeking both to make a life and to make peace, if at all possible, with their (and our) shared fate, while still alive, to find themselves (and ourselves) to exist as foundlings whose agency is often suspended in topographies and architectures of transition, uncannily marooned betwixt and between what Billy-Ray Belcourt's extract at the outset of this preface calls the arrival of "the undead past and the still-to-be-determined future," necessarily fated to exist in that tense space and that tensed present moment of waiting in the meantime, where all the sadness of life exists.[19]

This gathering of critical essays also loosely coheres because my critical reflections commingle textual examples of the uncanny/unhomely with the leitmotif of spectrality, this materializing in the essays that follow as a theme, a trope, or image, and as a scabrous tonality or atmospheric affect.[20] In the pages that follow, spectrality, this portmanteau term and concept, will emerge both as virtual and material spectral residue or traces: in dreams and memories; in photographs and relics of the dead; in abandoned and ruined architectural structures; in the spectral flows of electronic capital. Spectrality also will emerge in these essays in the form of unrequited specters—as the "undead" revenants, the community of the already dead and gone who yet are symbolically alive, these restless, minatory spirits haunting individual and collective lives in the living present. We shall also encounter in these essays the uncanny literary effect repeated by couplings of the specular (the narrator or character's scanning gaze; the technological gaze of surveillance capitalism) with specularity (images of doubling, such as mirrors and other reflecting surfaces) and speculation, this trope evident both in the interpretive projections made by narrators and characters and, thematically, via textual allusions to late capitalism's transition to a predominantly postindustrial finance economy (insurance and risk; commodity futures markets; real estate development; currency exchanges and cryptocurrency). Finally, in several essays readers will encounter representations centering on the impact of spectralization: how in postmodernity the so-called real has become shrouded by simulations and simulacra and how global banking and investment sectors and stock markets have fostered the dematerialization and reduction of marginalized human subjects to such analytical abstractions as "labor power" or "labor units."

Methodologically speaking, as my parenthetical insertions in the above paragraph suggest, this leitmotif of spectrality is vital for this investigation insofar as its explicit and implicit presence in representations of homelessness provides a path to navigate between, on the one hand, textual and, on the other hand, general economies of production—especially as these are grounded, as Freud does in his 1919 essay on the uncanny, in the architectural trope of the house or home. In any case, all of the above permutations of spectrality I enumerate above bring us full circle to the hauntology inherent in the uncanny/unhomely dyad. Consider in this context Fredric Jameson's claim, for example, that "the ghost story is indeed virtually the architectural genre par excellence, wedded as it is to rooms and buildings ineradicably stained with the memory of gruesome events, material structures in which the past literally weighs like a nightmare on the brains of the living."[21] Moreover, Jameson further defines the ghost story as one characterized by "the barely perceptible agitations in the air of a past abolished socially and collectively, yet still attempting to be reborn."[22] So the key point he introduces is that such "barely perceptible" disturbances in the atmosphere of ghost stories are crucially "wedded" to the material substance of lived spaces—to the specific settings of human history.[23] Such as the ruins of residential and commercial structures, the constantly evolving scenography of roadside architecture, and the proliferation of architectural junkspaces (see the "Junkspaces" and "Urbicide" essays).

"The ghosts are swarming at the moment," Mark Fisher observes, before raising and then answering a question raised by this claim: "Why hauntology now? Well, has there ever been a time when finding gaps in the seamless surface of 'reality' has ever felt more pressing? Excessive presence leaves no traces. Hauntology's absent presence [as in ghosts and revenants of the past], meanwhile, is nothing but traces."[24] For his part, writing about Jacques Derrida's conceptualization of hauntology, Kanien'kehaka (Mohawk) multimedia artist and cultural theorist Jackson 2Bears solicits us to recognize two things: how "there is a distinct difference between a spirit and a specter in that the latter comes back (revenant) with ill wishes and insidious intentions to haunt the living" and how "turning your back on the ghost only produces more specters, or an 'accumulation of ghostly layers.'"[25] Thus what is needed, as 2Bears argues, is "the conjuration and invocation of the specters for which one (or a culture) is possessed or haunted." What is needed, I hasten to add, in order to "speak to the specters" in our new Gilded Age and attempt to exorcise them, is to stay with rather than get past the past, stay with the melancholy rather than complete the mourning process, stay with the accumulated ressentiments so as to expose and bear witness to, rather than ignore or deny or sanitize, a "common spectral adversary, a collective hauntology."[26] In this spirit of critical provocation, then, I offer this critical prose collage of unhomely American Wests arranged in an alphabetic order, one that yet also I hope constitutes a call out to the reader's own vagabond imaginings.

An alphabet of unhomely wests

> The alphabetical order erases everything, banishes every origin.... At certain moments the alphabet calls you to order (to disorder) and says: *Cut! Resume the story another way.*
> —Roland Barthes, *Roland Barthes* (1977)

Alphabet/Abecedario, una ofrenda

EXTRACTS

The alphabetical order erases everything, banishes every origin.... At certain moments the alphabet calls you to order (to disorder) and says: *Cut! Resume the story another way.*
—Roland Barthes, *Roland Barthes* (1977)

Aside from my sister, or maybe Lonnie, I hadn't a clue as to who would be writing me. It was a one-page letter written on a church notepad sheet, and I spent days trying to decipher the cursive writing, tracing words to understand which alphabets they were, figuring slowly by sounds what the sentence was. It was in English but the writing was shaky, which made it even harder to read.
—Jimmy Baca, *A Place to Stand* (2001)

The majority of the names engraved on the mausoleum and on the large marble staffs were those Turtle recognized as street names: Hollenbeck, Lankershim, Van Nuys, Bixby.... Turtle discovered a marble-gated crypt that belonged to Robert E. Ross, who was born in Clarke County, Ohio, on August 15, 1836, and died March 31, 1884, in Los Angeles, California. It looked livable. Slabbed walls, a roof, and a floor that was completely dried. A for *Act like the natives*, accept and adapt. Turtle pushed the rusted old gate in and entered the Ross crypt.
—Helena María Viramontes, *Their Dogs Came with Them* (2007)

And these names I remembered every time I peed out in the open like a wild beast. I remembered their names and imagined they were coming out of me, and I tried to write their initials

in the dust, different ones each time, so I wouldn't ever forget
their names and so that the ground would also remember them.
CC for Chief Cochise
CL for Chief Loco
CN for Chief Nana
S for the priest woman called Saliva
MC for Mangas Coloradas
And a big G for Geronimo.
 —Valeria Luiselli, *Lost Children Archive* (2019)

1. "*Tracing words to understand which alphabets they were.*" Published in early 2022, the *Abecedario de Juárez* represents the collaborative work of photojournalist Julián Cardona and artist Alice Leora Briggs. As its subtitle suggests, this book provides "An Illustrated Lexicon" of slang words and phrases spawned by the femicides and drug cartel violence in Juárez, especially during the 2006–12 years of Mexican president Felipe Calderón's administration.[1] As we see exemplified by the illustration in figure 1 introducing the lexicon's various entries for the letter *A*, each of the alphabet's letters is introduced by one of Briggs's sgraffito illustrations. Within each letter heading or section the various individual entries are themselves arranged in alphabetical order, depending on the first letter of the word or the phrase. An anatomical overview (pun intended) of the entries in the letter *A* section of the lexicon, for example, reveals thirty-four individual entries, beginning with the term *abatir*, "to kill," a euphemism used by the Mexican army, and ending with the term *los azules*, the Spanish word for the color blue repurposed so as to refer to the Mexican federal police who wear blue uniforms. Each of the individual entries is formatted in the same way throughout the lexicon: there is the individual word or phrase itself, followed by its slang meaning; then a brief or lengthy exposition of the term's origin and context followed by its literal meaning; and finally, a list of "Related terms" appears, directing the reader to relevant entries in other sections of the *Abecedario*. And it is by means of the striking contrasts between a slang term's unofficial meaning and its dominant literal meaning that one of the revelatory themes forwarded by the *Abecedario* emerges: how the drug cartel subculture uncannily poaches on and appropriates the familiar rituals of everyday life in Juárez, especially

FIG. 1. Alice Leora Briggs, *A*, from *Abecedario de Juárez*, 2010. Sgraffito drawing on clay panel, 10 in. x 8 in. Courtesy of the artist and Evoke Contemporary, Santa Fe NM. Tia Collection, Santa Fe NM. © All rights reserved.

those associated with cooking and cuisine (for example, carne asada, literally "grilled meat," in this lexicon is a coded phrase meaning to kill, torture, and bury someone who has been kidnapped).

Another distinctive feature of this lexicon's format centers on how Cardona's various longform journalistic narratives about the state of emergency in Juárez—these typically based on named or anonymous persons who either are implicated in or victims of the narcoeconomy—are themselves broken into segments and then dispersed over the course of several different, but related, entries under various alphabet letter headings. As Briggs notes with regard to the *Abecedario* format, this lexicon periodically "explodes into first-hand accounts of extortion, kidnapping, torture and murder, provided by victims, witnesses, perpetrators, and media accounts."[2] So the texture of Cardona's prose discourse in the *Abecedario* is both polyvocal and polytonal, this feature paralleled by Briggs's deployment of intra- and intertextual imagery in her sgraffito illustrations (more on that below). So this "minefield" of slang words and phrases exposes an entire ecosystem produced by the labor and administration of a hegemonic parastatal and transnational criminal economy.

And as Briggs concisely puts the matter in the "Authors' Note," a second major theme forwarded in the *Abecedario* is that in addition to the gangs and cartels, "the Mexican State sponsors much of this crime. When not committed by the State, the government's policy of near impunity condones the crimes of others."[3] Throughout the length of the *Abecedario*, stories chronicled by Cardona keep popping up and fissuring the prevailing *doxa*, shedding light where there has been darkness and exposing more complex and irreducible truths than the official discourse circulated by commercial news outlets and the Mexican state's media apparatus, institutions whose iterative explanations and solutions for the border crisis wittingly and unwittingly sponsor an organized forgetting, one that—like any euphemism or the numbing abstraction promoted by a reliance on statistics—deflects attention from or represses the stark reality of the continuous state of emergency in Juárez and elsewhere in the U.S.-Mexico borderlands.[4] Briggs thus articulates the primary ambition of the *Abecedario* is that of bearing witness: "It's a record of what took place in a particular city during a particular time period. And it is, like it or not, a record of what human beings are capable of. And I think we need to look at this stuff."[5]

2. "*Cut! Resume the story another way.*" Like any archive, a lexicon presented in alphabetic order provides a structure—a syntax, so to speak—for presenting whatever stuff we need to look at in linear fashion from the alphabet's first to its final letter. As Roland Barthes puts the matter, "At certain moments the alphabet calls you to order (disorder)."[6] Both the agency Barthes accords here to the alphabet (it calls) and his recourse to the imperative mood presume that the reader will answer the call and find it acceptable—perhaps even pleasurable—to experience structure and organization amid our often-chaotic everyday life. After all, the promissory note attached to archival or alphabetic records is that historical and social and personal memories can be preserved, their meanings clarified—and hence existing power relationships normalized.

Nevertheless, just like any archive, any alphabet is also inherently contradictory in character. For even as some diachronic or sequential order is established (as in from past to present or from A–Z), the alphabet falsely suggests there might be a place for everything within its physical and conceptual boundaries.[7] As a result, the issue then becomes not merely how an alphabetic ordering of material can preserve historical, social, and personal memories and, at least temporarily, stabilize their meanings. Rather, the crucial issue centers on how an alphabetic ordering of material can appropriate and transform, restrict, and even erase or ignore alternative or oppositional "stuff" from the historical record. And it is precisely this gap between an implicit utopian promise of order and the reality of alternative and continuously accumulating evidence that—as Barthes's parenthetical aside in the above quote discloses—we should also regard any alphabetic call to order as simultaneously a call to disorder. A call that Barthes articulates as an editing demand or a stage direction: "Cut! Resume the story another way."

The other way that the *Abecedario* advances the story about the Calderón administration centers on how its specific format and contents produce a kind rogue archive. Literally, in the sense that its archival record centers on a dynamic subcultural argot that heretofore "has never been and would likely never be contained in traditional memory institutions" (for example, museums, libraries, commercial and corporate archives, state and federal historical societies).[8] And figuratively, a type of rogue archive in the sense that this lexicon's verbal and visual discourses solicit the reader to proceed through the length of the *Abecedario* in an errant or vagabond fashion. Indeed, while the lexicon's alphabetic order obviously (like this alphabet book of essays) maps an itinerary for the reader to follow, both the inclusion of related terms and the dispersal of Cardona's journalistic narratives into fragments throughout the *Abecedario* solicit the reader to cut into, rearrange, and hence performatively produce an alternative text from the material that has been prepared for the reader and contained in a print or digital archive. Take the slang term *los feos*, for example, which refers to the Mexican federal police as "the ugly ones." Since one of the related terms for los feos is *los azules*, a reader could decide to leave the lexicon's entries under the letter *F* and return to the final entry for the letter *A*, *los azules*, a term both alluding to the blue uniforms of the federal police and related to such other terms as La Placa (the badge), *policholos* (a hybrid of police and gangsters), and *la farola* (literally, streetlight; but its slang usage refers to flashing lights atop the cab of police trucks).

Los feos → los azules → La Placa → la farola: this particular nonlinear pathway returns us not only to the last lexicon entry for the letter *A* but also to the Briggs illustration introducing this section of the *Abecedario*. This particular illustration features two local or perhaps federal police officers processing a crime scene, their truck parked behind them and a corpse lying below them on a sidewalk or street. As is the case with forensic criminal investigations, the reader navigating the *Abecedario* discovers a truth or set of truths through a process of disclosure. Truth appears, then, not only as bearing witness but also as *aletheia*, a hermeneutic of emergence or unveiling, a concept directly opposed to the connotation of its etymological Greek root word *lethe*, which binds together the covering up or hiding of something (or of some truth) with the concept of forgetting or forgetfulness. From this perspective, then, the additional question to explore when considering the *Abecedario* as a type of rogue archive centers on "what havens and temporary escapes from the realm of necessity" might be provided through verbal and visual discursive means?[9]

3. "A *for* Act like the natives, *accept and adapt*." The "territory of images" produced by Alice Leora Briggs in the *Abecedario* displays three enmeshed features.[10] First, in her signature sgraffito illustrations there appear various scratches and scrapings of a prepared black surface. Such incisions expose both straight and curved and cross-hatched white lines of varied length and width and breadth. In any given illustration some passages will be notable

for their dense clutter, while others remarkable for their white blank space. Often a noirish chiaroscuro effect gets vividly revealed in her graphic rendering of the drapes and the folds of clothing, the creases and the wrinkles of animal and human flesh, and of banquet tables grotesquely laden with food and drink. Her technique creates a visual rhetoric of layering that, on one level, functions as a counterpoint to the horizontal spread and sprawl of both the lexicon's entries and Cardona's segmented journalistic narratives. Second, her illustrations are aesthetically invested in intertextuality, as we witness in the several illustrations that suture contemporary Juárez scenes with other scenes and motifs drawn from medieval and early modern art history. And third, her visual aesthetic is further distinguished by the recursive presentation of selected images, their repetition and return to the text at periodic intervals in the pages of the *Abecedario* underscoring how this lexicon is all about echoing the continuous, kaleidoscopic transformation of this ephemeral subcultural argot. As the "Authors' Note" soberly reminds us, "As with any attempt to capture slang, our efforts became history before these pages were bound."[11]

With these predominant features of her aesthetic in mind, let us consider as a representative example, the repetition with a variation of the above illustration introducing the lexicon's entries for the letter *A*. This time around, though, the illustration of the two uniformed police or soldiers conducting a forensic investigation of a crime scene accompanies the lexicon's entry for *la limpia*, a term that literally refers to "the cleansing" while its slang meaning alludes to "a series of extrajudicial killings in an area or territory that is reportedly administered by one or more authorities, such as the president of the Republic, state governors, mayors, or police chiefs."[12] And this recursive return of the illustration in the *L* section of the *Abecedario* is juxtaposed with a lengthy narrative based on Julián Cardona's 2010 interview with a retired *sicario*. We learn from this interview that this sicario distinguishes his work as a cartel contract killer from the government-sponsored extrajudicial executions conducted by various paramilitary groups such as the secret Special Operation Forces situated within the Mexican Marines and Army. With this context before us, the atmospheric tonality of this illustration, titled "Narcoinsurgencia," is edgy. On the one hand, there is the violence associated with the Mexican state's ghostly *operativos negros* to accomplish

FIG. 2. Alice Leora Briggs, *Narcoinsurgencia*, 2010. Sgraffito drawing on clay panel, 8 in. x 10 in. Courtesy of the artist and Evoke Contemporary, Santa Fe NM. Private Collection. © All rights reserved.

both la limpia against *narcotraficantes* and *la limpieza social*, or "social cleansing," against "Juárez citizens who are deemed undesirable" (for example: drug addicts, sex workers, and the homeless).[13] On the other hand, there is the violence associated with the drug cartel insurgency revolt against these measures prosecuted during the Calderón administration years.

Just as this illustration both ghosts and is ghosted internally by the verbal discourse that surrounds its positioning in the *L* section of the lexicon, so too it is ghosted by Briggs's addition of an intertextual graft drawn from early modern art history. A vital influence both in Briggs's creation of the "Alphabet of Juárez, 2010" and the illustrations for the more recent *Abecedario* is Hans Holbein's *The Dance of Death*, originally published in France in 1538 and whose series of woodblocks in later editions included additional figures, one of whom is called "The Soldier." The artist Arnold Birckmann's heirs published his woodcut edition of Holbein's *The Dance of Death* in 1555. Approximately a century later another German artist, Wenceslaus Hollar, published thirty of his own copperplates from *The Dance of Death* in a 1651 book titled *Mortalium Nobilitas*.[14]

As we see here, the mid-ground plane of Briggs's Narcoinsurgencia is dominated, as it is in Hollar's adaptation of Holbein's "The Soldier" woodcut, by two spectral figures: a living (for the moment) helmeted soldier with an upraised sword battles with a skeletal figure who represents Death. Meanwhile, near the top of the frame, another skeleton appears, this undead figure pounding a bass drum and leading still other soldiers into battle. These soldiers march at an oblique angle toward the battle being waged before and below them by this singular helmeted soldier and this skeletal figure of Death, whose legs or bones are entangled with the dead who have fallen—one of whom is positioned so that his gaze appears to be looking toward the anonymous corpse lying in the foreground between the two contemporary uniformed Mexican police processing the crime scene. Their upright postures framing both the corpse who lies at their feet, as well as the spectral figures behind them who have been parachuted into the present from another century. Briggs's overall compositionality and the sharp edges of her incised lines produce a contact zone binding together all these corporeal forms—the living, the dead, and the pair of *calaveras*. Whatever the kinetic energy supplied by this illustration's horizontal lines of force (for example: the thrust and parry of weapons; the outstretched arms and legs of the quick and the dead) these three distinct but overlapping human assemblages are sutured together to create a sort of vertical pyramid, one which rises up from the bottom edge to the top edge of the illustration's flattened perspectival plane.

Thus it is as if this graphic spectacle of violence (and its aftermath) juxtaposes the three tableaus not so much to underscore difference, but instead—precisely in the contact zone where their incised lines intersect and overlap—to dramatize an ongoing transgression of temporal and spatial boundaries. As Briggs herself has remarked, in this instance about the 2020 exhibition of her collaboration with Julián Cardona titled *The Writing on the Wall*, this art installation (and, by extension, the *Abecedario*'s later-published illustration) "contains overlapping bodies of work that focus on the cocktail of frailty and strength that alternately sustains and destroys our humanity. It is not a new idea. We have been drinking and swimming through this cocktail for centuries."[15] Whatever the differences that need to be recognized and

FIG. 3. Wenceslaus Hollar (1607–77), after Hans Holbein the younger (German, ca. 1497–1543), *The Knight and Death, from The Dance of Death*, 1651. Etching in black on ivory wove paper, sheet trimmed within platemark, 7.1 cm x 5.2 cm (2 13/16 in. x 2 1/16 in.). Courtesy the Wallace L. DeWolf and Joseph Brooks Fair Collections, Art Institute of Chicago.

honored between the then (of the Protestant Reformation and the Inquisition) and the now (of global capitalism, both its legal and illegal sides) and the there (of Europe) and the here (the local contemporary Juárez and the U.S.-Mexico borderland crisis)—there nevertheless exists here, in Briggs's graphic configuration of "this cocktail of frailty and strength," sameness or identity, a similitude. This similitude underlined here by Briggs's deployment of the uncanny motif of "the double" or doppelganger figure as a result of her image's mirroring of corpses in both the fore- and mid-ground passages of this illustration. It is as if we are bearing witness to the haunting return in an emergent conjunctural now of presentness of a past plague of traumatic violence.

So then, let us recognize this point: that in the very instant of our looking at this particular illustration, its space overdetermined by a compositionality forwarding a dialogue between arrivals (the soldiers led by the skeleton pounding on a drum; the uniformed Mexican authorities) and departures (the fallen dead), both the utopian promise of and desire for law and order and the reality of contagious violent disorder commingle. In this jarring juxtaposition of the exemplary (a local historical event in Juárez) and the explanatory level afforded by an allegorical "dance of death," we bear witness to time's harrowing and to the harrowing of time: to things as they are now, to things as they were then, to things as they will become or have already become, all this simultaneously happening as the sand in the hourglass empties and the bodies begin to decompose and Death's drummer continues to march onward, ever dancing with and ever in search of ever more victims. His errant path leading not only toward the paired human assemblages depicted inside this illustration's borders but also toward the viewer situated outside the frame, not yet a part of but nevertheless eventually fated to join the community of the dead.

The repetition and return (with an intertextual variant) of this image in the *L* section of the *Abecedario* forwards an uncanny economy of revenance: here there is both a reminder (of the continuous contagious violence underwriting human history) and a remainder (the accursed excess of violence that, like a plague or a viral pandemic, can't be contained or controlled).[16] Moreover, Briggs's graphic representation of such an uncanny economy of revenance liberates meaning in the *Abecedario de Juárez* from fixity and finitude. So here we are—here where there be ghosts and ghostly affects. Where there be las calaveras, both the dead and the glistening white bones of skeletons. And where there be the diffused light of a textured, white null space, this light hovering between and wrapping around both the quick and the dead exposed to our gaze. Like a Barthian punctum troubling any easy passage between visual signifiers and their meaning, Briggs's intertextual graft, with its doppelganger motif and its uncanny economy of revenance solicits the viewer to explore the troubling question as to whether the contagious violence in view here is primarily historically specific (a primary theme of her collaborator Cardona's longform journalistic narratives) or but one more example of a pattern of human suffering, this dance of and with death, that has existed for centuries.

4. "*So I wouldn't ever forget their names and so that the ground would also remember them.*" The first entry in the *Abecedario* for the letter *C* is calaveras, and within this section alone there are five Briggs illustrations portraying her collaborator Julián Cardona sitting at a table in a Juárez coffee shop where, as we learn elsewhere in the lexicon, the two collaborators would often meet to discuss their work and Cardona himself would meet to interview his informants. By my rough count, there are nearly thirty images in the entire *Abecedario* of Cardona, and twenty-two of them repeat this format: a medium shot of him sitting behind a table, facing an unseen friend and colleague (such as Briggs) sitting across from him (and the reader/viewer outside the frame who looks at the image). His upper torso and arms and hands are in view, and while his face sometimes will appear in these images of him at the table, typically Briggs will crop these images so we do not see the entirety of his face. Two things change throughout the repetitions of this image in the lexicon: the types of objects that appear on the table in the foreground before him (for example: sheaves of paper money, pieces of paper with writing on them, snakes and ladders, a mask of a pig head); the types of scenography that appear behind him (for example: a fragment of the coffee shop's interior, a crime scene, barb wire coils), these sites alluding to his longform journalistic narratives that either frame or are framed by one or more of Briggs's illustrations.

Now within the pages devoted to the lexicon's entries for the letter *C*, there are five images alone of a man sitting at the coffee shop table, one of which appears twice. Titled *Musica (Julián Cardona)*, this repeated image

FIG. 4. Alice Leora Briggs, *Musica (Julián Cardona)*, 2018. Sgraffito drawing on clay panel, 10 in. x 18 in. Courtesy of the artist and Evoke Contemporary, Santa Fe NM. © All rights reserved.

features Cardona seated at the table and surrounded by las calaveras. But this time around, Death's presence is not depicted as a singular skeleton or skull—like the image either of Santa Muerte that appears elsewhere in the *Abecedario* or in Hollar's allegorical figure discussed above. Rather, here we see a riotous, magpie assemblage of skeletal hands and arms and ribcages and vertebrae, of white skulls bearing/baring teeth and of white bones depicted on the belt buckles and sombrero rims of this undead mariachi band's attire, all this whiteness juxtaposed to the darker tones Briggs deploys to represent another assemblage of calaveras, these imprinted on what looks to be a lithograph displayed on the table upon which Cardona's hands rest, this sheet of white paper that composes an image embedded in the foreground of the larger image.

Once upon a time, in the time before this time of the femicides and the cartel violence and Calderón's Mexican "war on drugs," with its sham *efecto cucaracha*, we can imagine these musical calaveras as living human beings with flesh covering their skeletons and organs. As living human beings playing music at Día de Muertos and Mexican Independence Day commemorations or at weddings and baptisms and birthday parties. Perhaps even at funerals. Such a retrospective projection of their fictive existential status constitutes

FIG. 5. José Guadalupe Posada (1852–1913), *This Is About Don Quixote the First, the Matchless, the Giant Calavera (Esta es de Don Quijote la primera, las sin par la Gigante calavera)*, after 1891. Broadside with relief engraving and letterpress. Composition 22 1/16 in. x 13 7/16 in. (56 cm x 34.2 cm); sheet: 23 9/16 in. x 16 in. (59.8 x 40.7 cm). Inter-American Fund. Courtesy Museum of Modern Art.

the "what has been," that past from which certain moments get grafted onto the here and now of Juárez, this volatile laboratory of our future. But what about that lithograph Briggs represents as printed on white paper and being displayed on the table before the seated Cardona, this image rotated so that it is right side up facing an unseen someone sitting across from Cardona, as well as the viewer outside the frame? This collection of skeletons who represent—just as do the standing mariachi calaveras who surround this illustration's left and right margins—a thanatopic presence. A presence, it turns out, that also pushes the timeline of the "what has been" informing this illustration, and by extension the *Abecedario* itself, further back in history, both to the time before and during the Mexican Revolution and to the earlier time of Spanish colonialism. For Briggs's sgraffito version of this lithograph pays homage to the artistry of José Guadalupe Posada (1852–1913), a legendary printmaker of political cartoons, posters, illustrations, and topical broadsides during his life, whose artwork after his death during the third year of the Mexican Revolution, influenced such later Mexican artists as Diego Rivera and José Clemente Orozco.

The specific Posada illustration that Briggs reproduces and embeds into the surface of her own mariachi calaveras illustration is a ca. 1910–13 broadside titled *Esta es de Don Quijote la primera, la sin par, la Gigante calavera*. During Posada's era such broadsides usually were printed as single sheets, their content centering on that era's politics, religious controversies, and popular entertainments. The graphic art featured in a particular broadside usually was accompanied by a ballad or poem or corrido, and broadsides that included calaveras also were prepared in October and November for distribution around the time of Día de Muertos. In this particular Posada that Briggs incorporates into her *Musica* illustration, two calaveras on horseback appear. At the top of the sheet is "Don Quixote the first, the matchless, the giant skull," riding the calavera of his horse Rocinante, his lance extended as he charges through other calaveras, some of them shown being trampled and others being thrown in the air. Meanwhile, at the bottom of the sheet, in an illustration prepared by Posada's colleague Manuel Minella, two calaveras, one on horseback, are depicted outside a cemetery's gates, as if in pursuit of or restraining a group of mourners from entering the cemetery.

"Even madmen, delinquents and misfits can find a welcome in the new towns, that is, in the rationality of modern society," writes French philosopher

Jean Baudrillard, while "little by little, the dead cease to exist," exiled "further away from the group of the living . . . further and further from the center towards the periphery, finally having nowhere to go at all, as in the new town or the contemporary metropolis."[17] In modern society, then, with regard to the relationality of life and death, the situation is that now "there is in our system of values no reversibility: what is positive is on the side of life, what is negative is on the side of death; death is the end of life, its opposite, whereas in the symbolic universe the terms are, strictly speaking, exchanged."[18] As in, say, the "symbolic universe" of pre-Columbian or Meso-American peoples, such as the Aztecs and the Toltecs, where a dialectical rather than dualistic relationship between the "properties" of the living and the dead predominates.

Consider how the racks of skulls (*tzompantlis*) associated with rituals of blood sacrifice or how various symbolic rituals of exchange (for example, a skull in return for a blessing from a god) reveals how the dead, whose status is clearly different than that of the living, are nevertheless still regarded as a vital presence in the here and now, rather than—as Baudrillard asserts—distinguished from and expelled both to a different metaphysical plane of reality and to the geographical margins of "modern society." Let us consider also how the first entry in the letter *C* section of the *Abecedario* is calaveras, from the Latin *calvāria*, a combination of *calvus* ("bald") and the suffix *-aria*, literally meaning the dome or roof of the skull. If capitalized as Calvāria, the word translated into English means "Calvary," referring to the domed hill outside of Jerusalem, where tradition holds that Jesus Christ was crucified. This place sacred to Christians also known as Golgotha, one of whose connotations is that of a charnel house, a vault or building in which the bones of the dead are preserved and laid up, analogous to items inventoried in a ledger's final accounting. In addition to its particular etymology, the meanings and usage of calaveras underscore the dialectical rather than dualistic relationship that exists between life and death, the sacred and profane.

As several art historians and cultural studies scholars have noted, Posada's various prints popularizing las calaveras display a hybridization of pre-Columbian, modern, and vernacular or colloquial art traditions. Like Holbein's *Dance of Death*, Posada's various calaveras function as a sobering, albeit at times playful and soaring, reminder of the mortal fate that we all share, regardless of our station in life. More specifically, his Don Quixote calaveras symbolically function on two levels: on the one hand, as a kind of return of the repressed symbol of the Old World's colonial projects, the entry of Spain's conquistadores to the New World echoed here by the entry of Don Quixote and Rocinante into a Juárez coffee shop; and, on the other hand, as a reincarnated figure of the blessed "fool" whose "mad" visions and behaviors unconcealed the stark realities of the Spanish Conquest's continuous exploitation of Indigenous peoples and the earth in the name of God and country. I have come to think it is precisely this symbolic duality that *Musica* solicits us to recognize about the Cardona-Briggs collaborative project. A verbal and visual project of bearing witness whose repetitious quotation of Posada's calaveras in the *Abecedario* extends still another project: the return of death from the margins of the living to the center of modern society.[19] A project waged not just to contend against consumer capitalism's organized or selective forgetting of the past, but also one that provides an incisive and yet errant, as in purposeful straying, errand on behalf of a utopian dream of future justice, both for the quick and the dead.

5. *"To learn to live with ghosts is to rethink ourselves through the dead."* And through the dance of and with the dead—which is to say through *la musicá*. The bass line or percussive quality of *Musica* is afforded primarily by the predominance here of vertical lines of force, this accruing from these undead musicians' upright posture and spatial positioning on either side of Cardona's seated presence. The centering effect of this compositionality is further supported, on the left, by the angled line of the vocalist's hand and, behind him, the musician whose grasp of his trumpet directs our gaze toward Cardona, just as, on the right side of the image, does the slant of the fiddler's bow. Such framing details composing this image's foundational bass line are counterpointed by the visual evidence of a competing, more improvisational desire, this shaped by the restive imbalance of the experiential worlds both within and without this illustration's borders. Briggs herself improvises, plays over and under this illustration's percussive bass line through a poetics of movement based on a formal commitment to errancy. Here I am thinking about that vortex of motion conveyed by the swirling lines representing the various underbrims of the mariachi sombreros. I am thinking also about the assorted human and animal calaveras in the lithograph displayed on the table in the foreground of *Musica*, the horizontal line of energy created by the skeletal knight-errant in motion toward this illustration's right border. I am thinking here about the visible imbalance in the grouping of this mariachi band's seven calaveras, the denser clustering of four of las calaveras in the bottom right half of the frame that functions to shift the illustration's balancing center away from its geometrical center.

And here I am thinking about the kinetic energy created by Briggs's cropping of this illustration's content: how Cardona's facial features above his mouth and chin are eclipsed by the illustration's top border; how there is an elision of the crowns or brims of four of the seven sombreros worn by las calaveras, the two figures seemingly trundling into view at the top of the frame in this charged moment and the two calaveras populating the foreground at the frame's left and right corners; how both the guitar neck and the right half of the prominent skeletal mariachi at the bottom right corner of this frame are also beyond the illustration's visual field. Does not such a cropping technique solicit us to imagine what exists beyond the edges of the existing frame, which is to say imagine the cinematic movements of these clothed calaveras and the conical beauty of their sombreros, the fluid resonance of this perhaps grateful dead's soundscape produced by this one mariachi's breathing into the trumpet's mouth and another band member's scraping of a bow across a fiddle's strings and the vocalist's performative pose in the left foreground, his mouth open and his hand placed over what would be his heart if he still had one, all this movement underway both inside and, we can imagine, outside this illustration's permeable border, all this kinetic energy and sound erupting resulting from this image's phantasmagoric commingling of the living and the dead, of the playful and the deadly serious, and all this contrapuntal interplay between the what has been and that which will survive beyond this irruption of the undead's presence in the living present?

To my way of seeing it is as if the eternal, vagabond restlessness of the world sounds here, these undead mariachi players seemingly caught, like a camera's still shot, and yet simultaneously released, their clothed skeletal remains tumbling and inclining toward its audience outside the frame, the protective parenthesis formed by their corporeal positionality on either side of the late Julián Cardona now in the process of unraveling into commas, undone by the flick of a bow and the sound of the (last) trumpet and the sound of a singer who transforms the sheer act of breathing into music, these calaveras now turning to face their audience, toward any one of us who can imagine entering this frame and occupying that seat we cannot see before us but know that it exists on the opposite side of the table bearing the lithograph of the mounted knight-errant, turning toward any one of us who just might realize, whatever the degree of melancholia prompted by this graphic vision of our shared mortuary fate, that we not only behold but also are immersed in a compelling scene of recognition, one in which such animated calaveras just might conjure up both memories of our past losses as well as forecast our losses to come, just might perhaps put us on edge, perhaps even make us feel as restless as these antic calaveras—and perhaps also cause us to remember this: that it is the sound of music, whether or not we dare to imagine it as originating, as if by magic, from beyond the grave, which conspires to fill the world's abiding, melancholy emptiness. As the aphorism goes, "Out of oblivion spring narratives."[20] And song and dance. And, for better or worse, vagabond thoughts and sentences.

[**Exposure**; **Diapers**; **Junkspaces**; **Lipstick**; **Queues**; **Television**; **X-ray**; **Zombieland**]

Boredoms, generational and otherwise

EXTRACTS

Boredom is always counter-revolutionary. Always.
—Guy Debord, "The Bad Old Days Will End" (1963)

At no point have I ever been able successfully to keep a diary; my approach to daily life ranges from the grossly negligent to the merely absent, and on those few occasions when I have tried dutifully to record a day's events, boredom has so overcome me that the results are mysterious at best. What is this business about "shopping, typing piece, dinner with E, depressed?" Shopping for what? Who is E? Was this "E" depressed, or was I depressed? Who cares?
—Joan Didion, *Slouching Towards Bethlehem* (1968)

You sat in the dark, smoking, sobbing with loneliness and boredom. My mama, Madame Bovary. You read plays. You wished you had been an actress. Noel Coward. *Gaslight.* Anything the Lunts were in, memorizing the lines and saying them out loud while you washed the dishes. "*Oh*! I thought it was your step behind me, Conrad . . . No. Oh, I *thought* it was your step behind me, Conrad."
—Lucia Berlin, *A Manual for Cleaning Women* (2015)

My friends are all either married, boring, and depressed; single, bored, and depressed; or moved out of town to avoid boredom and depression. And some of them have bought houses, which has to be the kiss of death, personality-wise. When someone tells you they've just bought a house, they might as well tell you they no longer have a personality . . . . And the *worst* part of it is that people in their houses don't even *like* where they're living.

> What few happy moments they possess are those gleaned from dreams of *upgrading*.
> —Douglas Coupland, *Generation X* (1991)

1. "*Sobbing with loneliness and boredom.*" Here's a go at writing about boredom, hopefully without becoming either bored or boring. As we witness in the above extract by Joan Didion, for example, both the task of diary writing and her belated attempt to decode its cryptic entries "overcome" her with boredom. This situational boredom prompts her turn to the interrogative mode, the emergent question "who cares?" signaling her overall indifference—her loss of the desire to desire.[1] Affiliated with such other terms associated with the modern (and postmodern) human condition as alienation, the blasé mode, ennui, and malaise, *boredom* refers to that feeling of emptiness following on one's awareness of the tedium of everyday life: its being drained of meaningful experiences and relationships; its being drained of any interest and hence of any reason to care.[2] So Didion's response discloses how that feeling state identified as boredom reveals any bored human subject's heightened self-awareness and hence proclivity for a critical self-assessment that can border on self-loathing. So in this particular instance we also witness how boredom "declares itself an aesthetic or intellectual or emotional category, not an ethical one."[3]

Take the above extract from Douglas Coupland's novel *Generation X*, where the serial repetition of the phrase "boring and depressed" by the first-person narrator (a character named Andy) underscores stylistically, as well as thematically, his judgment that his former friends still living in Portland have experienced "the kiss of death, personality-wise" upon their having achieved the so-called American dream through home ownership. Even worse, he asserts that these "people in their houses don't even *like* where they're living." Whether his friends are married or single, whether settled in place or constantly on the move, Andy supposes they are either, on the one hand, in denial about their bored state, or, on the other hand, demonstrating a kind of existentialist bad faith achieved by sublimating their present unhappiness in the suburbs and replacing such an ugly feeling with consumerist fantasies of a new, improved, or "upgraded" future house and lifestyle to come. Hence mort + gage = "dead pledge."

His exasperated tone and faux concern about the nature of his friends' lifestyle choices; his pose of cynical detachment; his condescending summary judgments (for example, the supposed fact that home ownership must mean one's having lost any spontaneity and originality)—such rhetorical and affective features intensify Andy's particular critique to a degree that a protective defense mechanism seems at work here in his enunciation. One that functions both to camouflage his emergent melancholia and immunize him from the contagion of boredom he diagnoses as having overtaken his friends' adult lives. Such rhetorical and affective features qualify him for membership in what Patricia Meyer Spacks, in her book on literary representations of boredom, has termed "the aristocracy of boredom."[4] Such features uncannily betray not just his abiding anxiety about whether his present life has relapsed into a bored state without his becoming aware of it, they also disclose his anticipatory anxiety—as he approaches his thirtieth birthday—about whether his future life will be genuinely interesting or, heaven forbid, full of loneliness and self-destructive obsessions. For even as this excerpted moment from *Generation X* opens with his judgment that his former friends are living "bored and depressed" lives, it concludes with a grudging confession about how "profoundly" depressed he has become simply as the result of his conjuring up the specter of their inauthentic lives.

In one direction, then, his heightened self-awareness turns his developing critique inward. But in another direction, this critique targets external factors—not so much fate or chance in this instance, but rather specific socioeconomic contexts and cultural or class or caste expectations for success. And given how his critique fastens securely on the fact of his friends having mortgaged the real state of their lives to a purchase of real estate, are we not solicited also to recognize how, for Andy at least, they ought to be regarded as homeless persons? Not literally houseless, living without a fixed abode or dwelling, but rather as existing—amid all their privileges and creature comforts—in a state of metaphysical or "transcendental homelessness."[5] As George Lukács details in his *The Theory of the Novel* (1920), transcendental homelessness is exemplified by the failed quests of various protagonists in canonical modern novels to discover and inhabit a spiritual and/or emotional home in an everyday world increasingly ruled by capitalism's principle of commodity accumulation. In *Generation X*, this condition of transcendental homelessness emerges, on one level, as either a cause or an effect of what Lukács terms a "nameless, shapeless, object-less boredom," which is to say a kind of chronic generalized anxiety about the future that afflicts not only new suburban homeowners but also the novel's three main protagonists (Andy and his friends Claire and Dag).[6] But on another level, transcendental homelessness also emerges in the novel either as a specific cause or effect of that larger "historical moment at which the commodity completes its colonization of social life" and spawns a specific type of boredom linked with satiety: "When one gets too much of the same thing and everything becomes banal."[7] As Claire succinctly puts the matter, an obsession with commodity accumulation is problematic because such an addiction will "only remind you that all you're doing with your life is collecting objects. Nothing else."[8]

Whether defined as situational or as the result of satiety; whether its advent forecloses on desire or promotes an active passion—boredom's symptoms include both the suspension of one's agency or desire (as we see with Didion's "who cares?" question) and one's tendency to dwell in the subjunctive or conditional as if or if only mood, with its liminal temporality of waiting in the meantime. So the narrator's mother in the Lucia Berlin short story titled "Panteón de Dolores" sits in solitude in the darkness of a mining shack's claustrophobic space, barely warmed by a coal stove and "sobbing with loneliness and boredom," unable in this fraught moment to realize that she is "waiting for something without knowing exactly what it might be," and that it could arrive and remedy the situation at hand.[9] And even though the unhappy suburban homeowners that Andy targets with his verbal rant apparently know what they are waiting for—the twinned arrival both of upgraded homes and of more convivial and interesting personalities—they also, like the Madame Bovary mother figure in Berlin's short story, remain uncomfortably "pinioned forever between a disintegrating, irrecoverable, half remembered past and an always uncertain future."[10]

The larger point I want to make, with these various examples in mind, has two valences. From the perspectives offered by the above extracts, we witness how a braiding together of different types of boredom overlaps with a profound or existential type of boredom. Thus as psychoanalyst Adam Phillips reminds us, "We should speak not of boredom but of the boredoms, because the notion itself includes a multiplicity of moods and feelings that resist analysis."[11] Furthermore, as Claire's phrase "nothing else," which I quoted above, reveals, the intensified commodity accumulation that is critiqued in *Generation X* indexes that historical moment when the leading ontological question in philosophy is being transformed. As theorist Jean Baudrillard claims, "The traditional philosophical question used to be 'Why is there anything at all, rather than nothing?' [Whereas] the real question today is 'Why is there nothing rather than something?'"[12]

2. *"Boredom has so overcome me."* Titled "The Sun is Your Enemy," the opening chapter of *Generation X* concludes with a scene in which Andy, Dag, and Claire—the key members of a self-described "poverty jet set"—have gathered on the front lanai of Andy's rented bungalow in Palm Springs, California, to await the dawn of another day in the desert.[13] As the sun begins to rise over "the lavender mountain of Joshua," the trio, as Andy describes the scene's affective atmosphere, "are just a bit too cool for our own good; we can't just let the moment happen." So Dag intervenes with "a gloomy aubade: 'What do you think of when you see the sun? Quick. Before you think about it too much and kill your response.'"[14] Claire responds with a short story about a farmer in Russia driving a tractor in a wheat field who slumps over the tractor's steering wheel and starts crying after realizing the sun emits an odor causing his crop to die "of history poisoning." Dag relates a story about an eighteen-year-old Australian surf bunny sunbathing on Bondi Beach who discovers "her first keratosis lesion on her shin." For his part, Andy imagines "a place in Antarctica called Lake Vanda, where the rain hasn't fallen in more than two million years."[15]

Andy describes this jet-set trio's spontaneous swerve from looking at the sunrise to telling fictional stories about various apocalyptic vignettes as exemplifying "the carapace of coolness." As the word "carapace" suggests, to perform "coolness" one must produce a protective, stylized mask that camouflages one's feelings or emotions. Indeed, as he later discloses to Dag and Claire, "because the three of us are so tight assed about revealing our emotions," his favorite model for narration emerged during his time in Alcoholics Anonymous. There, the basic meeting rules were "no interruptions" and "no criticism." Such rules fostered the kind of noncritical atmosphere necessary for telling stories in this newer Palm Springs setting. But as Claire reminds them, it's not enough to live life as a succession of isolated cool moments: "Either our lives become stories, or there's just no way to get through them." Dag and Andy agree with her imperative, with Andy then revealing, as the short chapter concludes, "that this is why we the three of us left our lives behind us and came to the desert—to tell stories and to make our own lives worthwhile in the process."[16]

So the "carapace of coolness" here is enmeshed with completed narratives that have the potential for making lives "worthwhile" rather than revealed through a "succession of isolated cool moments." It is precisely this distinction between "coolness" and "cool moments" that especially troubles Dag as he approaches his thirtieth birthday. For he has become convinced he is experiencing a "Mid-Twenties Breakdown": "the failure of youth but also a failure of class and of sex and the future and I *still* don't know what."[17] He regards his life story heretofore as a failure because it appears to proceed as "a series of scary incidents that simply weren't stringing together to make for an interesting book, and *God* you get old so quickly. Time was (and is) running out."[18]

"And I *still* don't know what": This peroration to Dag's confession of his serial losses discloses the overall uncertainty and the suspension of agency that symptomizes the onset of profound or existential boredom, where it seems "impossible to make any clear distinction between the respective contributions made by the subject and object to boredom."[19] In profound or existential boredom there is instead "a longing for any desire at all" to emerge—and a desire for the arrival of any "small moment that proves you're alive."[20] Or, to use Claire's words, to prove that your life is "worthwhile." Unlike the kinds of bodily language attached to other types of boredom—the acts of yawning or fidgeting in one's seat or pointedly checking and rechecking one's watch—the existential boredom in *Generation X* centers on being devoid of expression. As is the case with what Andy calls the face of "'what-am-I-going-to-do-with-my-life?' semi-clinical depression," Dag's narrative poses of detachment and his deadpan tonality serve self-protectively—just as does any mask or carapace of "coolness"—both to flatten this human subject's sense of "failure" and to project to the waiting world an illusion of this bored subject's emotional self-control rather than its abiding fragility.[21]

In the hope of remedying this depressing existential situation, Andy, Dag, and Claire light out for the desert, "where the weather is hot and dry and where the cigarettes are cheap," to live in the "quiet sanctuary from the bulk of middle-class life" of Palm Springs. Their choice to lead "small lives on the periphery" is labeled "Occupational Slumming," a Coupland neologism that means "taking a job beneath one's skills or education level as a means of retreat from adult responsibilities and/or avoiding possible failure in one's true occupation" (Andy and Dag work part-time as bartenders; Claire works at the Chanel counter of the local I. Magnin store).[22] So instead of the tragic fate faced by the Russian wheat farmer in Claire's story, whose wheat crop dies of "history poisoning" due to the sun's odor smelling like old *Life* magazines, all three, at various moments in the novel, aspire instead to achieve "Historical Underdosing": that state of living "in a period of time when *nothing seems to happen*. Major symptoms include addiction to newspapers, magazines, and TV news broadcasts."[23] Hence the paradoxical desire emanating from the possible connotation of the *X* in *Generation X* as signifying erasure. On the one hand, a deep-seated fear that one's relatively comfortable middle-class existence is a "kiss of death, personality-wise." On the other hand, a deep-seated desire for the zero-degree or blank state, this underscored by the novel's repetitious imagery of the "clean slate" or of the need for "emptying" out one's mind. No wonder, then, that this particular "poverty jet set trio" desires to emulate the "existential cool" of philosopher Albert Camus, who is namechecked in the novel because of his stated desire, during his existential crisis, "to imagine a first man who starts at zero."[24]

And so, by these stages, I return to the function provided by "the carapace of cool," exemplified by the bedtime stories the poverty jet-set trio tell each other throughout the novel. As Andy describes the situation, these "pretend" stories told "to each other under the hot buzzing sun next to vacant lots" essentially occur in "alternately forked universes [that] might still bear the gracious desert homes of such motion pictures stars as Mr. William Holden and Miss Grace Kelly," homes that would be repurposed by this Generation X trio for "swims, gossip, and frosty rum drinks the color of a Hollywood, California sunset." The extent and extant of such "pretend" stories' content, Andy believes, hopefully will produce a "more welcoming universe" than the degraded setting where their stories are shared: the desert landscape of West Palm Springs, which is "barren—the equivalent of blank space at the end of a chapter—and a land so empty that all objects placed on its breathing, hot skin become objects of irony."[25] Through an improvisational narrative creation of more "welcoming" universes, then, one just might experience a more redemptive, "existential cool" structure of feeling than that of profound existential boredom. And whether understood as an attitude or style, a technique or mode of being in the world, it is precisely the performance of "existential coolness" that models "a way to express an archaic interval, lag, play, or slack between a people and their society."[26] Just as the desert location for the bedtime stories itself provides a temporal and spatial interval from either society's abandoned junk spaces or its architectures of consumerism, the narration of "alternate forked universes" via bedtime stories potentially opens up a utopian space of possibility instead of a suffocating accommodation to necessity. As Alan Liu has suggested more specifically, the function of various "cool" techniques (in this novel's context, narrative detachment and irony and deadpan tonality) is to create "a slack that opens up between the ethos and counter-ethos of postindustrial information work, between knowledge work and the 'ethos of the unknown.'"[27]

"The ethos of the unknown": in that liminal space and temporality of potentiality existing "between a people and their society," the bedtime stories detailed in *Generation X* reveal how *X* connotes not just erasure but also an *unknown variable* on the margins of the barren desert of the Real. Put differently, it is the potential transformation of profound existential boredom into the "cultural play" of existential cool that just might reveal how, as Walter Benjamin lyrically suggests in his essay "The Storyteller," boredom can spawn "the dream bird that hatches the egg of experience."[28] Or, as Andy comments, channeling the poet Rilke, any anxiety accruing from any type of boredom can be alleviated if we never forget "that all of us are born with a letter inside us, and that only if we are true to ourselves, may we be allowed to read it before we die."[29] "If only we are true to ourselves": notwithstanding the subjunctive mood signaled by the "if" here, the reigning assumptions determining this jet-set trio's everyday life—as well as the overall stakes involved in their sharing of bedtime stories—hatch right before our eyes. So this trio's fervent dissatisfaction with everyday life centers on its inauthenticity. But due to the mediation of meaningful relationships both by consumerism and the reign of simulations and simulacra, a reality effect dominates experience rather than any genuine encounter with one's authentic, singular essence, much less some elusive Real itself.

And unlike other types of boredom, this existential situation in turn can lead to a productive creative boredom—the telling and listening to fictional "bedtime" stories—that will aid and abet a lifelong quest to read that "singular letter" addressed to one's true self and calling. As we will see below, this quest for contact with Real life and the truth of one's real personhood manifests itself in scenes involving not only storytelling but also both literal and figurative blood sacrifices, singular events that, at least momentarily, serve to spawn a nascent sense of community rather than a chronic case of individual alienation. So, these scenes on one level underscore how creative boredom, contra Debord's claim, can be redemptive if not also revolutionary. On another level, as if foreshadowed here by Andy's allusion to Rilke and the attendant imagery of textuality (the secret letter) that will return at the novel's conclusion, Coupland's representation of the jet-set trio's encounters with the Real instead expose that an aporia, or abyss, still remains. Regardless of these characters' predilection for irony and for the detachment afforded by a carapace of coolness, they uncannily will continue to dwell within the confines of theatrical spectacle, a fate that exposes how a regressive, romanticized, and escapist nostalgia both informs their existential boredom and fuels their escapist bedtime stories.

3. *"What few happy moments they possess."* Generation X opens with Andy telling a story that dates back to the late-1970s, when he was fifteen years old and decided to use his savings to buy an airplane ticket and fly to Brandon, Manitoba, in order to witness a total eclipse of the sun. On the morning of the eclipse, he takes a public bus to the edge of the small city and then walks down a dirt road and enters a farmer's field. And "in that field, when the appointed hour, minute, and second of the darkness came," Andy lies down on the ground, "surrounded by the tall pithy grain stalks and the faint sound of insects," holds his breath, and experiences "a mood of darkness and inevitability and fascination—a mood that surely must have been held by most young people since the dawn of time as they have crooked their necks, stared at the heavens, and watched their sky go out."[30] In the novel's final chapter titled "Jan. 01, 2000," Andy tells another travel story about his drive from Palm Springs to Calexico, California, where he will cross the U.S.-Mexico border and continue driving to west to Mexico's Baja peninsula and the village of

San Felipe. There he will reunite with Dag and Claire and the three of them will prosecute their plan to open a small hotel "for friends and eccentrics only" and spend their nights "washing zinc salves from each other's noses, drinking rum drinks, and telling stories."[31] But about fifteen miles from the border, as he nears the town of Brawley in California's Imperial Valley, "an unusual incident" occurs—one that he "must talk about." It is an event that not only occupies most of his travel narrative in this chapter but also hearkens back to the novel's opening chapter. This time around, the event is not a solar eclipse, but rather the sight of what he initially imagines must be "a thermonuclear cloud—as high in the sky as the horizon is far away—angry and thick, with an anvil-shaped head the size of a medieval kingdom and as black as a bedroom at night. . . . It was that same cloud I'd been dreaming of steadily since I was five, shameless, exhausted, and gloating."[32]

Given the end-of-the-world leitmotif evident in the bedtime stories told throughout *Generation X*, it is hardly surprising that Andy sees this "stratospheric black monster" and panics, thinking that a nuclear detonation has truly accomplished what an eclipse of the sun also foreshadows: that day the "sky goes out." But a few minutes later and a few miles farther on down the road, he sees that this mushroom-shaped black cloud was produced by farmers burning off their fields' stubble. This post-harvest ritual fire event causes the highway traffic to slow and, in the lee of the wind that blows the fire's smoke toward the horizon, Andy notices how the fields had become "carbonized to an absolute matte black of a hue that seemed more stellar in origin than anything on the planet." To witness better this "hot, dry silk black sheet, this marvel of antipurity," he pulls onto the shoulder of the highway and gets out of his car, joining others before him who had stopped and were now leaning against their cars, gazing at this "accidental wonder before them."

He is soon joined by "a dozen or so mentally retarded teenagers," who are discharged by their chaperone from a large passenger van just as a "cocaine white egret" flies in from the west, circling the burned-off fields, "its jet-white contrast with the carbonized field . . . so astounding, so extreme, as to elicit gasps" from the teenagers as well as other parked further down the road. The white egret then alters its flight path and flies toward the gathering of onlookers either standing at the wooden fence bordering the fields or next to their vehicles, swoops down, and grazes Andy's head, one of its claws ripping his scalp and drawing blood. As he feels his scalp and begins to consider the blood on his fingers, he bows down to one of the teenage girls who offers him a "healing staccato caress" with her hands on his head, the "faith-healing gesture of a child" in Andy's estimation. Then he suddenly is "dog-piled" by "the instant family" of the teenagers, their somewhat painful but nevertheless truly "adoring, healing, uncritical embrace" embodying "a crush of love" that, he judges, was "unlike anything I had ever known."[33]

Like "regionality" itself, which Kathleen Stewart defines as that "geography of what happens," Andy's story here fastens on the singular event of becoming in and of a place as affective and haptic "intensities pass from body to body—human bodies, animal bodies, machine bodies, bodies of thought, ecosystems, visceralities, and noumena."[34] Thus both substantial things and material human and animal bodies become enmeshed, producing in the process a "contact aesthetic."[35] This aesthetic grounds itself on three encounters: there is the encounter between a great egret's claw and Andy's scalp; there is the encounter between his singular human head and a teenager's laying on of hands; and then, finally, there is the encounter between these two human bodies and the other teenagers who had piled out of their group's travel van earlier in the sequence and who now collectively form a "dog pile," a group hug of bodies loosely arranged, one imagines, in concentric circles that radiate outward from the epicenter formed by Andy's corporeal pose of supplication. The cinematic rush of images in this sequence proceeds, in short, as an "energetics of tension and release, build up and lateral shift." Andy's mood state shifts from apprehension, to comprehension, and then to respectful wonder. His heretofore solitary state evolves, temporarily at least, into membership in an "instant family"; and his protective carapace of coolness gets replaced by the paradoxically painful pleasure he calls "this crush of love."[36]

This sequence's corporeal imagery of bowing down and kneeling and laying on of hands; this sequence's acts of scarification and drawing of blood; and this sequence's rhetoric of election, grounded by Andy's sense of having been "chosen" for special dispensation by a divine messenger god, this great white egret which appears to belong "more to the Ganges or the Nile rather than America"—it is as if this emergent assemblage endows this small secular happening—which takes place outdoors, adjacent to a wire fence and near the limit posed by the horizon and the nearby U.S.-Mexico border—with the atmosphere of a religious communion service.[37] The full participation in which seemingly fulfills Andy's desire, per his gloss of a Rilke poem at an earlier point in the novel, to look out "into the evening that is full of things happening" and "to feel what is going on there" in such a way that "his whole situation drops from him as from a dead man, although he stands in the very midst of life."[38] As if for Andy this singular event provides redemptive proof of his passage, exemplifies a "small moment" in his life that *"proves you're really alive,"* rather than being bored, lonely, and depressed.[39]

4. *"Such was the moment's beauty."* Earlier in the novel, in response to a challenge posed by a character named Elvissa to tell a story about a singular moment that "defines what it's like to be alive on this planet," Andy tells a family story about a time when he fried bacon for his six siblings and parents on a Sunday morning, his "forearms getting splattered by little pinpricks of hot bacon grease" and his eyes tearing up because he began "feeling homesick for the event while it was happening."[40] And at the end of the novel's penultimate chapter, which takes place chronologically after the novel's final chapter, in which the great egret draws blood from Andy's scalp, he narrates still another story about such an existential moment when one feels truly alive on this planet. This story centers on what he imagines his prospective arrival at the end of his car trip to the Baja peninsula will be like: he will lie down on one of the "the razory brain-shaped rocks" that edge the coastline and these rocks—like the great egret's claw in the earlier moment near Brawley—will cut his flesh and draw his blood under a burning "chemical sun" and his brain will morph into a "thin white cord stretched skyward up into the ozone layer" and his ears will fasten on the sound of wings beating. And then "a great big dopey, happy-looking pelican" will land near his prone, bleeding body and will waddle over and, instead of eating his liver as in the classic version of the Promethean myth, will offer him "the gift of a small silvery fish."[41]

As is the case with the story he tells in the novel's final chapter about the black smoke cloud and the white egret and the teenager's redemptive laying on of hands, these two stories similarly disclose the melancholia engendered by an ephemeral but nevertheless beautiful moment; an abiding desire for true sociality or intimacy; and the emergence of a freely given gift economy or sacrificial exchange that substitutes for the market-driven exchange of commodities that mediates human relationships. The scarification of the human body by rocks or bird; the pain of hot bacon grease on one's forearms or the pleasurable pain rendered by the teenage group's loving embrace—such constituent features of these three linked stories in *Generation X* surely manifest here, as they also do in Alfred Hitchcock's memorable film *The Birds* (1963), a passion for "the direct experience of the Real as opposed to everyday social reality—the Real in its extreme violence as the price to be paid for peeling off the deceptive layers of reality."[42] The Real as that hard, resistant kernel (or rock or bird's claw) that awakens one from the hypnotic spells of our boredoms, whether situational or the effect of satiety. The Real whose shock or jolt—like the desperate practice of cutting the body with knives or razors so as to feel alive again—forecloses on "the unbearable anxiety of perceiving oneself as nonexistent," this status or condition that, as we have seen, defines the overarching existential boredom in *Generation X*.[43]

And yet there exists an inherent problem that lurks here with this desire for authenticity. It is one that motivates my occasional deployment in above paragraphs of the subjunctive or hypothetical mood via "as if" sentence openers. This problem occurs because the very reality of the Real centers on how its traumatic or excessive, unsettling, and disorienting character cannot be integrated into what we experience or essentially regard as our everyday reality, which, as the above quote claims, is composed of multiple layers of deceptive simulacra or carapaces that function as camouflage. Instead of the Real, the sublime event composed by the thermonuclear cloud produced by the burning off stubble after harvesting a field produces, by chance, a compelling roadside "tourist attraction." Andy compares the soil's smooth appearance as a result of the combined action of fire and wind and smoke not only to a "hot, dry silk black sheet" but also to a "marvel of antipurity." Indeed, such is the spectacle created by this singular event that the "supergravitational blackness" of the field's "matte black of hue" leads Andy to wonder if the color has an otherworldly, stellar origin. But he immediately revises that comparison as he processes what his gaze records. In a manner similar to this poverty jet-set trio's earlier enunciated desire to transmute their boring lives into worthwhile tales (for example, to the alternate universe of a textuality that just might have a proper beginning, middle, and end), he describes this burned-over, flat earth as if he were discussing the flattened plane of, say, one of Mark Rothko's monochromatic canvases.⁴⁴ Andy describes this field's carbonized soil as a "matte black of hue," which in turn looks like "black snow that defied XYZ perspective and that rested in front of the viewer's eye like a cut-out paper trapezoid."⁴⁵ What we experience in the end, then, as well as from the beginning of *Generation X*, is a version of creative and existential boredoms that disclose what Slavoj Žižek observes is the "fundamental paradox of the 'passion for the Real': it culminates in its apparent opposite, the "pure semblance of the *spectacular effect of the Real*."⁴⁶

[**I**dyll; **J**unkspaces; **P**sychometropolis; **Y**ellow ribbons; **V**agabondage; **Z**ombieland]

Cryptography, or the architectonics of the crypt

EXTRACTS

He stood and crossed the road and walked up into the cemetery past the old stonework crypt and past the little headstones and their small remembrances, the sunfaded paper flowers, a china vase, a broken celluloid Virgin. The names he knew or had known. Villareal, Sosa, Reyes. Jesuita Holguín. Nació. Falleció. A china crane. A chipped milkglass vase. The rolling parklands beyond, wind in the cedars. Armendares. Ornelos. Tiodosa Tarín, Salomer Jáquez. Epitacio Villareal Cuéllar.
—Cormac McCarthy, *All the Pretty Horses* (1992)

He listened to the magical recording of a Spokane Indian elder telling a traditional story. A true Spokane. She spoke fractured English, which Mather could barely understand, but her fluent Spokane was being translated by a Bureau of Indian Affairs agent. The story was about Coyote, the trickster, and it echoed through the cluttered basement. Boxes of various artifacts were stacked in tall piles. A maze of doors, small rooms, and hallways. Some rooms had not been opened since the early part of the century, and exploring the basement involved a contemporary sort of archeology. The basement even had its own mythology. Chief Seattle's bones were supposedly lost somewhere in the labyrinth. And the bones of dozens of other Indians were said to be stored in a hidden room.
—Sherman Alexie, *Indian Killer* (1996)

This was the first time the earth's insanity had affected her. The Little Town was riddled with bullet holes and tunnels bored by five centuries of voracious silver lust, and from time to time some poor soul accidentally discovered just what a half-assed

job they'd done of covering them over. A few houses had already been sent packing to the underworld, as had a soccer pitch and half an empty school.... She had a quick peek over the precipice, empathized with the poor soul on his way to hell. Happy trails, she said without irony, and then muttered Best be on my errand.
—Yuri Herrera, *Signs Preceding the End of the World* (2015)

To learn to live with ghosts is to rethink ourselves through the dead or, rather, through the return
of the dead (in us) and thus through haunting.
—Jodey Castricano, "Cryptomimesis" (2000)

1. *"A contemporary form of archaeology."* The word "cryptography" variously connotes the art of writing in codes or ciphers to protect sensitive information, the study of such encrypted writing ("cryptograms"), and the analysis of methods for either encrypting or decrypting secret communications ("cryptoanalysis"). Contemporary cryptography centers on information security and privacy in such areas as electronic commerce, military communications and government surveillance, digital currencies (cryptocurrency), and computer passwords and software programming. The word itself comes from the Ancient Greek words, *kryptós* (hidden or secret) and *graphein* (to write). Derived from the feminine form of kryptós, the Greek word *krypte* (a vault or secret place) spawns the Latin *crypta* (grotto or cavern), from which the English word *crypt* is derived to connote a subterranean cell or cave or an above ground vault for the interment of bodies, such as in the catacombs or burial vaults of a church or a mausoleum in a cemetery.

Depending on its context, however, the word *crypt* may also refer to any non-ecclesiastical architectural structure (or earthen form) whose spatiality resembles that of a cellular, receptacle-like, or recessed space of containment. Such as, in the built environment, above-ground mausoleums or below-ground catacombs in cemeteries, basements and cellars and hidden rooms and closets in a house, the tunnels of an urban railway station, or the sump hole in an underground mine and the mud pits in oil drilling rigs. Such as, to consider earthen forms, caves, pockets, or the sandstone amphitheaters and overhanging ledges of desert ecosystems. Such as playas or depressions in desert basins that hold water from underground aquifers or hidden springs and seeps. Such as deep arroyos, these trenches sometimes lined with traprocks or stone tinajas, whose shallow basins hold seasonal water that can reflect the stars inhabiting the overarching dark vault or crypt of the night sky.

Furthermore, as exemplified by the graphic inscriptions on human skin made by tattoos or body art, we can consider a corporeal cryptography composed by human anatomy: small depressions or cavities either evident on the human body's surface (the skin, orifices, or even the eye sockets) or hidden from view, such as the glandular cavities found in certain internal organs. And we can consider how certain bodily postures model a corporeal cryptography. Take, for instance, the performative cringe embodied by marginalized human subjects who are regarded as wasted people living wasted lives. Such as the homeless people depicted living in an encampment on Crown Hill in downtown Los Angeles in Héctor Tobar's 1998 novel *The Tattooed Soldier*, their "hunched posture" making them look "like walking question marks" in the eyes of one of this novel's main characters.[1] This simile compares human corporeality to a punctuation mark whose contorted graphic shape both literally signals the interrogative mode's inherent field of indeterminacy (a question without an answer or answers) and figuratively relays this particular homeless demographic's unknowable Otherness.

Another way to understand cryptography is to consider how the architectonics of the crypt are evident in the interior psychic space of human subjects. As Nicolas Abraham and Maria Torok have theorized, an intrapsychic crypt produced by trauma comes complete with its "own topography" and exists as "an enclave" space between the dynamic unconsciousness and the ego (whose very function they liken to that of "a cemetery guard") in which are entombed the memory traces of words, scenes, and affective responses attached to a lost object, thing, or person of value. Such "secrets" are buried alive and yet preserved in the human subject's psychic crypt "like the living dead" or, better yet in this context, like the undead, those objects (like the sled in the film *Citizen Kane*) or those valued humans and nonhumans (dogs) who are literally dead but belatedly resurrected in symbolic or figurative form.[2] Thought about as a psychological defense mechanism spatialized as an enclave space like a sepulcher or vault, then, the intrapsychic crypt marks a cleft or splitting in the human subject's psychic space in the wake of actual or remembered trauma.

But Abraham and Torok's crucial point about such entombed "secrets"—and what will concern this essay, which focuses on examples of cryptography in Tobar's *The Tattooed Soldier*—is this: in a manner similar to the haunting return to consciousness of repressed fears and anxieties that Freud theorizes as the uncanny, such encrypted and entombed "secrets" in the intrapsychic crypt typically manifest themselves, due to experiential triggers in the human subject's present moment, as corporeal and textual or linguistic repetition compulsions. Though on one level the intrapsychic crypt functions to conceal or hide the psychic residue of the traumatic past (and hence protect the grieving subject), such psychic residue nevertheless might be displaced into visible forms of corporeal cryptography (such as a tic disorder, catatonia, vertigo, or repetition compulsions) or disclosed by what Abraham and Torok call cryptonymy or "haunted language," which refers "to what is unspeakable through ellipsis, indirection, and detour, or fragmentation and deformation," in short to the disintegration of meaning or grammar or semantic or rhetorical coherence.[3]

Cryptography, then, as an uncanny writing on and about the traumatized body, as in tattoos on human skin. Cryptography, then, as exemplified by or through architectonics of the crypt in the built environment. Cryptography, then, as a version of posthumous writing about the dead or disappeared, as in messages secreted in the envelopes of "dead letters" or the inscriptions literally etched on gravestones or the stone faces of above-ground crypts. And cryptography, then, linked with cryptonymy, as in *The Tattooed Soldier*, where prose stylistics and textual representations of architectural forms of the crypt transform, at novel's end, the dark space of an abandoned railway tunnel, its entrance covered with graffiti, into an intrauterine architectural structure that paradoxically assembles the features of the womb as well as the tomb.

2. "*Slippery bitch of a city.*" In parts one and three of Tobar's *The Tattooed Soldier*, both cryptography and the architectonics of the crypt literally and figuratively dominate four key scenes, the first three of them linked by a singular leitmotif in which the Guatemalan exile Antonio Bernal gazes at photographs either sent to him by his mother who still lives in Guatemala or hidden in a photo album itself secreted in a dresser drawer in the Los Angeles apartment of Guillermo Longoria, the tattooed soldier of the novel's title. Though this novel's plot eventually migrates toward a conventional revenge plot, its overall trajectory is catalyzed by this leitmotif and the crucial presence of various forms of architectural, corporeal, and stylistic cryptography.

The first scene occurs on the morning of the event that inaugurates the novel: Antonio's eviction, along with that of his roommate José Juan Grijalva, from their Bixel Gardens apartment in downtown Los Angeles by their Korean immigrant landlord. While hastily stuffing his few possessions into a black Hefty bag before leaving the apartment, he discovers a stack of unopened letters from his mother. Wedged between two of the envelopes, he notices "a forgotten photograph of his wife and son, taken years ago in Quetzaltenango against a painted backdrop of fanciful lakes and volcanoes." It is this very image, he decides, that encapsulates *"the sadness of me, the tragedy of me."*[4] Three days later—after he and José Juan have settled into a makeshift shelter on the margin of a homeless camp on Crown Hill—Antonio once again rummages through his black Hefty garbage bag, searching for this vacation snapshot from his Guatemalan past life. Unsettled by his failure to find it, his memory becomes "pinpointed" on still another, even more devastating day of displacement and loss: that day seven years before, when he was "standing in the central square of San Cristóbal Acatapán, the box at his feet . . . taking the first step in the journey that would lead, eventually, to Los Angeles. He was leaving behind a house with floors that were covered with reddish black blood. He had wandered through that house like a sleepwalker, his shoes sticking to the tiles." This trek eventually delivered him to the corpses of his wife and young son, their bodies having been dragged through the house, "painting the floors with their blood," and then left on its front steps by members of the infamous death squad known as the Jaguar Battalion of the Guatemalan army.[5] And it is on this very day in January 1985, that Antonio, after boarding the bus that will take him away from this San Cristóbal house crime scene, gazes out the bus window prior to the bus's departure and sees a man with an obvious military bearing sitting on a cast-iron bench and eating an ice cream cone in the town's central plaza, his left arm displaying "a tattoo of a yellow animal with its jaws open."[6]

And now, on a sunny day in 1992, Antonio and José Juan leave the Crown Hill homeless camp and visit MacArthur Park. In this park, seven years after he began his long journey from Guatemala to Los Angeles, Antonio experiences an uncanny repetition of his initial glimpse of the tattooed soldier in the central plaza of San Cristóbal. Sitting at one of the chess tables in this Los Angeles park, dressed in civilian clothes, he sees this very man bearing the death squad emblem of the jaguar tattoo. In zoology, crypsis is a term derived, like the English word "crypt," from the feminine form of the Greek kryptós, and it describes the body markings, colors, and behaviors that an animal deploys to protect it from predators. But as we see here in this uncanny "double" of the original recognition scene in Guatemala, the corporeal cryptography represented by the tattoo of the jaguar—one of the most important animal figures in the Quiché Mayan *Popul Vuh*—publicizes, rather than conceals, the soldier's identity, at least to Antonio and other Guatemalan refugees in Los Angeles. And with this renewed recognition of his wife and son's murderer, "Antonio spun in the flux between decades and countries, time and space distorted."[7]

The vertiginous effect on Antonio upon his second catalytic sighting of the tattooed soldier exemplifies how his subjectivity is suddenly subjected to what Jodey Castricano terms, in her discussion of Jacques Derrida's "ghost writing" as a form of cryptomimesis, "an uncanny economy of revenance."[8] The apparitional presence who has suddenly appeared before Antonio's gaze as if he were "watching a statue or hunting trophy come to life," embodies a haunting reminder of the Guatemalan civil war.[9] Moreover, the contagious violence of this conflict's war crimes produces a remainder—a traumatic residue of memory traces—that now has emerged from Antonio's intrapsychic crypt in the corporeal form of the tattooed soldier. And just as Antonio spins "in the flux," disoriented by this recognition scene's collapse of spatial and temporal borders, so too does Tobar's prose begin to unravel and trouble conventional distinctions between grammatical and syntactical units: "He was in a park in Guatemala, a park in Los Angeles. The present, the past, somewhere in between."[10]

Tobar's brief prose cryptonymy here establishes a syntactical parallelism that blurs the difference between two parks and two geographical locations, even as this enunciation devolves from an opening independent clause into a phrase fragment ("a park in Los Angeles") shorn of the conjunction "and" that would make this statement a compound sentence instead of, technically speaking, an example of the grammatical error known as the comma splice. This syntactical enjambment is then followed by three successive phrase fragments shorn of verbs but nevertheless punctuated as a complete sentence, the declension of his fragmentary thoughts into the staccato rhythm of a serial list ultimately unable, in the immediacy of this event, to ascend to the level of the explanatory. The liminal spatiality and temporality connoted by his feeling caught "somewhere in between" discloses how his life continues to unfold in the future anterior tense, as if he is "pinioned forever between a disintegrating, irrecoverable, half remembered past and an always uncertain future."[11]

3. *"The tragedy of me."* Part 2 of *The Tattooed Soldier* intervenes in the novel's 1992 narrative present in Los Angeles by returning to Guatemala in 1985 and reconstructing the main characters' life histories, especially detailing the intersection of their lives on the fateful day when Antonio's wife and son were murdered. The novel's part 3 then resumes the plot in Los Angeles immediately after Antonio recognizes the tattooed soldier in MacArthur Park. In this section's opening chapter, titled "Fire Escape," we witness Antonio once again searching the Hefty garbage bag in the hope of locating the once forgotten and now missing photograph of his wife and son taken during their family vacation in Quetzaltenango. During the second search of the same garbage bag that he conducts at the Crown Hill homeless camp, he notices an envelope that seems thicker than any of the other unread letters his mother in Guatemala has sent him. Inspecting this envelope's contents, he discovers still another photograph, this one new to him and taken in what he surmises to be the San Cristóbal cemetery. At the center of this photograph, he sees two white marble crypts surrounded by a few other crypts displaying the names of the dead written on them in crayon or pencil. And he also notices how this small grouping of white marble crypts at the center of the picture is surrounded by numerous pauper's graves, most likely filled by peasants "killed on the highways and slum children who died of dysentery and malnutrition."[12]

Confused by the presence of this particular photo of graveyard crypts hidden inside this miniaturized crypt of a paper envelope, Antonio begins to read his mother's cover letter and quickly learns that the two white marble crypts centered in the image contain the corpses of his wife and son. And he further learns that—as his mother had been told by one of his friends, a Belgian priest—at first there were no crypts, much less markers, for the burial sites of his wife and son in this cemetery. Upon hearing this news, she provided the priest with the money needed both to install the two white marble crypts and also to cover the cost of writing his wife and son's names "with gold-leaf letters and swirling flowers" upon their blank white surfaces.[13] With this explanation resolving the enigma of the photograph's presence in one of his mother's letters to him, Antonio initially feels "bitter shame" for not having fulfilled his duty as a father and husband to make these burial arrangements. But then, a second glance at this photograph fills him with renewed anger at his mother "for taking upon herself a duty that should have been left to him." Vowing never to read one of his mother's letters again, he tears the letter into pieces. But he keeps the photograph, putting it in his shirt pocket—an action that, while putting this visual record of their crypts out of sight, nevertheless simultaneously retains it as a secret close to his heart, a memento mori. These particular remains of the dead—this visual and discursive cryptographic evidence calling to him both from and beyond the grave—add to what we may (and he does) recognize as his debilitating sense of having inherited an unresolved debt: "I didn't bury them properly. Even after they were dead I failed them." Failing them in death and failing them after death: it is at this point in his ongoing internal dialogue of self-recrimination that his inner voice swerves to ventriloquize Elena's voice speaking to him from beyond the grave: "'Of course you didn't remember to bury us, Antonio,' Elena would have said. 'You always forgot everything.'"[14]

Occasioned by the symbolic return, through the medium of photography, of the literal dead (his wife and son) and the actual undead (the tattooed soldier), resurrected before his gaze and his consciousness, this ventriloquism of Elena's voice symptomizes the intrapsychic splitting of Antonio's haunted subjectivity in the wake of the serial historical traumas in Guatemala and Los Angeles. Antonio's ventriloquism of Elena's voice underscores Derrida's working definition of the crypt as a "foreigner incorporated in the crypt of the Self"—the spectral Other who lives on in the intrapsychic crypt formed in the wake of past trauma and who now surfaces as a phantom—as "'the buried speech' of another which returns itself in 'the person of the subject.'"[15] Thus, through both the mediation provided by such written signifiers on the page (his mother's letters) and by the photographic representation of the white marble crypts with their etched cryptography, what emerges in the novel's part 3 is the transformation of the Crown Hill mise-en-scène into a joint Crown Hill-Guatemala mise en abyme (or abyss). The uncanny economy of revenance emerging as a result of these scenes featuring corporeal and discursive cryptography essentially relocates the primal scene away from the domestic family and home into a Guatemalan cemetery and a Los Angeles park and homeless camp, where the affective atmosphere and theme of these latter settings is overdetermined literally and psychologically by Antonio's uncanny economy of indebtedness. So, he remains suspended in the melancholy state of refused mourning "somewhere in between," neither here nor there, neither now nor then.

4. *"Lost in the labyrinth."* In part 3 Antonio learns the tattooed soldier's address and his name—Longoria. One evening he breaks into Longoria's apartment and, while casing the premises, discovers a cache of grisly photos taken during the Guatemalan civil war in his bottom dresser drawer. In the wake of recognizing the tattooed soldier playing chess in McArthur Park, Antonio "had thought about killing the soldier, but only in the abstract."[16] But after seeing the secret war crime pictures of several victims of the Los Jaguares murder squad, Antonio realizes that the "anonymous cadavers" he knew "only as photographs" had been murdered "with no living witnesses" to testify against them in a courtroom.[17] And so he begins to believe—nearly a week after his original encounter with the tattooed soldier in MacArthur Park—that he could not only avenge his wife's and son's deaths by killing Longoria but also with such an act achieve justice "for the massacred who had been left without fathers, husbands, or brothers to avenge them."[18]

In the novel's final sequence, Antonio eventually achieves his vengeance, shooting the tattooed soldier with a small caliber pistol and leaving him for dead on the sidewalk outside his apartment building during the height of the Rodney King riots. But the wounded Longoria rises up and, though bleeding to death, begins following Antonio back toward the homeless camp, now relocated at the site of an abandoned tunnel and station of the old Pacific

Electric Railway below Crown Hill. Eventually Antonio realizes he is being followed and picks up Longoria's stumbling and bleeding body and carries him away from the rioters and the soldiers, intending to hide "him in the muddy crypt of the tunnel so that he would finally die."[19] In his near-death state, Longoria hallucinates the graffiti-covered tunnel entrance as being at "the foot of a green mountain, wild plants and shrubs all around them, forlorn palm trees and tall milkweed."[20] But when Antonio enters the railway tunnel carrying Longoria on his back, the "concrete floor beneath yields to mud," and Longoria loses sight of the sky, "as if someone were shutting a coffin."[21] Longoria loses feeling in his feet and hands, and as his blood seeps out of his wound, this earlier impression of having reached a green mountain with wild plants and shrubs morphs into a vision of a cornfield, glowing golden even in the tunnel's darkness, its stalks rising from the tunnel's mud and its "fleshy leaves shining, tiny husks bursting like green embryos."[22] And then he sees a "dark woman," whom he believes to be his mother, hoeing the rows of green corn. He sees her stop her work and turn toward him, gesturing with an outstretched arm and hand for him to rise up and join her in the field:

> With invisible strings she pulls him up, and now he is walking toward her through rows of corn. Leaves brush his face, cool and moist. Rainbow-colored trousers hang loosely from his waist, fabric she wove at the loom. On his feet are sandals, strips of old leather held together with wire and twine. He smiles at his dirty toes, mud caked in the nails. So strange and happy, after all these years, to be wearing his peasant clothes again. And now words from his mother in a language he has nearly forgotten. "*Balam,*" she says.[23]

In this threshold moment between life and death and in this threshold space where golden light commingles with darkness of the crypt formed by an abandoned railway tunnel, a singular human representative of the dead welcomes the dying and delusional Longoria into their community. Tobar's assemblage here of Longoria's visionary return to the green earth and to the mother begins to define the tattooed soldier's final conscious thought as an act of expiation for his offenses. For disobeying his mother while running an errand for her in his youth and going into a movie theater's dark space, where he is kidnapped—along with other able-bodied males of all ages—and forced into the Guatemalan army. For his role as an adult both ordering and participating in his death squad's massacre of peasant families, including all their children, whose death throes compose the haunting soundscape of his life as an exile in Los Angeles. As a result, his final thoughts here stress the matter of things and things that matter in terms of providing protection or security or support in his fallen world: a mother's offered hand; the caress supplied by leaves of corn; the feel of rainbow-colored trousers and leather sandals; the sight of this good earth's mud caking his toenails.

All this description is augmented by Longoria's allegedly feeling "so strange and happy," a simple judgment providing a pause before the magical narrative transformations that begin to unfurl here, at his end and close to the novel's end. In Longoria's case, he transforms from prone to standing and then walking position as he hallucinates being pulled upward by the "invisible strings" of his mother's invitation to labor with her in a field of corn. With regard to the novel's mise-en-scène, the muddy floor of the railway tunnel crypt transforms into an imaginary cornfield's muddy soil, where this emergent matrix of water, earth, and corn—both its shining fleshy leaves and its green husks—recycles key features of the Mayan K'iche' creation myth with its promissory note of redemption. And perhaps most importantly, in his final moment of consciousness, Longoria envisions his mother addressing him as *balam*, the Mayan word for "jaguar." Where once the jaguar signified a dreaded hunter and killer—the totem animal, of course, for whom Longoria's death squad is named—now, in this imagined green world being cared for by a mother, balam refers instead to the mythical jaguar figure as an agricultural god, as the protector of cornfields and hence also of the people who work the earth with their labor of hands.

So in this final scene involving the architectonics of the crypt in *The Tattooed Soldier*, we witness how cryptography designates a place of passage or transition: a type of "intrauterine architecture" in which features of the tomb (here the dark tunnel as a double of/for the subject's death) become enmeshed with the utopian fantasy of a redemptive return to the womb (both the body of the mother and of an originary first nature that sustains the web of life).[24] As Anthony Vidler hastens to reminds us, this utopian fantasy of a return to an intrauterine existence represents an impossible desire underwritten by nostalgia. The adult Longoria's dying vision exemplifies this fantasy, as his nostalgia mode projects a "homesickness" for what is imagined to be a past conceived both as the spatial and temporal location of the true family, the organic village collective, and that earlier, more instinctual stage of one's existence associated with childhood and youth. Given that this imagined past is also privileged over one's fallen present in this reactionary nostalgic mode, it is as if time itself is not only experienced as fragmented or segmented, rather than being seamless, but also as ghostly. In this mode of nostalgia, one's present moment is in effect under erasure, harrowed both by memory traces of past trauma and by an emergent recognition that the future will prove the past as, in the end, inherently unrepeatable. As if it were possible to return to the womb after one's birth. As if it were possible to undo the historical transformation of a primal first nature into a second and even third nature as a result of the industrial and post-industrial revolutions.[25]

5. "*Small remembrances, the sunfaded paper flowers, a china vase, a broken celluloid Virgin.*" "Debris, that unorganized residue of the physical and metaphysical homes we construct for ourselves," Peter Schwenger writes, "finds its most melancholy incarnation in the corpse."[26] Amid the mud of the tunnel floor and the debris of a brand-new clock radio, soot-stained coffee pot, a bleach white sweatshirt, and piles of discarded clothing, Antonio conducts a night watch over the additional debris constituted by Longoria's corpse, reflecting on the possibility of his having achieved some degree of restorative justice by shooting the tattooed soldier. He concludes that his countryman possesses "no redeeming qualities" whatsoever and that "while the blood of Los Angeles might soon begin to fade," the blood of Guatemala was indelible.[27] Indelible like the ink of a tattoo. Indelible like traumatic memories occasioned by the sight of war crimes. At dawn, convinced that Longoria was truly dead, Antonio leaves the abandoned railway tunnel full of debris from prior homeless camps and begins walking, soon crossing paths with an army of Central American people holding brooms, "harvesting mounds of pale green glass, teasing them into dust pans and shovels, lifting them into boxes and trash bins."[28] This debris had accrued from the previous night's riot. Whereas earlier in the novel Antonio looks at a group of Guatemalan women in traditional dress, so far distant from even "the memory of corn," here he watches a harvest of "pale green glass" being conducted by other

Central American refugees and judges their removal of the riot's debris "an act of love" exemplifying, here in early the morning light of a new day, "the true brotherhood of the city."[29]

As he has done throughout the novel, Tobar renders the narrative's final movement predominantly through a conjunctive rhetoric and grammar of parataxis: the blood of Los Angeles and the blood of Guatemala; a park in Los Angeles and a park in Guatemala; the accumulated debris below ground in an abandoned railway tunnel under the streets of south-central Los Angeles and the toxic waste of an illegal landfill in Guatemala. Through such parallelism, the novel elaborates its leitmotif of the uncanny double, in the process linking the history and fates of people in Guatemala (and Central America more generally) and that of the United States. On one level, the manner in which events transpiring in Los Angeles represent an uncanny repetition of the Guatemalan past arguably solicits us to recognize how Longoria himself represents a victim of political and economic foreign policies that originated during the Cold War and extended into the era of rampant global neocolonialism. But on the other hand, the crucial point to make with regard to this repetition of pastoral imagery—Longoria's dying vision of laboring in the field with his mother; the people harvesting the debris of glass produced during the riot—solicits us to differentiate Longoria's nostalgia for the stillborn past from Antonio's more reflective nostalgia for an alternative future, one informed by his recollection of his dead wife Elena's periodic allusions to Che Guevara's concept of "revolutionary love."[30]

The string of losses and failures Antonio experiences in *The Tattooed Soldier* testifies in the end to how he is both done and undone by those he knows and grieves for and by all those nameless and faceless deaths that form the background of his (and, by extension, our) social world. While Antonio doesn't profess to understand fully what his wife Elena's invocation of "revolutionary love" signifies, he nevertheless continues to believe that "If she were alive, Elena would put her arms around him and whisper all the answers in his ear."[31] As is the case with his nascent sense that the cleaning up of the riot's debris is an "act of true love," so too does this shift to the conditional mood in the novel's final sentence announce the arrival of what Neil Campbell elsewhere calls "pensiveness": an affective and cognitive state that denies any heroic closure or narrative resolution; that functions "to suspend narrative logic in favor of an indeterminate expressive logic"; and that propels the novel's plot trajectory toward "that which we have yet to know." Such as all that unfinished business of choices and of relations yet to come in that future community of the living who are waiting "somewhere out there in all that dark."[32] As the sweeping and cleaning of debris continues around him, then, Antonio self-consciously validates his own role in hastening Longoria's death. And he begins to redefine his personal obligation to the dead as not so much a validation of where and what he already is or has been, which is the case, as we saw in that earlier scene where he looks at the photograph of Elena's and his son's crypts. Rather, he revises that earlier sense of his indebtedness so that he envisions an orientation toward a future becoming. An obligation to foster the arrival of all those hoped-for posthumous "people to come" that will have developed a point of identification with everyday suffering—and whose struggles and sacrifices will assume collective responsibility for the lives (and the deaths) of others similarly engaged in "revolutionary love." And it is precisely this orientation, what we might call a hopeful nostalgia for the future not the past, that motivates him as he walks forward into his future.

[Diapers; Exposure; Graves; Idyll; Junkspaces; Lipstick; Urbicide; Television]

Diapers and loading docks

EXTRACTS

"Yeah. Got a homeless mother and her child living in it. I mean I actually went down to talk to her. At first I thought, shit, if they screw up the upholstery . . . I was gonna go down there, blow 'em away. I put my life into that car. But then, I thought, she might actually take care of it for me. You know, in return for finding her a place."
—Karen Tei Yamashita, *Tropic of Orange* (1997)

"Yes sir." He turned one foot a little, pleased with the waxy glint from the Cole Haan shoe which retailed at $300 plus, but which his uncle Tambourine Bapp had fished from a donation box left at the loading dock of his thrift shop on the outer banks of Colfax Avenue.
—Annie Proulx, *That Old Ace in the Hole* (2003)

They sat on the bus bench, canvas bags beside them, filled with the day's essentials: fearlessness scrambled with huevos con chorizo and wrapped in a tortilla as thin as the documents they carried to prove legality. Neatly packed burritos in a container bought at a Tupperware party hosted by a co-worker or a cousin or the boss's wife and so they felt obliged to buy. Some carried jars of cool tap water con canela as Lollie's mother did (for cleansing your bladder from infections by not being able to get up from the sewing machine to "make water"). Others carried embroidery projects or knitting for the one- or two- or two-and-a-half-hour bus rides that took them away from their families and familiarities from sunup to sundown.
—Helena María Viramontes, *Their Dogs Came with Them* (2007)

Diana la cazadora des choferes. A bus passenger who appeared to be a middle-aged woman with dyed blond hair shot and killed two Juárez ruta 4 bus drivers (forty-five-year-old Roberto Flores

Carrera and thirty-two-year-old Freddy Zárate), on two consecutive mornings in late-August 2013. . . . It is not known if the murdered drivers abused women or were randomly selected to pay for the abuse of others. Another line of investigation suggested that they had refused to transport *burritos* or other drugs on their buses. None of these theories were pursued by law enforcement.
Literal meaning: Diana, the hunter of bus drivers.
Related terms: *burritos, feminicidio*
—Julián Cardona and Alice Leora Briggs, *Abecedario de Juárez* (2022)

1. "*Got a homeless mother and her child living in it.*" Although the homeless male was not constituted as a category until the mid-1930s during the height of the Great Depression, the homeless, statistically speaking, have been around since the beginnings of industrial modernity: they were labeled drifters, bums, hoboes, vagrants, and tramps.[1] The discourse on and the constitution of homelessness during the so-called Progressive Era was especially responsive to social, economic, and political anxieties about the impacts of immigration and urbanization, where fears regarding the homeless city focused on the potential for violent revolution. From this perspective, the proto-revolutionary Army of the Homeless on the move in Silko's *Almanac of the Dead* (1991) represents a latter-day version of the Industrial Army movement of 1894, the western contingents of which marched on Washington, as tracked in the diary of a young Jack London. Discourse about such homeless male figures produced a double vision of such vagabondage. On the one hand, the long-standing social construction and legal definition of vagrants and vagrancy rendered a person without a fixed abode as constituting a criminal threat to the sedentary spaces of domestic order. On the other hand, the tramp's mobility could also connote a liberation from the alienation spawned by urban industrial modernity. Consider the textual lineage from Walt Whitman's "Song of the Open Road" (1856) to Charles Lummis's *A Tramp Across the Continent* (1892), London's *The Road* (1907), and on to Jack Kerouac's *On the Road* (1957), where adventurous vagabondage configures the chronotope of the street and road as an imaginative zone of regeneration for the bourgeois white male, whose quest for masculine freedom and self-reliance through sheer velocities of movement reproduces the nation's continuous mythic romance with rugged individualism.[2]

Unlike their tramp and hobo predecessors, the so-called new homeless and working poor of the 1980s most affected by a new round of deindustrialization and technological innovation were the peripheral low-wage temporary employees and the chronically unemployed—a demographic dominated more by women and ethnic minority men.[3] Furthermore, even as literary discourse at times reproduced the symbols, icons, and rhetoric associated with Depression-era documentary realism (e.g., the photographs of Dorothea Lange), the critical discourse emerging in a globalizing world system significantly entangled the themes and imagery of circulation and flows (of people, images, commodities, and capital) with an attention to immobility: repetitious vagabondages to nowhere, circular departures and uncanny returns marked affectively by "the continuous sliding between states of terror, amusement, and sheer banality."[4] An alternative narrative of globalization on the border emerges, one focusing on laboring bodies embedded in local survival circuits. Such as: the ramshackle colonias networked by dirt tracks and badly paved roads with the illegal garbage dumps and the factories and warehouses; the animal rendering plants; the tiendas and strip malls; and the *barras*. Such as: the North American Free Trade Agreement's transnational spaces of production and consumption defined by the presence of both a phantom proletariat laboring in a nocturnal, low wage service economy (e.g., nannies, maids, janitors, repairmen, bartenders, and sex workers) and its anonymous daytime ghost workers (temporary clerical help, line cooks and waitstaff positions, assembly-line labor in factories and warehouses) whose minimum wage labor is attached to machines and whose bodies are susceptible to the "slow violence" of neoliberal flows of capital. All this physical and affective labor, all this entangled mobility and immobility symptomizing what Charles Bowden, in *Dreamland: The Way Out of Juárez*, calls "the real production line . . . the conveyor belt of flesh."[5]

2. *"Fished from a donation box left at the loading dock of his thrift shop."* A vignette emerging early in the pages of *Dreamland* exemplifies just such an alternative narrative of globalization's impact on laboring bodies. The textual moment I have in mind occurs when Bowden's prose swerves from the book's primary investigation of events surrounding the belated discovery of bodies buried in the backyard of a drug cartel's so-called "death house" in

a middle-class neighborhood in Cuidad Juárez. A leitmotif of hands in both Alice Leora Brigg's sgraffito illustrations and Bowden's prose frames this textual vignette, which opens with the phrase "Reach for it, always reach for it." Both in this Mexican border city and in "the small towns and tired crossroads" in "faraway places," Bowden writes, there are hands growing and harvesting and transporting the product, and there are hands rolling the cigarette papers and composing a line of cocaine on a flat surface and striking a match to heat the "product" in a spoon and pushing a syringe into a vein. And as this vignette concludes, hands make an appearance shooting a gun or strangling a man with a cord and then opening bags of lime "to hasten the body on its way to rot" below the patio in the cartel death house's back yard. "Reach for it, always reach for it." All this activity of reaching and grasping and holding things and bodies, whether of the quick or the dead, all this activity accruing from both legal and illegal desires exposing how "the city never really sleeps but moves product or schemes product," its production line of hands and bodies continuously in motion servicing the disparate "hungers" of this "wide world" filled with people who desperately "crave an end to the emptiness" of their lives, all this illegal traffic in "product," whether it is consumed locally or in "faraway places," never "understood" or "discussed" or "noticed," for "all is unmentioned, everything it seems is unmentioned."[6]

Even though this "product" and the "it" and the "all" and the "everything" enmeshed with the "conveyor belt of flesh" seem to be hiding in plain sight, both unconsciously denied and consciously ignored, what can be seen and mentioned and perhaps even understood is a particular type of class-bound and gendered vagabondage. For in this city, where the sewage trickles down the streets and black funnels of smoke rise from burning tires, all while "the poor fire mud and dream of bricks," there always will be:

> The woman walking through the dust with a plastic bag of groceries in one hand and her ankles swollen and her face tired and still she trudges on and she is everywhere going about her errands, journeys never understood or noted but travels that fill the city with motion as the poor stagger along to get the few things that they need, that roll of toilet paper, that bundle of diapers, the quart of milk, the stack of tortillas, the small bag of chiles, and, of course, eggs and lard and the ankles are so thick and it is difficult

to imagine those very ankles once held up a lithe young girl, a person now replaced by a tired face, an old sweater, sagging slacks and those thick ankles, swollen and yet never mentioned, not once mentioned in speech or newspapers or in any other media, a silence about the ankles and the aging women and the dust and those little plastic bags of items that are carried for miles and then put on an old table in a shack made of cardboard that sits in a dirt yard surrounded by pallets from loading docks.[7]

Regardless of this passage's content, it would be difficult not to notice its form: how it unfurls across the book's columnar format as a lengthy, single compound sentence, its vivid descriptive details subordinated to the narrative mode. In what appears to be this passage's predominant narrative thread, the third-person narrator's gaze tracks an anonymous woman's pedestrian transit across Juárez's commercial and industrial precincts. Through references to the object world constituted by the city's public transportation grid, to this woman's clothing and the plastic shopping bag she carries, and, crucially, to the warehouse loading dock with its nearby discarded pallets and cardboard boxes, this passage surges through Juárez's various zones of consumption and production and waste, this "swarm of vitalities at play" testifying to the transnational maquila economy that both defines this city and overdetermines the fate of this woman's corporeal presence in the world.[8] The true subject or theme of this passage (and the whole of *Dreamland* for that matter), then, centers on the modalities of a force that transforms human subjects into things. A force that has the power not only to produce corpses but also—even while the human subject is alive—to figuratively murder bodies and souls.[9] A force that we also glimpse in Bowden's choreographing of this lengthy sentence through the irregular repetitions and returns to the textual surface of certain words, phrases, and clauses, producing a synonymy between different temporal and spatial scales.

This observation brings us to this passage's second or embedded narrative, which, keyed by the periodic stalling out in this long sentence, dilates the duration of this localized travel narrative. I am thinking here specifically about that moment midway through the above passage when the gaze of Bowden's narrative persona zooms in, for a second time, to note this prematurely aging woman's swollen ankles in order to highlight that they are "so thick." On the one hand, this phrase fragment functions as a rhetorical hinge, its insertion enmeshed here with a serial list of the items in the plastic shopping bag the woman carries. On the other hand, this phrase fragment introduces a swerve in what heretofore has been an enunciation relayed in the continuous present tense. For what follows this iterative enunciation of thick or swollen ankles is a highly condensed narrative nested within the dominant travel narrative unfolding in the now of narration. This narrative within the larger narrative embeds her past ("a lithe young girl, a person") into her present circumstances; the narrative's end circles back to repeat, with a slight variation, its opening phrase fragment ("those thick ankles").

The immediate point I want to make here, then, is that such specific repetitions of the repeated phrase "thick, swollen ankles," along with the overall devolution of the sentence into a series of words or phrase fragments, parallels how our detached narrative persona's gaze of surveillance itself shifts from an opening medium shot ("a woman walks," "a lithe young woman") into a close up focus on discrete body parts (the "tired face," ankles). This woman's whole corporeal being, in short, becomes disarticulated into discrete body parts, and the body parts then rearticulated and equated—due to the serial grammar—with the old sweater and slacks that, one can imagine, sag in the same manner as her prematurely aging facial and neck skin. So it is that Bowden here (and elsewhere) in *Dreamland* relentlessly reimagines forms of human embodiment in our contemporary state of emergency as "unthinkable as wholes and [yet] unthinkable apart from each other."[10] Thus, as we see here in this passage's panoramic view of an anonymous woman's iterative journey (the narrative mode says once what we can infer happens on a daily basis), Bowden's signature prose aesthetic gets defined by startling juxtapositions, serial grammar and syntax, and a disarticulation/rearticulation dynamic process in which human corporeality is fragmented into various body parts and then, by means of metonymic logic of sheer proximity, reassembled as but one more commodity populating the object world of capitalism.[11]

The epistemological and ontological struggles he announces in *Dreamland* with regard to his ability or inability to map Juárez and its environs—this laboratory of our future—are reflected aesthetically by his uncanny stylistics, the key features of which trouble any conventional desire for coherence and expectation of closure. In this exemplary passage, all the accumulating restatements and amplifying appositions, all the agglutinative details and prose fragments attached both to this anonymous woman's portrait and to the narrative progress of her everyday pilgrimage, branch off, to use an anatomical image, like ribs from the main spine of a simple everyday quest narrative centered on survival. As Bowden's prose oscillates between concretizing our attention (through granular descriptions) and then dispersing it—by means of abrupt and at times abstract summary judgments that often are immediately qualified or withdrawn—an atmospheric affectation of precarity emerges. A sense of creative stammering that literally and figuratively challenges our understanding of what constitutes the limits or even the differences between, say, a sentence fragment and a complete sentence, between a sentence and a paragraph, between a paragraph and a larger textual sequence, and between the conventional generic boundaries demarcating fiction and nonfiction. As if, in the end, as Bowden puts the matter, anything and everything that seems solid will vanish in "this city with dust in the air and men and women in the ground," since the hard fact is that "no one ever hears anything. Or sees anything. Or smells anything. Or reports anything."[12]

Let us ponder this jeremiad, its melancholic tonality and the manner in which Bowden's pronouncement doubles the oblivion of the final days to come—days that will see the city shrouded with dust both above and below the earth's surface—with a steadfast recognition of an ongoing cognitive and psychological oblivion in the present. As if to underscore how we inhabit a waking dream that fatally insulates us from reality. As if that waking dream itself is not recognized as a living nightmare. And let us further consider how this magisterial pronouncement begins to falter as it draws toward its own end, as if to mirror the attrition or entropy attributed to this woman's tired face and sagging clothes. Toward an end in which a complete declarative sentence beginning with "no one" is succeeded by three sentence fragments. Each fragment shorn of the grammatical subject "no one." Each fragment specifying the loss of a particular human sensory ability—and of human agency itself (our inability "to report"). Each fragment independent, separated by periods, but bound to the two prior fragments by means of a syntactical parallelism and the repetition of an introductory "or" and the final "anything." This overall interplay among fragments via regular accented sound repetitions operatically manifesting this narrator's chronic failure to unify the past, present, and future of a homeless stranger's biographical experience and psychic life.[13]

3. *"All the sounds and smells and all the deaths and loves are details in this fact."* As this particular *Dreamland* vignette concludes, Bowden's narrative persona makes this observation: "The world now is said to be global, and all the sounds and smells and all the deaths and loves are details in this fact."[14] Those who seemingly are doomed to be local are subject both to visible and invisible predations, their lives overdetermined by the vast, seemingly instantaneous accumulation of wealth accrued by the sorcery of the global market's unjust and unequal, spectral flows of capital, its transits spawning Bowden's portrait of and reflections about this representative figure of "the poor," who walks the streets of Juárez toward a cardboard shack adjacent to the loading docks of a warehouse supplying the trucks that will deliver commodities across the U.S.-Mexico border. This figure who is largely invisible to people in more affluent circumstances. This figure whose "tired face" and "swollen ankles" and labored gait foreshadow the future of all the young "girls who emerge at first light from shacks built of pallets stolen from loading docks."[15] This figure who for miles has carried a plastic shopping bag filled with familiar domestic commodities: a toilet paper roll; diapers and milk; tortillas and chiles; eggs and lard. All these familiar, domestic commodities collected and itemized, heaped together according to a metonymic part-part logic of sheer proximity. All these domestic commodities inside the plastic bag grammatically and syntactically equated with the other objects and actions described outside the bag: this anonymous woman's swollen ankles and her tired face; the sheer physiological labor expended during her pedestrian journey; the swirling motion of dust circling around her aging body; the wooden table inside her cardboard shack and wooden pallets stacked near loading docks of a maquiladora warehouse.

As Bowden claims in this vignette, this female figure represents the city's "poor," a demographic whose presence is essentially both invisible and also misunderstood. Bowden himself cannot escape this ethical and epistemological crisis, for as he confesses at another juncture in *Dreamland*, concerning the plague of contagious violence and exploitation of labor that defines Juárez, "I can't decide if I am hearing the cries of a hard birth, or something more like a death rattle."[16] Nevertheless, what Bowden's quasi-allegorical rendering of this anonymous woman's pedestrian journey does make visible—precisely at the point where his omniscient gaze itemizes the contents of this woman's plastic bag—is a gendered sexual economy in which women do not just perform productive labor with their hands and bodies, but also are tasked with performing reproductive and affective labor: food preparation, child care, and the emotional caretaking of the family unit. All this reproductive and affective labor is never remunerated, never accounted for "in speech or newspaper or in any other media." This absence surely also symptomizes the continuing repression constituted by the spectacular and sexualized toxic male violence against women's and children's bodies, exemplified by those who literally have disappeared during the years of the femicides.

It remains true that our critical labor, in this North American Free Trade Agreement (NAFTA) era of "global capital flows in which a 'borderless' world enables transnational capitalism and neoliberal definitions of freedom," becomes, Krista Comer has argued, that of distinguishing critical regionalist modalities of mobility from "the spatial behaviors of finance capital as well as the legacies of settler spatial spreadings."[17] In Bowden's thematic and stylistic interplay of a mobility/immobility binary in *Dreamland*, the stakes of a truly critical regionalism center on a bearing witness, on the one hand, to the unhomely pathos of a local situation in which the possibility of a radical alternative to a globalizing world system seems to have decisively receded. Hence the melancholy tonality of *Dreamland*. And if this observation represents a fair assessment of the stakes associated with a critical regionalism, then Bowden's particular prose aesthetic solicits us to ponder crucial questions about the ethics as well as epistemology of representation. For even as his portrait of *Dreamland* presents a harrowing, concretized acknowledgment (and bitter indictment) of the complex realities of everyday life in the U.S.-Mexico borderlands, does not his turn to a quasi-allegorical mode of representation risk erasing the burdens of history borne by specific actors?[18]

Fredric Jameson, for one, further suggests that the allegorical mode—which itself risks becoming but one more abstraction analogous to the spectral abstraction produced by late-capitalism's shift to finance capital—can mitigate the problem of creating a cognitive map of our present historical moment, such as we see in Bowden's inability to decide whether what he chronicles in contemporary Juárez represents birth pains or a death rattle. This is because the allegorical mode demonstrates how "the most random, minute, or isolated landscapes [can] function as a figurative machinery in which questions about the system and its control over the local ceaselessly rise and fall."[19] Certainly, for Bowden, the "local" is Juárez itself, a place that he calls, in another of his books, "the laboratory" in which we witness in the present moment a preview of our precarious global as well as local futures. And certainly in *Dreamland*, the architectural truth center of Juárez, this simultaneously local and global city, is represented by a local drug cartel's "House of Death," as well as by this local woman's cardboard shack situated adjacent to the truck loading docks of a maquiladora. These are two strategic and unhomely, minute locales, and their presence in *Dreamland* produces a friction or a counterweight that interrupts the celebratory fictions about globalization voiced by the neoliberal order's most ardent defenders. Indeed, as Jameson further suggests, it is precisely in this present state of emergency that, "One is tempted to resuscitate here the old Marxist 'humanist' opposition of 'relations between things' and 'relations between persons': in the much-celebrated free circulation opened up by global capitalism, it is 'things' (commodities) which freely circulate, while the circulation of 'persons' is more and more controlled."[20]

And so we arrive here at Jameson's explicit naming of what I earlier called Bowden's true subject: the power of a force (global capitalism) to transform and deform certain persons into (disposable) things. This is one reading forwarded by this textual moment from *Dreamland* that constitutes the center of this essay. But another reading is possible: that there is another force also at work here, one as unnoticed and misunderstood as is this allegorical female figure and her daily quest for survival on the streets of Juárez, a force accruing from a certain male gaze's externalization of this walking woman's transitive being in the world, its catachrestical reduction of her to the status of an assemblage of corporeal part-objects. The open question that this second reading solicits us to consider centers on the degree to which her visible reduction to a "tired face"—especially given the fact she is accorded no name, no voice, no conscious thoughts—effaces her personhood.[21]

[**A**lphabet/Abecedario; **L**ipstick; **Q**ueues; **S**cene of the Crime; **U**rbicide; **X**-ray; **T**elevision]

Exposure, a poetics of

EXTRACTS

Lecha: "An airplane. What's left of a Beachcraft Bonanza. We lost the pilot, one geologist, and a quarter-million-dollar sensor unit." The insurance adjustor spread the other eight-by-tens on the fold-down trays in front of both of them. The corpses had been draped with blankets. The focal point of the photographs seemed to be the scattered, mangled electronic equipment. Against the snow, the bundles of wires torn loose from the shattered black metal boxes reminded her of intestines. Engine oil appeared like black pools of what might have been blood.... In the close-ups, an arm dangled out of the front section of the wreckage.
 —Leslie Marmon Silko, *Almanac of the Dead* (1991)

John Smith: Olivia and Daniel Smith look at the jumpsuit man, who is holding a camera. Flash, flash. Click of the shutter. Whirr of advancing film. All of them wait for a photograph to form, for light to emerge from shadow, for an image to burn itself into paper.
 —Sherman Alexie, *Indian Killer* (1996)

Antonio: At the end of the album, taped to the back cover, there was a white envelope. When Antonio pulled on the flap, which was tucked in but unsealed, a small stack of photographs fell to the floor. He put the album on the bed and scrambled to pick them up. He was squatting to look under the dresser when he saw the bodies, three corpses lined up on a cement floor. Scattered all over the green linoleum, everywhere, were pictures of corpses. A morgue had fallen from the album and spilled around his feet. Corpses with their eyes open. Corpses with their pants pulled down, the seahorses of their genitals exposed. Corpses with their arms folded over their chests. Corpses with hands missing. Peasants in green shirts. Living men, in camouflage, posing with the corpses, as if to say, We're alive and they're dead. And here is the tattooed soldier, the painted killer, standing over a child lying face down on a dirt path.

—Héctor Tobar, *The Tattooed Soldier* (1998)

Ermila: Who was it that told her everything went up into thin air but never quite disappeared? Something always remained behind, like the photographs of her parents, like the formidable mass of oil on the asphalt where the van had once been parked.

—Helena María Viramontes, *Their Dogs Came with Them* (2008)

1. "*The focal point of the photographs seemed to be the scattered, mangled electronic equipment.*" Drawn from novels depicting homelessness as theme, trope, and image, these selected extracts foreground the twin senses of photography as a medium and the inherent contradictions bound up with a poetics of exposure. In the brief extract from *Indian Killer* photography as a medium is regarded primarily as a technological apparatus: "Flash, flash. Click of the shutter. Whirr of advancing film." And since the whirr of advancing film in the crypt of a camera body eventually results in a graphic image for viewing, photography represents a technological process that both captures and preserves emanations of light from some "there" and "then." The photographic image thus potentially fosters an exchange of affective intensities between the affecting subject or object represented in the photograph and the affected viewer who gazes at the product of the photochemical process. Hence the second sense of photography as a medium: the camera's apparatus and the photochemical or digital process of developing an image enables our communion with the spectral avatars of the already dead, especially those who have endured "the dual impact of historical violence and the structural dislocations of capitalist modernity."[1] Which is the case in the above extract from Héctor Tobar's novel *The Tattooed Soldier*, where a main character, Antonio, scrambles after dropping the titular tattooed soldier's secret stash of photographic trophies from the recent Guatemalan civil war on the floor of the soldier's rented apartment in downtown Los Angeles. He then finds

himself gazing not at the photographic prints per se, its paper medium, but rather at "the bodies, three corpses lined up on a cement floor."

And as the extract from Silko's novel *Almanac of the Dead* particularly underlines, a character named Lecha also is graphically exposed by photographic images to the hard fact of the world's resistant externality, its elemental opacity. Consider the uncanny category confusion that emerges as she processes eight-by-ten photographs of an Alaskan aviation accident in which what is normally out of sight (on the "inside") now has become exposed to view against the blank whiteness of snow on the ground (the outside): viscous engine oil looks like spilled blood; the wires and cables of mangled electronic equipment remind her of human intestines. Lecha's exposure to forensic photographs of this accident site through the medium of photography exposes more than just the possibility of a virtual communion with the dead, whose corpses are, in this instance, covered by blankets. Such photographic exposure to the sight of death also diagnoses how there exists an inherent gap between the past moment of light captured in and by a camera and the moment of our looking at the printed or digitally produced image. The theoretical bond between viewer and viewed produced as a result of photographic exposure, then, simultaneously exposes an unsettling absence or distance literally exemplified by the temporal lag associated with the speed of light as well as, by the description here of the corpses covered in blankets, these human victims who are clearly not the focal point of this series of photographs. Whether exemplified by a family snapshot, cinematography, or an x-ray, then, the poetics of exposure constitutes a paradoxical "bond of the furthest apart," to cite Sharon Cameron, who was writing in another context. To be sure, our exposure to photographs compels our regard "even or rather especially, in the absence of an orienting perspective that would make what is seen precisely recognizable."[2] After all, in the intensely immersive scene from *The Tattooed Soldier*, it is as if Antonio's existential being in the world, and the numbing tonality of the notational prose description Tobar creates, reveals an emergent dissociative disorder, one whose symptoms are a shock estrangement from his present scene of recognition and the suspension of his agency. After all, the blue photo album he has discovered has "spilled" its grisly contents "around his feet" and is likened to a morgue. After all, what is exposed to his gaze assumes the paradoxical reality of specters both present to his sight in this moment and like ghosts, "who don't appear in photos, or vampires, who don't appear in mirrors, because they're not actually there" and hence remain hauntingly inscrutable, beyond his cognitive apprehension.[3]

2. *"For an image to burn itself into paper."* Exposure as the state of being exposed to all manner of substances and material agencies—like to the sun and rain and dirt and toxins to which homeless bodies are relentlessly exposed. Exposure as the facing of an ontological condition: parental abandonment, in the character Ermila's case; the world's abiding pain, suffering, and death, in the character John Smith's case. Exposure as a pedagogy, a learning encounter that leads to new knowledge, for better or worse. Take Lecha's differential response (than that of the insurance adjustor who sits beside her on a flight to Alaska) to the forensic photographs of the wreckage from mysterious plane crashes, her assumption that the bits of wreckage, more so than a human arm dangling from the front of the plane, represent the focal point of such photographs. Take John Smith's affective unsettlement in that temporal interregnum between the click of the camera's shutter and the somewhat magical chemical burning of an image on photographic paper. It is as if the characters in these selected extracts have themselves become photographic plates, their sensoria so finely attuned to what is happening before their eyes; as if these characters have been gifted with second sight, its blessing and curse, as they face the ontological and epistemological challenges of making one's life out of "bits of wreckage. Some bones. The words of the dead. How make a world of this? How live in that world once made?"[4] Through this key verb *burn*, deployed in *Indian Killer* both to describe the photochemical process and to announce a paranoid main character's psychological obsession, at least at the outset of the novel, with fire and flames, we witness how the serial physical and mental wounds and material wreckage enmeshed with the trauma of the historical Real (abandonment and loss; dismemberment and death) cauterizes the human psyche, just as visible light itself cauterizes the exposed chemical skin of the photographic plate or paper.

In the novels referenced here whose excerpts compose this essay's extracts, the poetics of exposure in the unhomely urban U.S. West gets entangled with the imagery of haunting/being haunted by the corporeal, technological, and topographical forms of what we can call encrypted, sepulchral spaces:

a camera's closeted interior; the black boxes from the wrecked fuselage of a Beechcraft Bonanza airplane; a dresser drawer hiding a blue photo album, itself described as a "morgue" containing photographs of dead corpses with their killers. As is the case with the "morgue" created by the photo album's front and back covers in Tobar's description, the cluster of four sentence fragments each beginning with the word *corpses*, which follow the appearance of the word *morgue*, are paralleled by another quartet of sentence fragments that end the passage by exposing to view another type of fragment: body parts, such as a silver tooth; a woman's fists; a man's shoulder in rigor mortis; another dead man's skin color and his hair, sticky and stiff with dried blood. The parallelism of these two quartets of sentence fragments appearing on either side of the complete sentence that belatedly injects the tattooed soldier's presence in the frame, effectively encloses and embalms this sight of death, at the center of which poses the tattooed soldier. Tobar's prose technique here produces a force field of energy that passes from gazes to gazes, bodies to bodies, and from bodies as objects to material objects as themselves having agency. The visceral, rote repetition of *corpses*; the at-times tortured syntax and the amputation of sentences into sentence fragments; the haptic materiality of both body parts and part-objects—does not the focalization of Antonio's shock exposure to the sight of death here uncannily take on a life of its own as it unfurls, during this catalytic moment, with a heightened intensity to the degree that the look and the gaze, the living and the dead or disappeared who once lived under the light of sun and moon, are irrevocably bonded together?

3. *"Like black pools of what might have been blood."* In her book *Beyond Pleasure*, Margaret Iversen draws a useful distinction between the "traumatic photograph" and the "simulacral photograph."[5] Through an elaboration of Jacques Lacan's theoretical shift from mirror imagery to that of anamorphosis (the distorted projection of an image's real appearance on a plane or curved surface), Iverson suggests how, in the traumatic photograph, the historical Real breaks through the defensive shield of the viewer's consciousness, exploiting the inherent dissonance between one's being positioned as a sovereign subject of sight and, simultaneously, as the corporeal object of the gaze of human and nonhuman Others. We are fated always to look from one point or perspective, whereas human and nonhuman Others in the world also can gaze at us from all sides. Before the specific look of the individual subject, then, there already exists the gaze of others at us: which is to say, the regard both of humans and of nonhumans and of things inhabiting our present world; and, in the visual arts, the regard of posed figures and of things from the past looking out toward our space of viewing beyond the visual field of the image. So, Lacan theorizes, no originary point of vision exists, an optical fact undermining the illusion of mastery forwarded by the simulacral photograph, the visual field of which is organized according to the law of perspective, as this develops from a singular point of view. The self-reflective masterful desire of consciousness propped up by the simulacral photograph is founded on a misrecognition, in particular a blanking out of the uncanny realization that the viewing subject is not just a subjectivity but also a subject, both to the unconscious—with its repressed desires, fears, and anxieties and its introjection of how we imagine others are regarding us—and by the blind spot inherent in any visual field.

With this Lacanian perspective in mind, then, let us return to consider the excerpt from Viramontes's *Their Dogs Came with Them*, at the point where Ermila recalls someone telling her that "everything went up into thin air but never quite disappeared": "Like the photographs of her parents, like the formidable mass of oil on the asphalt where the van once had parked." Ermila's look at a traumatic photograph elaborates three key points. Looking at a family photograph of her absentee parents is traumatizing, to be sure, in large part because possessing this photograph entwines her spectatorship of it with her parents' pose of directly looking out toward a camera and, by extension, the space of the viewer beyond the frame. This particular entangled encounter of look and gaze reactivates a primal scene for Ermila, one in which her subjectivity is subject to a volatile intersection of both projected desires and introjected anxieties. As if the primal scene of her childhood abandonment by her parents will shape her present and future psychic life as a repetition of the desire for recognition from "the lost parental gaze."[6] And let us further note how the dynamic of photographic exposure rendered in this scene of misrecognition is tethered to the equally haunted, dark materiality of oil on an asphalt driveway, this literal stain figuratively surfacing as a metonym for both the mental residue of her past trauma that cannot be assimilated or explained away and the L.A. petroculture and the urbicide spawned by the economic rhythms of capitalist modernity, where the law of eminent domain and new freeway design and construction have transformed her domestic home and her familiar neighborhood into an unhomely space of abjection.

4. "This was too much to see. Too much to know and hold inside your head":[7]

> Black pools of engine oil on an asphalt pavement.
> Black pools of engine oil that might have been blood.
> Black hair of a corpse sticky and stiff with blood.

5. "*Something always remained behind.*" Writing about the Gothic themes and tropes in Jacques Derrida's "ghost writing," Jodey Castricano notes how the theme of the revenant bears a special relation to economy. This is not only because the English word "revenant" relates to the word "revenue" but also because of its etymological linkage with the French verb *revenir*, meaning both "to come back" (say, as a ghost) and "to amount to" something (as a return on an investment).[8] The spectral dead depend on the living to keep them alive in their hearts so as to preserve their influence. The living uncannily rely on the dead as well: even as the living give the dead a future, the dead in turn endow the living with a genealogical past through which they may come to know and place themselves on a continuum between the past and present. It is not so much that every journey in life takes place in the haunted company of the dead, as the gypsy in Cormac McCarthy's *The Crossing* believes, as that such journeys, rightly seen, transpire in the company of undead revenants: the literal dead and gone who yet are symbolically alive, their spectral existence embedded in such material things as photographic images as well as the memory traces lodged in human hearts. Assembling specters (the photographic traces of the dead), the spectral (dreams and memories), and speculation (insurance and risk; resource extraction; real estate development) with specularity (the projected gaze at and from within the photographic frame), these selected novels' overall poetics of exposure produces an economy of revenance testifying to the historic violence and hemispheric dislocations of capitalist modernity and postmodernity.[9] As Silko's novel reveals, photographs and other technologies of visual surveillance represent crucial weapons of containment and control for regimes

pursuing what Achille Mbembe has termed *necropolitics*: that condition where regimes in power exercise their sovereign authority both through disciplinary technologies of control and surveillance and through the production of spaces organized by a dominant logic of death. Through spatial segregation, for example, those marginalized populations regarded by the dominant group as being disposable (the refugee, the exile, the ethnic immigrant Other, the homeless) become targeted for the operation of terror and death and by policies that refuse them basic social services or protections.[10]

However, like the waste matter and wasted lives spun off as the surplus remainder of capitalist production, it is also imperative that we ponder Ermila's hard-earned lesson that "Something is always left behind" in the bones, the bits of wreckage, and the words and the photographs of the undead. Here we should consider further Silko's *Almanac of the Dead*, where it turns out that in the photographs of the various men charged by federal authorities over the years with being Geronimo, one anonymous man's face uncannily glimmers in the frame, presenting to viewers a mysterious spectral image "where the faces of the other Geronimos should have been."[11] In this example, as well as in the related example in Silko's novel when Lecha views photographs of the strewn wreckage of an airplane, we witness how the photograph, as material object or relic of the dead, always traffics in competing forces: between the drive for the fixity or closure of meaning (containment) and the pleasure bound up with the unruly, libidinal play or excess of meaning inherent in all visual signifiers; between rational and magical thinking; and between the demands of matter and spirit. The fluid, at times volatile, osmosis between viewing subject and photographic object does not just signal an ontological or epistemological uncertainty—an ambiguity that can forward in the viewing subject a sense of suspended agency. Rather, this osmotic space of mediation exemplified by the photograph implies the possibility of change and transformation. It performs this mission by indirectly exposing the traumatic stain that activates the terrain of memory and of history for those marginalized, but not finally defeated, by the continuing coloniality of power. In John Beck's words, as a result of this spectral presence in the photographic framing of the various Geronimos, "The novel develops a counter epistemology in forwarding the process of image production as not limited to documentary certification or mimetic representation."[12] This haunting ghost in the photographic machine thus exposes "a metaphysical power somehow finding a passage into the world" and, as a result of this literal and figurative exposure, momentarily destabilizes the disciplinary mechanisms and technologies of control exercised by the presiding coloniality of power.[13] "Because the differences created with each iteration of 'Geronimo' remain entangled in representations of the people's struggle to survive that Silko maps in her fiction," Audrey Goodman rightly observes, "each scene enacts a new or modified strategy of visual resistance."[14]

[**Cryptography**; **Psychometropolis**; **Scene** of the Crime; **Television**; **Urbicide**; **X**-ray]

Freeways and highways, a literary collision

EXTRACTS

Method of this project: literary montage. I needn't say anything. Merely show.

—Walter Benjamin

Any text is constructed as a mosaic of quotations; any text is the absorption and transformation of another. The notion of *intertextuality* replaces that of intersubjectivity, and poetic language is read as at least double.

—Julia Kristeva

Audio tracks

1. "We both fall silent, or perhaps fall into a kind of noise, distracted by sudden demands of the route: highways merging, speed checks, roadwork ahead, dangerous curves, a tollbooth—look for spare change and pass the coffee."[1]
2. "'I think we're lost,' she said. 'We're not that lost,' he said. 'You can hear the freeway. Listen.'"
3. "Sirens, horns, the din of speeding cars, such racket of steel and gas and industrial innovation and the ingenuity of imagination all reduced to freeway traffic."
4. "Uphill and invisible, traffic out on the boulevard to and from the freeway uttered tuneful exhaust phrases which went echoing out to sea, where crews of oil tankers sliding along, hearing them, could have figured it for wildlife taking care of nighttime business on an exotic coast."
"They entered the transition tunnel to the eastbound Santa Monica Freeway, where the radio, which had been playing the Byrds' 'Eight Miles High,' lost the signal."

5. "An insular tale of loss of the formative terra cognita that exists in the song only as memory, a map written in the darkness of your guts, readable in a cross section of your autopsied heart."

Bones

6. "As if driving itself, the car left the freeway and started up the hill, an ascension."
7. "As if their home cemetery in some way still did exist, in a land where you could somehow walk, and not need the East San Narciso Freeway, and bones could still rest in peace, nourishing ghosts of dandelions, no one to plow them up. As if the dead really do persist, even in a bottle of wine."
8. "While the construction men were building the freeway, they found bones. Telling no one, they just threw the skulls into the wet cement and kept on working."
9. "Who is to know the fate of his bones, or how often he is to be buried?"

Concrete

10. "Sleep was essential if she was to be on the freeway by ten o'clock. Sometimes the freeway ran out, in a scrap metal yard in San Pedro or on the main street of Palmdale or out somewhere no place at all where the flawless burning concrete just stopped, turned into common road, abandoned construction sheds rusting beside it."
11. "She exited and ended up in an unfamiliar city block of boarded-up warehouses. She drove beneath the overpass at the edges of a no-man's-land where a single eucalyptus tree stood tall and slight, an anomaly of nature. Otherwise, the deserted area revealed the congealed remnants of squatters like scabs on a wound . . . people bequeathing cold and blackened wood chips to campfires; abandoned makeshift cardboard beds; forsaken newspapers. They squirreled away bundles of clothes or bottles collected for deposit money inside the concrete catacomb of pillar and girder."
12. "She twirled her index finger on the smudged glass, moss-covered cedars along the highway casting shape-shifting shadows across her face, like dark clouds passing over, then breaking wide again."

13. "The whoosh of the city's vehicles, the broken-up silence from faraway night, made her feel that they lived on an island, the freeways closing in on them like ocean waves, the tierra firme vanishing swiftly."
14. "So one learns to proceed with a strange and exhilarating mixture of long-range confidence and close-range wariness."

Dogs

15. "Above the woven arteries of freeways, a copter's searchlight swept over the roadblocks to catch a lone stray running out of the edge of light. The bitch zigzagged across the pavement of First Street, its underbelly droopy with nursing nipples."
16. "When the dog had worn himself down we headed back over the freeway, and once again sat and waited near the house. Then we went over the freeway for the last time and walked the short distance to the Walgreens they had just built."
17. "We laughed a lot, even after we tried to take a shortcut through a dog kennel. Climbing a fence with Dobermans barking and snarling beneath us. Abbott and Costello. No one would pick us up when we got to the freeway. Not true, some guy in a truck finally did, but we were almost there, waved him on."
18. "Then the night was very quiet again—not even the distant freeway traffic could be heard, or the footpads of coyotes, or the slither of snakes."
19. "Vacant lots like missing teeth gave a rough grin to the streets we haunted."

Embankments

20. "*Danger Landscaping Ahead*—one can still be grateful for this sustained programme of planting and improvement that has made the freeway embankments and cuttings a visible environmental asset to the city (even if freeway noise and dirt are not)."
21. "On lunch hour I'd go with Ruth to collect weed bouquets, scrambling hot and sweaty up the freeway embankment for Queen Anne's lace and tobacco weed. Rocks in our shoes."
22. "The arbutus trees rustled in the wind, and the undersides of their leaves—the sides that gather oxygen—were flashing sage-colored

against the freeway's embankment.... And I kept thinking of some of the fields I had just seen, now barely turning green, and how those fields reminded me of fears I had when I was younger—fears that nature might simply decide not to wake up one year. Nature would open her eyes, go back to sleep and never return."

23. "Her sneakers stood beneath miles of earth that had been heaved up, plowed aside, carted off and carried away in preparation for the rolling asphalt of the Interstate 710 Long Beach and Pomona freeways. Severed tree roots jutted from mud walls. It was another planet altogether and she gazed above her at the high ridge and marveled at how far down the tree roots had grown. Except for the horizon being erased by the night, she saw nothing above them. Out of sight, out of mind, and over the embankment, everything was forgotten. Nonexistent."

Frontage

24. "He stopped at a fish market. Stay here, be right back. Then the freeway and hot gusts of air. Down onto a ribbon of hot macadam road where they never saw another car. One slow red tractor. Windmills. Hereford cattle knee deep in Indian paintbrush."

25. "Across the road and across a dry wash a hundred yards was what looked like a huge mobile-home town, with a factory or a refinery of some kind lit up behind it and in full swing. There were lights on in a lot of the mobile homes, and there were cars moving along an access road that ended near the freeway overpass a mile the other way."

26. "We take the next exit from the freeway, hoping it will lead somewhere, and soon are on bumpy blacktop with ruts and loose gravel. I go slowly. Streetlamps overhead throw swinging arcs of sodium lights through the sheets of rain. We pass from light into shadow into light into shadow again without a single sign of welcome anywhere. A sign announces 'STOP' to our left, but does not tell which way to turn. One way looks as dark as the other. We could go endlessly through these streets and not find anything and now not even find the freeway again."

Ghosts

27. "Everything happens as though the streets and facades of the city keep to themselves the unconscious of the event, the insurrectional moment as trace."
28. "Like haunted houses, like the whole highway was a long ghost town."
29. "The building would be haunted forever then. The foreman would finish the last skyscraper in the city and move on to his government job. He would be working on a freeway exit in the Cascade Mountains when he saw his first ghost."
30. "All I see in hindsight is the chaos of history repeated, over and over, reenacted, reinterpreted, the world, its fucked-up heart palpitating beneath us, failing, messing up again and again as it winds its way around a sun. And in the middle of it all, tribes, families, people, all beautiful things falling apart, debris, dust, erasure.... Perhaps I'm also chasing ghosts and echoes. Except mine are not in history books, and not in cemeteries."

Helicopters

31. "Ten years later the child becomes the young woman who will recognize the invading engines of the Quarantine Authority helicopters because their whir of blades above the roof of her home, their earth-rattling explosive motors, will surpass in volume the combustion of engines driving the bulldozer tractors, slowly, methodically unspooling the six freeways."
32. "Helicopters were always landing on the roof at UCLA, suggesting trauma all over Southern California, remote scenes of highway carnage, distant falling cranes, bad days ahead for the husband or wife or mother or father who had not yet (even as the helicopter landed and the trauma team rushed the stretcher into triage) gotten the call."

Incidents

33. "The Loop has electronic sensors embedded every half-mile out there in the pavement itself, each sensor counting the crossing cars every twenty seconds. The Loop has its own mind, a Xerox

Sigma V computer which prints out, all day and night, twenty-second readings on what is and is not moving in each of the Loop's eight lanes. It is the Xerox Sigma V that makes the big board flash red when traffic out there drops below fifteen miles an hour. It is the Xerox Sigma V that tells the Operations crew when they have an 'incident' out there. An 'incident' is the heart attack on the San Diego, the jackknifed truck on the Harbor, the Camaro just now tearing out the Cyclone fence on the Santa Monica. 'Out there' is where incidents happen."

Jams

34. "'Where are you?' 'Doing the Joan Didion freeway thang. You know, slouching around L.A. Sorry, but it's hard to feel exhilarated going five miles an hour.'"

35. "Stuck behind the bumper of a mammoth Mayflower moving truck and unable to see what was ahead, tired of seeing the driver on her left picking his nose, the driver on her right applying lipstick on her mouth. Motorcycle riders, mere flashes on her rearview mirror, slalomed in between the stalled, throbbing stoppage of cars, hundreds, thousands, filed in neat rows. The cars and trucks began to crowd her until a wild impatience moved her to set her signaling blinkers on and aim the car in a crawl toward the closest runaway exit out of the Pomona 60 West."

36. "In both directions of the freeway, spread across ten lanes, hundreds of cars piled one into the other in an almost endless jam of shrieking notes. Perhaps, perhaps someone had caught it all on video. There was always someone out there catching unsightly things on video. Perhaps not."

Knots

37. "The freeway interchange right above their apartment looped like knots of asphalt and cement and the cars swerved into unexpected steep turns with squeals of braking tires. Sunlight glistened off the bending steel guardrails of the ramps."

38. "Gnarls of freeway flotsam from the bleached glass meridians of the Santa Monica freeway: plastic lawn chairs, Styrofoam cooler lids, and broken skis—cheap, vulgar, toxic items that will either decompose in minutes or remain essentially unchanged until our galaxy goes supernova."
39. "She stepped to the edge of the roadway. Forty feet below her, blocks of asphalt swam in the river, muddy water swirling around them. The bridge supports, pillars of thick steel blackened by dynamite, had taken up a gnarled, snakelike dance."

Lanes

40. "They went across the road and into the trees, struggling up the refuse-choked bank to the freeway fence, and then, with La Migra right behind them, they went up and over the fence and onto the shoulder of the freeway. The cars streamed by in a rush, even at this hour. Four lanes in each direction, the torrent of headlights, sixty-five and seventy miles an hour: suicide."
41. "The eastbound lanes teemed with VW buses in jittering paisleys, primer-coated street hemis, woodies of authentic Dearborn pine, TV-star-piloted Porsches, Cadillacs carrying dentists to extramarital trysts, windowless vans with lurid teen dramas in progress inside, pickups with mattresses full of country cousins from the San Joaquin, all wheeling along together down into these great horizonless fields of housing, under the power transmission lines, everybody's radios lasing on the same AM stations, under a sky like watered milk, and the white bombardment of a sun smogged into only a smear of probability."
42. "They walked a few hundred feet to a two-lane transition road where cars passed under a bridge and into a tunnel, the sound of their engines echoing into a fluttering roar. To reach the shelters they would have to cross the transition road, which was filled with rush-hour traffic, two lanes of cars snaking past them at about twenty miles an hour. Inside the cars, everyone seemed to be wearing sunglasses."

Maps

43. "*There are maps and there are maps and there are maps.* The uncanny thing was that he could see all of them at once, filter some, pick them out like transparent windows and place them even delicately and consecutively in a complex grid of pattern, discernment, body politic. For each of the maps was a layer of music, a clef, an instrument, a musical instruction, a change of measure, a coda.... On the surface, the complexity of layers should drown an ordinary person, but ordinary persons never bother to notice, never bother to notice the historic grid of land usage and property, the great overlays of transport—sidewalks, bicycle paths, roads, freeways, systems of transit both ground and air a thousand natural and man-made divisions, variations both dynamic and stagnant, patterns and connections by every conceivable definition from the distribution of wealth to race, from patterns of climate, to the curious blueprint of the skies."

44. "It maps a baroquely layered but ultimately one-dimensional reality (Marcuse à la Klein bottle?) in which the city is at once an endless text always promising meaning but ultimately only offering hints and signs of a possible and final reality . . . like printed circuit or a freeway."

45. "I follow long lines, red or yellow or black, to beautiful names like Memphis, to names unseemly—Truth or Consequences, Shakespeare—to old names now resignified by new mythologies: Arizona, Apache, Cochise Stronghold. And when I glance up from my map, I see the long, straight line of the highway thrusting us forward into an uncertain future."

Necropolises

46. "Drive along the highways of Vietnam for any extended distance and you may notice, if you are looking for them, the cemeteries abutting the roads. Marking each one is an obelisk, a monument, or a sculpture, usually a trio of heroes, sometimes including a heroine, tall enough to be visible from a distance. Draw closer and you will

see a stone stela, engraved with the names of the dead. Every town and village have their own necropolis, devoted to the martyrs who died in the twentieth-century wars to unify and liberate the country. These burial grounds exist in America, too, and perhaps if I drove its freeways and thoroughfares looking for them, I would see them and think that America was preoccupied with its sacrificed warriors."

47. "We pull over in front of a large sign, which the boy reads aloud as we unbuckle our seat belts:

Apache Prisoner-of-War Cemeteries.
We unlock doors, step out of the car.

On a metal plaque fixed into a stone at the entrance to the cemetery, there is some kind of explanation of what we're about to see. The boy is in charge, he knows, of reading site-specific information. He stands in front of it and reads aloud, his prosody well attuned to the necrological hypocrisy of the plaque. It explains that three hundred Chiricahua Apaches rest in that cemetery, where they were buried as prisoners of war after they surrendered to the US Army in 1894, and commemorates 'their industry and perseverance on their long road to a new way of life.'"

48. "I remembered the souvenirs in the gift shop of the atomic museum, the little chocolates shaped like Fat Man and Little Boy. . . . I turned to the person next to me. Earlier I had seen him leading a foreign camera crew. He was in his late-fifties. He stood very quietly, hands behind his back, posture ramrod straight but not rigid. Without expression he watched the cenotaph. He was Japanese. It is possible to feel at once hollow and aflame, like a ghost burning."

Overpass

49. "Toward the small hours of the morning the traffic on the freeway slacked and the rain stopped. He sat up shivering and hitched the blanket about his shoulders. He'd put some crackers from the roadside diner in the pocket of his coat and he sat eating them and watching the gray light flush out the raw wet fields beyond the

roadway. He thought he heard the distant cries of cranes where they would be headed north to their summering grounds in Canada and he thought of them asleep in a flooded field in Mexico in a dawn long ago, standing single-footed in the wetlands with their bills tucked, gray figures aligned in rows like hooded monks at prayer. When he looked across the overpass to the far side of the turnpike he saw another such as he sitting also solitary and alone."

50. "They reached the freeway and stood underneath it, dwarfed by the immensity of the structure. This overpass was higher than most, an underbelly of concrete covered with a fine network of leafless ivy branches that spread out like capillaries across the gray surface. Water oozed like blood from the cement, and the damp air around them smelled of feces and urine."

51. "In the distance, they see thunderclouds gathering, and they walk in that direction. Toward what now, they do not know. Away from the darkness behind them. North into the heart of light they walk."

Petrotopia

52. "Sun glimmers on fragments of abandoned earthquake-ravaged freeway held up to the sky by uncollapsed poles—like the sculpture garden at the Ridgecrest Mall. The traffic jams abruptly. Lolling here in the glorious West makes me think of photos of those dead factory towns in other parts of the world . . . cities so big and dead as to have their own complete cosmologies of the afterworld. Now, contrast these visions with the shiny turquoise buildings of the West: blue-jeaned employee babies learning Japanese in corporate crèches, freeways brimming with the success stories of the New Order—software, jets, and submarines; white bond paper, vaccines, and slasher movies."

53. "'I'm going to LA,' Orville finished with an air of triumph. 'Yeah,' said Bert, getting into it. 'Hollywood and Vine, Sunset Strip, teeny-boppers, Homes of the Stars.' 'Not that LA,' said Orville, without rancor, lost in his dream. 'Little America. Wyoming. The world's largest service station, over a hundred pumps. Restaurants, showers, dozens of rest rooms, novelty stands, electric shavers. . . .' His voice

trailed off, overcome by the grandeur of it. 'My own pump, premium and regular, four hoses, two on each side, a niche for myself, better than that supermarket I worked in when I was sixteen.'"

Quite often

54. "During the past several years I have felt myself a sleepwalker, moving through the world unconscious of the moment's high issues, oblivious to its data, alert only to the stuff of bad dreams, the children burning in the locked car in the supermarket parking lot, the bike boys stripping down stolen cars on the captive cripple's ranch, the freeway sniper who feels 'real bad' about picking off the family of five, the hustlers, the insane, the cunning Okie faces that turn up in military investigations, the sullen lurking in doorways, the lost children, all the ignorant armies jostling in the night."

Refrains

55. "Sleep under the freeway. It was almost a refrain in the neighborhood."
56. "Fffffffffffffhhh, cars driving past on highways. Ffhhhhhhhhhhhh, cars we hear from inside the motel."
57. "We know the sound of freeways better than we do rivers, the howl of distant trains better than wolf howls, we know the smell of gas and freshly wet concrete and burned rubber better than we do the smell of cedar or sage or even fry bread—which isn't traditional, like reservations aren't traditional, but nothing is original, everything comes from something that came before, which was once nothing. Everything is new and doomed."
58. "So only transit, transfer, translation and difference. It is not the house passing away, like a mobile home or shepherd's hut, it is in passing that we dwell."

Signs

59. "How many grids overlap other grids overlap other grids? Aqueducts, power lines, freeways, signage . . . like those ones with felt-pen-on-cardboard signs saying Will Work for Food."

60. "One of the huge freeway signs had fallen or been knocked down, and now lay on the ground, propped up by a pair of dead sycamore trees. With the trees, it formed a massive lean-to."
61. "Inside the car, I've grown accustomed to our smell, to the intermittent silence between us, to instant coffee. But never to the road signs planted like omens along the road: Adultery Is a Sin; Sponsor a Highway; Gun Show This Weekend! Never habituated, either, to seeing the cemeteries of plastic toys abandoned on front lawns on reservations, or the melancholy adults waiting in line, like children, to refill their large plastic cups with bright-colored sodas in gas station shops, or those resilient water towers in small towns, which remind me of the equipment we used in school during science lab classes. All of that leaves me in firefly mode."

Trash

62. "Quilted-steel catering trucks crisscross in the afternoon. Their ripples shine like a lake of potable water after hard desert passage. It's a Collection Day, and the garbage trucks are all heading north toward the Ventura Freeway, a catharsis of dumpsters, all hues, shapes and batterings."
63. "For an hour she prowled among the sunless, concrete underpinnings of the freeway, finding drunks, bums, pedestrians, pederasts, hookers, walking psychotics, no secret mailbox. But at last in the shadows she did come on a can with a swinging trapezoidal top, the kind you throw trash in: old and green, nearly four feet high. On the swinging part were hand-painted the initials W.A.S.T.E."

Underneath it all

64. "It was night and raining when she arrived downtown and parked and began looking for the girl. There were thousands of people living on the streets there: staying under overpasses or sleeping in cars or worn-down old Winnebagos and camper vans, covered in tarps outside of closed businesses or sleeping in vacant lots or squatting in empty buildings. There were alcoholics and drug addicts,

schizophrenics and sociopaths, ex-cons and war veterans, prostitutes and hustlers, gutter punks, runaways, and street kids."

65. "She was south of the freeway now, and was decidedly anxious. . . . But already the streets looked different than they did to the north of the freeway. The large old bungalows were replaced by liquor stores, discount clothing shops, fast-food places. On the left she saw the Korean Catholic Church, Doug's Wine and Spirits, and a burned-out gas station. On the right, Mama's Soul Food, Victory Guns, two storefront churches, and a store sign that said—she looked twice to make sure—'98 cent Housewives etc.'"

66. "Lightning illuminates a turquoise mural on a freeway underpass. I can hear the TV blaring up above. There are two hacksaws in a sink filled with pink water and suds and I smile to myself, hungry. Whenever I hear about some young guy on the news who was found near the beach, maybe part of his body, an arm or leg or a torso, sucked clean in a bag near a freeway underpass, I have to whisper to myself, 'Dirk.'"

Vertigo

67. "I feel along my mouth with my tongue and watch the passing cars enter the freeway, and the gamy taste brings with it the heavy feelings of sunlight on my skin, the layers and layers of lush greenery, the soft chirring sounds that were part of the silence."

68. "I sit on the porch stoop, the light above the door to the cabin turned on because it's still dark out. First, I study the map, locate where we are now. We're much further away from home than I thought—a vertigo swells slow in my stomach, like a crescent moon tide."

69. "I looked down at the floor, too, at the swirls of cream in the gray of the linoleum. And the darker gray and the small black spots a vertigo surprise once you noticed. I perused the floor, memorizing the randomness.
    Why would he kill her? Dad?"

West, the storied direction

70. "And as we pushed westward, patches of what the garage-man called 'sage brush' appeared, and then the mysterious outlines of table-like hills, and then red bluffs ink-blotted with junipers, and then a mountain range, dun grading into blue, and blue into dream, and the desert would meet us with a steady gale, dust, gray thorn bushes, and hideous bits of tissue paper mimicking pale flowers among the prickles of wind-tortured withered stalks all along the highway; in the middle of which there sometimes stood simple cows, immobilized in a position (tail left, white eyelashes right) cutting across all human rules of traffic."

71. "Anyhow, today we're going to be telling bedtime stories on our picnic, and on Indian Avenue we're just about to turn off onto the Interstate 10 freeway to head west, riding in the clapped-out ancient red Saab."

72. "Stories that make the familiar strange again, like those that revealed the lost landscapes, lost cemeteries, lost species around my home. Conversations that make everything around them disappear. Dreams that I forget until I realize they have colored everything."

73. "The challenge is how to tell two stories at once: the history of revolutionary violence that has unfolded in the space of the city; and the history of that other violence enacted by the economic production of urban space—all the disappearances, demolitions, and expulsions that accompany mindless urban renovation, and the generally insipid, hygienic, inevitably boring, and sterile constructions that are thrown up in its wake. The two stories are of course not unrelated."

X as erasure

74. "A man on the side of the road was stepping out of an old red truck. A woman sat on the passenger seat, staring straight ahead. The girl knew what the woman was staring at. She was staring at nothing. There was nothing out there to see. The man kicked the door of the truck over and over again as the steam rose up from under the hood.

'That's right, just kick and kick,' said the girl. A raven flew across the sky and then the truck disappeared. Her brother tapped her arm. 'What is it?' 'Trampled,' he said. 'That man was trampled.' He licked the tip of his finger and drew an *X* through the dust on the window."

75. "On a Monday morning the workers would find:

MR SPEEDY X POOR X SIDE; BROOKLYN DIABLOS C/S; RUEBEN, ERNIE, RALPH; EL CHINO JOCKEY X LOTE M/ LIL LIZARD, SANTOS X MCBRIDE QUE RIFA; RUDY LOVES LA CAT BERNIECE POR VIDA.

The boys would never know that in thirty years from tonight, the tags would crack from earthquakes, the weight of vehicles, the force of muscular tree roots, from the tramplings of passersby, become as faded as ancient engravings, as old as the concrete itself, as cold and clammy as a morgue table. Not even concrete engravings would guarantee immortality, though tonight they would feel immortal."

Yuppie cartography

76. "Mental geographies betray class prejudice. In the trendy-chic L.A. Weekly's 'Best of Los Angeles' guide, one of the 'Ten Best of the Best' is the Robertson Boulevard off-ramp of the Santa Monica Freeway near Beverly Hills: where the air starts to clear of smog and the true heaven of the Westside begins. In Yuppie deli-map consciousness, landscapes tend to compress logarithmically as soon as one leaves the terrain of luxury lifestyles."

77. "Back on the freeway I pushed the truck through the limeade air, climbed over a pass, and dropped into an urbanized desert: overflow strip malls and endless pods of pastel housing within commuting distance of San Bernardino and Riverside—suburbs of suburbs, bedrooms of bedroom communities, absorbing the quality-of-life refugees until the refuge grew into an epicenter. Nothing remained undeveloped except the cemeteries. Only the dead had open space."

Zero-degree writing

78. "There were also strange road signs saying things like Caution: Dust Storms May Exist and another one saying Zero Visibility Possible, which I knew meant something about bad weather conditions, but I smiled to myself thinking it was like a good-luck sign for us because we'd have to be invisible now that were going to enter a town full of strangers."

79. "After a while, even thoughts lose shape and float like ghosts. Things are explained, but the sentences have no subject, only a hint of a verb, and after a while, even the object is a muddled thing. . . . Memory ebbs, and the cavalcade of the vanished and of the dead disappears from sight and becomes some ghost column winding through the city streets that no one professes to see."

Coda: list of sources

1. Valeria Luiselli, *Lost Children Archive*, 45.
2. Sherman Alexie, *Indian Killer*, 203.
3. Helena Viramontes, *Their Dogs Came with Them*, 209.
4. Thomas Pynchon, *Inherent Vice*, 4, 135.
5. Rebecca Solnit, *A Field Guide to Getting Lost*, 121.
6. Luis Alberto Urrea, *Into the Beautiful North*, 242.
7. Pynchon, *The Crying of Lot 49*, 79.
8. Viramontes, *Dogs*, 157.
9. W. G. Sebald, *The Rings of Saturn*, 11.
10. Joan Didion, *Play It as It Lays*, 17.
11. Viramontes, *Dogs*, 276.
12. Attica Locke, *The Cutting Season*, 50.
13. Viramontes, *Dogs*, 316–17.
14. Reyner Banham, *Los Angeles*, 197.
15. Viramontes, *Dogs*, 77.
16. Willy Vlautin, *The Motel Life*, 145.
17. Lucia Berlin, *A Manual for Cleaning Women*, 282.
18. Pynchon, *Inherent Vice*, 70.
19. Solnit, *Field Guide*, 88.
20. Banham, *Los Angeles*, 70.

21. Berlin, *Manual*, 264.
22. Douglas Coupland, *Polaroids from the Dead*, 97.
23. Viramontes, *Dogs*, 225–26.
24. Berlin, *Manual*, 198.
25. Richard Ford, *Rock Springs*, 20.
26. Robert Pirsig, *Zen and the Art of Motorcycle Maintenance*, 389.
27. Kristin Ross, "Parisian Noir," 90.
28. Urrea, *The Water Museum*, 54–55.
29. Alexie, *Indian Killer*, 405.
30. Luiselli, *Lost Children Archive*, 146.
31. Viramontes, *Dogs*, 12.
32. Didion, *The Year of Magical Thinking*, 135–36.
33. Didion, *We Tell Ourselves Stories in Order to Live*, 236.
34. Karen Tei Yamashita, *Tropic of Orange*, 58.
35. Viramontes, *Dogs*, 276.
36. Yamashita, *Tropic*, 55.
37. Viramontes, *Under the Feet of Jesus*, 16.
38. Coupland, *Generation X*, 81.
39. Héctor Tobar, *The Tattooed Soldier*, 112.
40. T. Coraghessan Boyle, *The Tortilla Curtain*, 170.
41. Pynchon, *Inherent Vice*, 19.
42. Tobar, *Tattooed Soldier*, 11.
43. Yamashita, *Tropic*, 56–57.
44. Mike Davis, *City of Quartz*, 67.
45. Luiselli, *Lost Children*, 39.
46. Viet Thanh Nguyen, *Nothing Ever Dies*, 23.
47. Luiselli, *Lost Children*, 137–38.
48. Ellen Meloy, *Last Cheater's Waltz*, 223.
49. Cormac McCarthy, from *Cities of the Plain*, as quoted in *The Border Trilogy*, 266.
50. Tobar, *Tattooed Soldier*, 10–11.
51. Luiselli, *Lost Children*, 316.
52. Coupland, *Shampoo Planet*, 217–18.
53. Rob Swigart, *Little America*, 10–11.
54. Didion, *We Tell Ourselves Stories*, 277–78.
55. Tobar, *Tattooed Soldier*, 7.
56. Luiselli, *Lost Children*, 343.
57. Tommy Orange, *There There*, 11.

58. Jean-François Lyotard, from "Domus and Megapolis," quoted in *Rethinking Architecture*, 275.
59. Coupland, *Generation X*, 91.
60. Octavia Butler, *Parable of the Sower*, 199.
61. Luiselli, *Lost Children*, 178.
62. Pynchon, *Gravity's Rainbow*, 772.
63. Pynchon, *The Crying of Lot 49*, 105.
64. Vlautin, *The Free*, 255.
65. Nine Revoyr, *Southland*, 58.
66. Ellis, *Imperial Bedrooms*, 101, 184.
67. Nic Pizzolatto, *Galveston*, 150.
68. Luiselli, *Lost Children*, 141–42.
69. Louise Erdrich, *The Round House*, 163.
70. Vladimir Nabokov, *Lolita*, 153.
71. Coupland, *Generation X*, 14.
72. Solnit, *Field Guide*, 13.
73. Ross, "Parisian Noir," 101.
74. Julie Otsuka, *When the Emperor Was Divine*, 40–41.
75. Viramontes, *Dogs*, 164.
76. Davis, *City of Quartz*, 375.
77. Meloy, *The Anthropology of Turquoise*, 34.
78. Luiselli, *Lost Children*, 273.
79. Charles Bowden, *Murder City*, 129, 42.

[**I**dyll; **J**unkspaces; **M**otel noir; **N**oir motel; **O**il rich; **P**sychometropolis; **U**rbicide; **W**indows]

Graves and gravestones

EXTRACTS

There was one grave I hadn't looked at yet. It was marked with a white wooden cross just tall enough to stand above the weeds which grew up around it. Although I couldn't see it, there would be an unpainted wooden border around the grave. A circle of Styrofoam hung from the top point of the cross. From the bottom of the circle, pointing down, a piece of wire wrapped in green, and, below that, a faded paper flower barely visible in the weeds. There was no headstone, no name, no dates. My brother.
—James Welch, *Winter in the Blood* (1974)

The family cemetery was surrounded by a low, crumbling wall of ocean cobblestones. Wire fencing, now rusting and sagging, enclosed the entire west and north sides where the wall had fallen and stone was scattered over the ground. The recent graves were still mounded high. The white wood crosses that marked them were entwined with red and yellow plastic roses and plastic wreathes of green ferns and pink carnations. Graves in the older section were marked with flat wedges of dark basalt from the low volcanic peaks, *cerros*, they'd passed driving from San Isidro. Some of the black stones had been patterned with crude white crosses gradually weathering away. Around the stone markers the plastic roses and carnations had been planted into the white dune sand as if they had always grown there.
—Leslie Marmon Silko, *Almanac of the Dead* (1991)

And still the graves pile tiny hump next to tiny hump. Did the wind snatch all these children up? Drought? Influenza? Poisoned air or water? There is no other sign that anyone lived here once. There is nothing like a church, a bar, or even the foundations of a church or bar. There is no sign that there were owners of these children. And beyond the cemetery fence nothing but ancient slabs of cow manure, rock-hard pebbles from sheep, and a high, lonely wind off the ridge. The sound underfoot is like the pitiless crunch you hear on old made-for-television Westerns—either crusty snow or flinty soil, nothing soft or lullaby here.

—Alexandra Fuller, *The Legend of Colton H. Bryant* (2008)

The Indian Agent nodded.
The lights on Ghost Ridge.
They weren't ghosts as Marsh had suggested. No, there was a naturalist's explanation: flammable breaths of gas rising from the pockets of decomposing flesh. Because the Indians had been buried in a mass grave. And something about the temperature of the air above that grave?

—Stephen Graham Jones, *Ledfeather* (2008)

1. *An Unhomely Graveside Grammar.* There is no. There was no. There is no other. There is no sign, no names and dates, no headstone. There is nothing like no. There is no thing. There was no thing. There is nothing. There was nothing. There has been nothing. There would be nothing. There would be nothing to know except the empty gray sky and bare trees and white dune sand. A circle of Styrofoam and a faded paper flower and white crosses painted on flat wedges of dark basalt. Nothing soft or lullaby here, nothing but the lonesome sound of the high winds coming down from the mountain ridges, this cold caress. Nothing here but the pitiless crunch of our steps taken on all the ocean cobblestones that have come to ground here, down from those selfsame ridges. Right here amid all the dust clouds and all the ancient slabs of cow manure, the stench of all the dead cattle and all the dogs who run away at our approach. Right here amid all the toppled gravestones and all the recent graves mounded high, pale hump next to pale hump, as if they had always grown here. Here on this plot of earth where there is something about the temperature of the air above the graves and the lights on Ghost Ridge.

Where there is, was, and always will be this constant weathering away, this crumbling and rusting, all this sagging and scattering. Here in this world that "seemed to care nothing for the old or young or rich or poor or dark or pale or he or she. Nothing for their struggles, nothing for their names. Nothing for the living or the dead."[1]

2. "*Some apparition out of the vanished past.*" At the center of Cormac McCarthy's fiction exists that which "is constant in history": all the "greed and foolishness and a love of blood," as the Duena Alfonsa defines it during her final conversation with John Grady Cole in *All the Pretty Horses*.[2] As her use of the word "constant" signals, the unrelenting course of traumatic events coring the heart of McCarthy's fictional Border Trilogy gets structured by uncanny, haunting repetitions and returns of contagious violent encounters. These encounters typically either transpire within or are seen subsequently to produce cordoned-off topographies of abandonment and ruin: derelict cemeteries, deserted estancias, and demolished churches. And among the possible corporeal effects of these violent encounters spawned by humankind's "love of blood," are scars, the last existence of which, as Alfonsa exclaims during her first extended conversation with John Grady, "have the strange power to remind us that our past is real. The events that cause them can never be forgotten, can they?"[3]

By novel's end, as an encampment of Indians watch this pale rider "vanish upon that landscape solely because he was passing" before a blood red sun, John Grady Cole's serial history of losses that "can never be forgotten" include the deaths of his grandfather and father, as well as of his Abuela who raised him; the assassination of Jimmy Blevins; his killing of the *cuchillero* in a Saltillo prison; and the loss of his family home as well as what he more generally calls "my country."[4] Moreover, during his doomed quest in Mexico to discover some semblance of the pastoral life he has known while growing up on his maternal grandfather's ranch in West Texas, he eventually endures the loss of his beloved Alejandra, who prophetically remarks to John Grady at dawn in Zacatecas, on what will turn out to be their last day together, "I saw you dead in a dream."[5] Given his condition of literal and metaphysical homelessness that develops over the course of the novel, it is hardly surprising that, when Cole recrosses the border and enters Langtry, Texas, during an early afternoon rain, he appears, at least to two local men trying to start a stalled pickup truck, as if an "apparition out of the vanished past."[6]

In the penultimate scene of *All the Pretty Horses*, John Grady Cole rides his horse Redbo and leads Blevins's horse to the Knickerbocker, Texas, Catholic cemetery in order to witness his Abuela's funeral. On this cool and windy day, a funeral procession of a few cars and trucks and a Packard hearse arrives at the cemetery, and—while he watches with hat in hand from across the blacktop road—"a priest and a boy in a white gown ringing a bell" conduct the burial rites. Only after all the mourners and the two men tasked with filling the grave site with dirt depart does he cross the narrow road and then walk "into the cemetery past the old stonework crypt and past the little headstones and their small remembrances." Shifting his gaze once during his walk to consider "the rolling parklands beyond, the wind in the cedars," he arrives at "the unmarked earth" of her cemetery plot. His own "small remembrance" of his dead abuela emerges as he stands over her gravesite, a genealogical memory trace honoring her lifelong care for the Grady family, from "the wild Grady boys who were his mother's uncles and who had all died so long ago" to his mother's father, the patriarch who represents the first man to die in the family's ranch house, built in 1872. As this scene concludes, he calls her "his Abuela," says his farewell to her in Spanish, and then turns his "wet face to the wind," holding "out his hands as if to steady himself or as if to bless the ground there or perhaps as if to slow the world that was rushing away."[7]

With regard to the novel's abiding episodic structure, this scene binds together its concluding moments and its opening scene, which centers on the funeral of John Grady Cole's maternal grandfather, whose Grady surname "was buried with that old man the day the norther blew the lawn chairs over the dead cemetery grass."[8] In both of this novel's cemetery scenes, John Grady is exposed to the elements, as if the relentless motion of the wind over the rolling prairie's low grass and the "spits of snow in the air with blowing dust" provide an objective correlative for the temporary vertigo that besets him as he once again faces the hard fact of human (and animal) finitude. In the wake of that first funeral on another blustery day in West Texas, McCarthy's narrator describes John Grady riding "out near sunset on the westernmost section of the ranch," then dismounting on "the crest of a low rise" and, while contemplating a bleached horse skull he holds in his hands, standing there "like a man come to the end of something."⁹ And here in the novel's final funeral scene, we witness how John Grady once again both exposes and is exposed to things that matter and to the spectral matter of all things: there and then, a bleached horse skull; here and now, an above-ground stone crypt, various family grave markers, and such material "remembrances as china and chipped milk glass vases, a china crane, sun faded paper flowers, 'a broken celluloid Virgin.'"¹⁰

Such chipped, broken, and faded human-made matter, along with the serial list of names he reads on the headstones he passes, all these things exist ephemerally in John Grady's consciousness and are acknowledged simply in notational form, as a serial checklist of what meets his gaze, these phrase fragments unscrolling without judgment, comment, or adjudication of value by either this character or this narrator who speaks. John Grady's emergent capacity to acknowledge the way of all flesh materializes in just such enigmatic souvenirs, mementos, and relics that decorate both the named and the unnamed dead who inhabit the graves and the crypts both above and below this cemetery's rolling prairie earth, this heaping together of proper names and common nouns lacking any context or depth other than that associated with an incantatory soundscape, the enigma of this assemblage underscoring his suspended agency and wounded interiority as he faces the absent presence of death.¹¹

3. "*In the company of the undead.*" As John Grady Cole eventually stands over the material residue and smell of the freshly upturned earth outline of his Abuela's gravesite, this singular funeral scene metastasizes into an affective scene of mourning. Precisely at the rhetorical hinge produced by the phrase describing his turning "his wet face to the wind," this final funeral scene's heretofore energies of narration and description abruptly pivot stylistically (to more layered, lyrical prose) and spatially, swerving from the merely local and notational here to the expansive there of the "unmarked earth," which, as the narrator ventriloquizes John Grady's interpretation, signifies "oblivion." We are called out to bear witness to John Grady being called out, so to speak, by this as yet unmarked gravesite, the sight of which, during his short walk to it through the cemetery's other graves and gravestones, prompts his reflections to ascend to the larger frame of remembered human

history, its inherent oscillation between beginnings and "coming to the end of something." On one level, his initial reflections while standing over his Abuela's unmarked grave perhaps suggest what any grief-exposed subject would hope to discover: that some degree of consolation may arrive as the result of one's renewed understanding of a family's biological continuity, its genealogical narrative, into which one can insert one's own partial history and thus knit together the past and present, as well as imagine a possible future beyond the evidence of all the losses in the present. But, of course, at this fraught moment during his return to Texas in the wake of his deadly serious Mexican adventure, both his bodily and his mental composure are as brittle as a chipped china vase. John Grady's communion with the dead effectively shifts from the illegibility of the face of death to the tactile sensations of the visible skin and body—to all that "overflows the face": such as the flow of tears down one's cheek; such as the physical gesture of holding out his hands "as if to steady himself" during the sudden onset of vertigo that threatens to suspend his agency as well as his balance.[12]

So the rather abstract simile uttered in the novel's opening moments about John Grady seeming to have come "to the end of something" gets fleshed out in this cemetery scene's final sentence, McCarthy's prose extending across the page via both its recursive syntax and its repetitious deployment of the word *nothing*, the falling meter of the three dactyls it inaugurates in the final phrase fragment arriving at the final word *dead* ("Nothing for the living or the dead"). McCarthy's narrator describes Abuela's gravesite in the Knickerbocker cemetery as "the unmarked earth," a judgment that is both true and untrue. That is, her gravesite is "unmarked" in the sense that it does not yet have a headstone whose blank slate could get resolved through the inscription of a name, dates, or an epitaph. Hence, the potential terror associated with the powerful metaphor of the unmarked grave, where "the reunion with the mother [earth]" happens, but "with no corresponding regeneration of the symbolic."[13] Yet, on the other hand, this burial plot created by humans who work the prairie earth with their shovels does in point of fact demarcate his Abuela's final resting place, distinguish it from the surrounding prairie earth, much less all the other graves in the cemetery. Though literally unmarked, his Abuela's gravesite constitutes a paradoxical space: it simultaneously marks both her absence (to sight) and her presence (to mind)—just as do the other gravesites with their headstones and all those "small remembrances" whose containing or receptacle shapes, like the flower vase, serve as miniaturized, material analogues of the old above-ground stone crypt John Grady first regards when entering the Knickerbocker cemetery. We might well consider, then, how the very materiality of a gravesite's heaped-up or mounded earth testifies not only to the fact of decomposition in progress. Its visibility also reminds us of how the earth offers a coffer from which humans like John Grady Cole can "preserve and retrieve legacies, open crypts and folds of human time in the midst of nature's transcendence."[14]

From this perspective, John Grady remembers his Abuela in this moment as one of the undead—that is, a figure literally dead but symbolically alive—tethered, unlike himself, to a place defined by memento mori, the various decorations and statues and tombstones, the mounded earth marking the new gravesites. After all, as Robert Pogue Harrison observes, "A grave marks the mortality of its creators even more distinctly than it marks the resting place of the dead. It is not for nothing that the Greek word for 'sign,' *sema*, is also the word for 'grave.'"[15] So these "small remembrances," these singular names on headstones, these signs and wonders occasioning John Grady's accumulating memories epitomize how, through the work of mourning, the dead "must be detached from their remains so that their image finds its place in the afterlife of the imagination."[16] His reaching out with his hands as if to steady himself thus resembles a kind of conjuring act desiring to separate out the deceased's corporeal remains from the mourner's phantasmatic imagination, so as to facilitate the transit of the dearly departed beyond the boundary between the living and dead. Moreover, when the narrator decodes John Grady's vertiginous gesture of hands "as if to bless the world," are we not summoned to consider how a vital contract of mutual indebtedness exists between the living and the dead?

In the end, it appears to be the case that every journey on the road does not necessarily take place, as the gypsy in McCarthy's novel *The Crossing* says to Billy Parham, "in the company of the dead."[17] Such journeys occur rather in the company of the undead, whose spectral traces become materially embodied not only in the architectural form of an old stone crypt in a Texas cemetery but also, say, in the various darkly lit, nested, or cellular interior spaces that John Grady and, at times, Lacey Rawlins inhabit or pass through on foot or horseback. Such as the receptacles or crypt-like containing spaces of open gravesites, concrete water troughs, and stone tinajas. Such as the traprocks lining the bottoms of ravines with their shallow basins holding water that reflects, like an eye, the overhead vault of stars in the night sky. Such as the screened or enshrouded spaces created by screens of trees along a waterway or road, like the one where Jimmy Blevins is delivered by his captors for his execution. Such archeological and architectural and geological apparitional traces get sedimented as well in spectral material things and performances throughout McCarthy's Border Trilogy: bones, photographs, corridos, portraits, monuments, memories, and dreams. Dreams that uncannily return to haunt the living, we who are admonished to regard the fact that we ultimately inhabit an indifferent world, one that "seemed to care nothing for the old or young or rich or poor or dark or pale or he or she. Nothing for their struggles, nothing for their names. Nothing for the living or the dead."

[**A**lphabet/Abecedario; **C**ryptography; **K**otex; **Q**ueues; **U**rbicide; **Z**ombieland]

Hotel life

EXTRACTS

Remnants of individuals slip into the nirvana of relaxation, faces disappear behind newspapers, and the artificial continuous light illuminates nothing but mannequins. It is the coming and going of unfamiliar people who have become empty forms because they have lost their password, and who now file by as ungraspable flat ghosts. If they possessed an interior, it would have no windows at all, and they would perish aware of their endless abandonment, instead of knowing of their homeland as the [religious] congregation does.
 —Siegfried Kracauer, "The Hotel Lobby" (ca. 1922–25)

I watched Robert Kennedy's funeral on a verandah at the Royal Hawaiian Hotel in Honolulu, and also the first reports from My Lai. I reread all of George Orwell on the Royal Hawaiian Beach, and I also read, in the papers that came one day late from the mainland, the story of Betty Lansdown Fouquet, a 26-year-old woman with faded blond hair who put her five-year-old daughter out to die on the center divider of Interstate 5 some miles south of the last Bakersfield exit. The child, whose fingers had to be pried loose from the Cyclone fence when she was rescued twelve hours later by the California Highway Patrol, reported that she had run after the car carrying her mother and stepfather and brother and sister for "a long time." Certain of these images did not fit into any narrative that I knew.
 —Joan Didion, *The White Album* (1979)

They hurt me so much I could never become one of them, drove me to books, drove me within myself, drove me to run away from that Colorado town, and sometimes, Camilla, when

> I see their faces I feel the hurt all over again, the old ache there, and sometimes I am glad they are here, dying in the sun, . . . the same faces, the same set, hard mouths, faces from my home town, fulfilling the emptiness of their lives under a blazing sun. I see them in the lobbies of hotels, I see them sunning in the parks, and limping out of ugly little churches, their faces bleak from proximity with their strange gods, out of Aimee's Temple, out of the Church of the Great I Am.
>
> —John Fante, *Ask the Dust* (1980)

1. *"Faces disappear behind newspapers."* "In tasteful lounge chairs a civilization intent on rationalization comes to an end," writes Siegfried Kracauer in his 1920s meditation on the significance of the hotel lobby.[1] The transient and ultimately valueless "comings and goings" of humans "who have become empty forms," the voyeuristic gazes of surveillance, and above all the overall fragmentation and anonymity of social relations—these themes populate Kracauer's phenomenology and sociology of the hotel lobby, this microcosmic interior space that manifests the macrocosmic transcendental or metaphysical homelessness wrought by industrial modernity's "rationalization," its focus on maximizing the efficiency of production to increase institutional profits. Hence Kracauer's scathing diction and imagery: "remnants of individuals"; "mannequins"; "ungraspable flat ghosts"; "endless abandonment"; "instead of knowing their homeland." Hence his deployment of the conditional mood in the sentence that begins, "If they possessed an interior" life, which underscores the modern human subject's abiding alienation from self and community.

Approximately six decades after Simmel's essay, Fredric Jameson comments on the phenomenology of hotel life in his 1984 essay "Postmodernism; or, the Cultural Logic of Late Capitalism." To support his argument that a decisive break has occurred not just in the history of capitalism (its transition to a multinational corporate stage) but also between modernism and an emergent postmodernism aesthetic, Jameson discusses architect John Portman's design for the Hotel Bonaventura in downtown Los Angeles, focusing particularly on the "postmodern hyperspace" realized by its soaring, reflecting glass-clad external towers and the labyrinthine interior design of its lower floors where the lobby and retail stores are located. The problem Jameson diagnoses is precisely this: the hotel's architecture challenges "the capacity of the individual human body to locate itself . . . and cognitively to map its position in a mappable external world."[2] With this claim in mind, let us recall the above extract to this critical essay where Joan Didion remarks on the challenge of "knowing one's homeland" as she reflects, during her stay at the Royal Hawaiian Hotel, on a news story about a young California mother who abandoned her five-year-old daughter on an interstate highway median near Bakersfield. The image of the girl running after the family's car "for a long time," she adds, certainly "did not fit into any narrative that I knew."

2. *"Out in the street on our butts."* "'Now come to find out we got this new landlord. This Enchanted Seas Corporation. If it was enchanted sea*sons*, maybe I could deal with that, season this place into an enchanted restaurant. But who's got a business incorporating enchanted seas?' My thumb points to me, the boss. 'I been to enchanted seas. Hey, I been to *dis*enchanted seas. What does a corporation know about an international hotel like this one? They could turn it into a five-star enchanted castle with a sea moat, and where we gonna be? Out in the street on our butts.'"[3]

3. *"I see them in the lobbies of hotels."* Seven years later, in his 1991 critique of Frank Gehry's redesigned Santa Monica, California, house, Jameson judged that this architect has achieved a "novel spatial intervention." Just as Portman's hotel design exemplified for Jameson key features of an emergent postmodern aesthetic, so too had Gehry's use of "the cube" transformed the classic California bungalow design into a version of postmodern pastiche. Even so, given how Gehry's architectural pastiche included corrugated aluminum and chain link fencing as external design elements, Jameson's critique pivots from a focus on aesthetic issues to underscore how such construction materials signify "the junk or Third World side of American life today."[4] Now while the word *junk* potentially conjures up architect Rem Koolhaas's concept of *junkspace*, Jameson's pairing of this word with the term "Third World" focuses our attention on "the production of poverty and misery, people not only out of work but without a place to live, bag people, waste and industrial pollution, squalor, garbage, and obsolescent machinery."[5]

What the material cladding of Third World architectural junk at the Gehry house signifies, then, is both postmodern kitsch and "demographic shifts out of all proportion with historical precedent, which now invest the urban sphere"—especially the downtown center with its ethnic "towns" or precincts and the once-thriving petty bourgeois residential sector—both with an "incalculable diversity of 'cultures'" and an emergent, "contentious internal liminality."[6] Contentious, that is, because the massive multinational corporate investments in urban reconstruction and gentrification require the disciplinary control and management of the actual junkspace architectural structures and public spaces that remain in place. Structures and spaces that are increasingly occupied by newly arrived legal and undocumented immigrants, by the resettlement of diasporic communities, by the urban homeless (or, as Jameson puts it "the bag people"), and by the minimum wage service economy laborers sentenced to live in on the margins of the gleaming new downtown district or the now-decaying first-ring suburbs. Internal liminality, that is, because, as Mike Davis documents in his book *City of Quartz*, the production of an "Oz-like archipelago of Westside pleasure domes—a continuum of tony malls, arts centers, and gourmet retail strips—is reciprocally dependent upon the social imprisonment of the third-world service proletariat who live in increasingly repressive ghettos and barrios."[7]

4. *"What the city had to offer had a home in the hotel."* The hybrid narrative form, the polyvocality, and the plots in the ten novellas that comprise Yamashita's *I Hotel* (2010) center on the vagabond flows of labor, capital, and of both aesthetic and political ideologies through various architectural nodal points in San Francisco between 1968 and 1977: the I Hotel, the Monkey Block, the Ferry Building, Angel Island, and Alcatraz. Centered on an architectural structure whose seventy-year history spans the temporal distance between Kracauer's and Jameson's writings, Yamashita's novel's tracks such flows into and through the I Hotel, "its regional locus of migrants, their cultural practices, and local histories" registering, just as Jameson implicitly argues regarding the significance of Gehry's domestic revision of the California bungalow aesthetic, "a whole transnational, global regionality . . . that builds *outward* and *inward* as we respond to the diverse refrains of coloniality and capital, of migration and violence, internment and Cuba, Black Power, and

Asian American cultures."[8] Centering on the legal, forced eviction of the I Hotel's mostly elderly Filipino and Chinese bachelors after its purchase by the Enchanted Seas Corporation based in Asia, the second chapter of the novel's final novella ("Where Will You Live When You Get Old?") traces how an algorithmic expansion of an original frontier town's trading posts, saloons, and lodging houses eventually reached a point where "city life could perhaps be translated as hotel life":

> And we could see how city life and hotel life were inextricably connected, that what the city had to offer had a home in the hotel. Over time, we'd forgotten that hotels in our city have long served as temporary but also permanent homes, that living in hotels had been a normal consequence of living in our city. From the inception of our city, our city life could perhaps be translated as hotel life, the way that we as young, single, and independent people could arrive to find work in the industry of the city, find the small cafés and bars, theaters and social clubs, laundries, shops, and bookstores, all within walking distance or perhaps a cable car stop away. Even if we did not actually live in hotels, we may have participated in, if not considered the simple luxuries of hotel life: the bustling social life of our streets, the hotels' communal restaurants and social galas, the convenience of maid service and bedsheets changed, the possibility of being completely freed from any housework, the possible leisure to think or to create, and finally the anonymity and privacy of a room of our own. Hotel life defined the freedom of the city, but such freedom has been for some reason suspect, and there are always those who want to police our freedom.[9]

Whether regarded as a temporary or permanent home, "hotel life" signifies, as we witness in this excerpt's final sentence, two entangled ideologies: on the one hand, "the freedom of the city"; but on the other hand, "those who want to police freedom." As was the case with the wandering tramps and hoboes of the turn of the twentieth century, historian Frederick Jackson Turner and novelist Frank Norris's era, the very transitory nature of hotel residents' lives has made them both morally and socially "suspect," effectively defined them, at least from the dominant class perspective, as "the displaced people in the city's plan to impose a particular meaning of *home* and of *nation*."[10]

Through such trespassing of geographical scales, Yamashita's narrator—speaking here as a collective "we" and "our"—explores how the "particular" boundaries establishing the limits of home, region, and nation produce an agitated, internal liminality comparable to the one Jameson sees embedded in the montage of building materials found in the Gehry house. As is the case with the homeless urban Indians whom Sherman Alexie describes in the Seattle setting of *Indian Killer*, so it is for Yamashita writing about San Francisco, where displaced hotel residents and homeless persons represent the precipitate of policies, tax codes, urban renewal, and global real estate investment by a dominant social formation founded on exclusion rather than inclusion in its quest for profit and power. The I Hotel, the first floor of which housed the offices of several activist movements during the Civil Rights era, constitutes an interstitial, residual space from which to speak both of and for those displaced by "a system that served the few and propertied and wealthy, a social system that had failed our immigrant parents and grandparents, had denied their human rights because of their class and color."[11]

5. *"Who now file by as ungraspable flat ghosts."* In this prose archive of unhomely Wests, we learn an enduring, haunting lesson about the precarity of existence: no one, no matter how well educated and behaved, is guaranteed shelter and sovereign rights—for at any time, "anyone can be cast out." Moreover, as we witness in the spatial archeology of landfills and the vagabondage of the homeless, the working poor, and the elderly, all of whom are "cast out on their butts" in *I Hotel* (but not without resistance), another enduring lesson emerges: that everyone, not just the actual homeless, "lives only their relation to production and consumption, trading in their human relationships for 'an immense accumulation of commodities,' tied less to each other than to their overflowing shopping carts," whose uncanny Other materializes in the sight of spectral homeless figures who push shopping carts full of castoff belongings.[12] Thematically dramatizing an organic oppositional resistance to the major trends in both modern and postmodern urban renewal projects that either invest in demolition to create tabula rasa environments or in a sanitized nostalgia for so-called heritage industry-type preservation, *I Hotel* forwards an alternative counter-memory literally and figuratively grounded by leitmotifs of the burial and return, the excavation and exposure, and of both

archeological narrative projects and architectural structures.[13] In opposition to public memory, and even as "we tumble into the gravesite left by its [the I Hotel] demolition," through counter-memory resistance there may yet be rebuilt "a great layered and labyrinthine, now imagined international hotel of many rooms, the urban experiment of a homeless community built to house the needs of temporary lives. And for what? To resist death and dementia. To haunt a disappearing landscape."[14]

Both in its formal structural design and its themes, the novel exemplifies placemaking as "worlding," which Krista Comer conceives as a particularly feminist, critical regionalist "political and knowledge practice sensitive to issues of place across spatial scales," or "globalization from below."[15] Yamashita's vision of a future "international hotel of many rooms" created through a recovered counter-history memory archive extends the connotation of *worlding* to refer to a utopian space: a kind of inchoate future-anterior work already in progress. Like a revenant, this utopian vision haunts, reminding us that the struggle against the virulent legacies of settler-colonial conquest continues well beyond so-called first contact with or the end of the frontier. This vision echoes that belief that through a re-envisioned critical regionalism that travels over and under the national scale there exists the potential for new political alliances—such as those forged during the 1960s and 1970s on the various first floor spaces of the I Hotel. As the archive of contemporary representations of the homeless in U.S. West literature attests, this political ecology centers on both naming individual and collective trauma, on recovering the memory of sustained oppositional subcultures, and on recovering the work of organic intellectuals (e.g., Mayan prophetic texts, the Black Panthers' manifestos). As modeled by the mise-en-scène in *I Hotel*, then, this utopian vision of what comes next sketches the emergence of a resilient "positional identity politics," one where political solidarity with others gets realized through groups' similar positionality in the struggle for specific social and environmental justice demands.

[Cryptography; Idyll; Motel noir; Noir motel; Psychometropolis; Urbicide]

Idyll of the idle

EXTRACTS

The real crackpots of Los Angeles in the "thirties" were the individuals who ordered tons of oranges and vegetables dumped in the bed of the Los Angeles River, while thousands of people were unemployed, hungry, and homeless.
—Carey McWilliams, *Southern California* (1946)

The Oz-like archipelago of Westside pleasure domes—a continuum of tony malls, arts centers and gourmet strips—is reciprocally dependent upon the social imprisonment of the third-world service proletariat who live in increasingly repressive ghettos and barrios.
—Mike Davis, *City of Quartz* (1992)

Downtown Los Angeles, on the other hand, is almost pure spectacle, of business and commerce, of extreme wealth and poverty, of clashing cultures and rigidly contained ethnicities. Boredom is assuaged by overindulgence and the bombardment of artificial stimulation; while despair is controlled and contained by the omnipresence of authority and spatial surveillance, the ultimate in the substitution of police for *polis*. Young householders are virtually non-existent. In their place are the homeless, who are coming close to being half the central city's resident population despite vigorous attempts at gentrification and dispersal.
—Edward Soja, *Thirdspace* (1996)

1. "*Voy a ser uno de los 'homeless.'*" I'm going to be one of the homeless, thinks Guatemalan refugee Antonio Bernal as he is evicted from his Los Angeles apartment at the outset of Héctor Tobar's novel *The Tattooed Solder* (1998). Initially pondering the cognitive dissonance opened up by the disjuncture

between his self-image and "this ugly word," Antonio realizes that the word *homeless* provides a "logical conclusion to living for [six] years in this cold, alien country." Since he cannot conjure up a Spanish equivalent to capture "the shame and sooty desperation of his condition," this "compound, borrowed word would have to do: home-less."[1] Here in this moment, as well as throughout the novel, *home-less* not only connotes poverty and unemployment, it also designates: a status (of disaffiliation from kin, family, and citizenship); an existential condition ("sooty desperation"); and an affective mode of being (shame, humiliation). Because he carries "the unbearable burden" of feeling responsible for the 1985 deaths of his wife and son, both murdered by a Guatemalan army death squad, becoming homeless in 1992 Los Angeles also signifies, through an uncanny repetition of his earlier loss and displacement in Guatemala, the entanglement of local and global spatial scales. Both his body's cringe and his facial expression make legible, so he believes, his history of failure in Los Angeles. And yet, these corporeal signs of his internal state of affairs are described as being "sooty." This word to describe his corporeal appearance thus signifies on two levels: as connoting both matter—literally in the form of dirt; figuratively as a sign of impurity—and as describing his inner being's elemental opacity. On the one hand, soot both makes visible his abjection and contrasts with the jaguar tattoo inscribed on the forearm of the soldier who killed his family. On the other hand, soot exemplifies one of this novel's leitmotifs: that of the invisibility or illegibility of the homeless.

The discourse of homelessness in the early 1980s frequently invoked "the new homeless" to underline the differences in age, race, gender, and ethnicity between this emergent population during the Reagan-Bush years and the mostly white male homeless population spatially segregated into urban skid row areas during the years of the Great Depression and World War II.[2] But as we witness in the case of Antonio's forced political exile and his later forcible eviction from his apartment, another world becomes visible in contemporary U.S. West prose works, one that has "more to do with the uncanny literary and social effects of enforced social accommodation, or historical migrations and cultural relocations."[3] In its dialectical interplay with the concepts of home and homesteading, homelessness as theme and trope in *The Tattooed Soldier* also signifies the uneven economic development, the territorial divisions of labor, and the deracination attendant upon gender, racial, and class inequalities in a transnational U.S. West. As exemplified by moments in the novel when he gazes at reflecting surfaces, such as storefront windows, and doesn't recognize himself, Antonio's unhomely estrangement, as the novel's plot discloses, ultimately underscores the dissolution of spatial and temporal boundaries, including those between his everyday life and the lifeworld of a globalizing world system, between private life and public spheres, and between the traumatic events transpiring between his past in Guatemala and his seven-year exile in Los Angeles.

Initially intending to sleep in one of the concrete hollows of a freeway interchange, the newly homeless Antonio Bernal and his Mexican roommate José Juan Grijalva eventually discover a homeless camp spread across a flat, empty space at the top of a small rise named Crown Hill in downtown Los Angeles. A couple of days later, after the two men had left their new blue tarp-covered shelter in the Crown Hill homeless camp in order to walk to a Unitarian church food bank and pick up a frozen chicken, Antonio finds himself reflecting on their return journey:

> There were so many Latinos in Los Angeles now, thousands upon thousands of Mexicanos, Guatemaltecos, and Salvadoreños, more than he ever imagined. He had come to the States expecting to be surrounded by blond, blue-eyed gringos, not a Spanish-talking sea of brown faces. Even the Mayan Indians of his country, people who had lived in the same little *aldeas* in Guatemala since before the Spaniards came—even they were here. He remembered coming across a group of Indian women one day, not far from the vacant lot where he and José Juan now lived. They were wearing their traditional dress, embroidered *huipiles* and long rainbow-striped skirts. He watched them, these ancient people of the corn, as they walked through a canyon of brick tenements, their leather sandals scraping along the oil-stained sidewalk on Bixel Street. What where they doing here, in this place where not a single stalk of corn could grow? It saddened him to find so many of his countrymen transported, as if by some dark magic, to this freeway-covered plain, wandering about Los Angeles in an amnesiac daze, far from even the memory of the soil.[4]

"As if by some dark magic": From a macroeconomic systems theory perspective, Antonio's urban scenography discloses, in the first place, how minorities and Indigenous immigrants from the hemispheric margins have come to occupy the very center of what Manuel Castells has called the "informational city," one whose general economy has shifted from manufacturing and durable goods production to the liquid flows through it of multinational capital's speculative investments in data harvesting, in real estate, and in financial services.[5] What is further remarkable about this passage is Antonio's speculation that these traditionally dressed women were "wandering about Los Angeles in an amnesiac daze, far from even the memory of the soil." Antonio's particular description and then deep wonderment about what these "ancient people of the corn" were doing, here in this world city where the words *canyons* and *plains* do not connote natural landforms, disclose a crucial reality of everyday life in Los Angeles: the "encircling networks of multinational capital that actually direct the system exceed the capacities of any perception."[6] But unlike the "amnesiac daze" he projects onto the Mayan women he sees on the streets of this world city, Antonio carries "the unbearable burden of what he had seen at his house in San Cristóbal so many years ago," the memory traces of which hang over him "like a blood-stained cloth," polluting his consciousness with that "inescapable sense of having failed Elena, his first and only love; of having failed Carlos, his son; of having allowed them to die alone."[7] For as the novel's first part proceeds, we learn how, seven years after his hasty departure from his native country in fear for his life, his Guatemalan memories have become even stronger and more debilitating in the wake of each occupational failure he experiences in Los Angeles and now, in 1992, the year marked by the Rodney King riots.

2. "*An archaeology of signs.*" While looking for an open space on the hill's flat plain to build their temporary shelter, Antonio and José Juan discover—on "the muddy lot beneath them green with weeds grown thick from recent rains"—the architectural footprint of a demolished home. It turns out that this architectural ruin is but one of several residences comprising "a forgotten neighborhood built with brick and cement" underneath the homeless encampment's structures of wood, cardboard, and tarpaulin. The next morning, as they temporarily leave the encampment to search for food, they discover a broken cyclone fence with an attached sign announcing, "*Coming Soon: Crown Hill Hotel and Finance Park.*" Later in the day, while walking this "lush

knoll of wild plants and grasses in the middle of the city," they discover an old couch, positioned so the camp's homeless residents can enjoy, "like a suburbanite entertaining a guest in his living room," a panoramic view of the Financial District's skyscrapers, city hall, and the Harbor Freeway.[8] And then, in the third week of their stay at the homeless camp, police and sanitation workers with bulldozers and garbage trucks evict Antonio and other homeless residents camping on Crown Hill's flat plain, their exodus taking them to the concrete entrance of an abandoned rail tunnel at the base of the hill.

"In the case of the ruin," Georg Simmel observes, "the fact that life, with its wealth and its changes, once dwelled here constitutes an immediately perceived presence. The ruin creates the present form of a past life, not according to the contents or remnants of that life, but according to its past as such."[9] The archaeological palimpsest that defines Crown Hill's past—the multiple historical layers of its inhabitation over time—constitutes a reminder of a once-thriving neighborhood. The broken-up pieces of concrete testifying to the placement of concrete sidewalks, stairs, and the neighborhood's streets; the shards of bathroom, kitchen floor, and wall tiles; the brickwork rubble—such material traces of the past reveal the boom-and-bust rhythms of capitalist development, which preceded and anticipated the ruination Antonio encounters in his Los Angeles exile in the late 1980s and early 1990s. Such material evidence of ruination in this deceptively pastoral setting, Antonio recognizes, indexes the multiple layers of historical meaning Crown Hill embodies. There was the cycle of building and then demolishing the Crown Hill houses built by what he calls the "lost community" during the Gilded Era. Such material evidence, as Antonio and José Juan discover during their sojourn on Crown Hill, also indexes the 1870s "tramp crisis," which, as it turned out, emblematized the struggles wrought by industrialization during the late nineteenth century, just as the social problem of homelessness approximately a century later, represented by Antonio's displacement from Guatemala to Los Angeles, encapsulates the struggle over the economic and cultural rhythms, and hence the impact, of globalization.

This same social, political, and cultural struggle plays out, for instance, in Frederick Jackson Turner's historiography of the frontier and the U.S. West. In the year after the 1910 national census (and thus two decades after the key 1890 census, which declared the frontier "closed"), Turner's essay

"Social Forces in American History" reiterated a major theme from his earlier 1893 essay, "The Significance of the Frontier in American History," about the need for the West, and the nation at large, for that matter, to adapt to the new conditions and challenges in the aftermath of the frontier experience, one which was grounded by the presence and then the eventual exhaustion of what he called the frontier's "free lands." More specifically, he observes how, by 1910, the contemporary western and national "problem" centers in fact on two other transformative developments: "The familiar facts of the massing of population in the cities and the contemporaneous increase of urban power, and of the massing of capital and production in fewer and vastly greater industrial units, especially attest the revolution."[10] Thought about from the side of capital, the problem of the West for Turner is best realized at the turn of the twentieth century by those emergent captains of industry who controlled the nation's industrial production and banking and investment houses. Thought about from the side of labor, it is a problem that Turner sees embodied in the form of nascent labor unions and political parties, like the Populists in such plains states as Kansas and Nebraska, and in the larger public discourse about the threats to the family home posed by the West's population of seasonal homeless refugees laboring on what was then called the "wageworker's frontier."[11]

On the one hand, such dominant cultural concerns over chronic poverty, the threats to family life posed by economic displacement, and the changing patterns of labor and social relations during periods of economic change link these two histories of Crown Hill's development, demolition, and reoccupation. On the other hand, in *The Tattooed Soldier*, the spatial juxtaposition of Crown Hill's lush green knoll with the Financial District's towering skyscrapers underscores how the entwined growth of cities and of homeless populations during the Reagan-Bush years is fundamentally different from the earlier moment of industrial modernity. Urbanization now largely has been decoupled from industrialization per se, and economic policies promoting agricultural "deregulation and depeasantization" have accelerated the national and transnational exodus of surplus rural labor to urban areas "even as cities ceased to be job machines."[12] Antonio's discovery of the material traces of a past Crown Hill neighborhood trigger memories of his succession of low-paying restaurant and street vendor jobs since his arrival in Los Angeles in 1985 after fleeing his native Guatemala. And with the bulldozing of the homeless camp built on this the vacant, lush, and wild land near downtown Los Angeles to prepare for its transformation into a hotel and financial park, *The Tattooed Soldier* explicitly illustrates how the combination of bank deregulation and multinational corporations' purchasing of undervalued property, where the working poor and homeless live, produces what Manuel Castells has called the "dual city" spawned by the global economy: a city where a new sociology of power centered on finance and banking services, data collection, insurance, and real estate development exists alongside both a service economy of minimum-wage laborers comprised of new migrants and immigrants, ethnic minorities, and the working poor and an informal underground economy linked with the homeless.

3. "*Couch Time.*" Deindustrialization and the shift to an information or financial services economy; the emergent "festival marketplace" of performing arts and athletic arenas, of museum and entertainment districts; the indoor and outdoor shopping mega-mall; the renovation and repurposing of decaying warehouse and manufacturing buildings into expensive townhouses and lofts—these features of contemporary urban architecture dramatically elide the predominant capitalist chronotope of labor. That is to say: time becomes spatialized. Primarily, it emerges as places for entertainment and consumption in newly revitalized downtown business and financial districts, this transformation of urban space transpiring despite the competing claims on it made by the homeless and working poor. At one point in Tobar's novel, there is a remarkable scene that depicts homeless men lounging on an old couch on the precipice of Crown Hill's vacant lots, watching for the occasional car wreck on the nearby freeway interchange, their pose compared to that of suburbanites entertaining guests in their living rooms. Given Tobar's deployment of pastoral imagery to describe Crown Hill and the way this imagery ironizes suburban leisure entertainment, the couch scene embodies the "idyll of the idle," to use Vivian Sobchack's phrase for what she calls the "lounge time" ethos of film noir: that time-space intersection grounding the meaning of everyday life "for the uprooted, the unemployed, the loose and the existentially paralyzed."[13]

By representing the phenomenology of urban homeless space as an inverted pastoral and by deploying the motif of the auto accident, couch time simultaneously dramatizes the pleasure of the homeless as they gather on a hill and survey spectacular accidents happening below this forward observation post, such random collisions underscoring one of our contemporary society's contingent dangers. Through Tobar's limited third-person narration of Antonio's cognition and affective mode of being in this scene, we also witness his dark pain accruing from an inability to imagine being at home anywhere in the world amid all the accumulating accidents of local and global economic and political history.

[Cryptography; Freeways; Hotel life; Junkspaces; Urbicide; Vagabondage; Zombieland]

Junkspaces, outtakes from an unhomely archive

File Document #1: An extract from *Into the Beautiful North*, a 2009 novel by Luis Alberto Urrea in which a nineteen-year-old Mexican woman living in a rural village journeys north across the border to recruit her own "Siete Magníficos" to return with her to her hometown and help defend it from the bad guys who want to take control of it in the absence of the village's men, who have migrated north in search of gainful employment:

> Their drive to Las Vegas through the American desert was vividly dull. Dead gas stations. Outposts of I-Don't-Want-to-Live-Here sat in ruin beside the road. Border Patrol trucks puttered ignored around the off-ramps as Mexicans in wasted cars passed them in reeking oil smoke. The dense brown cloud of Los Angeles exhalations felt its way out across abandoned drive-ins and peeling ice cream stands. White men in pickups with ear-flapping big dogs in the back. Old trailers faded to white. Industrial buildings and dying palm trees, alkaline flats and military bases. Vast blacktop lots of abandoned RVs, the pale boxes arrayed like iron cows in a feed lot. Small triangular flags in vivid plastic colors rattled in the endless wind. And rocks, rocks piled upon rocks, whole hillsides of nothing but rocks.[1]

File Notes: Once upon a time, an urban "network of monuments"—arches, columns, gates, statues, museums, and government buildings—composed "a complex mental map of significance by which the [traditional] city might be recognized as 'home.'"[2] Such architectural monuments, in short, were both material artifacts and conveyors of symbolic meanings that served to orient the citizens of a traditional city in their collective urban space and to their collective history. But as a result of the accelerated economic and cultural rhythms of globalization throughout the twentieth century, the production of urban space, as Jean Baudrillard argues in his road trip book *America*, became identified with both the "mobile deserts" of suburban and exurban spread and sprawl development and the triumph of "simulacra and simulation": hence, "no oases, no monuments; infinite panning shots over mineral landscapes and freeways. Everywhere: Los Angeles or Twenty-Nine Palms, Las Vegas or Borrego Springs."³ Baudrillard's nonhierarchical serial grammar here conflates desert city place names, underscoring how "everywhere" looks the same: a homogenous space comprised of highways and mineral landscapes of "rocks, rocks piled upon rocks, whole hillsides of nothing but rocks." And as this excerpt from *Into the Beautiful North* puts the matter, the unhomely algorithm of these surface features multiplies and repeats from horizon to horizon, from here to infinity and beyond, with neither comfort ("no oases") nor historical depth ("no monuments"). Or of any interest: "Their drive to Las Vegas was vividly dull."

In his book *Postmetropolis*, cultural geographer Edward Soja observes how the "geohistory" of urbanism from the mid-eighteenth century to the present "can be told through the increasingly globalized economic and cultural rhythms of capitalist development and the associated interplay of modernization and modernism."⁴ Soja explains how the pace and duration of these various "rhythms of capitalist development" depend on technological developments and transformative changes in the dominant energy regime. Like that historical transition from steam to fossil fuel extraction, especially of oil and natural gas, whose refinement into various gasoline and aviation fuels and petrochemicals (e.g., plastic products like polyvinyl chloride; pesticides and herbicides) define what Soja calls both "modernization" (economic development) and "modernism" (the structure of feeling spawned by the experience of modernity). In this context we can consider the example provided by the field of architecture and urban design, which exemplifies the braiding together of economic and cultural/aesthetic considerations with technological advances in building materials and transportation logistics to produce the time signature of a particular rhythm of capitalist and cultural development. Such as, after World War II, the emergence of what Stephanie LeMenager has called "petrotopia," "the now ordinary U.S. landscape of highways, low-density suburbs, strip malls, fast food and gasoline service islands, and shopping centers ringed by parking lots or parking towers."⁵

These same "increasingly globalized economic and cultural rhythms of capitalist development" also have destabilized "the longstanding conceptual division between city and region," to the degree that the contemporary postmetropolis, Soja further argues, should be regarded as "some variant on city-region, urban-region, or more broadly regional urbanism."[6] To take but one example: consider the city-region state or regional urbanism composed by Los Angeles and Las Vegas, cities not only linked historically by rail and highway corridors but now by their networked entertainment, tourism, and military-industrial research and the development of advanced digital effect technologies, robotics, and animatronics.[7] In our now increasingly globalized economy and culture, local or regional styles and architectural forms and structures, if they materialize at all, inevitably constitute, as critic and theorist Hal Foster observes, "a trace souvenir of the old culture, a token at a remove."[8] Now the phrase "a token at a remove" could be referring to how any "trace souvenir of the old culture" is enmeshed with the perennial human impulse for nostalgia. Nevertheless, this excerpt from Urrea's novel models for us how a "trace souvenir of the old culture" also can be discovered by means of a ground-level view—not infinite panning shots from above—of the roadside junkspace architecture that offers a corrective to Baudrillard's postmodern perspective that the American West's urban and rural "mobile deserts" exemplify the loss of history. For as we witness in this brief extract from *Into the Beautiful North*, the residual traces of an "old culture" appear in junkspace roadside architectural structures built during an earlier phase of petrocapitalism's historical development, such as the now abandoned gas stations and the closed drive-in movie theaters and the deteriorating trailers parked in (im)mobile home parks and the asphalt parking lots filled with abandoned RVs. There are first-generation industrial warehouses bordering the highway and, in the distance, U.S. Air Force military bases established during the Cold War era. On the interstate highway itself there are Border Patrol trucks and the "wasted cars" of Mexican laborers emitting "oil smoke," air pollution that parallels the "dense brown cloud" of Los Angeles smog migrating from Los Angeles into the rural desert basins beyond the San Gabriel Mountains.

The atmospheric affects forwarded by Urrea's prose assemblage here are those of malaise and precarity, of fatigue and decline. Everything that once had value is now in the process of becoming, or already has become, just so much worthless junk. With the exception of the triangular-shaped flags fluttering in the desert's "endless wind," deceleration rather than acceleration dominates this abandoned and ruined landscape: the gas stations are "dead," the trucks merely "putter," the house paint fades and peels, palm trees wither in the desert's alkaline soil. All things are passing and being passed, monuments to transit and transience. As such, these serially presented fragments of past, present, and future junkspaces to come are simultaneously dispersed in horizontal fashion and yet bound together by this novel's narrative gaze of surveillance, its inventory of the material culture fragments comprising this miscellaneous heap of things ultimately unable to reproduce the larger context or whole of which they each are a part.⁹

File Document #2: An extract from a 2001 short story by Wanda Coleman titled "Backcity Transit by Day," published in her 2008 collection titled *Jazz and Twelve O'Clock Tales: New Stories*. In this story the first-person female narrator looks through windows of a public bus and a commuter train car as she returns home from work in Los Angeles.

> And this, too, infects me as I stare without focus at the passing landscape which, with the exception of a shopping mall or two, is a depressing spectacle of dilapidated pastel A-frames and gritty-gray public housing projects with shabby roofs, junk-filled lawns, un-mendable fences, and dented primer-splatted jalopies blooming on the blacktop. These are the neighborhoods I once knew and cannot forget.¹⁰

File Notes: At one point in his *Los Angeles: Four Ecologies* (1971), architectural historian Reyner Banham discusses the "blocks of neat little houses in tidy gardens" and the "dingbat" apartment complexes that populate the "flat plains" of Los Angeles—the "heartland of the city's Id." As if channeling historian Frederick Jackson Turner's 1893 frontier thesis, he concludes that such prevalent architectural forms represent how "the plainsman's dream of urban homesteading can still be made real."¹¹ In contrast, Wanda Coleman's document in this unhomely archive regards the scenography of the Los Angeles flatlands through which her female protagonist travels by public transit on her way home to South Los Angeles as constituting a "depressing spectacle," rather than any updated pioneer dream of utopian freedom. Take the adjectives she deploys before all the nouns that name types of dwellings, lawns, fences, and vehicles: "dilapidated," "gritty," "shabby," "junk-filled," "un-mendable," and "dented." Take the natural/unnatural exchange of properties between nature and culture revealed by her image of a "primer-splattered jalopy" that appears to be "blooming" on the blacktop. Indeed, take the verb "infect" that opens this passage of melancholy recognitions.

This dystopian vision of junkspace existing outside the bus window provides an objective correlative of this character's inner state during her journey. She has been lulled into a "mild catatonic pose" by the rhythms of the bus as it passes through this rather cartographic void of urban space, all these "neighborhoods I once knew and cannot forget." She sees neighborhoods situated between a shopping mall and the "cement structures" of public housing projects "rising and falling across a palm-dotted distance." Such neighborhoods that she stares at "without focus" in her state of reverie ultimately constitute "a haunting absence, not a haunting presence."[12] Along with the descriptive mode, Coleman's first-person narrator-protagonist in this brief prose fragment ventures also onto the philosophical terrain of epistemology and ontology here as her narrative persona admits both to her limited knowledge ("I once knew") and to her being haunted ("cannot forget") during this day's and as well as her entire life's journey to date. All told, we witness how her reflections, to quote Avery Gordon writing in another context, relay "the peculiar temporality of the shadowing of lost and better futures that insinuates itself... sometimes as nostalgia, sometimes as regret."[13]

And we further witness how her gaze of surveillance fixes on architectural junkspaces whose presence affirms a paradoxical "disjunctive inclusion" that defines how the spatial archaeology of the urban American West "has to include places whose existence is not part of its 'ideal-ego,' places that are *disjoined* from an idealized image of itself."[14] Such as the utopian dream of urban homesteading that Banham sees manifested in the "dingbat" architecture of the Los Angeles plains. Such as the "self-conscious architecture" of urban redevelopment, manifested in performing arts spaces, museum districts, upscale retail shopping, and festival marketplaces (farmer's markets; living traditions folk festivals), that exists in dialectical relationship with the viaducts and freeway underpasses and the public parks and sidewalks and parking strips colonized by the urban homeless. Such as the literally dilapidated, junk-filled spaces of the neighborhoods Coleman's narrator once knew intimately, whose counterpart beyond the "rising and falling" public housing projects, beyond the concrete riverbed and highway sound-dampening cement walls, is the drosscape comprised of former industrial sites and steel factories and railroad yards and meat packing plants; of waste transfer and recycling facilities; of inland ports and distribution warehouses; of container stores and storage units. All these large and small decorated sheds signifying transit and transience, simultaneously conjoined with and yet disjoined from the newly renovated downtown and the freeways and the gleaming hotels and motels and car rental hubs that surround both local and international airports.

File Document #3: An extract from Douglas Coupland's novel *Generation X* (1991). A character named Dag, nearing his thirtieth birthday, believes he suffers from a "Mid-Twenties Breakdown": "the failure of youth but also a failure of class and of sex and the future and I *still* don't know what."[15] In this excerpt, he is calling his friends Andy and Claire, who also live in Palm Springs, from a telephone booth in Scotty's Junction, Nevada. He tells them a fictional story about a man named Otis who suffers from "bomb anxiety" and how, at one point during his auto tour of the nuclear American West, he has an epiphany as he views an Arizona freeway's roadside architecture:

> It happened this way: he was driving home to California on Interstate 10 and passing by a shopping mall outside of Phoenix. He was idly thinking about the vast, arrogant block forms of shopping mall architecture and how they make as little visual sense in the landscape as nuclear cooling towers. He then drove past a new yuppie housing development—one of those strange new developments with hundreds of blockish, equally senseless and enormous coral pink houses, all of them with an inch of space in between and located about three feet from the highway. And Otis got to thinking: "Hey! these aren't houses at all—these are *malls in disguise.*"[16]

File Notes: This excerpt drawn from Dag's short story references four architectural forms relevant to any consideration of junkspace: an interstate highway and interchange; a shopping mall anchored by a big box store; nuclear power plant cooling towers; and a "new yuppie housing development" of coral pink houses bordering the highway. These sites form not so much a literal junkspace but rather a scenography in keeping with architect theorist Rem Koolhaas's polemical notion of junkspace.[17] For Koolhaas, junkspace is not really architecture, but rather a sorry product resulting from the adaptation of new building technologies and materials merely to satisfy the needs of an intensified consumer capitalism that emerged after World War II. Thus junkspace for him is exemplified by modular, cellular, and often temporary (non)architectural forms: highway systems; the homogenous blocks of residential apartment or townhouses or condominiums (like Dag sees being built outside the Phoenix downtown area); themed retail shopping malls and single-story, commercial strip malls; and the faux pastoral spectacle of corporate campuses or research parks, the ones typically located near tier one universities to interface with research faculty. Junkspace is also characterized by materials such as concrete, stucco, plywood, sheetrock, adhesives, and manufactured or composite wood. Its exterior surfaces "smooth, mirrored and polished, its interiors air-conditioned"; its formal logic "one of addition, proliferation, successive transformation, and spatial continuity" in support of an economic model based on "constant expansion and mutation of corporate capitalism."[18] Whether exemplified by a hotel lobby with a four-story atrium or by the VIP lounge at an airport or by the food courts and water fountain features in themed shopping mall concourses, junkspace flourishes in a society that values speed, mobility, flexibility—and the disposability of both commodities and relationships.

As David Spurr further elaborates the specifics of Koolhaas's satirical manifesto, junkspace not only intends to foster comfort and pleasure at the point of consumption. It also fosters the "disorientation and the suspension of the critical faculty."[19] An ambition that of course is not fulfilled by Dag's story of Otis, a character whose cognitive status transforms in this extract from "idly thinking" while he drives on U.S. Interstate 10 to his anxiety-ridden projection that both the "new yuppie housing developments" he sees as his journey unfolds are actually *"malls in disguise"*—and that shopping malls themselves, in turn, look like the cooling towers of nuclear power plants. Whatever the degree of disorientation we might attribute to these somewhat paranoid visions, his critical faculties nevertheless remain strong, as exemplified by his rhetoric's summary judgment: "vast, arrogant block forms"; "strange"; "little visual sense"; "equally senseless."

Furthermore, his construction of an analogy between shopping mall and nuclear power plant architectures reveals how the fictional Otis's story actually tells Dag's story. As the character named Andy, the novel's primary narrator, informs us elsewhere in the novel, all the stories Dag shares with his two friends feature an uncanny, recurring motif of the end times: "eschatological You-Are-There accounts of what it's like to be Bombed, lovingly detailed, and told in deadpan voice."[20] Indeed, Dag's intense "bomb anxiety" leads him to seek relief by traveling "the Nuclear Road" from southern Nevada to Alamagordo and Las Cruces, including a stop in southwestern Utah to visit the site of a John Wayne movie that was filmed during the above-ground era of nuclear testing at the nearby Nevada Test Site (more than half the people involved in the film's production eventually died of cancer). Instead of providing relief, however, Dag's road trip triggers a "scary realization," one that gets translated into the "hot and scary idea" that Otis, Dag's fictional doppelganger, conjures up during his drive through the Phoenix area: that "if these [yuppie] people mentally can convert their houses into shopping malls, then these same people are just as capable of mentally equating atomic bombs with regular bombs."[21]

Realizing this uncanny conjunction between the boredom he associates with the cookie-cutter nature of the architectures of commodity consumption and his abiding paranoia, sharpened by the prospect of nuclear apocalypse, Otis's (and, by extension, Dag's) internal and external worlds—both now colonized by the ubiquitous presence of junkspace in all its replicant forms—uncannily have become "scary once more."[22] And given how Dag's comparison of the architectural form of a shopping mall with that of a nuclear plant's cooling towers strains the comparative logic inherent in metaphorical figures of speech, his vision of nuclear apocalypse prompted by the sight of roadside architectural junkspace arguably expresses a parallel dystopia in communication itself. A crisis in signification, in short, that raises the question as to what narrative forms and rhetorical figures can even begin to capture the "scary" experiential reality of an everyday life ruled by commodity consumption, let along the specter of nuclear apocalypse.

File Document #4: A prose excerpt from Charles Bowden's work of creative nonfiction/documentary journalism *Dreamland: The Way Out of Juárez* (2010).

On the strip where the hotel looms, the road is lined with Domino's, Peter Piper, McDonald's, Applebee's, Carl's Jr., and Burger King. Every signal meeting the eye says safety. In the midst of this commercial barrage is a club called Hooligan's. One fall a few years back, five men sat at a table there. One danced with a pretty woman. Apparently her boyfriend took offense. The five men left the club but were detained by Mexican police who beat four of them to death. The boyfriend was rumored to have deep ties to the Juárez cartel but this has never been explored and the dead have been largely forgotten. The boyfriend did marry the pretty woman shortly after the incident, so some good came of the evening.[23]

File Notes: "Every signal meeting the eye says safety," Charles Bowden judges after he briefly describes a Juárez commercial strip full of familiar, name-brand fast-food franchises and one combination pub and eatery. I say "familiar" here because the setting he describes exemplifies one of the architectural forms that Rem Koolhaas defines as junkspace: hotel franchises with their "now ordinary" lobbies and "seemingly safe" atriums. The Juárez hotel Bowden alludes to here, it turns out, is a part of the Radisson hotel chain. It caters mainly to businessmen "who have come to Juárez to feast off the North American Free Trade Agreement," its lobby filled with soundscapes of "warm" music and featuring both a sushi bar and a café under its four-story atrium. Furthermore, eastward-facing rooms on its top floors provide an aerial view of a nearby middle-class condominium development on Calle Parsioneros. One of its unassuming stucco-covered duplexes became known as "The House of Death" after the January 2004 discovery of the corpses of twelve men who had been tortured, murdered, and then buried beneath its backyard patio. The signals relayed by the "now ordinary" surface amenities and architectural forms of urban hotel life as well as these nearby condominiums turn out to be illusory safe havens. For, as Bowden also reports, four of five men socializing at a presumably "safe" Hooligan's establishment near the Radisson Hotel were beaten to death by the Mexican police after one of these men had danced with a young woman whose boyfriend, it turned out, was not only extremely jealous but also had close ties to the Juárez cartel.

Once upon a time, before the drug cartels held sway and before this beige two-story condominium with a backyard patio in the Juárez neighborhood called Los Acequias was known as "The House of Death," a woman named Erika rented it. And in this neighborhood, populated mostly by the families of middle managers who worked in the maquiladoras, a grocery store clerk remembered her as a young mother buying food and drinks for her child's birthday party. This grocery store, Bowden observes, "is new and sparkling clean. It is part of the promise of the modern nation that joins a modern world in a modern global trade."[24] At a later moment in this condominium's history, however, we learn that still another type of shopping spree for another type of fiesta occurred. On the first day after the construction of the house—which was secretly owned by a cartel—was completed, the cartel's specialized labor force realized they did not yet possess the necessary tools to begin their killing trade in this house. Out of necessity, they scurried about the neighborhood, searching for supplies of duct tape, rope, and extension cords, of garbage bags and bags of lime. They found these and other items at a local hardware store that had "a comforting feel, the aisles piled high with sledgehammers, paint, cement, air coolers, wood stoves, flues, nails, screws. Here men come for the things necessary for home improvement."[25]

As Bowden's prose montage in *Dreamland* oscillates between narrative fragments, journalistic exposition, and still-life vignettes, an uncanny irony emerges: that the labor of housekeeping projects at the cartel death house produces a grotesque inversion of everyday consumerism and domesticity.[26] Everyday domestic chores that take place in such domestic spaces as kitchens and bathrooms—food purchasing, preparation, and cooking; matters of hygiene and waste disposal—become uncannily transformed into their uncanny opposites, functioning as nightmarish doubles of their normative intended use. Bathtubs, showers, and sinks are handy for drowning or electrocuting their victims; hair curlers and steam irons and cooktop surfaces are useful for burning their victims' flesh; kitchen sinks with garbage disposals become useful for maiming human hands. Duct tape and plastic shopping bags act as crucial items for binding and suffocating humans; telephone and lamp cords serve as convenient ligatures for strangulation; large plastic garbage bags are vital for holding body parts and bodily waste matter and fluids; newspapers and tarps help protect floors and walls from blood pools and spatters; lime hastens the decomposition of bodies. Shovels become necessary to dig graves rather than holes to plant seeds for a garden. Drywall, spackling compound, and house paint are necessary to repair unhomely crime scenes and, if a backyard burial site becomes filled to capacity, cover any corpses that might end up propped between the vertical wall studs in so-called living rooms and hallway corridors and bedrooms and rooms for home entertainment.

The "House of Death" is "now an archaeological dig closed to new customers," Bowden writes, and a brass plaque reading "House of Life" is now bolted to one of its exterior walls, a plaque that the neighbors at first averted their eyes from "because it questions their necessary fantasy, just as it questions our own."[27] This plaque represents a necessary fantasy, Bowden claims, because not only the immediate neighbors but all of us need to regard the formerly titled house of death as "a spot of unique evil." Rather than see it for what it really symptomizes—one more discordant and perennial chord sounding in the uneven rhythm of current economic and cultural capitalist development—this new geography "based less on names and places and lines and national boundaries and more on forces and appetites and torrents of people."[28] Furthermore, as is the case with memorial markers and any and all surviving relics or keepsakes of the dead, this newly installed brass plaque bolted to a wall at the Juárez house of death—even as its presence attempts to disavow or rewrite this junkspace architecture's status as a crime scene—simultaneously and paradoxically serves to exhume this house's haunted history. The question Bowden interrogates implicitly here and explicitly elsewhere in *Dreamland* centers on whether or not such houses built of stucco and concrete and vinyl will not only represent "a medical and psychical metaphor for all the possible erosion of bourgeois bodily and social well-being" but also become recognized as "a culture's amnesiac memory bank upon which we should constantly work in order better to understand ourselves."[29]

[Alphabet/Abecedario; **Exposure**; Freeways; **Idyll**; Lipstick; **Queues**; Urbicide]

Kotex, Keds, ketchup, and dead kids

EXTRACTS

I did the loops several times over and found myself at an adoption agency, an orphanage, and a miserable shantytown of abandoned children on the edges of a vast dump. If I took one lead down one road, it brought me around to the same road again. Impoverished kids, orphaned kids, street kids, dead kids, disappeared kids. The whole system was a damn cloverleaf, and I began to have this nauseating sense of moving constantly to no good purpose.
—Karen Tei Yamashita, *Tropic of Orange* (1997)

Used to be us Indians had nothing to throw away—we used it all up to the last scrap. Now we have a lot of casino trash, of course, and used diapers, disposable and yet eternal, like the rest of the country. Keep this up and we'll all one day be a landfill of diapers, living as adults right on top of our own baby shit.
—Louise Erdrich, *The Antelope Wife* (2012)

Various features of your journey north might include police corruption; violence in the form of beatings, rape, murder, torture, road accidents; theft; incarceration. Additionally, you might experience loneliness, fear, exhaustion, sorrow, cold, heat, diarrhea, thirst, hunger. There is no medical attention available to you. There isn't even Kotex.
—Luis Alberto Urrea, *Across the Wire* (1993)

1. "*Disposable and yet eternal, like the rest of the country.*" "The shape of the contemporary city," writes Sze Tsung Leong, "is no longer cohered by physical, visible characteristics, such as form, iconography, or density, but arrived at by default, as the residue of ulterior motives," chief among which is control.¹ Control space connotes a mobile, flexible map of information gathering grounded by computer technologies designed for surveillance: "smart" credit cards; radio frequency identity chips (RFID); more sophisticated commercial and residential forms of audiovisual surveillance such as tracking devices that monitor the mobility of commodities and consumers. The new digital technologies developed to understand and shape new patterns of urban spatiality thus produce more of a cartographic augmented reality conceivably providing an infinite amount of data for any given spatial coordinate. To the degree, then, that contour maps no longer signify geological configurations but rather reveal, say, the distribution of wealth and an estimated spending potential of a certain zip code, urban spatiality no longer is "*visualized* or *composed* as much as it is empirically *computed*."²

Control space is motivated by "the desire to understand, predict, and even fashion the ever-changing, often imperceptible, processes of urban life."³ Consider the heat map, a cartographic representation of a given locale on a computer screen whose varying plumes of color identify wealth (amount spent on retail) and shopping intensities (frequency and time of day) of specific postal zip codes. Consider the now ubiquitous presence of preferred customer cards and self-checkout machines, which track consumer spending habits and preferences, leading to the targeted delivery by regular mail or email messaging of store coupons and special offers, as well as customer surveys. As a result of such technological innovations, the emergent spectral cartography of control space effectively exposes the granular details of the inner workings of our consumer life, and in the process abolishes the distinction between public and private spaces. As Leong and other recent observers of this technological reformation of urban spatiality have noted, this reformation is anything but benign. "Just as industrial civilization flourished at the expense of nature and now threatens to cost us the Earth," Shoshana Zuboff argues, "an information civilization shaped by surveillance capitalism and its new instrumentarian power will thrive at the expense of human nature and threaten to cost us our humanity."⁴

Driven by ulterior or hidden motives tied to the controlling spaces of consumption and the regulation of the movement of human subjects, "control space" will foreground, for example, certain zip codes based on its technological deep mining of data on lifestyles, income, population demographics, and even crime rates. Driven by the ulterior motive of regulating the movement of human subjects through explicit surveillance, other locales will become more or less invisible from an economic and even political perspective. Thus "control space" inherently exists in dialectical relation to what Leong calls "residual spaces," which are those spaces subject to obsolescence or even erasure as technological innovations appear and then get superseded, as population demographics shift, and as the periodic crises endemic to capitalism occur, leading to infrastructural transformations in banking and investment, housing, and transportation networks. Here, we can consider shuttered big box retail stores and enclosed shopping malls and first-generation strip malls and downtown manufacturing factories, the service stations replaced by minimarts or fast-food franchises, and, as we have seen in Héctor Tobar's novel *The Tattooed Soldier*, an abandoned neighborhood on Crown Hill facing the downtown Los Angeles financial skyscrapers and the current site of a homeless encampment. These architectures of abandonment and ruin exist in both urban and now first-ring suburban zones, spawned by the ongoing redistribution of capital investments and the new territorial divisions of labor, by arterial highway expansion and new airport and inland port construction, and by residential sprawl encroaching on the drossscape represented by toxic industries and petroleum refineries, car wrecking yards and sand/gravel pits, and even landfills or waste management transfer and recycling facilities.

Such residual spaces, within and around which the debris of consumer capitalism accumulates, display our dominant social formation's valuation of instantaneity and disposability.[5] Such values in the realm of commodity production and consumption lead to a monumental waste problem. Such waste testifies to the transit and transience both of social relations and our affective attachments to commodities, thus exposing a glimpse of a capitalist social totality founded on exclusion and the ephemeral.[6] As sociologist Zygmunt Bauman observes in his *Wasted Lives*, "The liquid modern life is a daily rehearsal of universal transience. . . . A specter hovers over the denizens of the liquid modern world and all their labors and creations: the specter of redundancy. Liquid modernity is a civilization of excess, redundancy, waste and waste disposal."[7]

2. "*A landfill of diapers.*" An auto-ethnographical account of life and death in a shanty town adjacent to Tijuana, Mexico, Luis Alberto Urrea's *By the Lake*

of Sleeping Children describes in its title essay how a mountain of trash from both sides of the U.S.-Mexico border had sealed off the "little Edward Abbey desert canyon" that had been used as a landfill, creating an artificial lake and turning the hillside slopes above its water level into a morass of stinking mud. "The canyon itself, as we know, was long gone," he writes. Instead of a riparian ecosystem defined by the presence of hawks and owls, coyotes and wild goats, "Kotex, Keds, Kalimán comic books, and ketchup bottles frolicked there now."[8] As this essay unfolds, Urrea pauses the predominant narrative mode detailing his exploration of this canyon so as to present descriptive vignettes, these keyed to the trajectory of his first-person narrator's scanning gaze. As one such vignette explains:

> The slopes of this vale, small as it was, were crowded with the sad wooden crosses of the dead children's graves. The whole area was full of nameless, abandoned, forgotten, sleeping little corpses. Plastic flowers faded from blue to pink by the sun. A toy or two. Cribs. . . . And the water ate away at the slope, the clay and sand coming loose and the little crosses toppling and falling into the water to float around like model sailboats. And other crosses, those in the bottom of the vale, stood in the water at angles, reflecting on the still surface. It looked like a Pink Floyd album cover, actually.[9]

Urrea's narrative persona stands here on the edge of the canyon's hillside, gazing down its slope toward the lake, both noticing the makeshift wooden crosses that mark the graves of dead children and, as his gaze lowers, how some of the other crosses have fallen down the hillside into the water, now seen to be floating and moving with the current, while others somehow stand upright, though at different angles, in the lake's muddy shallows. In this scenography where water erodes the earthen embankment, the corpses of the nameless, abandoned children remain absent from sight. But their presence nevertheless is conjured up by visible objects: wooden crosses; faded plastic flowers; toys; cribs.

Urrea's serial grammar here structurally equates the "sleeping little corpses" with these named material objects, and along with this passage's aural repetitions and its figurative language (i.e., the similes "like model sailboats" and "like a Pink Floyd album cover"), language becomes thickened, in the process calling attention to its potential for affective unsettlement. This potential is realized with Urrea's use of the present participle "reflecting." On the one hand, this verb form refers to the shadows cast by the crosses standing in the water at weird angles; but, on the other hand, it also can be read as Urrea's sly attribution of subjectivity (and agency) to these quasi-object/quasi-subject statuses, their standing and pensively reflecting on the water's still surface. "Like a Pink Floyd album cover, actually": the overall linguistic and imagistic weirdness of Urrea's prose description exemplifies what Michael Taussig says elsewhere about bogs or swamps, how their abject "weirdness" ultimately represents "nothing more and nothing less than the weirdness of language, so slippery yet firm . . . where the provocation of meaning created by this sliding back and forth between literality and metaphor occurs, so to speak, as a process of depetrifaction, the very process we might now call *miasmatic*."[10]

Hence Urrea's rhetorical stress in the second vignette, his narrative persona this time around positioned at the edge of the artificial lake, on the miasma of shit and mud and the corrosive solvent composed by toxic water. His gaze in one direction focuses on the weirdness attached to how some of the fallen crosses floating in the water display the cryptography of dead children's names, these "peering up at him." His gaze in another direction stares at three mammoth tractor tires positioned as if they were "march[ing] into the water in a row."[11] When his gaze then shifts to look down into this noxious, cloudy water, Urrea is startled by the sight of the lake's submerged detritus apparently drifting toward the lake's surface. What then emerges before his gaze of surveillance is a grotesque, anti-pastoral vision that ironizes the resurrection of the dead and the ritual feast of sacramental communion: "And we looked: looked at the shore, where the ground was swelling with this noxious water and crumbling. And we looked in, deep, where the bed of this lake was mud, and mud was drifting up, and the rotten soil was broken, and the coffins, the cardboard boxes, the pillowcases, the wooden crates, the winding sheets, were coming up. They were coming up. The children themselves were rising, expanding into the water, and the gulls were eating them."[12]

In this harrowing moment of recognition, incommensurate things heap together through their sheer juxtaposition or contiguity in space. This montage-type compositionality is made to cohere, though, by Urrea's serial grammar (the chaining together of clauses by the use of the conjunction *and*) and by the rhythmic repetitions of clauses in the continuous present tense. The result is that in this profane resurrection, human and nonhuman things are happening—they are drifting and coming up and rising and expanding and eating. Corporeal decomposition is doing its silent work; the lake's toxic waters are making the lakeshore crumble and swell up, like the bloated corpses, causing all the named things in view here to perform their roles in a bloody feast of communion in which the dead children's necrotic flesh is offered up to supplicant seagulls who have made their pilgrimage from the nearby sea.

3. *"Abandoned children on the edges of a vast dump."* Such discarded objects as Keds and toys and comic books and floating wooden crosses compel our attention primarily because they possess, by means of Urrea's surreal rendering of this residual space, an auratic quality. These cribs as crypts; these pillowcases and winding sheets—the aura emanating from these relics of the dead randomly scattered on the slopes above and on the shores of this landfill's artificial lake centers on how such stuff conjures up one's own intimate recollections of childhood. But here we are, on the shores of Tijuana's lake of sleeping children, where the substantial and dynamic materiality of these objects continuously on the move functions to rupture any desire to idealize childhood as a rather benign state of object relations. In a manner similar to what Margaret Iversen has said of Edward Hopper's painting *House by the Railroad* (1925), Urrea's positioning of the spectator on the shore of a Gothic, transformed and transforming miasmatic landscape conjures up the unhomely return of the past "as a kind of denatured nostalgia."[13] For as the corpses of children rise up, as wooden crosses topple into and reflect on still water, as discarded tractor tires seemingly march together in lockstep fashion, and as the seagulls feast on the corpses of childhood in broad daylight, the unresolved historical traumas and the contradictions of capitalism as experienced by abject populations uncannily hover into view. In this description of a depetrification process underway, Urrea's animated assemblage of embodied waste and dead children transgresses that "sacrosanct boundary between the embodied self and the rest of the world," thus producing an atmospheric effect of attraction and repulsion, "an equally unique mixture of awe and fear."[14]

All this so-called weird activity transpiring under "a perfect blue southern California sky," Urrea further notes—the same sky that enshrouds similar garbage dumps in such hemispheric neighboring places as Mexico

City, Mexicali, Matamoras, and Cuidad Juárez; El Salvador, Honduras, and Guatemala. Linking together the then and now in Tijuana with the there and then of such other nodal points in the transnational circuitry of production and consumption and waste, Urrea's prose shifts to the imperative mood to offer up this final judgment: *"Jump in—you own it: it's Lake Nafta."*[15] As this descriptive sequence's final italicized sentence renames the garbage dump as *"Lake Nafta,"* the overall phantasmagoria devolving here from Urrea's assembled object world of waste matter and wasted lives effectively grafts onto the exemplary (the massiveness of an object world) the register of the explanatory. Thus the potent truth conveyed by such everyday strange stuff assembled in and by the landfill and its lake can only be known and experienced through Urrea's (and our) entwined attention to and speculation about an emergent "process geography" of agential quasi-objects/quasi-subjects and diasporic human subjects, their entangled motion producing in *By the Lake of Sleeping Children* a layered, "cross-cutting map" of waste flows as a reminder and excess remainder accruing from global capitalism's flows of commodities and capital and living people (as well as the corpses of the dead) on the move.[16] Flows erupting from and circulating through and beyond this "residual space" that challenges the utopian dream of any "control space" that might be implemented under legislation like Proposition 187, or the construction of "a new Berlin Wall at the border," or by "microchips injected into the backs of our hands, read by circling Landsat satellites." As Urrea rhetorically asks, "You think they're going to work? You think they can possibly work?"[17]

[Alphabet/Abecedario; Cryptography; Diapers; Idyll; Junkspaces; Urbicide; Zombieland]

Lipstick traces

EXTRACTS

These locales, which we call *pickup sites*, represent the end of a multiday trip and are near rendezvous points where *coyotes* have arranged for vehicle transportations. Between 2009 and 2013 we documented forty-eight of these sites, which yielded hundreds of thousands of objects. These areas contained high proportions of backpacks and clothes, as well as diverse assemblages of hygiene, cosmetic, electronic, and personal items.

—Jason De Leon, *The Land of Open Graves* (2015)

Midway through February, in an alley in the center of the city, some garbagemen found another dead woman. She was about thirty and dressed in a black skirt and low-cut white blouse. She had been stabbed to death, although contusions from multiple blows were visible about her face and abdomen. In her purse was a ticket for the nine-a.m. bus to Tucson, a bus she would never catch. Also found were a lipstick, powder, eyeliner, Kleenex, a half-empty pack of cigarettes, and a package of condoms.

—Roberto Bolaño, *2666* (2009)

As she was soaping herself she heard someone else come into the bathroom, heard the same someone take two steps and stop, heard them deliberating and heard their hands dip into Makina's rucksack and rootle through her things. She poked her head out. It was a woman in her second youth; she looked tired. She had Makina's lipstick in one hand and started to apply it and didn't stop despite the fact that Makina was watching her and the woman could see she was.

—Yuri Herrera, *Signs Preceding the End of the World* (2015)

Dreamland Context 1: Lipstick makes a handful of noteworthy appearances in Charles Bowden and Alice Leora Briggs's *Dreamland: The Way Out of Juárez*. Its material and semiotic presence enters the text initially during one of Bowden's journeys to a wildlife refuge—unnamed, but most likely the Buenos Aires National Wildlife Refuge—in southern Arizona during the month of June. Walking the well-worn immigrant trail about a mile north of the U.S.-Mexico border and the Mexican town of Sasabe, he discovers a woman's bright green jacket, its color not yet faded due to the desert sunlight, its pockets containing "a new tube of lipstick and a compact of fresh eye shadow."[1] Inferring that this garment's location marks the very spot where an anonymous woman needed to lighten her load in order to survive her arduous and dangerous journey north, Bowden comments that in this very act of relinquishment "she became an American, she tasted the new Middle Passage that ground away earlier lives." Whatever the shape of the dreams that motivated her desert pilgrimage, this was the place and the moment when "the whole feel of this passage slapped her in the face." The feel of the summer heat. The feel of mesquite branches raking her face. The feel of her fellow travelers' indifference. And the feel of having entered, under the cover of darkness, "a no-man's-land where only people with guns have force and anyone else is prey."[2]

Later in the day, Bowden stops to rest during his hike. As he sits in the dirt near the stone footing of an abandoned settler's cabin, he smells the perfume rising off the lipstick tube he had removed from the green jacket and now holds in his hand. This olfactory trigger prompts him to consider this cylindrical material object as constituting the fragment of a hieroglyph yet to be successfully translated—an encrypted signifier that, if it were able to be successfully interpreted, would allow us a glimpse of this anonymous woman's recent history and to know better her active desires and dreams for the future. He then shifts from such speculation to offer up this summary judgment: "So many of us suffer from the weight of numbers on the groaning ground."[3] All this pensive reflection and all this attribution of judgment occurs as he rests on the trail in close proximity to another sort of hieroglyph: an architectural ruin attesting to the failed ranching dreams of an earlier generation of immigrants in this area.

Immediately before this moment Bowden reports feeling an intensifying "thunder in his head," this phrase forwarding a metonym drawn on a natural world sound (thunder) to represent the status of his interior being in the world. But here, in this summary judgment, his soundscape image gets recast: it is the sentient desert earth itself groaning from the accumulated weight of all the suffering bodies it has borne and continues to bear in the present tense of *Dreamland*. Such rhetorical chiasmus or boundary transgressions (inner/outer; human/nonhuman natural world) underscore the emergent empathetic unsettlement of Bowden's narrative persona ("so many of us suffer"). Such aural imagery and rhetorical boundary transgressions also anticipate this entire sequence's unsettling conclusion. For the reciprocal, call-and-response sound of the pain and suffering shared by both the human collective ("us") and the unnatural natural world immediately metastasizes into Bowden's confession of his interpretive paralysis: "I can't decide if I am hearing the cries of a hard birth, or something more like a death rattle."[4] Thus, a discarded, barely used lipstick tube functions—as is the case with any homeopathic substance—as both cure and poison, its fetching perfumed fragrance provoking here a rhetorical metalepsis, or swerve, a transgressive blurring of boundaries among narrative, epistemological, and corporeal or bodily registers. Dreams and reality, blessings and profanations, prospects for a new life and the likelihood of an extinction of that very prospect—these antithetical opposites become sutured together and embodied in this lipstick tube's material presence, this once-forsaken commodity literally and figuratively lost and then found in the no-man's-land that defines both the geopolitical border and the hybrid text of *Dreamland*.

Dreamland Context 2: Four months later, Bowden returns to this same border site "where Mexicans trudge through the wildlife refuge seeking the golden shore." Once again, he walks the old trail where, during the previous June, he had discovered an anonymous woman's green jacket containing lipstick and eye shadow in its pockets. Now, however, in the late afternoon October sunlight, he watches a doe moving through the mesquite trees that border the fence line of the abandoned ranch's family cemetery, where he discovers plastic flowers decorate sixteen of the graves. And in one of the mesquite tree's branches, he discovers both a woman's rose-colored knit blouse, its sleeves flapping in the wind, and discarded empty plastic water bottles strewn around its trunk. He then notices a stranded bullet-ridden black van, whose interior, upon inspection, contains a child's red sweatshirt as well as an empty long-neck bottle of Bud Light, its elongated shape—as one of Alice Leora Brigg's illustrations underscores—echoing the shape of a lipstick tube and a rifle or automatic weapon's bullet. "The man carrying the baby in the June heat," he speculates, "passed by here on his way north. And today hundreds are probably on the march all around me. As are drug smugglers. And vaqueros who cut the border fence in order to graze their stock illegally on the tall grass of the refuge."[5]

Dreamland Context 3: In between these opening and closing descriptions of his journeys in June and October to the same wildlife refuge on the U.S.-Mexico border west of Juárez, Bowden specifically references lipstick and, more generally, cosmetics for a third time in *Dreamland*. Triggered by the sight and smell of a massive forest fire burning through the Pinaleño Range near Wilcox, Arizona—its outbreak consuming an old-growth forest that had thrived there for over three centuries—he reflects on the parallel apocalypses represented by both this climatic event and the human history of migration that has occurred and still occurs in these borderlands. There is, on the northern horizon, a forest fire, the sonic landscape of which solicits his and our attention: "Ah, hear the screams as the flames lick." His resort here to the rhetorical figure of personification signifies, he muses, how this particular biotic community's evolutionary "universe of dreams and hungers [are] going up like a torch." Just as is the case with some of the migrants he had earlier described making the "Middle Passage" across a no-man's-land to a new life in the United States, migrants whom he imagines crossing the desert basin beneath this mountain range on fire, "creeping north, hundreds of thousands of migrants, that fabled 'them,' brown, hot and thirsty, the women dragging their lipstick and eye shadow through the new and deadly ground."[6]

Bowden's narrative, prompted by sight and smell of the forest fire, then swerves to describe these entangled human and ecological histories as composing a mixtape of "white noise." Just as white noise results when different sonic frequencies are combined, this borderland mixtape assembles together the noise of a planet undergoing global warming; the noise produced by the victims tortured and murdered by drug cartel sicarios; and the noise created by the multitudes of the "fabled 'them,' brown, hot and thirsty" and by the multitudes of drugs and weapons continuously crossing and recrossing the border. The forest fire's red flames analogous to the red lipstick in plastic or metal tubes and the red blood shed by those bodies found dead on the immigrant trails and in the environs of Juárez, this mixtape of white noise, for Bowden, emblematizes the ecological, economic, and political holocaust underway in a world "now said to be global." This globalized world in which villages are destroyed, cattle turned into bones, and people hurled "from where they were born toward some place they have never been where they hope to survive."[7]

Dreamland Pedagogy 1: **a.** *Maquiladora*, feminine singular of *maquilador*, from *maquillar* (to assemble; to make), from *maquila* (to process for a fee) and *-dora* (a suffix used to create name of the place where the action is performed from the infinitive). A manufacturing plant in Mexico near the U.S. international border run by a foreign company and exporting its products to that company's country of origin.

b. *Maquillarse*, from Spanish verb maquillar, borrowed from French *maquiller*, to put on makeup, to apply cosmetics.[8] Cf. *masque* or "mask."

Dreamland Pedagogy 2: A parable from anthropologist Michael Taussig: "'What have you learned?' the reality asks of the writing. 'What remains as an excess that can't be assimilated and what are you going to do with the gift I bestow, I who am such strange stuff?'"[9] One thing Bowden has learned about the "strange stuff" of reality is that an inherent gap exists between any reality and the writing or visual art representation of it. There is reality itself, here in *Dreamland* comprised mainly by events transpiring simultaneously at the drug cartel "house of death" in Juárez, a forest fire on the mountain, and the travels of migrants north on the desert trails toward the United States. And there is his developing, exploratory train of verbal thought and discursive prose prompted by such real-life happenings—visible evidence fated always to be moving at a tangent to reality, this "strange stuff" and this "excess that can't be assimilated." Unlike historian Frederick Jackson Turner's vision of the western frontier as offering an escape from a bondage to the past, for

Bowden, writing a century after Turner's essays on the meaning of the frontier experience in United States history, discarded articles on an immigrant trail—such as clothing and cosmetics and plastic water bottles and bullet-ridden vans—represent anything but the kind of material evidence that would sustain a master narrative whose plot trajectory arcs from bondage to liberation. Instead, what one expresses during the act of shedding articles of clothing or ditching tubes of lipstick or compact cases of cosmetics during a desert pilgrimage to reach some fabled golden shore is the disheartening reality of "the new Middle Passage": the bodily and mental exploitation surely grinding away contemporary immigrant lives ("the fabled 'them,' brown and hot and thirsty") just as surely as slavery did for the "earlier lives" of Africans forced to make the original Middle Passage.[10]

Clothing and cosmetics: such everyday stuff is strange—alien and unhomely—precisely because it constitutes an "excess that can't be assimilated." The discarded pile of stuff deemed surplus on the immigrant trail materially counters any mythic adventure narrative whose teleology is oriented toward the production (and celebration) of the imminent arrival of a homogenous and composite nationality. So let us catalog, one final time, the assemblages of "everyday strange stuff" that Bowden presents during the course of his separate journeys away from Juárez to the wildlife refuge on the Arizona border with Mexico. A bright green jacket and a rose-colored knit blouse and a child's red sweatshirt. Mascara and a lipstick tube and makeup. Cigarettes and Bud Light bottles and a Dentyne Ice gum foil pack. Empty plastic water bottles and an abandoned cattle ranch's grave markers decorated with plastic flowers. A bullet-riddled cargo van.

It seems right to claim that such stuff found on the immigrant trail is strange precisely because such newly castoff matter is essentially homeless, out of place or context, representing an unnatural or at least unexpected presence in this desert ecosystem's no-man's-land. On another level, when regarded as attentively as Bowden does in his serial narration of his journeys of discovery along the immigrant trail, such "strange stuff" is also estranging. The affective impact on the human sensoria of lipstick's scent; the cognitive disorientation produced by the agency of a rose-colored blouse lodged in a mesquite tree, its sleeves flapping in the wind—such stuff estranges precisely because it is as if he encounters such things in the very process of their becoming regarded as waste or trash. This strange stuff estranges because its heaped-up material presence simultaneously occupies and exposes the fungible—hence volatile and transgressive—nature of whatever constitutes the dominant ideological categories of the valuable and valueless, the inalienable and alienable, the natural and the unnatural. And with this speculation in mind, perhaps we can better understand the obsessive fixation throughout the length of *Dreamland* on both the accumulated and the accumulating, performative "strange stuff," the reality of which effectively troubles the desire for the disciplinary production and monitoring of a militarized geopolitical borderland. And, too, the verbal and visual discursive strange stuff Bowden assembles throughout *Dreamland*, this textual signifier simultaneously connoting a book title, a leitmotif, and a threshold state of consciousness in which the properties of night and day, the moments of sleeping and waking, and the status of the reality and the dream blur together, commingle and exchange places, in the process beggaring the imagination like a black crow moaning.[11]

Dreamland Pedagogy 3: Bowden's reflections on the color of human blood and of the red hues painted on women's cheeks and lips eventually arrive at a historical episode from the early years of the Spanish conquest in the Americas. Based on his reading of texts by Bernal Díaz and Father Durán about the Spanish invasion of Mexico in the years 1518–19, Bowden recounts in expository fashion how the Aztecs greeted Hernan Cortés and his soldiers with gifts of gold, jewels, feathers, clothing, and virginal "young girls who are very beautiful and wear plumage." Girls whose long hair hung down and whose cheeks were painted red. Girls awarded to them, the Spanish soldiers were supposedly told, "so they [the Aztecs and Spaniards] could be brothers and the young fragrant women were to be brides."[12] Still, Bowden interjects, at this early moment in the history of the Spanish conquest, the artifice represented by red-painted cheeks and lips also could signify an alternative desire and an oppositional female agency to the Aztecs' disciplinary technique of marking girls' and women's cheeks and lips in preparation either for the sanctification of marriage or their sacrifice to a god. For at this very moment there still existed the residual power associated with the red-cheeked goddess of plants, Xochiquetzal—an Aztec nature deity known also as "the goddess of whores": "So it all tangles up together, soldiers, virgins, blood, whores, red, the gods, a bundle of passion that can only be accepted if proper, or damned if free appetite. Blood on the floor of the house in Juárez, red on the cheeks of a woman walking the *calles* and smiling at life itself."[13]

In this short summary passage that concludes the *Dreamland* leitmotif of cosmetics, Bowden offers a serial list of disparate stuff, both strange and familiar: various occupational statuses or identity markers; the chromatic hue we call red; the affective realm of various passions. This entangled assemblage testifies to Bowden's desire to apprehend some elusive and perhaps entirely unrepresentable "it." Now the abstraction introduced by the "it" in this passage is grounded by its proposed intimate relationality with both "a bundle of passion" and "life itself." What links these two domains together is the color red, which as we witness in the passage's enjambed phrase fragments, indexes the blood on the floor of a drug cartel house of death and the lipstick of a smiling woman who walks the *calles* of Juárez. Bowden thus envisions the color red as part of a "prismatic archive": as an errant archival domain of "unstable, changing sense impressions" that binds together "different historical moments, and involve[s] different actors" since the time of Cortés's excursion into the New World.[14] Put differently, his historiographical method conceives of the historical record as if it were a palimpsest, a layered assemblage of distinct temporalities and spatial locations simultaneously present. So what the writing of history can learn from the strange stuff of reality—this entangled "it" of historical things, persons, and events—will result from "a montage of memories as *slices in time* laid on top of one another—a *now* overlaid by a *back then*."[15] A now structured here by the paratactic juxtaposition of death's immobility with everyday life's pedestrian mobility, by the interiority of a death house with the exteriority of an everyday street scene, and by the juxtaposition of a corpse's rictus grin with a borderlands Mona Lisa's enigmatic smile. A back then emblematized as the time of Cortés and the Aztec empire with its gods, as the time of the migration of slaves via the Middle Passage, and as the time of the settler-colonial occupation and settlement in Arizona, this represented by the material evidence of a cattle ranch's ruins on an immigrant trail.

Evident through such paratactic juxtapositions of the here and there, the now and then, these functioning to render distinct epochs as simultaneously present, what I want to call the discursive vagabondage of Bowden's vagrant imagination and historiography extends to other registers in the text of *Dreamland*.¹⁶ Resisting any incremental, graded unfolding of events and things according to the logics of cause and effect or even of hierarchical segmentation, you see a transgressive impulse at work in both the overlap of semiotic codes (e.g., cosmetics as signifying both disciplinary obedience to patriarchy and as free appetite) and in the way his books are not so much plotted as structured by recurring patterns of imagery and of phrasing and of events. You see this centrifugal impulse at work even in the brief epitomizing statement quoted above, whose lean prose declarations are informed by his methodological and methodical condensation of the personal journal and field notes, the secondary source material and ethnographical records he consulted. And you feel this impulse in Bowden's signature stylistic feature, a lengthy compound sentence that also constitutes a paragraph. Such assemblages interrogate the formal limits posed by line and form, by grammar and syntax. And such assemblages—as we witness in the above passage linking Cortés with a woman walking the streets of contemporary Juárez—thematically underscore what Bowden's narrative persona articulates throughout *Dreamland*: the cognitive and affective disorientation that follows on the uncanny eruption into the present moment of an individual, collective, and national traumatic past.

At the same time, we might well consider the ethical risk that accompanies this aesthetic and its modeling of history. To the degree that Bowden's historiography conceives an entangled human and ecological history as essentially "one long catastrophe returning in new guises," the risk surely is, as Ben Lerner has noted in the context of discussing the late W. G. Sebald's writing, that "the work of historical reckoning can pass into a transhistorical fatalism." On the one hand, as Lerner's use of the word "fatalism" suggests, such a vision of history dangerously "denies both agency (that we might change, individually and collectively) and accident (that you might get struck by lightning without it meaning anything)." And as his use of the word "transhistorical" suggests, the potential problems are this: the degree that such a historiographical palimpsest dwells in such abstractions as "it" and "a woman" risks equating all historical tragedies.¹⁷

Dreamland Pedagogy 4: In this particular montage's serial assemblage of slices of time, there exists a deep structural affinity informing Bowden's concept of borderland history over the centuries. It is an affinity produced by the color red as a chromatic hue and material substance. Whether applied to faces or emanating from the strange stuff of commodities, red is a revelatory color because it connotes both the power of desire and the desire for power throughout the continuum of borderlands history. Linked with cosmetics housed in compacts, cases, and tubes, and whose substances are applied to eyelids, cheeks, and lips, the color red in *Dreamland* connotes—as we witness in the entwined etymology of "mascara" and "mask"—an artifice bound up with deceit and deception. Thought about as an artifice disguising reality, the color red exemplifies the title, imagery, and thematic matrix of *Dreamland*—a text obsessed with uncanny repetitions of imagery centered on secrets, concealment, camouflage, veiling, and disappearance—as well as the misrecognitions and denials of reality constructed by dreams and daydreams. As in the dreams of migrants about crossing desert and river and mountains to reach a fabled "golden shore." As in the dreams of drug mules and *narcotraficantes* paying homage to Santa Muerte, and in the dreams of corrupt federal police and Mexican army officers who want to believe you can "live outside the rules and you have a lot of money and you will live forever, even if you die young."[18] As in the waking dreams occurring on "the patio of the house of death [where] they shoveled over dreamers, and sweating men stood over the graves and kept dreaming and it goes on and on because that is how we avoid the hard reality."[19]

As the expression "to show one's true colors" reveals, however, colors such as red can signify authenticity as well as the artifice of deception. Things displaying red hues can signify our potential grasp both of the transgressive or resistant matter of real stuff and experiences, as well as of experiences and stuff that really matter. To the degree, then, that Bowden persuades us that Juárez houses a social collective essentially sleepwalking and daydreaming in order "to avoid the hard reality" represented by the entangled "it" of globalization's war machine, its drug cartel machine, and its overarching femicide machine, then the gift proffered by Bowden's writing (and Briggs's illustrations) is that of making us affectively respond to this hard reality. Theirs is a project bound up with dramatizing a situation, just like that revealed by the discovery of the drug cartel death house, "where a vulnerable space is opened up through which ghosts might make their appearance."[20] As in the "ghosts" of the colonial past that continue to haunt the women "smiling at life itself" while they walk the streets and ride the buses in the globalizing economic, political, and cultural system manifested by the maquila economy. Indeed, as Michael Taussig reminds us in his book *What Color Is the Sacred?*, "color is a colonial subject."[21] Take the signifying chain for "red" in the borderland context of *Dreamland*, one that undoubtedly includes the specific red hue known as carmine, also called cochineal, or—as the Aztec word names it—the "blood of the prickly pear." Produced by harvesting and crushing the female scale insects that live on the pads of prickly pear cacti in the U.S. Southwest, this red-colored dye was used for over two centuries in the textile trade monopolized by the Spanish in the Americas and Europe, at least until a French naturalist successfully smuggled prickly pear cactus pads out of Mexico to Haiti.[22]

To the degree, then, that Bowden's prose introduces such objects as tubes of red lipstick existing both as a materiality in history and as themselves materially embodying a continuous history of being made, consumed, and discursively represented, then the gift extended by *Dreamland* is to expose how this entangled "it" represents "the new geography, one based less on names and places and lines and national boundaries and more on forces and appetites and torrents of people."[23] Bowden's sustained discursive representation of the disruptive and disquieting power embodied in the discarded stuff of clothing and cosmetics strategically transgresses various semiotic codes and spatial and temporal scales in order to critique how the historical traffic among and exchange of women has grounded, and continues to ground, the inherently irrational and violent and exploitative quality of both early and late capital's colonial and neocolonial regimes of production and consumption.[24]

[Alphabet/Abecedario; Diapers; Queues; Television; Urbicide; X-ray; Zombieland]

Motel noir

EXTRACTS

Genevieve went over and kicked lightly at the front tire of her Dodge—to her the tire always looked low. The boys had made her remember what it was to be young. Once, before they had any kids, she and her husband Dan took off one weekend and drove to Raton, New Mexico. They stayed in a motel, lost twenty dollars at the horse races, made love six times in two days, and had dinner in the coffee shop of a fancy restaurant. She had even worn eye shadow. Romance might not last, but it was something while it did. She looked up the street and waved at Sam the Lion, but he was looking the other way and didn't notice her and she went back into the empty café, wishing for a few minutes that she was young again and free and could go rattling off across Texas toward the Rio Grande.

—Larry McMurtry, *The Last Picture Show* (1966)

Miracle Mile had a heyday once. The motel bungalows, blue kidney-shaped pools, tall palm trees, and hedges of pink oleander sprang up. Winter havens for house trailers stretched for acres. But years before either Seese or Cherie had ever seen Tucson, something had changed. The drought had left no green. In the dust-haze any lawns or grass that might have been alive was indistinguishable from the cement of buckling sidewalks.

—Leslie Marmon Silko, *Almanac of the Dead* (1991)

"I spent the night in a little mom-and-pop motel in the middle of nowhere. The walls had knotty pine paneling and fifties lamps and prints of deer on the wall—"
"Dag, get off the car. I feel really uncomfortable here"
"—and there was the smell of those little pink bars of motel soaps. God, I love the smell of those little things. So transient."

—Douglas Coupland, *Generation X* (1991)

1. "*So transient.*" In February or March 1957, Edward Hopper, nearing his seventy-fifth birthday, completed his painting *Western Motel* while serving as a fellow at the Huntington Hartford Foundation located in the Rustic Canyon area of Pacific Palisades, California. As his wife and model Jo Hopper simply describes it in her record book and diary, this oil painting's subject is a "deluxe green motel room, mahogany bed, pink cover, dark red chair with blue robe," its central female figure seated near the bed's footboard and gripping it with her right hand, looking like a "haughty blonde in dark red, her Buick outside window green."[1] What art historian Linda Nochlin has observed about the earlier Hopper 1940 painting *Gas* also seems applicable to our understanding of the compelling resonance of the later *Western Motel*: "The power of the painting lies in its ability to convince on the level of the factual, in its terse visual rendering of the evocative in the everyday, of that which is glimpsed and briefly remembered while passing through."[2]

Now by her phrase "terse visual rendering of the evocative in the everyday," I take Nochlin to be referencing how Hopper develops this painting's "level of the factual" through the two signature features that define his overall body of work: the rhythmic juxtapositions and repetitions of color that compose the paintings' visual field; the situating of enigmatic human bodies before or behind transparent glass window and door frames, their gazes manifesting a primary Hopper leitmotif. Certainly the "terse visual rendering" of certain passages of line and color in *Western Motel* illustrate how Hopper represents "the factual" both as the recognizable contents of the everyday real (e.g., configurations of brush stokes that readily signify, say, a bed or club chair or piece of luggage) and as a physical (and social) world that has been subtly transformed, to anticipate my argument here, into a disquieting orthogonal space. I am thinking, for example, of how his brushstrokes produce what we can readily recognize as, on the one hand, an image of a bed's mahogany footboard and also, on the other hand, a configuration of a regular rectangular block—this relatively abstract geometrical presence and its particular chromatic register repeated by both that portion of the bed's headboard visible above the horizontal, rounded mound of pillows beneath the pink bed covering and the bedside table on which a mahogany-colored clock rests. And with regard to this visual evidence of the painting's dual investment in the logic of mimetic representation and the lure of abstraction, let

FIG. 6. Edward Hopper (1882–1967), *Western Motel*, 1957. Oil on canvas, 30 ⅝ in. x 50½ in. (77.8 cm x 128.3 cm). Yale University Art Gallery, New Haven CT; bequest of Stephen Carlton Clark, BA, 1903.

us further consider how the slim, gooseneck-like table desk lamp's helmet or cowl inside the motel room uncannily iterates both the shape and the function of the headlamps on the green Buick parked outside the motel room's plate-glass window.

Such parallelism and contrapuntal relationality of lines, shapes, and chromatic registers disclose how Hopper's compositionality produces this painting's visual field as a permeable, threshold space of transit between what is portrayed as existing either inside or outside the motel room. Take Hopper's interplay of horizontal and vertical energies or lines of force. Along with the sage green interior walls framing the room's windows, the fore- and midground swath of mahogany, pink, and garnet tones traversing the painting's width—from the mahogany bed on the left to the club chair on the painting's right margin—comprise the dominant horizontal line of force in the painting's interior world. And outside the motel room, there is the parallel horizontal line configured by the front portion of the green Buick's hood and headlights, the horizontal slash of an unlined highway pavement in the near distance (its pale color picked up by the picture window's bottom threshold), and, in the far distance, the elongated horizontal lines and relatively smooth, sunlit tops of the mountains and mesas framed by a patch of light cerulean blue sky (its color echoed by that of the robe draped on the club chair inside the motel room). Contending against such layered or stacked, horizontal lines of force, however, is the verticality supplied by the anonymous woman seated on the bed slightly to the left of the painting's center, her upright pose itself framed by the open curtains hanging vertically on either side of the picture window immediately behind her (their yellow ochre color echoed by this woman's hair color, the lamp on the bedside table, and the sere or wheatgrass-colored desert land on either side of the highway). That she is neither positioned precisely at the painting's geometrical and balancing center nor centered within the window frame especially underlines how the power of the painting hinges not only on her presence and gaze (more on that below) but also on the motel room's plate-glass window.

Like all windows (and doors for that matter), this rectangular window functions as a threshold space, enabling the transit of our gaze between the inside and outside worlds depicted by the painting. It also functions as a second or double picture frame within the larger frame provided, of course, by the stretched canvas's boundaries, which demarcate the limits or horizon of the painting's visual field. The interplay of horizontal and vertical lines of force and its framing and cropping of the visual field provided by the inset window glass and frame can be regarded as promoting a double gaze of attention. Looking at this picture, in other words, we just might discover how our own performative gaze oscillates between focusing on this anonymous woman's somewhat magisterial presence—created by her slightly turned bodily pose—and her studied gaze, which is directed toward the viewing space both of the artist and the beholder of the painting. And on the other hand, even as our gaze may well be transfixed by her presence, are we not solicited also to bypass our surrogate within the room and consider what is outside of the window frame, these monolithic landforms and this vault of sky whose presence we can imagine as extending beyond what the visual field makes visible? Keyed for us by the motel room's transparent picture window, the transit of our gaze due both to Hopper's compositionality and handling of color in *Western Motel* troubles the categorical oppositions between inside and outside and between human architectures and nonhuman environments. Moreover, this window frame's function as a threshold space enabling the transit of our gaze complements the painting's subject matter: it permits the sight, to return to Nochlin's phrasing, of "that which is glimpsed and briefly remembered while passing through," a function in keeping with the inherently transient or transitional nature of motel residency as well as the sun's light.[3]

2. *"Wishing for a few minutes that she was young again and free."* As Wallace Jackson has written, the other major leitmotif in Hopper's artworks is that of waiting, which is to say, in the context of *Western Motel*, waiting in that hinged pause between having arrived and having departed when and where an existential uncertainty or indeterminacy often reigns.[4] In his book *Hopper*, the poet and art critic Mark Strand notes how in several Hopper scenes "an imprisoning, or at least a limiting, dark" predominates, one whose very opacity and identification with the night starkly raises questions regarding the existential temporal arrangements we all face as mortal humans: "What do we do with time and what does time do to us?" In Hopper's work, he further observes, human figures are repetitively portrayed as "characters whose parts have deserted them and now, trapped in the space of their waiting, must keep themselves company, with no clear place to go, no future."[5] Compared to such classic Hopper works as *Nighthawks* (1942) or *Hotel Lobby* (1943), however, *Western Motel* does not appear to be as invested in darkness. Rather, *Western Motel* seems more intent on forwarding a sense of spaciousness and an orientation toward a future life defined by the freedom accruing from mobility—this promissory note of desire signified here by the presence of the automobile and the open road outside the motel room's window. Indeed, for evidence that attests to this particular painting's relay of a sunnier affective structure of feeling, for example, we need look no further than Hopper's representation of cast shadows. Whether such shadows appear inside or outside this motel room, the painterly passages appear to be produced through Hopper's desaturation of his primarily green and yellow ochre hues with white or gray in order to lighten rather than darken their chromatic value.

Along with the relative absence of dark tones in *Western Motel*, there also exists this very rare thing in Hopper's artwork: the model (Hopper's wife Jo), who poses at the approximate center of the painting, gazes not outside the window behind her but rather toward the artist and viewer who exist beyond the frame.[6] Just like the painter, whose presence beyond the frame is implied, the viewer of *Western Motel* does not just gaze at a lone woman seated on the edge of a motel room's bed. We are also positioned as the recipient of her gaze (more on that below). This notable revision of Hopper's basic leitmotif of looking leads Strand to consider *Western Motel* as representing an exception to the usual critical judgment of Hopper as the painter of modernist alienation. For Strand, then, this lone woman's gaze acknowledges the "presence of another" beyond the picture's field of vision and, as a result, affords the painting "an amazing stillness." It is precisely the pairing of this emergent "amazing" moment of stillness with a betwixt and between temporality of waiting that leads Strand to offer this summary judgment about the painting's overall dynamic of looking: "We are the real reason everything seems to stop in the picture. We are the invisible force within the painting, and we are the occasion it honors. This may be the reason we do not feel excluded. We are not being urged on. The moment is ours."[7]

As Strand's phrasing suggests, it is as if for him the collective looking and being looked at in this painting's arrested "moment" realizes what art critic Michael Fried elsewhere has labelled "the presentational" mode rather than some more "actional kind of theatricality."[8] In its sustained investment in presentness ("the moment is ours"), *Western Motel* essentially resists imagining its depicted moment of waiting as either bound up with some past burden (the what has been) or overdetermined by some anticipated future (the not yet). Furthermore, given Strand's deployment of the adjective *amazing* to describe this painting's investment in the presentness of the now, it would appear that the presentness of the now should not be equated with, say, sheer instantaneousness. For within the very ephemerality and rootlessness of everyday life signified by the green Buick and the motel and the open highway, Hopper's painting heightens its mode of presentness through the transformation of the "we"—the "haughty" woman, the artist, and the viewer—into an "our," which is to say into a collective that realizes and shares this sheltered moment as a state of grace. Grace imagined as a renewed sense of intimacy with an Other. Grace imagined as an aesthetic of attunement—via the prolongation of the visible field in view here—to the environing world's abiding beauty. And grace imagined as an "arrested moment" with one's own self as well as with others, that models for us an authentic experience of sincerity: that ideal condition in which there exists no gap between what one regards and what one knows, between what one says and what one means and between what one sees and what other humans (and nonhumans, for that matter) see. Or, to paraphrase an old song lyric, though someone or something took my joy, I have found a way to get it back.

3. "*To her the tires always looked low.*" Is not such receipt of grace that beautiful thing Genevieve nostalgically desires in the above prose extract from Larry McMurtry's *The Last Picture Show*? That "wishing for a few minutes that she was young again and free and could go rattling off across Texas toward the Rio Grande," staying in motels along the way and romancing her lover as if, years later, she once again could dwell in the presentness of that particular grace known as true intimacy?[9] And yet, the pathos of this scene centering on the boys' final preparations to leave town accrues because Genevieve's wistful desire to renew an imagined past moment of full presence in her life is ruptured by signs and wonders attesting to her alienation. When McMurtry first introduces this character named Genevieve in *The Last Picture Show*, we learn that as a waitress working the graveyard shift in Sam the Lion's café in Thalia, Texas, she is subject to the admiring male gaze of assorted cowboys, oilfield workers, long-distance truckers, and local married men, as well as by local boys, such as Sonny Crawford and Duane Jackson, in training to be men more or less like their fathers before them.

But in this scene, which appears approximately halfway through the novel, Genevieve herself assumes the position of a spectator, watching these two boys, paychecks in hand, depart Thalia in an old pickup truck to make a weekend road trip to Matamoros, Mexico, across the border from Brownsville, Texas. And now, while she watches the boys depart in the middle of the night, she suddenly becomes overwhelmed by memories ranging in time from her youthful past to her present moment as an adult alone in the dark on Thalia's main street. McMurtry's serial narration of her cascading memories fastens on what it felt like, once upon a time, to be young and free and in love with her husband, Dan. That time before when she made a free-wheeling road trip with Dan and spent romantic nights in a roadside motel. That time before the kids came along. That time before all the regrets arrived in full force, before Dan passed on the opportunity to partner with a friend who eventually became oil rich. And that time before Dan got seriously injured in a drilling rig accident, forcing her to work as a waitress and late shift cook in Sam the Lion's café in order to support her entire family.

Unsettled here by the cumulative impact of an earlier moment when she started to cry as she took the boys' food order, by her watching them depart town in the narrative present, and by her recollection of her life's singular road trip adventure, Genevieve rues the yawning distance between her stranded present moment and her vividly recalled past, this temporal and affective dissonance grounded here by the stark contrast she draws between the "full" motel nights on the road back then and the "empty café" in the here and now that she pivots to reenter as the scene ends. Even as she visualizes an image of plenitude—true romance as indeed a substantial "something"—the enunciated tagline "while it lasted" exposes how her recognition of just such a pleasurable remembrance is simultaneously a misrecognition, irredeemably alienated from her present circumstances. And given the evidence here of this character's eruptive nostalgia, just in case we might ourselves misrecognize the pathos that saturates this scene, McMurtry stages its conclusion as a misfire of such a projective gaze of desire. For as the taillights of the boys' pickup truck begin to disappear in the distance, she notices Sam the Lion, further on up the empty street, also watching the boys' departure, and she waves at him before returning to the empty café to finish what remains of her night shift. The intended object of both her gaze and her wave, however, does not see her in the gathering darkness. This misfire of another's gaze—one that presumably would reciprocate and validate her own gaze and being in the world—just as surely undercuts her recollected past moment of plenitude as does the material presence of her own car's underinflated tires, these mute objects that have drawn her regard at the outset of this charged scene of arrival and departure. And that now, here at the end, symptomize her deflated inner state.

"While it lasted": so it happens that all the clipped memory traces she associates with her past youth and mobility constitute both "beautiful things" and, simultaneously, as Rilke puts the matter in his *Duino Elegies*, "nothing but the beginning of terror which we still are just able to endure."[10] In contrast to that emergent grace of presentness that Strand for one sees exemplified through the dynamic of looking in *Western Motel*, this scene from *The Last Picture Show* exemplifies how the nature of local knowledge—the personal and collective histories that constitute regionality itself—surface as a layered or entangled sense of time and space, of memory and event, history and story, affect and emotion, out of which McMurtry assembles "a critical regional presence/present, always already inflected by the past, haunted by memories, myths, and everyday realities."[11]

4. *"The crucial X always eludes us."* Although not directly concerned with this painting, Slavoj Žižek has noted how Hopper's art forwards several key features of the cinematic noir universe, especially "the way the *frame* operates in his painting."[12] In *Western Motel* we see, on the one hand, the contracted frame provided by the motel room walls demarcating the space of an inside. On the other hand, the large, transparent glass window and the visible sliver of a glass door to its right simultaneously enable our view of an outside. Nested within the outer frame provided by the dimensions of the canvas itself, Hopper's insertion of these two frames into the picture makes visible certain spaces and elements and, simultaneously, suggestively implies the existence of "spaces and elements beyond the limits of the scene itself, as if envisaging a wider field than the sphere the picture can surround."[13] My point here is that the effect produced by Hopper's framing and cropping of this particular motel scenography underscores the inherent instability of any perspectival vision. Such external supplements to the painting's pictorial reality as those portions of the green car and desert floor and mesa and the sky absent from the visual field, for example, exemplify how, in Žižek's words, in the end "the crucial X always eludes us, our vision is always 'framed.'"[14]

The primary focal point of what we look at in *Western Motel* is arguably the "haughty" unidentified woman, to return to Jo Hopper's description of this posed figure who sits on the bed, her right hand grasping its footboard, her body turned sideways, and her gaze directed toward our anonymous spectatorial presence outside the painting's visual field. Both the trajectory of her gaze and the window's material presence behind her—this framed object that also frames her and enables our visual passage across the painting's spatial planes—foreground the existence of plural viewpoints. Thus, this enigmatic woman bears our visual regard, and her corporeal presence conceivably fosters, as Strand has argued, the spectator's affective identification with and perhaps even a glimmer of desire for her (after all, this stilled moment is ours). Nevertheless, such a noir leitmotif as "the frame" also serves as "a reminder that to look does not protect against being looked at."¹⁵ The woman who bears our projected gaze also is a human subject who looks back at us and, I suggest, remains beyond anyone's projective desire for full knowledge, and hence presumptive mastery, of her and the visual field. For one thing, her corporeal pose itself is ambiguous: her presence strikes me as being simultaneously revealed and concealed, both approachable and withdrawn. For another thing, it is neither entirely evident that this woman can be said to be reciprocating any viewer's gaze nor that we, in our own performance of looking from beyond the picture frame, can ever truly be there for her, in this moment and in this space, to answer her visual call or invitation (if there be one at all).

With all this in mind, let us consider how Hopper's rendering of her face models a carapace of pure exteriority: that her face—shall I say her poker face?—registers an emptiness rather than, say, offers a discernible external look or facial expression that would reliably communicate the status of this enigmatic female Other's internal world.¹⁶ As a result of the uncertainty or utter elusiveness of any facial signifier that could provide us with such evidence, then, *Western Motel* produces an "*unoccupiable* point, the point at which the subject disappears"—where the proprietary "'belongs to me' aspect of our looking is suddenly drained from representation."¹⁷ This painting's leitmotif of looking thus looms up before our eyes as an uncanny, unstable visual fable of projective desire, the tensely rendered nature of her pose and her blank facial affect deflecting any viewer's potential scopophilic drive to experience the pleasure to be derived either from one's visual surveillance of another person or from one's gaze being returned, and hence validated, by that of other person who exists over there waiting silently on the edge of the bed. Like Genevieve, in McMurtry's *The Last Picture Show*, watching Sam the Lion, who himself is caught out watching the taillights of the boys' old pickup disappear as they drive away from Thalia after darkness, so too in *Western Motel* all of us who are caught out looking here in the end dwell in "those spaces that open between what we see and what we know of what we see," as well as "between what we see and the *other* sees."¹⁸

5. "*In the dust-haze any lawns or grass that might have been alive.*" Regardless of the evident "sunniness" that irradiates *Western Motel*, its leitmotif of the

gaze conveys what the noir features of other Hopper paintings more obviously underscore: that "we as spectators are often barred from, refused access to the full seeing of others depicted on the canvas. Whatever we abstract from the field of the painting is never anything more than our own construction and thus the expression of our own expectations."[19] Even as the clear glass frame provided by this motel room's window allows the viewer a glimpse of the external world, it also functions, conversely, as a mirror that reflects the viewer's performative projection of desire. Moreover, as I noted above, Hopper's framing and cropping of the painting's visual field subtly exploits the dynamic of recognition/misrecognition: the subject who looks also is the object of surveillance by others. So the visual field in *Western Motel* emerges as a faulted and divided space, one relaying an uncanny aura of mystery, as Walter Benjamin more generally describes this optical issue. The key word here is *object*. One might be tempted to confine its meaning to the framed art object in our purview. But what Benjamin has in mind here is something more resonant and complex. He argues that our experience of the aura of an object testifies to the emergence of what he calls an "unconscious optics" in which "a response characteristic of human relationships is transposed to the relationship between humans and inanimate or natural objects."[20] On one level, then, Benjamin's theorizing of an "unconscious optics" asks us to consider objects as abiding in an intimate relationality with human subjects. On another level, though, with his verb *transpose* and his phrase "a response characteristic of human relationships," he refers to another foundational feature defining human subjectivity: that human propensity or unconscious desire to project onto objects the agency both to look back at us and to feel like us.

With Žižek's observations about the noir features in Hopper's artworks and Benjamin's notion of an object's aura as enmeshed with an "unconscious optics" in mind, then, let us consider the presence of still another gaze in *Western Motel*. Both within the periphery of the painting's visual field and yet out beyond the motel room's window, there exists the massive auratic presence of mute inanimate or natural objects: the automobile and the ribbon of highway, of course, and in the distance the inhuman, physical presence of the desert floor, the monolithic landforms of mesa and mountain, and the overarching canopy of blue sky. Visibly present in the painting's visual field and to the mind's eye as it imagines the materiality of such objects extending beyond the painting's frame, the presence of these landforms and this vault of sky conjures up the inherent difference between the partial views of all the human subjects involved in this painting's leitmotif of looking and, let us say, the more panoramic gaze of these material presences mutely testifying to the geological scale of deep time. As if realizing an uncanny double of the "unoccupiable point" represented inside the motel room by the posed woman's facial mask of exteriority, here outside the window and extending beyond the painting's framed visual field is a nonhuman other similarly exemplifying an unbounded, rather than partial, non-psychological point of view.

So here I am, closing in on an identification and naming of the unsettling specter that has been hiding in plain sight during my critical exploration Hopper's *Western Motel*. My arrival at this belated recognition of the indecipherable gaze of the material world Other—this non-psychological fourth gaze—in this painting has compelled me to reflect upon the sheer contingency and ephemerality of not only my own life but also that of wood and glass and paint, of steel and asphalt and rubber. To reflect on all the transient human lives collectively journeying on the (lost?) highways of this visible world. To reflect on the fact that, in the end, it is this inscrutable, nonhuman Other's gaze that will continue apace and bear witness to still another future and still another world, one undoubtedly emptied of any motels and automobiles and concrete highways—and of any human presence (excepting our trail of so-called forever plastics, I suppose). A future world absent any and all humans whose shared mortuary fate, I venture to say, is foreshadowed here by this stilled moment in waiting—in this suspended pause between any arrival and departure on our separate journeys toward the community of the already dead and gone, toward those who signify the fleeting "what has been" and who perhaps, further on down the road, await our arrival.

[**Exposure**; **Freeways**; **Junkspaces**; **Hotel life**; **Noir motel**; **Vagabondage**; **Windows**]

Noir motel

EXTRACTS

"That film noir stuff is passé. Don't you get it?" Emi told Gabriel over her Bloody Mary. . . . "Stop being such a film buff. Raymond Chandler. Alfred Hitchcock. Film nostalgia. I don't give a damn if *Chinatown*, *The Player*, or everybody in Hollywood owes these old farts their asses. I'll give you this: at least they're in color."
—Karen Tei Yamashita, *Tropic of Orange* (1997)

The night it happened I was drunk, almost passed out, and I swear to God a bird came flying through my motel room window. It was maybe five degrees out and the bird, some sorta duck, was suddenly on my floor surrounded in glass. The window must have killed it. It would have scared me to death if I hadn't been so drunk. All I could do was get up, turn on the light, and throw it back out the window.
—Willy Vlautin, *The Motel Life* (2007)

More and more, my presence here, on this trip with my family, driving toward a future we most probably won't share, settling into motel bedrooms for the night, feels ghostly, a life witnessed and not lived. I know I'm here, with them, but also, I am not. I behave like those visitors who are always packing and repacking, always getting ready to leave the next day but then don't; or like ancestors in bad magical realist literature, who die but then forget to leave.
—Valeria Luiselli, *Lost Children Archive* (2019)

1. "*Stop being such a film buff.*" In director, writer, and actor Orson Welles's baroque film noir *Touch of Evil*—released in 1958, the year after Edward

Hopper completed *Western Motel*—there is a crucial motel scene that intensifies the uncanny potential inherent in Hopper's twin leitmotifs of waiting and the unconscious optics of the gaze. *Touch of Evil* dramatizes a story of murder, kidnapping, and political and legal corruption in the fictionalized U.S.-Mexico border town of Los Robles. As the film opens, Mexican narcotics detective Ramon Miguel ("Mike") Vargas (Charlton Heston) and his American wife Susie (Janet Leigh) are strolling late at night from Los Robles back to the U.S. side of the border during a honeymoon escape from their life in Mexico City. When a bomb explodes in an American building contractor's convertible just moments after crossing over into the United States (and having passed by the newlywed couple on foot), Vargas is assigned by the Mexican government to liaise in the ensuing investigation with Captain Hank Quinlan (Orson Welles), thus delaying the couple's return to Mexico City and, crucially, his resumption of an ongoing criminal investigation into the Grandi family crime organization, one of whose key members, Joe Grandi, heads up the Los Robles branch.

Vargas quickly realizes that Quinlan and Pete Menzies, his sergeant, are corrupt, but at the outset of the murder investigation he is unaware that both of these men are complicit with Joe Grandi's scheme to frame both Vargas and his wife as drug addicts in order to derail the investigation underway in Mexico City. After accusing Quinlan of planting evidence to frame the primary car bomb suspect, Vargas fears there might be reprisals against Susie. He is persuaded to have her sequestered at the Mirador Motel, its isolated set of cabins on the American side of the border situated next to a single two-lane road that courses through a high desert plain surrounded by low-lying mountain ranges and mesas. After she has been dropped off and left alone at the motel, Susie anxiously begins to inspect her new surroundings, at one point raising the blinds of her motel room to survey the empty, mostly barren, and forbidden landscape, its stark nonhuman physical presence supplying a natural world correlative to her inner world's increasingly agitated condition.

When translated from Spanish into English, this motel's name—*mirador*—connotes both an architectural structure, such as a balcony or bay window, as well as the act of gazing from such a location. As she peers out the motel cabin's window in this medium shot, Susie's face and bare shoulders are framed by the camera, just as—unbeknownst to her—the Grandi crime family has

FIG. 7. Susie Vargas (Janet Leigh) at the Mirador Motel in *Touch of Evil*, 1958. Produced by Albert Zugsmith. Directed and written by Orson Welles. Universal-International Pictures.

set in motion its plot to frame her as a drug addict and murderer. Though obviously transparent, rather than translucent or opaque, this glass window, like the massive picture window in painter Edward Hopper's *Western Motel*, enables the transit of her apprehensive gaze between the room's interior and the outside world that mushrooms up before her eyes.

This still shot's formal composition exemplifies how modalities of the uncanny coalesce to produce the visual field as a topology of displacement and disorientation and eventually, as the sequence unfolds, of vertigo. The compositionality of this image is asymmetrical rather than balanced and proportional. Its crisscross of regular geometrical lines (for example, the canted line of the window frame's bottom edge; the horizontal line of the desert plain) intersects with the irregular geometry evident in the contours both of her body before the window and by the mountain range in the distance, creating a jagged force field that complements her jangled, nervous energy. And there is the classic film noir chiaroscuro effect created as this shot grafts together—via a recursive play of shadows and reflections—the motel room's interior space and furnishings with the exterior spaces visible outside the window frame. As a result of Welles's investment here in mirroring effects and spatial doublings, what we—as well as Susie—might initially regard as a recognizable rustic motel mise-en-scène gets transformed instead into an uncanny mise en abyme (to put into the abyss). To be more accurate in my description of this still shot, the external natural world that Susie Vargas glimpses out there, both beyond this window's frame and what extends beyond image's visual field, seems simultaneously to exist—thanks to the flattening of the visual plane's surface and the motif of reflections—inside her room, not just before her gaze but also behind her body as she stands at the window. Let us also consider the rather weird effect created as the angled shadow of Susie's upraised right hand and forearm produces the illusion that, as she moves to raise the window blinds, her shadow—this uncanny double of her corporeality—appears as if it is about to penetrate and break the window's glass membrane. Furthermore, because of the contrast formed by the square of shed light that frames this dark shadow's appearance at the center of the image, it weirdly appears as if the window glass is, on the one hand, a seamless sheet of plate glass and, on the other hand, a sheet of plate glass divided into a trio of identically sized regular square segments.

One effect of both this serial visual repetition of reflections and this interplay of chromatic contrasts is to segment the visual field's framed and bounded space into a sort of cubist collage, a collision of warped shapes and irregular forms (with the exception of that ominous mazelike spiral of the cabin's loudspeaker that formally underscores the unraveling of Susie's mental composure from a state of confusion into a state of dread). It is as if, then, on the level of the film's intertextual allusions, that the resulting mise en abyme produced by this noir leitmotif of reflections and chromatic contrasts solicits us to recall the famous house of mirrors sequence in Welles's film *The Lady from Shanghai* (1947).

2. "*Settling into motel bedrooms for the night, feels ghostly, a life witnessed and not lived.*" What Imogen Sara Smith has called "Welles's chameleon-like camera" also contributes to the uncanny atmospheric affect in *Touch of Evil*.[1] In this still shot of Susie Vargas at the motel window, the camera's perspective is slightly elevated and positioned at an oblique angle just outside and above the motel window, this visualization of the scene thus produced by an unoccupied or de-anthropomorphized gaze divorced from being possessed by or attributed to any of the characters in the film's diegesis. In short, it is a voyeuristic object look that itself objectifies Susie Vargas just as surely as do the gazes of the film's assorted characters and of spectators in crowd scenes, all of whom stand in as surrogates for the viewer. As an object of constant surveillance and manipulation, the characterization of Susie Vargas introduces how a paranoid Cold War imaginary emerges whenever one's own visual field becomes illegible or foreign or unstable. Epistemological confusion regarding what is truth or falsehood essentially reigns in a corrupt world of political and economic conspirators fomenting secret plots, criminal conspiracies, blackmail, and slander. And as we can infer from the strained intensity of her projective gaze out the motel room window in this still shot, Susie Vargas, in her spatial displacement, appears uncertain, if not confused, about exactly what it is she is feeling—and, furthermore, whether she is entitled to such feelings and whatever judgments that arise in their wake. Her projective gaze out the window embodies how her emergent field of anxiety is anticipatory or futural, the edges of its estate overgrown with an increasing dread about being left alone and being potentially touched by the evil of whatever threat might arrive and take shape either inside the motel room space or out there in the dark night to come.[2]

All this affective and cognitive disorientation and all this anticipatory anxiety produced by the visual field's instability and captured by the camera's kaleidoscopic perspective illustrates how, to cite Anthony Vidler on the modalities of the architectural uncanny, "the field of anxiety is framed by the uncanny, so to speak, even as the uncanny itself is framed as a sudden apparition seen, as it were, through a window."[3] As it turns out, a "sudden apparition" does appear in Susie's immediate future, first, in the form of the Mirador Motel's night manager (Dennis Weaver) who voyeuristically stares at her from outside the motel cabin's windows and who blasts invasive, cacophonous music from his office into her cabin's loudspeaker. Soon, another sudden apparition arrives in the form of a gang of black leather-jacketed youths from Los Robles who terrorize her initially by their antic surveillance from outside the motel room's windows and then invade her room and surround her as she lies on her bed in her nightgown in a panic state. Sent to the Mirador

Motel by Joe Grandi, the male gang members lift her struggling body in the air above her bed, as if she were a kind of ill-gotten trophy, all this activity unfolding as the camera slowly zooms back from the claustrophobic interior of the motel room and the scene fades to black.

3. *"A bird came flying through my motel room window."* This cinematic sequence at the Mirador Motel culminates in a carnivalesque scene of queer baiting that grafts together the sadistic and voyeuristic elements inherent in the male gaze with a visual coding of her assailants as alien Others, a hybridized assemblage of ethnoracial and queer juvenile delinquents clad in black leather motorcycle jackets. The result of this cinematic assemblage in this film's motel sequence is an unsettling, somewhat ghoulish excursion in the travails and paradoxes accruing from noir spectatorship. Certainly with her butch haircut, black leather motorcycle jacket, and hard facial features, the sinister bull dyke (Mercedes McCambridge) who belatedly enters the motel room to aid in Susie's harassment embodies a version of mainstream Hollywood cinema's historically negative image of lesbianism. Nevertheless, when she informs everyone gathered in the motel room that she is there solely to watch the action unfold, we become immersed as viewers in the inherent ambivalence and paradoxes that accrue from noir spectatorship. On the one hand, when Welles's camera and editing decisions focalize this final scene of the motel room sequence through this lesbian character's voyeuristic gaze, this stereotypically-coded deviant individual functions as our surrogate viewer. On the other hand, when the camera shifts to medium shot of the whole room or focalizes what is happening through Susie Vargas's fearful gaze, we are invited to empathize with this major character's precarious situation. But given the camera's reverse zoom from this motel room's interior and the closing of the motel cabin's door as the scene fades to black, it turns out that we don't exactly know what our various spectatorial surrogates (one of which is the motel's night manager, who lurks outside the motel cabin's window) ultimately witness. The sight of whatever painful touches of evil that Susie Vargas seems destined to endure becomes apparitional, left to the film viewer to imagine. So the rather unsettling sadism spectacularly evident in the film's representation of the multiple voyeuristic gazes at Susie Vargas gets redirected from her toward the viewer, who is lured into imagining the

worst-case scenario—her rape and murder—is being prosecuted behind the closed door.

Given the evidence of a terrorist car bomb conspiracy that both inaugurates the film's investigative plot and underscores its paranoid atmosphere, such formal editing and cinematographic decisions regarding how to present the concluding moments of the Mirador Motel sequence explicitly reveal this film's investment in secrecy. In *Touch of Evil*, secrecy represents a key theme (this noir world's truths are hidden from sight; reality is specular and speculative); secrecy serves as the structural logic for film's criminal conspiracy plot; and, when regarded as a political, financial, or erotic desire, secrecy overdetermines the film's visual leitmotifs (such as the mirroring effect where reflections spawn uncanny disorientation and displacement), underlining the instability and deceptiveness of what meets the eye. Nevertheless, it turns out that the secret regarding the truth of what actually happens to Susie behind the motel room's closed door is, well, no secret at all. Neither is this motel a "safe house." Rather, it is owned and operated by the Grandi crime syndicate across the border in Mexico, whose criminal plot dictates that the gang of youth not rape and murder Susie Vargas, but rather sedate her with drugs and return her to a Grandi-owned boarding house across the border in Los Robles, where eventually she will awaken from her drug-induced stupor only to discover, as she lies in a strange bed in yet another room designed to accommodate transience, a murder victim hanging from the room's ceiling above her.

From its beginning at the Mirador Motel to its conclusion in this Los Robles boarding house, this sequence underscores a crucial insight: that the sudden apparition framing any uncanny field of anxiety does not solely exist as a spectral terrorist person or act whose arrival is from the outside, beyond the motel window, much less beyond the nation-state's geopolitical border. Such sudden apparitions haunting the here and now can be thought about as always having existed, hiding in plain sight, so to speak, inside the "home," whether that haunt (to employ the old usage of home as a place visited frequently) be represented on the scale of the corporeal body that houses the unconscious; the scale of an architectural built environment; or the scale of the transnational nation state, whose geopolitical borders literally and figuratively define the homeland. When the paranoid imaginary of an anxious subject manifests itself in the uncanny spectacle of a world warped by various private and public boundary transgressions, then the familiar, domestic space of a motel room's interior just might transform into a panic space. Indeed, in this situation—as we see with the example of Susie Vargas before us—everyday life will appear to the anxious human subject as if "all limits [have] become blurred in a thick, almost palpable substance," as if a cognitive and affective miasma "has substituted itself, almost imperceptibly, for traditional architecture."[4]

As we witness in *Touch of Evil*, that "thick, almost palpable substance" may manifest itself through the warped architectural spatiality of mirror reflections and distorted geometrical shapes and soundscapes. It may manifest itself as an affective and cognitive dysphoria: as a mental fog or ghostly haze produced by shock and fear that constrains a human subject from being able "to organize past and future into coherent experience."[5] Or as we see at the end of the motel room sequence when the impending violence threatening Susie Vargas gets foreclosed because the scene fades into darkness, the "thick, almost impalpable substance" that substitutes for the traditional architecture of a domestic motel room may manifest itself as a "blinding afterimage" of a youth gang holding her scantily clad body in the air above a motel room's bed, the sight of which produces a disturbing memory trace in the viewer's imagination "long after the stimulus that has caused it has ceased" to be present.[6]

4. "*Like ancestors in bad magical realist literature, who die but then forget to leave.*" Is it not the case that any paranoid anxiety arising from the arrival of "sudden apparitions" that transform domestic architectures into panic spaces should not just be relegated to a psychological matter where all "actions and events come to be interpreted in relation to the self"?[7] After all, the source of internal paranoid feelings—especially in relation, I should think, to anxieties about and fears of secret conspiracies—also can be traced to contemporary socioeconomic and sociocultural developments. Let us consider, for example, Mike Vargas's pronouncement to his wife in the concluding scene of *Touch of Evil*: "I'm taking you home." On one level, that he makes such a statement succinctly represents his desire for and achievement of both narrative and ideological closure as a result of his successful resolution of the car bomb murder and the Grandi family's conspiracy to frame him and his wife as criminals and drug addicts. On another level, however, this somewhat patronizing statement also discloses how he too suffers to a degree from cognitive and affective miasma. For "home" here at the film's conclusion presumably connotes this couple's return to their Mexico City residence. However, even with this setback to their financial and political power in the Los Robles-El Paso borderland, Mexico City remains the home base of the still-active Grandi family criminal organization. So with all this in mind, as well as the enigmas that the film introduces but never resolves, the trajectory of the criminal conspiracy plot that concludes with Vargas's closing statement arguably represents a "process whereby otherwise dangerous protopolitical impulses are 'managed' and defused, rechanneled and offered spurious objects."[8] Dangerous protopolitical impulses in this film are ultimately managed and defused, as Mike Vargas embodies through his actions and words such as the objective to restore home, family, and nation sustained by "the propriety of patriarchal domestic economy."[9]

Nevertheless, if we accept Mike Vargas's offering of a spurious object as a utopian desire, we might recognize something else in addition to his drive for "comprehension and control." We might better recognize, for example, how, at the end of the film, a crucial paradox emerges, one that Oliver Harris more generally has argued explains our fascination with film noir: "that blindness within vision itself makes possible a kind of vision in blindness."[10] Given Mike Vargas's apparent "blindness," then, what manner of "vision" might we discover embedded in the investigative plot trajectory of *Touch of Evil*? To begin to answer to such a question, let us first consider how the vision that emerges throughout the accumulating evidence of blindness (obtuseness; opacity; secrecy) in this film is shaped by two major post–World War II sociohistorical and economic developments. As I mentioned briefly earlier in this essay, one development centers the advent of the Cold War structure of feeling, this dominated by various affective categories of fear (paranoia; dread). The other key development is the highly visible and accelerated transformation of capitalist urban (and new suburban) spaces during this same era. As Julian Murphet has argued, the film noir genre's vision of such production of space "rests inalienably on both a racist *and* sexist distribution of power and population."[11] For Murphet, the key aspect of film noir's racial and political unconscious is the post–World War II African American majority presence in major inner-city areas, a historical fact of human migration that represents a literal and figurative black hole in film noir, an absent cause. And "if Noir refrains from pointing the finger directly at African-Americans, and offers more 'acceptable targets' (women, Communism), it is because the entire noir effect depends upon that primary repression" (i.e., "of well-nigh hysterical fantasies about black occupation of the inner cities").[12]

As we witness in the spatial choreography of human movement in *Touch of Evil*, women like Susie Vargas become "acceptable targets" of "well-nigh hysterical fantasies" because it dramatizes the threat posed by the ongoing transfer of "private being (desire, drive) from its classical 'home' in the bourgeois house to the thoroughly commodified urban lifeworld of late capitalism."[13] It is a transfer evidenced architecturally in Los Robles by networked grid of streets and roads and back alleys that delivers various female bodies to the unhomely transient spaces of nightclubs and hotel lounges, to motel cabins and dilapidated boarding houses and brothels, and all-night diners with jukeboxes. Her cringed posture as she walks by her husband's side at the film's conclusion indexes not only her post-traumatic stress. Her pose also reveals what Sianne Ngai argues is the gender problem at the very heart of political thrillers and classic film noir narratives: that conspiracy theory itself—this structure of feeling underpinned by the affective category of paranoid anxiety—ironically safeguards these two genres as distinctively male forms of knowledge production, even as the "knowledge-seeking trajectories of male protagonists" in them exposes how "they are small subjects caught in larger systems extending beyond their comprehension and control."[14]

5. *"This precarious life."* I suppose I could end this essay just like this, by pointing out how the frisson *Touch of Evil* generates—primarily by means of the voyeuristic display of Janet Leigh's body and the stereotypically negative Hollywood image of lesbian bodies—represents "patriarchal capitalism's ongoing disciplinary effort to control women's sexuality and independence."[15] True enough. But beside the possibility that such a critique may well represent a relatively familiar or standard one, I remain haunted not only by the uncanny resonance of this film, released over sixty years ago, both by the blinding afterimage of Susie Vargas's body as it is raised in the air by the teenage gang invading her Mirador Motel cabin and then by the sight of her cringe

of abjection in the film's final scene. And I am also struck by how this film's characterization of Susie Vargas's paranoid anxiety fits neither the stereotypically masculine model of persecutory paranoia nor the stereotypically female form of paranoia fueled by jealousy. Is it possible, then, that Susie Vargas embodies an alternative mode of knowledge production even as she embodies a pose of abjection due to the weight of circumstances set in motion by the car bomb at the border crossing? Is there still another way we might understand (and learn from) the implications, in a life lived under the sign of precarity, of one's being touched by evil? Rather than ask why her mental and physical trauma causes her to mourn, we might consider, in short, what her cringe of abjection can teach us about the power of mourning.

Reflecting on such questions prompted by this film's portrayal of Susie Vargas's trauma, I find myself thinking about Judith Butler's important book *Precarious Life* (2004). Writing in the context of the endless war on terrorism being waged in the wake of the events of 9/11, she reminds us that it is precisely because this body we inhabit constitutes a crucial component of our identity that violence represents "a *touch* of the worst order, a way a primary human vulnerability to other humans is exposed in its most terrifying way, a way in which we are given over, without control, to the will of another, a way in which life itself can be expunged by the willful action of another."[16] Now given this "primary human vulnerability," when we voluntarily or involuntarily recognize how all bodily lives are by necessity vulnerable to the claims of some Other—especially, in the context of *Touch of Evil*, either to those sudden apparitions arriving from outside or those already existing inside any putative local or national home—two consequences follow. One is that our own exposure as viewers to the trauma endured by Susie Vargas potentially can foster our complicity with it (say, our writing it off as a temporary derailment of the narrative's trajectory toward the restoration of justice). And, secondly, that such violence targeted against women drives home the primary lesson that "we are, as bodies, outside ourselves and for one another," and this lesson in turn spawns another recognition: there remains "something to be learned about the geopolitical distribution of corporeal vulnerability."[17] That is, something to be learned about the distribution of "corporeal vulnerability" during both the Cold War era context of *Touch of Evil* and, to take Butler's specific test case, the post–9/11 War on Terror. Historical moments when paranoid anxiety seemingly reigns as the normative condition. Historical moments then and now when the geopolitical distribution of corporeal vulnerability exposed by, say, acts of genocide and urbicide and domestic violence underline how a reified "hierarchy of grief" continuously relegates some losses and some lives as being of value, while other types of losses and lives, especially those of women and ethno-racial minorities, are considered to be of lesser value.[18]

If, rather than resolving the vertiginous grief that attends any visceral sense of loss with a palliative speech act belatedly promising a return to some nominal home, we instead stay with the blinding afterimages that accrue from Susie Vargas's vertiginous ontological and epistemological and corporeal dispositioning in the world, then, these are some of the questions that perhaps emerge as we continue to confront an "open future of infinite war in the name of a 'war on terrorism'": Will we be "left feeling only passive and powerless, as some fear?" Or will we instead—thanks to Orson Welles's chameleon-like camera and Susie Vargas's traumatized mode of knowledge production—be reminded not only of our human vulnerability, but also of "our collective responsibility for the physical lives of another?"[19] Such questions touch on the ethical stakes dramatized in *Touch of Evil*, this movie interrogating that uncanny sense of disorientation that arises when one realizes they are a small subject in a larger system of domination. This movie whose conspiratorial agents represent the "ancestral ghosts" that continue to haunt the conduct of the seemingly endless war on both foreign and domestic terrorism, on drugs and human trafficking in and beyond the U.S.-Mexico borderlands.

[Alphabet/Abecedario; **J**unkspaces; **L**ipstick; **M**otel noir; **R**ivers; **S**cene of the Crime; **W**indows]

Oil rich, core samples from a personal ledger

—for my parents

EXTRACTS

Oil (n.). "late 12thc., 'olive oil,' from Anglo-French and Old North French *olie*, uile 'oil' (12c. Modern French *huile*), from Latin *oleum*, "oil, olive oil" . . . from Greek *elaion* "olive tree," from *elaia* (see *olive*). . . . In English it meant 'olive oil' exclusively till c. 1300, when the word began to be extended to any fatty, greasy liquid substance. Use for "petroleum" is recorded from 1520s but not common until 19thc."
   —from the *Online Etymological Dictionary*

Petroleum (n.). "Early 15thc., 'petroleum, rock oil, oily inflammable substance occurring naturally in certain rock beds' (mid-14thc. in Anglo-French), from Medieval Latin *petroleum*, from Latin *petra* 'rock' (see petrous) + *oleum* 'oil,' see *oil* (n.)."
   —from the *Online Etymological Dictionary*

Ledger (n.). "[Akin to D. *legger* layer, daybook (fr. *leggen*, to lay, *liggen* to lie), E. *ledge*, *lie*. See **Lie** to be prostrate.] **1.** A book in which a summary of accounts is laid up or preserved; the final book of record in business transactions, in which all debits and credits from the journal, etc., are placed under appropriate heads. **2.** (Arch.) **(a)** A large flat stone, esp. one laid over a tomb. *Oxf. Gloss.* **(b)** A horizontal piece of timber secured to the uprights and supporting floor timbers, a staircase, scaffolding, or the like."
   —from *Webster's Unabridged Dictionary of the English Language (1913)*

1. Red Lodge, Montana—Winter 1952.

> Since that pioneer time the country had become trammeled and gnawed, stippled with cattle, coal mines, oil wells and gas rigs, striated with pipelines.
>
> —Annie Proulx, *Fine Just the Way It Is* (2008)

That the etymology of and the possible connotations for the word *ledger* braid together the notion of a final book of record, one in which accounts are "laid up or preserved," along with the finality signaled by a flat stone laid over a grave or tomb—all this suggests we regard any ledger as a death book.

My father unexpectedly died in early September 2007 at his home in Sarasota, Florida, this place so distant from his Texas origins, this place where he chose to retire after his career as a petroleum geologist, as an owner of an independent oil well drilling company, and as an oil and natural gas producer in Montana, Illinois, and Ohio. He was eighty-one years old and in relatively good health for a man his age, this sudden death most likely caused by an aortic or cerebral brain aneurism. To die in one's home while watching the evening news on television and holding a glass of Scotch and water, all the while sitting next to his (third) wife, who made the emergency call for help from the paramedics—this manner of death strikes me now, as the years have passed, as an exemplary good death. A manner of death that perhaps we all hope for, whenever and at whatever age an intense awareness of one's mortality surfaces and punctuates our everyday life's seeming endlessness, its repetitive routines and familiar demands on our time.

Certainly, his passing seems to me a more desirable death than that experienced by my mother, his first wife, who died in March 2013, at the age of eighty-four, in the Mercy Medical Center at Canton, Ohio. She suffered from Parkinson's disease, with which she had been diagnosed in the summer of 2006, the year before her first and only husband's death. In what became the final year of her life, though I and my own family were living—as we had been for several decades—nearly two thousand miles distant from her Canton residence, I was able to visit her, and my sisters who also lived in Canton, on four occasions. Due to the time that elapsed between each of my visits, the incremental stages of her decline became dramatically visible: the need for her to leave her house and enter an assisted living facility; the loss of her mobility;

the dementia that overwhelmed her in her final weeks and months. The status of the living person with just such a neurological disease, this person whom one beholds and, whenever possible, cares for, this person who desires a death with dignity—this person is fated to become, simultaneously, neither herself as one has known her through the years, nor not quite yet dead and gone. This person fated both to announce her desire to seek out death, and fated to experience how death itself, as a matter of course, will flee any such approach until a time and place of its own choosing.[1]

By the time I arrived for what turned out to be my final visit to be with her, hospice caregivers had been given notice and palliative care was the protocol of the day. During these visits I would look to our past—even as I was thinking of my and our family's future without her—at least as this past was manifested in the albums of family photographs she stored in a bookcase in her house. With her beside me, sitting in a chair next to her bed, I would stare at the dozens of black-and-white snapshots of our family's past in Ellis County and then Grayson County, Texas, and I would become fixated on the snapshots taken of me in the summer and fall months of 1949, not long after I was born in Sherman, Texas.

On the last morning of my final visit, amid the pile of photographs that had been removed from their clear plastic sleeves in the photo albums, I find myself staring at a small, square, black-and-white photograph framed by scalloped white edges. I am looking straight ahead at the camera while sitting atop a white plastic insert placed on a white toilet seat to accommodate my small frame. The lighting is dim, and I suppose it is the winter before my third birthday in April. I am shirtless and, given my spindly legs in view dangling on either side of the toilet, presumably I am naked from the waist down. Behind the toilet is a back wall composed of logs with mortar chinking, evidence of the original house, once owned by a coal miner in Red Lodge, Montana, the county seat of Carbon County, just north and east of the Beartooth Mountains in the south-central part of the state. White settlers began moving to the area after an 1882 treaty agreement between the U.S. government and the Crow Nation.

On the floor to my left is a small collection of glass bottles with cleaning fluids, and to my right is a metal diaper pail, painted white. It is night, and given the combination of my unsmiling, sleepy-eyed look and my straddling the toilet seat, presumably I have been awakened by my mother as a feature of a more advanced stage of toilet training than that stage represented by the soiled diapers inside the covered white pail, these items associated with my younger brother, born the previous summer in Red Lodge. That we are in Red Lodge at all is because my father, with the assistance of the G.I. Bill, had become the first in his family both to attend college and to graduate, in his case with a degree in petroleum geology from Wichita State. After graduation he had immediately been hired by the Cities Service company from Bartlesville, Oklahoma, and assigned to do the geological work for their drilling rigs operating in the Dry Creek and Elk Basin oil fields near Red Lodge. That my mother took this photograph at all says something about her sense of humor. That she took the photo at all suggests that her people—farmers who knew what it was like during the depression years to have little or nothing on the table—did not caution her against the old folk taboo against publicly attending to toilet needs, especially inside the house. And the fact that she took the picture at all during a dark winter night reveals, as I would also learn during the years to come, how often she was alone while her husband was sitting in a travel trailer or in a drilling crew's doghouse during the rig's evening or graveyard tour, tasked with decoding the earth's geological hieroglyphics for evidence of an underground reservoir of oil. This potential revelatory evidence deposited in the shards of cuttings from rock formations produced by the rotary drill bit's action and by the circular core samples brought to the earth's surface whenever the crew would change out the drill string of pipe and replace the worn drill bit.

Years later I would learn the name of the strong smell permeating that rustic bathroom in this old family photograph was from a bottle of Lestoil, a then-popular heavy-duty grease, stain, and linoleum floor cleaner made from a toxic mixture of petroleum-derived ingredients and chemicals, all potential carcinogens. Years later I would figure out the source of the sulfurous odor that seemed always to permeate this small house in Red Lodge, especially during these cold weather months when the windows and doors would be as tightly closed as possible. It wasn't the smell from the house's propane heater, but rather one linked to my father's dirty working clothes in the laundry hamper, his khaki shirts and pants and sometimes even the T-shirts that he wore over his U.S. Navy dog tags, all these articles of clothing stained by grease and by dried clots both of the earth's mud and the viscous gray mixture of bentonite clay, barite, and chemicals that formed the drilling mud necessary to lubricate the rig's drill stem and bit so as to circulate rock cuttings back to the earth's surface.

But as I looked at this old photograph with her sitting by my side in the assisted living facility during the week before her death, I began thinking about how this snapshot of me sitting on a toilet lays up and preserves, like any written ledger, my introduction to the paradoxical nature of this world into which we all are thrown. Here is a bathroom, this space where both hygiene practices and waste matter disposal occur. And here too, exposed to view in this closeted space is material evidence, on the cusp of the coming petrochemical revolution inaugurated by plastics, of petroleum's paradoxical presence, one that can be seen as well as said to produce and sustain the modern world. On the one hand, there is petroleum's presence as black gold, a material blessing that sustained this first house in Red Lodge and all the future houses in my family's life. On the other hand, there is petroleum's fabled presence as the "devil's blood or excrement," as either organic or refined matter capable of casting a curse at any time on any of these various houses and the everyday lives of their inhabitants.[2]

2. Olney, Illinois, Richland County ("Little Egypt"), Spring 1957.

> Wonder what all they're doin back home? Rawlins said.
> John Grady leaned and spat. Well, he said, probably they're havin the biggest time in the world. Probably struck oil. I'd say they're in town about now pickin out their new cars and all.
> —Cormac McCarthy, *All the Pretty Horses* (1992)

It is night in the spring of 1957, and I am eight years old and sitting in the passenger seat of my father's Willys Jeep Utility Wagon. We were on our way from our small house on Mill Street in Olney, Illinois, not far from the B & O Railroad tracks, to a drilling rig on a farmer's field in nearby Clay County. The rig's borehole had been drilled to its projected pay zone depth and its owner-operator now had to decide whether to pump cement into the hole between the borehole's earthen walls and the outside of the drill pipe and move the drilling operation forward into the completion phase of production, or to decide instead to abandon the well in the belief that it would prove not to be profitable enough to cover the drilling and completion costs. The shoulder season between winter and spring was known as "mud season," for good reason, and before leaving the asphalt pavement, my father got out and turned the front wheel hubs to engage the Willys Jeep's four-wheel drive. We then drove about a half a mile to the drilling rig, with him smiling and even laughing while having to push the engine's RPMs to maintain speed and control the steering wheel, which seemed to have a mind of its own as we careened through the soybean field, whose deep rows of newly upturned earth, bisected by various vehicle tracks, had not yet frozen as night descended and the temperature dropped.

Upon reaching the drilling rig, we were first assaulted by the sound of the diesel-powered draw works and the smell of its exhaust plumes and the skunk-like smells from the mud pits near the derrick floor. And then I watched as my father took a seat on a steel bench under an overhead yellow light inside the rig's doghouse. While the driller and the toolpusher were summarizing that day's drilling report, he pored over the rig's logging history and smelled and rubbed all the rock core samples that had been brought up to the earth's surface during the drilling operation. His job: to grade this "show" of evidence as either good, fair, or poor—with regard to disclosing the potential subterranean presence of oil and natural gas—and then make a recommendation about whether to proceed with or abort the drilling operation.

A few years before this outing on this early spring night, Cities Service had transferred him from Red Lodge to Olney, the seat of Richland County, about two hours by car directly east of St. Louis on U.S. Highway 50. Richland County is one of the sixteen southern Illinois counties that collectively were called "Little Egypt," whose so-called capital city was Cairo, situated on a bluff overlooking the convergence of the Mississippi and Ohio Rivers. And on this outing to the drilling rig on that cold night in early 1957, when I was nearing my eighth birthday, I saw my father as I came to think of him throughout his life. Both the way he drove that Willys Jeep and the way he seemed to take pleasure in poring over the geological evidence brought to the surface by the rig's diamond drill bits epitomized how he was always in a hurry, impatient to be on his way toward something or somewhere else. Always focused on the potential future earnings of a well's pay zone or, as his career evolved, how to line up oil leases and potential investors to form limited partnerships that would underwrite the drilling of a series of wells. He never seemed closely bound to any given present moment, but rather was always already elsewhere, assessing whether or not any actions in the present moment would further his working plan about what a desirable future could look and feel like. So it was that he had left Cities Service and, during the mid-1950s, formed both the Tatco Petroleum and Tip Top Drilling companies.

What my ledger account hasn't yet mentioned is that my father was the owner-operator of this rig we visited that night in the Willys Jeep Utility Wagon and, yes, the cumulative geological record of this particular well's "show" he judged good enough to warrant bringing it to completion. Within a short time frame he began to exchange his work khakis and steel-toed boots for tailored suits and cowboy boots, turn in his company car and the Willys Jeep for a new Cadillac each year, and join the local Petroleum Club and golf club and Elks Club. My mother quit ironing patches on the holes in my Lee blue jeans and began scheduling quarterly shopping trips to St. Louis, not only for clothing but also, when the time soon came to build a new house from scratch, to buy salvaged brick and antique furniture and lighting for the new house that would rise up on the northern edge of Olney, adjacent to the property of the Tippet family, whose patriarch, decades before, had saved the town's last breeding pair of albino squirrels from extinction by shooting a raccoon stalking them in his wooded lot, a part of which was now the site of our new home.

3. Northern Wyoming to Southern California—Summer 1960.

> They said that it was no accident of circumstance that a man be born in a certain country and not some other and they said that the weathers and seasons that form a land form also the inner fortunes of men in their generations and are passed on to their children and are not so easily come by otherwise.
>
> —Cormac McCarthy, *All the Pretty Horses* (1992)

She was called Betty Clyde Christian, born on April 2, 1928, in Sherman, Texas, the child of Bonnie and Clyde Christian, her middle name a tribute to her father, who had been hoping their first-born child would be a boy. Her people were named Doyle and Williams on her mother's side, Christian and Barnes on her father's side. The Christians had settled in Westover Parish, Virginia, and then migrated to Goochland County, northwest of Richmond, in the early 1700s. A century later, a branch of the Christian family had settled in Warren County, Tennessee, and sometime in the 1890s its members had arrived in northeast Texas, settling in Sherman, the seat of Grayson County. As for the Doyles, in the early 1700s they had migrated from Ireland's County Wicklow and landed in Fairfax, Virginia. By the early 1850s, one of this lot had arrived in Texas, settling in Hill County, south of Dallas, where Betty Clyde Christian's paternal great-grandfather, Joseph Harrison Doyle, was born in 1853. He died a month before his namesake son was born in 1879. His wife married a Confederate Army veteran five years later, and this couple, along with Joseph Harrison Doyle Jr., settled in rural Ellis County, where Joseph Harrison Doyle Jr. eventually became a farmer in the Red Oak area, then called Possum Trot by its original settlers.

He was called Lee Robert Tatum, born in Sherman, Texas, on December 10, 1925, the second son and third of five children born to Louis Edward and Cora Lee Tatum. His first name obviously alludes to his mother's middle name, while his middle name honored the memory of his paternal grandfather. His mother Cora Lee was born in 1890 in Bartow County, Georgia, and by the time of the 1900 U.S. Census, this branch of the Dyer family was living in rural Grayson County, Texas, where she eventually met and married her second husband, Louis Tatum, in 1920. Louis Tatum's forbears had begun their westward migration from Virginia in the 1700s and arrived in Grayson County two centuries later, after stops in North Carolina, Georgia, and then southwestern Missouri, where Louis was born on a family farm near the Ozark mountains in 1891.

By 1917 Louis Tatum was living in Denison, Texas, a few miles north of Sherman. Though he sought an exemption from serving in World War I because, as his World War I draft registration card revealed, he "don't want to cross water." Nevertheless, he was drafted and in late 1917 embarked on a troop ship from Hoboken, New Jersey, as private first-class in the Camp Travis Medical Replacement, Company 46. He returned from Europe and married Cora Lee Dyer in 1920 after having abandoned an earlier wife, one son, and two daughters. As an adult, Louis Tatum worked, by turns, as a master boiler's helper and then a painter for the Missouri-Kansas-Texas (MKT) or "Katy" Railroad in Denison. In the early years of the Great Depression, he abruptly abandoned his wife Cora Lee and their family of four sons and one daughter, just as he had abandoned his first wife and family years before. He would remain in the Sherman area, a self-proclaimed café proprietor during and after World War II, before eventually moving to San Angelo, Texas, where he died in 1958. Years later, however, as I learned from my favorite uncle who had married my mother's only sibling, Louis Tatum's café was in reality more of a front for an illegal saloon operating in plain sight in "dry" Grayson County. On my father's part, an immense silence came to pass about these years of his youth, an absence that especially centered on his scofflaw father's later life and fate, this paternal grandfather I never met.

For the most part, both sides of this family tree worked the land as they continuously moved westward across the southern tier of states, eventually arriving in the Blackland Prairie ecoregion of northeast and north central Tejas or—as it came to be called after December 29, 1845—Texas. But in the end, they never possessed the land. During the late-1920s and the 1930s, the combined impact of drought and a boll weevil plague drove these rural kinfolks off the land and into towns such as Sherman, Denison, and Waxahachie— and in one instance even further west of the Dallas-Fort Worth area, toward Ranger in Eastland County, a town that had experienced an oil boom between 1917 and 1920. These were working men and union members, laboring in a Katy railroad shop, or a Hardwick-Etter cotton gin, or in a Quaker Oats mill making corn syrup, or operating a combination Deep Rock gas station and hardware store in downtown Sherman. The women would do clerical work or make and serve food in school cafeterias or become elementary school teachers. Years later, other great aunts and uncles, siblings of my grandmother Bonnie Doyle Christian, would migrate to Garland and McKinney, both towns destined to become first-ring suburbs in the greater Dallas metroplex.

Immediately after World War II ended, my father's three brothers became part of the other great migration in the nation's twentieth-century social history when they moved their families from Texas to California, as had so many Oklahoma and Texas refugees from the Dust Bowl years over a decade before them. They settled in Long Beach and San Diego and the Sacramento area. They worked in the aircraft industry's manufacturing sector, by dealing poker to off-duty sailors and marines, or by becoming a civil servant for the state government. Their mother, my paternal grandmother Cora Lee, who well could have served as actress Jane Darwell's double in the 1940 *Grapes of Wrath* movie, eventually followed them to California and rented an apartment in the Saint Mary's neighborhood of Long Beach, just to the north of the city's downtown area and waterfront and just a few blocks south of the Long Beach Polytechnic High School and the Pacific Coast Highway.

By 1960 Tip Top Drilling Company and Tatco Petroleum had become important enough clients for the oil service company Magnet Cove Barium Company (Magcobar) to offer my father a paid family vacation trip to a dude ranch in the northern Wyoming mountains somewhere between Cody and Buffalo—and not all that far as the crow flies from his first job as a petroleum geologist in Red Lodge, Montana. Given the California migration of his mother and all of his siblings (excepting one older sister who remained in Texas) to California, he both accepted the offer and decided to expand both the duration and destination of a vacation road trip so as to visit his side of the family in southern California. In the end, he planned an epic road trip journey that would include, after the stay at the dude ranch in Wyoming, visiting the Yellowstone and the Grand Teton National Parks, Salt Lake City, and Las Vegas, spending a few days in each destination before we arrived in Long Beach.

Not the prodigal son but rather the favorite son smiled on by fortune, one wildly successful in his chosen profession and, even when in Las Vegas, as it happened, wildly successful at the craps tables—this would be his role to perform during this extraordinary month in our family's history, this epic, month-long road trip that would prove to be the only occasion when my father would take an extended vacation from work in the summer months when the oil patch drilling operations were at their peak.

This first trip to the far West was also extraordinary for how certain moments and sights along the way exposed the somewhat contradictory grafting together of the cultural imaginaries associated with the residue of the rural American West's pastoral or ranching economy and the now-globalized petroleum industry, the region's new dominant economic force. There was, of course, the fact of the dude ranch itself, where I learned to ride a horse and shudder at the thought of eating rainbow trout, this one owned by a leading oil field service company and located near the oil and gas field operations in the Bighorn Basin between the Shoshone and Bighorn National Forests. There was the fact that my entire experience at this ranch was shaped by my having devoured, a few years earlier, the Spin and Marty eleven-minute episodes that were part of Disney's after-school television series *The Mickey Mouse Club Show*. There was Las Vegas, whose hotel casinos capitalized on the themes associated with the frontier West and desert oasis fantasies, where our stay at the Sands Hotel and Casino, eventually acquired in 1967 by Howard Hughes, included a supper club show headlined by the comedian Red Skelton, who at one point in his act paused to introduce Dale Robertson, star of the *Tales of Wells Fargo* television show. And in Anaheim, there was the Frontierland attraction at Disneyland that capitalized on the popularity of actor Fess Parker's Disney television show *Davy Crockett* during this era of the film and television western's peak popularity.

There is also this fact to consider: like most of the built environment in or north of downtown Long Beach, my paternal grandmother's apartment was situated above the northern edge of the thirteen-mile long and three-mile-wide Wilmington Oil Field, the third largest oil field in the contiguous United States at this time. As we migrated by car between visits to her apartment and the house of our father's oldest brother in the Los Altos neighborhood, as well as our day trips to various southern California tourist sites, we occasionally would notice the aboveground pumpjacks and the occasional tank battery positioned behind fenced enclosures in vacant lots or in parking lots and the open land bordering freeway entrances and exits. I do not recall our family visiting the La Brea Tar Pits, and I don't suppose our father would have wanted to in any event, for by then he had become less connected to the earth and its geology and more involved in the business side of running a drilling company, the buying of mineral leases, and the courting of potential investors in limited partnerships, whose proposed drilling programs would be conducted by his own drilling company.

An oil basin below us and around us; a roadside architecture that included pumpjacks removing the basin's oil and, as they did so, triggering the need for further drilling to inject water into the empty pockets below the ground in order to combat soil subsidence; the deteriorating, toxic air quality that accompanied a rampant motorized culture in which freeways were regarded as the logical extension of the driveways that fronted suburban and exurban homes—these things not only dominated everyday life but also literally as well as figuratively became a part of us, though I did not know this yet. Just as I did not yet appreciate how the promise of mobility we experienced that summer in this nation's emergent "autopia" was predicated on our emergent affluence.³

4. Richland County, near Olney, Illinois ("Little Egypt"), Summer 1964.

> Sure, he could be this crew's chain monkey for a week or two. Yeah, he could sleep four to a doghouse with all these white boys, the wind rocking the trailer. No, he didn't mind being Chief, though he knew that, had he been around back in the days of raiding and running down buffalo, he'd have been a grunt then as well.
>
> —Stephen Graham Jones, *The Only Good Indians* (2020)

I am standing knee-deep in soybeans and freely sweating in the summer heat and humidity alongside my younger brother and a man named Blackwell, our father's chief toolpusher, who supervised the several rigs operated by Tip Top Drilling Company. I am sixteen and a sophomore in high school. The youngest of our three sisters had been born this past March, just a few weeks before I passed my driver's license test. We are standing in this field because my brother and I have been assigned by our father to ride along with this toolpusher on his daily check-in visits to one or more of the rigs—and to do the roustabout work of general maintenance as needed. On this day and at this particular drilling location, the rig officially began drilling operations by lowering the rotary drill bit into the borehole. My brother Chris and I are tasked with carrying and unrolling large coils of black plastic PVC pipe, the individual joints of which we would struggle to straighten as they baked in the soybean field's summer heat. By using hose clamps, we would connect all the separate joints together to create a pipe that would connect the new well pad and its mud pits to a gasoline-powered, skid-mounted water pump situated on the edge of a creek about a quarter of a mile away. The water reaching the well site from this creek would be mixed with drilling mud and pumped into the rig's drill string in the borehole.

Since the age of thirteen I had been working part-time jobs, mostly at a local men's clothing store. Whatever little pay I earned was not necessary to support our family's budget. And as I progressed through my high school years, it became clear to both my parents that their first-born son was not all that interested in following in his father's footsteps and becoming a petroleum geologist. That would be my younger brother's destiny, which partially explains, I later supposed, why were out in this field, chaperoned by this toolpusher for Tip Top Drilling Company, wrestling with black PVC pipe in the summer's heat and humidity. My younger brother would in a few years get his degree in petroleum geology and do the real work of a roughneck on the drilling company's rigs—later losing one eye, but not his life, when hit by one of the tongs on a rig's drilling floor in Northeast Ohio—and then eventually become a working partner with our father. Our family was never really privy to our father's rationale for any of his financial decisions, especially his extravagant expenditures on new cars, horses, a motor home, college tuition, or wedding expenses. He basically saw himself as the family's sole breadwinner and left all the affective labor necessary to sustain the family for our mother. Such a division of labor was neither unique nor exceptional for the time. From the beginning, he was basically distant and unreachable when he was around the home, except when giving out orders to do chores and doling out discipline, sometimes with a belt. Whatever affections he was incapable of expressing or loath to show were effectively displaced into all the extravagant expenditures or gifts that would suddenly show up at the house. I simultaneously was in thrall to his mystery and somewhat fearful of him.

Such expenditures also represented the paradox inherent in his early upbringing and his eventual achievement of becoming, as the saying goes, "oil rich." Coming of age during the Great Depression years, during which he was raised by a single mother and his older brother, he knew what poverty felt and looked like. Out of necessity, he had learned about the value of thrift and had internalized the importance of a strong work ethic. But in his youth, he had been exposed to other truths: that no matter how hard and long one worked and no matter how disciplined one was in sticking to an improvised plan for the future, the world could neither be controlled nor fully mastered. And that people, including one's family as well as total strangers, would usually disappoint you. Such as the everyday life he knew full well, one in which a father readily would abandon his wife and five children. Such as this selfsame hardscrabble world in which, at the age of thirteen, he would spend an entire summer chopping cotton, contributing some small portion of his earnings to the family's keep and then saved what remained so as, he hoped, to buy his first suit of clothes. But before he ever had a chance to wear the suit that he did end up buying before returning to school after the summer break, he discovered one day that one of his younger brothers had stolen it from their shared wardrobe closet and sold it to a pawnbroker in downtown Sherman.

And then there is the harsh reality inherent in his chosen profession—where one's quest for oil just might lead to a dry hole instead of a gusher. This world of petroleum where becoming "oil rich" referred to how any seemingly magical financial success just might vanish overnight, might disappear as abruptly, say, as a father from his family or a suit of clothes from his closet. Thus any improvement in one's class status would always be haunted by a chronic fear of failure. So even as our family became upper-middle class—thanks to my father's native intelligence, singular ambition, perseverance, and good fortune—I came to think, years later, that my own and my brother's presence as roustabouts in that soybean field in Little Egypt's oil patch during that summer embodied, in displaced fashion, his anticipatory anxiety about whether or not his children, amid all their new privileges, would ever come to understand and value the virtues of discipline and work itself, regardless of the nature of the task at hand. For if such an understanding or recognition did not materialize in tangible fashion, then how could such children learn to honor, much less respect his rags-to-riches history, about which he rarely spoke?

5. Northeast Holmes County, near Winesburg, and Canton, Ohio—1973–1975.

> Anxiety about the Saudi tidal wave had been a constant in the oil patch for years; nobody knew when it would come but everyone agreed that once it *did* come, ruin would be complete: no more platinum AmEx cards, no more frequent-flier miles, no more fun trips to Las Vegas or Bossier City.
>
> —Larry McMurtry, *Duane's Depressed* (1999)

It is a bitterly cold and dark and I am roughnecking on a Tip Top Drilling Company cable tool rig on an Amish farm near Winesburg, Ohio, a little less than an hour's drive on U.S. Highway 62 from Stark County and its main city of Canton, where my father had relocated both his business and the family in 1969. The petroleum boom underway in Ohio had begun in the mid-1960s and was centered mostly on natural gas production. By early 1973, the Nixon administration had introduced new policies aimed to increase domestic production and reduce the nation's dependence on imported oil and natural gas. And as it turned out, that same year saw the Arab members of the Organization of Petroleum Exporting Countries (OPEC) impose an embargo on exports to the United States, as a result of U.S. support for Israel during the so-called Yom Kippur war launched by Egypt and Syria in the hope of regaining territory lost during the previous Arab-Israeli war in 1967.

Such global geopolitical circumstances increased the demand for drilling rigs in Ohio, and as it turned out older, more primitive cable tool rigs, such as the one I worked on that winter near Winesburg, Ohio, were restored to service. Cable tool rigs were useful for drilling to shallow depths, which was often the case in the Ohio oil patch, and unlike rotary drilling rigs, cable tool drilling rigs neither required a large crew to operate nor a large inventory of drill pipe. On a typical cable tool rig, a drilling contractor only needed two crews, each with a roughneck and a driller, to work the two twelve-hour tours each day. On this particular cable tool rig it was just me and a man from West Virginia named Rich, who farmed during the growing season and worked as a driller on cable tool rigs in Ohio and Pennsylvania during the winter months. And regardless of the weather, he was a profane man and a prolific storyteller. And while we were operating the rig on this Amish farmer's land, he would save his bawdiest stories until the farmer's two young sons would walk to the rig most every night, bearing a tin pie plate holding slices of their mother's fresh-baked fruit pies for us to enjoy. His voice barely audible over the ambient noise created by the nearby cable tool chisel pounding away at the earth's hidden sand and rock formations, these boys would sit on the doghouse's bench while we ate, dressed in their culture's traditional clothing and broad-brimmed hats, totally engrossed in Rich's mad tales of his mostly sorry sexual escapades.

By 1973 my father's business dealings had expanded to include investing his own funds as a limited partner in various oil and gas drilling programs in

Michigan, Alabama, and Utah. He would make occasional trips to these states each year to meet with directors or managing partners of the funds. During this same period, he would travel on occasion to Africa, having signed on as a consultant in petroleum geology with the government of Chad, which had contracted with Conoco to search for and develop its oil reserves both in the Doba Basin and the Lake Chad area. He typically would catch connecting flights to Chad in Zurich, and because of the ongoing civil war in this country, as well as the coup d'état orchestrated by a rogue military junta, he would tell stories about his being pulled aside by Central Intelligence Agency (CIA) operatives during his airport layovers. They were questioning him to ascertain whether or not his petroleum consultancy provided cover for his secretly serving as a courier charged by this country's corrupt political or military leaders with depositing oil profits in private Swiss bank accounts.

I am living this winter of 1973 in the finished basement of my parents' home in Canton, making the hour-long drive on a two-lane highway to and from the well site on this particular Amish farm in the rolling hills near Winesburg, working the evening tour in the darkness, and then struggling to stay awake as I drove back home over the often ice-covered or snow-packed roads. At home I sleep through most of the daylight hours, then awake and get dressed and make a thermos of coffee and pack some food and then make the drive to the well site, where the derrick's lights glowed in the darkness or the rising fog of early evening, seductively producing an illusion of warmth and comfort awaiting my arrival. And within this long winter's daily routine, sometimes I would perform as a sort of courier. For in the few daylight hours of freedom between the time spent traveling to work, doing the roughneck chores, and sleeping, I found myself—after five years or so removed from the everyday fabric of my family's life—dutifully and willingly relaying status reports and miscellaneous everyday information and updates between my parents, who essentially were living separate lives while residing in the same house. The prospect of divorce clearly was visible on the horizon here in Ohio, as it surely was even a decade before in southern Illinois in the 1960s, when my younger brother and I were coming of age, our presence in the house and our ordinary teenage behaviors conveniently serving as lightning rods for their intense, loud arguments, their conflicts about parenting practices, and their extravagant spending patterns.

During this brief period in my life in Ohio, my father's eighty-four-year-old mother Cora Lee died in Long Beach in 1974. This mother and grandmother who had been a devout member of the evangelical Church of the Nazarene throughout her life—and yet who would never sleep at night without a telephone in her bed in case of a medical emergency. This mother and grandmother who would tell me stories about her second son, my father, during the few visits I was able to make to see her in the years after my first trip to southern California in 1961. And she enjoyed repeating the story about the time her local Nazarene church's congregation was bussed from Long Beach to Santa Monica in order to be extras in the audience for the pivotal tabernacle scene in *Elmer Gantry* (1960), a film adaptation loosely based on a 1926 Sinclair Lewis novel that starred Burt Lancaster as a con man peddling religion on the rural tent revival circuit.

6. Salt Lake City, Utah, 1975 and Allenwood, Pennsylvania, 1976–77.

> "Why Sam, he's bound to have lots of money," Duane said. "Mrs. Farrow's fur coat is supposed to be worth five thousand dollars."
>
> "Probably is," Sam said. "That's five thousand he don't have in cash, though. He's got lots of trucks and equipment and oil leases, too, but it ain't cash and there's no way of tellin' how much of it's his and how much is the bank's."
>
> —Larry McMurtry, *The Last Picture Show* (1966)

On December 29, 1975, the Denver Regional Office of the U.S. Securities and Exchange Commission (SEC) filed a complaint in the Salt Lake City federal court seeking to enjoin Bingham Silver Lead Company, along with its general partner and manager George Badger, from future violations of various antifraud sections of the Securities Act of 1933 and the Securities Exchange Act of 1934. Also named in this SEC complaint were two other men who had invested in this limited partnership, one of whom was "L. Robert Tatum, of Canton, Ohio." Within a few months my father would exchange his business suit and tie for the khaki clothing issued to him at the onset of a two-year stint he would serve at the minimum security Allenwood Federal Prison Camp in north-central Pennsylvania, approximately a three-hour drive from Titusville, the birthplace of the petroleum industry in the United States. Notable inmates at Allenwood during his time there were convicted Watergate conspirators Gordon Liddy and Jeb Stuart Magruder. The only oil-based product that he would come into contact with during his time at Allenwood, excepting of course the ubiquitous presence of plastic items, was the Neatsfoot oil he would apply to soften the animal hides he would fashion into belts and purses in the prison camp's workshop.

His particular transgression resulted from a crucial problem that faced anyone who invested in oil and gas limited partnerships during and after the 1973 Organization of the Petroleum Exporting Countries (OPEC) oil embargo. Regardless of the Bush administration's stated desire to reduce the nation's dependence on imported oil and gas, it typically would take one to two years for a successful natural gas well in Ohio to be connected to the pipeline infrastructure and then for royalties to be paid out to investors. Given this temporal lag between well completion and any receipt of royalties, my father, as an independent owner-operator, continuously struggled to make payroll for his employees, much less pay the high overhead costs to keep all the drilling rigs running nonstop, twenty-four hours a day and seven days a week. The legal problem that emerged during his solicitation of various banks for business loans was this: in filing the loan applications it appears that, like a recent former resident of the White House, he both inflated the value of his assets and used the same collateral to underwrite different loans. Both of these actions constituted chargeable civil offenses and eventually triggered court cases, the outcomes of which were his conviction and then sentencing to the Allenwood prison camp, which had been built expressly to house individuals who committed various white-collar crimes. And when the banks eventually foreclosed on the tangible property of the Tip Top Drilling Company that had been listed as collateral on his loan applications, he was forced to file for Chapter 11 bankruptcy.

So it came to pass that such a pronounced rustling in the leaves began to drive away the dream bird that had hatched the eggs of the oil rich experience, first in Montana and then in southern Illinois, the dream bird that, in retrospect, had reached its apogee during the oil boom in northeastern Ohio, this period in my life which began with a stint as a roughneck on a cable tool rig in the winter of 1973 and culminated two years later when my life partner and future spouse Kathy and I moved to Salt Lake City. [4] There, in the fall of 1975, my father would visit us during one of his regular business trips to Utah to meet with a man named George Badger, the general partner and manager of a limited partnership named Bingham Silver Lead Company, which had been created for investors interested in oil and gas exploration in northeastern Utah's Uinta Basin.

7. Salt Lake City, Utah—October 1976–February 1981.

> These were her people. Speculators and opportunists, carnival barkers and realtors, imagineers, cowards and dreamers and girls. . . . Eyes peeled for the flash of ore, the flash of camera, the wet flesh of fruit. Gold, fame, citrus. Every erotic currency harvested green or yellow or the profound underground black of oil gone red-brown when slid between two fingers.
> —Claire Vaye Watkins, *Gold Fame Citrus* (2015)

It is late morning on an early October day in 1976, and I am twenty-seven years old and sitting in a wooden pew at the rear of a cold federal courtroom on the second floor of the old post office building in Salt Lake City. My father sits beside me, dressed in a white dress shirt and a business suit and wearing a tie. He is here in this place at this time because he has been subpoenaed by the U.S. attorney for the District of Utah to testify for the plaintiffs, not as a defendant, in the *SEC v. Bingham Silver Lead Company* case. As a result, he has been granted a short leave from the Allenwood Federal Prison Camp. It has been nearly a year since the SEC had filed its complaint against his now ex-business partner George Badger as a result of alleged antifraud violations.

His presence on the witness stand this morning represents but one building block of the prosecution's case against Badger for three different violations of federal securities acts involving his creation of fraudulent schemes both for the sale of common stock in the Bingham Silver Lead Company and for the creation of limited partnerships in this company and for his aiding or assisting in the filing of false tax returns, especially in regard to the tax shelter aspects applied to mineral royalties. In response to the prosecuting attorney's questions, my father's brief testimony laid out how he was initially approached by Badger with a prospectus for a limited partnership that would focus on oil and gas production in Utah, how that prospectus itself, as he later realized, made false claims about probable, expected returns both on his investment and any tax shelter benefits, and how he finally fell out with Badger after losing his investment and then began to suspect Badger was manipulating the company's accounts in his capacity as general partner. When he finished his testimony as witness for the prosecution, upon cross-examination Badger's defense attorney only him asked one question: whether or not it was true that he was currently serving time at the Allenwood Federal Prison Camp.

On other days as this case proceeded, we learned more about Badger's checkered legal history and his modus operandi for prosecuting various fraudulent schemes that, as it turned out, he would continue to launch over the next three decades with the assistance of members of his immediate family. We learned, for example, that the Utah State Bar had found him guilty of practicing common law fraud a few years prior to the Bingham Silver Lead Company case in the mid-1970s. Badger also was barred from practicing law for two years, a decision upheld in 1972 by the Utah Supreme Court. We learned that the specific count against him alleging his conspiracy to defraud his partners in the Bingham Silver Lead Company case centered primarily on his activity of filing false tax returns. As a result of his illegal activity in the early 1970s, it turned out that the Internal Revenue Service (IRS) had begun working with the SEC in its investigation of Badger's business dealings.

We also learned this sensational fact: after the SEC complaint was filed in federal court in late 1975 against him and the Bingham Silver Lead Company, Badger—this married man and Mormon bishop—attempted to learn more about the status and the progress of the IRS investigations into his various business dealings. He identified a well-placed administrative assistant in the Ogden, Utah, office of the IRS and then initiated a clandestine relationship with her, taking her out on several dinner dates in the hope of obtaining insider information about the progress of case against Bingham Silver Lead Company. However, this person quickly became suspicious about the true nature of Badger's motivation for approaching her. So she informed her IRS colleagues, who fitted her with a wire when she went on such dates with Badger. In the end, the taped evidence the IRS collected was introduced in the court case that soon followed, and on October 26, 1976, Badger was found guilty of attempting to bribe this IRS agent and sentenced to federal prison. The federal judge's resolution of this case also addressed the original SEC complaint against him and the Bingham Silver Lead Company, as he issued a permanent civil injunction against Badger, prohibiting him from committing any future violations of the various antifraud, securities registration, and broker-dealer provisions of federal securities laws he had flouted.

While Badger was serving time in a federal prison for his attempted bribery of an IRS agent, a federal grand jury in Salt Lake City in March 1981 also returned a twenty-four-count indictment against him and another partner, one Assen Ivanoff, a resident of Switzerland, in connection with matters involving basically the same underlying fraudulent actions as those that had been uncovered by IRS investigators working the Bingham Silver Lead Company case five years earlier. What makes this 1981 grand jury indictment especially relevant is not just the fact that Badger once again was involved in a fraudulent scheme (and being investigated even while already serving a prison sentence). It is also that this indictment specifically identified him and his partner Ivanoff as having prepared federal tax returns for 1974 and 1975 "which falsely reflected deductible business expenses and losses."[5] So Badger was perpetrating the same fraud with still another partner at the same time he and my father were actively being investigated by both the SEC and the IRS for the Bingham Silver Lead Company's violations of antifraud securities acts and preparation of false tax returns.[6] Badger pleaded guilty to the various counts in the indictment on September 18, 1981, and a week later the U.S. District Judge for of Utah sentenced him to an additional five years in prison and fined him $10,000, the maximum amount allowed under the then-current conspiracy statute.

Just how one thing leads into another—how a certain belief or expectation is validated or, more likely, destroyed—sometimes the ordinary drift of things turns out to be exactly how you had begun to suspect they would, in the end, turn out.[7] George Badger certainly orchestrated a shakedown racket that played on my father's gullibility and his often-misplaced trust. But Badger himself in the end also got played: a *badger game* is prison slang for a shakedown racket in which a sucker is framed into being caught with a woman in a compromising position. In any case, Badger's dealings offer a cautionary tale exemplifying, as Alexandra Fuller has written about the boom and bust petroleum economy, how "you can't police the panic of a boom from rotting the soul out of a place because somewhere in the throes of an energy boom isn't so different from a person in the throes of an addiction: there's the denial that things are out of control; there's the sleeplessness and moral carelessness, and the fact that you know you're doing something that isn't good for you, but you just can't stop."[8] This stern judgment could be describing Badger's entire career, even if his obituary published in the local Salt Lake City newspapers after he died in 2021 at the age of ninety, made no mention of his moral carelessness and his commission of financial crimes that spawned felony charges and serial convictions. Indeed, he continued to face federal charges and served at least one additional stint in federal prison in the early 2000s, the news of which gratified my father in his retirement years in Sarasota, Florida. This man who, during the course of his career as a petroleum geologist, had found his trust primarily rewarded by the earth, this earth that "lies there still, and obeys certain rules." As Rick Bass has written about his own career as a petroleum geologist, it is this fundamental fact that perhaps explains "why geologists become so fervent about a particular prospect."[9]

9. Sarasota, Florida—1983–1993.

> When the sky was dark grey, the spruce trees in the forest along the road dark green and the asphalt on the road black, and all the other colors were dulled by the restrained light and the humidity, petrol sometimes lay on the road surface shimmering in the most fantastic and unusual colors. Petrol was so unlike anything else we knew that it could have come from another world. A magnificent world full of adventure, one had to imagine, brightly colored and bountiful. Bountiful because the petrol's play of colors, which appeared and disappeared seemingly at random, was connected to the emptiest and ugliest of places.
>
> —Karl Ove Knausgard, "Petrol," from *Autumn* (2017)

A year and a half later, in 1983, my father divorced his second wife and married a woman he had met in Sarasota, Florida. They proceeded to buy a one-story house with a screened-in swimming pool that was located in a housing development bordering the fairways of a new golf course east of downtown

Sarasota called Palm Aire. Not the swimming pool but rather the two lime and lemon trees growing in the yard, the garage workbench where he would continue to make leather items as gifts, and the patio table near the pool, where in the evening darkness he would often sit playing solitaire under the light cast by a single ceiling fixture—these things he would come to value in the years ahead. This house became his permanent residence, though he would continue until his full retirement to make business trips to Ohio and consult with my brother, who basically had been running Tatco Petroleum since our father's time in the Allenwood Federal Prison Camp.

A decade later, my father's house in Sarasota nearly burned to the ground from a fire that had started in his garage where he stored his wife's car and tools and a lawn mower and the gasoline to power it. The payout from his homeowner's insurance enabled him to restore the garage space and turn what had been an adjoining closet inside the house into a small office space. But over the next few years after his full retirement, he was forced to take out a total of three mortgages on this house and to take on part-time work at the Sarasota airport's Hertz rental car agency. Instead of playing golf at Palm Aire, he would play at a public golf course in nearby Bradenton, his and his wife's annual greens fees paid for by my younger sister and her husband.

In the historical usage of the word *oil* there exists a figurative expression about the act of pouring oil upon the water in order to appease some conflict or disturbance. This usage is based on a practice performed by ancient sailors, who would pour oil—olive or fish or whale or, later, even crude oil—on a sea's troubled waters to protect their ship and enable it to complete its voyage. Such a figurative expression is clearly inadequate to capture the narrative trajectory of my parents' marriage and divorce, much less the financial woes and legal troubles that accompanied my father during the boom-and-bust economic cycles of the petroleum industry over his entire career. Not the metaphorical wave dampening created by pouring oil on water, but the volatile fire created by a marriage of gasoline and matches—it seems to me that this petroleum metaphor more accurately represents this late period in his own and his family's life, all the singular events that transpired in the various houses and courthouses and drilling rig doghouses, and even, as it turned out at one point, in a federal prison camp dormitory.

10. Sarasota, Florida—September 2007.

> Tell the children to come inside,
> That your search goes on for something you lost—a name,
> A family album that fell from its own small matter
> Into another, a piece of the dark that might have been yours,
> You don't really know. Say that each of you tries
> To keep busy, learning how to lean down close and hear
> The careless breathing of earth and feel its available
> Languor come over you, wave after wave, sending
> Small tremors of love through your brief,
> Undeniable selves, into your days, and beyond.
>
> —Mark Strand, "The Continuous Life" (1991)

We are at a funeral home in Sarasota, standing before a heavy-duty cardboard coffin that rests on a cloth-covered shelf in an otherwise windowless, bare room dimly lit by an overhead yellow light fixture. My younger brother and three younger sisters and I, all together and yet alone now in our separate approaches to and our retreat from this cardboard box that holds our father's body prior to its cremation later that day. We will turn toward each other and exchange pained expressions of grief, as if we are practiced in this ritual of mourning, as if we are well-versed in assuming the appropriate position when confronted with such bodily evidence of loss, this slow dance between an immersion in and respectful distance from this site and sight of death. But we are not. Our somber, halting choreography is proof positive that no one experiences grief in the same way and not necessarily even at the same time and place. Tomorrow, the urn holding his ashes will be displayed at the funeral service in the Lutheran church where he had been serving as an usher for Sunday morning services. That he joined this local church and looked forward to performing such duties added but one more dimension to the mystery of this man. This man whom I recalled as rarely attending church services before his retirement years in Sarasota. This man who had always seemed allergic to pensive reflections about the status of his or anyone else's soul.

I am standing before his cardboard coffin, looking at his naked body resting on its right side, his arms crossed over his chest and knees drawn slightly upward toward his chest, his corpse pose now staged as an uncanny return to a fetal position, this body now bare of any rings or wristwatch or military dog tag. And I begin to sway slightly, momentarily confused about whether or not I am observing him as he sleeps As if I am caught between looking at a still life pose in this moment, rather than a permanently stilled life. And I am standing before this particular cardboard box in this dimly lit room and thinking about another cardboard box, this other box connected with an origin story rather than a death, the story about my father, age twenty-three, pausing his petroleum geology studies after my mother had become pregnant and, after moving back to Sherman, Texas, had begun working for the Wonder Bread company. That story about him driving to the St. Vincent's Hospital in one of this bread company's step vans to pick up my mother and me a couple of days after I was born, my mother standing next to him on the passenger side floor and leaning against the van's front bulkhead wall, holding a cardboard bread box in which my blanketed newborn form rested, cushioned by a few loaves of white sandwich bread in their plastic bags.

And I am standing before this cardboard box and thinking about the weekly phone call from my father, the one I had missed while running errands, as it turned out, on the day before he died. And I am also thinking about the phone call I did receive on the day of my father's death, this call from my younger brother living in northern Michigan, who relayed to me both this news of our father's death and how there was a plan in the works for immediate family to convene in Florida for his funeral. And I am standing before his cardboard coffin thinking about the difference in these two phone calls, the one I missed from my father (though thankfully he did talk briefly with my wife Kathy), this missed final call reminding me how time and spatial distance and the fact of my having become an adoptive father of two children—how such realities and transformative events had served to heal so many of the unspoken wounds that had accumulated during our adult lives.

And I am thinking also about the brief phone call from my brother, the first time I had heard his voice in several years, thinking about how time and spatial distance does not necessarily heal certain wounds, about how our own dysfunctional sibling relationship had come uncannily to repeat, a generation later, that very silence that defined our father's relationship with two of his three brothers, men with whom he did not communicate throughout most of his adult life, except perhaps when he and the rest of his siblings gathered in Long Beach on the occasion of their mother's death and funeral in 1974.

And I am standing in a hushed silence before this cardboard coffin and thinking about the prior deaths of my maternal great-grandparents and grandparents and of aunts and uncles, about the memorial services held for them at the funeral home and then at the family plot in the West Hill Cemetery in Sherman, Texas. And I am standing before this cardboard coffin in a Sarasota, Florida, funeral home thinking about the difference between those dead and departed kinfolk who were born and who later died and were buried in that certain place and not some other, and my father, lying here in this cardboard coffin, definitely born and raised in a certain place, yet whose migratory life and manner of death in this remote place underscored how he seemed never truly bound to a certain place, unless its particular geology indicated the possible presence of oil and natural gas reserves hidden beneath all its surface features, its weather, and its seasons. And I am thinking now about how this trip to Sarasota for his funeral will undoubtedly mark my final visit to this certain country where his ashes will reside in the columbarium at a certain Lutheran church.

And I am standing before this cardboard coffin and thinking now about how, in the days to come, there will be no location for my grief, no way really to map or account for its comings and goings, its frequent departures and surprise returns that, in the days to come, will occupy my continuous life until its fated end. Nothing I have prepared so far for the eulogy I will deliver tomorrow really addresses such a train of thoughts.

Where does grief go? How does grief travel? At one point in the first of his *Duino Elegies*, Rilke asks a version of these very questions. As he writes, "In the end, those who were carried off early no longer need us." But, he adds, for those who remain behind, those "who do need such great mysteries, we for whom grief is so often the source of our spirit's growth—: could we exist without *them*?"[10] Over the years and in the face of certain losses, personal and collective, my thoughts have fastened onto this short passage, especially its turn from the declarative to the interrogative mode, where its final existential question represents an invitation for us as individuals to think of ourselves as members of a collective "we." At the same time, Rilke's question regarding whether or not we, the living, could really exist without the dead is a rhetorical question whose implicit answer, we are called to recognize, is "no." That we the living cannot really exist without them, the community of the dead who, the lyric speaker asserts at the outset of this passage, do not really need us, the living, anymore. The truth here, of course, is that we the living literally could not exist, would never have been born, without the prior presence of our living or now departed forebears. But Rilke ups the ante by further claiming that we the living not just exist but cannot really exist without our dead ancestors, since it is precisely their perishing—and our subsequent grief work—that presumably will foster our spiritual growth.

I further honor how this question solicits us, even in the face of its naming of the dead as a *them*, to resist drawing any absolute distinctions between the metaphysical realms of the living and the dead. Instead of exiling the dead further and further away from both the mental and physical spaces of the living, hence out of sight and out of mind, Rilke's question enjoins us to consider how really existing means recognizing that a contract of mutual indebtedness exists between the living and the dead. So as I have pondered these lines, I began to reject this poet's initial claim that "the dead carried off early don't need us." Is it not rather the case that the community of the dead in point of fact do need us, we the living, to keep them alive symbolically—via our imagination and memories, our spoken or written words, and our ritual ceremonies—to lay up and preserve, like the final accounting in a ledger book, the dead's absent presence and continuing influence in our everyday lives? And, in turn, do not we the living depend on this great family of the dead into which, at some future moment, all of us will be admitted? For even as we the living presumably can provide a future for the dead, sustain their presence as the undead (literally dead but symbolically alive), it is this *them*, this community of the dead, who provide us with a past, the reconstruction of which through our imaginations and storied remembrances—and our genealogical searches—just might enable us to place ourselves, amid the accumulating fragments that define everyday life, in a temporal continuum from the remembered past, the knowledge of which potentially will shape our living present, into the living present that in turn will shape our imaginative projections of potential futures.

Within a few months after my father's funeral, and before my mother's Parkinson's disease really began to exact its heavy toll on her body and mind, she began giving away various heirlooms and everyday things she had been collecting over the years, large and small items sent to us through the mail or given to us in person during our occasional visits to see her when she was still living in her own house. Things like jewelry and family photographs and school memorabilia and antique furniture. Things like her father's windup wooden clock and her mother's huge cast iron skillet, used to make the cornbread for Thanksgiving dinners. And on one occasion before her death, as I was leaving her house to return to my home in Utah, she pressed into my hands Lee Robert Tatum's U.S. Navy dog tag. It was an old-school dog tag: a thin, silver-plated and oval shaped disk attached to a silver-plated necklace. All these years later, one could still barely make out the stamping on it of his full name and personal identification number, as well as the name and date of his enlistment in this branch of the U.S. military. The final piece of vital information stamped at the bottom of this dog tag, this piece of metal that I have worn every day of my life since my mother gifted it to me, was his blood type: O-.

Oil rich and O-blood. Like the circular or oval-shaped letter O and the number o, visual signs whose shape and symbolic meanings simultaneously gesture toward both the void of nothingness or absence and the promissory note of growth embodied by a seed, egg, or womb, this final core sample in this personal ledger now hearkens back to its origin, just as its origin, from the very beginning, has called out to this ending.

[**C**ryptography; **E**xposure; **F**reeways; **G**raves; **S**cene of the crime; **Y**ellow ribbons; **V**agabondage]

FIG. 8. Lee Robert Tatum (*lower right*) in San Antonio, Texas, 1945. Author's collection.

Psychometropolis

EXTRACTS

Officer Peone looked at John and wondered which mental illness he had. The Seattle streets were filled with the mostly crazy, half-crazy, nearly crazy, and soon-to-be-crazy Indian, white, Chicano, Asian, men, women, children. . . . In the end, the police had to do most of the work. Police did crisis counseling, transporting them howling to detox, the dangerous to jail, racing the sick to the hospitals, to a safer place. At the academy, Officer Peone figured he would be fighting bad guys. He did not imagine he would spend most of his time taking care of the refuse of the world.

—Sherman Alexie, *Indian Killer* (1996)

Eight legs, one pair of liver-colored galoshes, and his sister's legs parted, those thick stump thighs pressed against her secretarial skirt, breaking and entering, trampling on his brown beret, pleading for him to play fetch peacefully with the two Psychiatric Emergency Team workers. His arms shielded his *cerebral hemispheres* and the PET workers clasped his pencil-thin wrists and forced him up, stole *his frontal lobe; principal speech area, precentral gyrus or primary motor area*, took him howling like a scribble off the page of white paper, *I can't stand my own parietal lobe, temporal lobe, occipital lobe,* all the way back to the dim institution, where the walls were as gray as brain matter.

—Helena María Viramontes, *Their Dogs Came with Them* (2009)

Later you remember your mom saying to take drugs was like sneaking into the kingdom of heaven under the gates. It seemed to you more like the kingdom of hell, but maybe the kingdom is bigger and more terrifying than we could ever know. Maybe we've all been speaking the broken tongue of angels and demons too long to know that that's what we are, who we are, what we're speaking. Maybe we don't ever die but change, always in the State without hardly ever even knowing that we're in it.

—Tommy Orange, *There There* (2018)

1. "*A sleepwalker, moving through the world.*" Clay, the first-person narrator-protagonist in Brett Easton Ellis's novel *Less Than Zero* (1985), likes to watch. We see him looking out the windshields and the passenger side windows of various cars. Looking out the windows of the assorted houses and apartments and hotel rooms and business offices he visits during his excursions around the Los Angeles valley. Whenever driving or riding in a car on Hollywood Boulevard, he looks at a travel company's billboard, its slogan "Disappear Here" mirroring his own cognitive and affective unsettlement. We watch as he looks across the tables and out the windows of various bars, clubs, restaurants, and retail stores. At one beach club, he sits on a bench and "stares out at the expanse of sand that meets the water, where the land ends. Disappear here," he thinks to himself.[1] He cannot resist looking at his reflected image when he faces a mirror or walks by the reflective glass of storefront windows. On several occasions he lies on his bed and looks at a poster of Elvis Costello hanging on one of his bedroom's walls. So we watch as Clay watches an image of this musician who, in turn, is posed looking out from behind his sunglasses and looking at persons or things beyond the frame. One might want to believe that this grammar bound up with a (triple) act of looking confirms a blessed act of mutuality, as one's gaze is reciprocated. But what Clay projects onto this dynamic of looking is how Elvis Costello doesn't return the gaze. Instead, he interprets his surrogate figure inside the frame as "looking out the window, beyond, into the night," his facial expression "almost alarmed at what it might be seeing, the word 'Trust' above the worried face."[2] Exemplified by the aporia between the implied imperative of the word *Trust* here and a subjectivity worried about its inability to trust what the future out there beyond the window will bring, the motif of the gaze in *Less Than Zero* underscores not an attunement with but rather an abiding gap between what one sees and

what one knows and between what one sees and what others see, let alone what they know. Hence his characteristic pose of watching and waiting, his feeling of being sentenced to endure, as best he can, "the impossible experience of waiting for something without knowing exactly what it might be."³

Alone in his bedroom at night, he watches movies and music videos, usually muting the sound and listening to his recorded music or to radio talk shows. When tiring of such programs he will tune in to late-night evangelical religious talk shows and listen to their apocalyptic prophecies about a godless nation's dystopian future. And then on one particular rainy night in Los Angeles during his winter break from the college he attends back east, Clay receives three phone calls on the personal number of his bedroom phone. The anonymous caller refrains from speaking after Clay answers each call and then waits in the ensuing silence, sometimes for up to three minutes, before emitting an audible sigh and hanging up. After receiving the last of these three "weird silent calls" over the course of this singular rainy night, Clay breaks the silence by throwing a glass against a wall in his bedroom. Neither any family member nor any servant in the house bothered "to see what the sound was."

> Then I lie on the bed, awake, take twenty milligrams of Valium to come off the coke, but it doesn't get me to sleep. I turn MTV off and the radio on, but KNAC won't come in so I turn the radio off and stare out across the Valley and look at the canvas of neon and fluorescent lights lying beneath the purple night sky and I stand there, nude, by the window, watching the clouds pass and then I lie on my bed and try to remember how many days I've been home and then I get up and pace the room and light another cigarette and then the phone will ring. This is how the nights are when it rains.⁴

The temporality of this passage's core focus on the strung-out Clay's failure to fall asleep after snorting cocaine is itself dilated, strung out as its second sentence chains together a series of independent clauses by means of the repetition of the mantra "and" or "and then" to enumerate Clay's mundane actions on this rainy night: lying in bed; getting out of bed and standing by the window; getting back in bed; and then getting up from bed and pacing the room. This long compound sentence is framed on either side by Clay's mention of his bedroom's soundscape: the opening detail referencing Clay's watching and listening to music videos is complemented by the sound of a telephone ring closing this passage. We learn that what happens within the frame provided by such aural imagery is that, in point of fact, "nothing much happens" on nights such as this, as well as on those infrequent days when it rains in Los Angeles. Nothing, that is, but his restless circuit of his bedroom's claustrophobic space; his compulsive namechecking of various icons and brand names of consumer culture and products, including the call letters of local radio and television stations. Simultaneously constituting "nothing much" and yet all that seems important in his everyday life, Clay's cognition toggles between a sharpening and then sagging of attention in tandem with his drug-induced rapid mood swings between euphoria and a debilitating stupefaction.

But all this restless movement and these compulsive behaviors on display here finally reach a temporary pause when Clay's narration swerves to offer a summary judgment in a single simple sentence: This is how the nights are when it rains. Keyed here by both the nonspecific, singular demonstrative pronoun *this*, which rhetorically provides a spatial (here) and temporal (now) deixis, Clay's judgment attends specifically to this act of enunciation in this present moment in this particular local place. At the same time, the plurality of *nights* here asks us to accept that this phenomenological experience on this night is not in itself exceptional, but rather in accord with what happens on all rainy nights in Los Angeles. The iterative mode here—this saying once of what has happened plural times—prompts us to consider what happens during the other rainy days or nights that appear in the novel. Such as one rainy interlude Clay recalls, when a breakdown in communication was caused not by "weird, silent phone calls" but rather by traffic signals on Sunset Boulevard: these "short-circuited, so a yellow light will be flashing at an intersection and then a green one will blink on for a couple of seconds, followed by the yellow and then the red and green lights will start to shine at the same time."[5] These dysfunctional traffic lights on Sunset Boulevard parallel both the semiotic breakdown occurring inside Clay's bedroom (weird, silent phone calls; dysfunctional radio signals) and the contradictory signals transmitted to his body and increasingly agitated neurology due to his excessive alcohol and drug use. Regardless of his characteristic blank affect and deadpan delivery, then, such a line as "this is how the nights are when it rains" discloses how he suffers not just from boredom but from an increasing sense of dread, this affective status symptomized throughout the novel by his sleep deprivation and his episodes of sudden onset vertigo and his generalized anxiety disorder.

2. *"Mostly crazy, half-crazy, nearly crazy, and soon-to-be-crazy."* Less than Zero is a tightly networked intratextual production as a result of its presiding structural logic: the uncanny repetition of thematic, rhetorical, and physical topologies to which Clay's deadpan gaze of surveillance attends. As is the case with Freud's theorizing of the uncanny as a structure of feeling, a theme, and a trope, Clay's depression and anxiety will be externalized by references to architectural forms, especially that of the domestic home. In *Less than Zero*, the differently scaled threshold spaces composed by the surfaces of his house's glass skin volumes, by his own membrane of skin and by his drug- and alcohol-fueled sensorium, effectively dissolve the boundaries between inside/outside, the real/the simulated, and waking/dreaming. As a result, Clay is haunted by a fundamental spatial and temporal insecurity, and his everyday life takes on an oneiric quality, as if it has become dreamlike. On the very day he arrives home from college during the holiday break between semesters, for example, he looks through his bedroom window's venetian blinds and feels agitated by the sight of palm trees "shaking wildly, actually bending in the hot wind," the force of which makes the windows in his family's house rattle.[6] Seeking distraction, he shifts his gaze back inside his bedroom to watch television. But he can't get no relief, for the images from the MTV music videos streaming across the screen make him nauseous. In similar fashion, on another turbulent night the continuous rattling of the house's windows caused by gusting high winds awakens him. He becomes increasingly alarmed by what he reads in newspapers about "houses falling, slipping down in the middle of the night" during the Los Angeles monsoon season. Like a vampire wired on cocaine, he sometimes decides to stay up all night when it rains, so as "to make sure nothing happens to our house."[7]

And even on those rare occasions when he is able to sleep through the rainy nights, his increasingly morbid anxiety leads him to recollect a haunting childhood dream in which he initially feels calm and at peace. But then gray and white and purple clouds gather overhead, and a hard rain begins to fall. As the thunderstorm intensifies, he makes a run for shelter, and in his agitated state he trips and falls down on the soggy earth, and he begins to sink downward, mud filling his mouth and nose and eyes until, at last, he is "completely underground," as if this dreamwork translates his chronic morbid anxiety into an uncanny fear of premature death and burial.

3. "*It should be clear by now that the truth about the place is elusive and must be tracked with caution.*" Whether mesmerized by the sights of an old, deserted carnival or the old family house in Palm Springs or a dying coyote on Mulholland Drive or scenes from a supposed snuff film, Clay's journeys proceed inexorably to a deflating end, his narration increasingly taking on the generic features and tonality of a ghost story. He recycles rumors of werewolves and of cannibalistic acts and of a ghost boy who wanders a canyon near Rancho Mirage. We witness him as he ponders another rumor, published in a local magazine, about people driving on Sierra Bonita Street who would routinely see "apparitions of the Wild West," such as Indians on horseback, one throwing a tomahawk through an "open window" and another invading an elderly couple's suburban living room.[8] Along with these restless spectral figures, whose haunting of the present marks the return of a repressed genocidal past, Clay spies coyotes traversing the urban streets and preying upon domestic pets let loose in residential backyards, as well as the rattlesnakes discovered inside the garages of homes in both Los Angeles and Palm Springs. Whether he is encountering death, loss, and disappearance through his childhood dream of being buried alive or by his repeatedly sighting a "Disappear Here" caption on a Hollywood Avenue billboard, these and other examples of spectral apparitions in *Less Than Zero* inhabit the interiority of residential homes and commercial spaces and—as we have seen in the quoted passage at the center of this essay—of his consciousness. Such uncanny home invasions threaten to liquify both the mental composure of humans like Clay and the solid foundations of various commercial and residential architectural structures and natural world landforms through which he travels through as if he were sleepwalking.

"The ghost story is indeed virtually the architectural genre par excellence," Fredric Jameson proposes, "wedded as it is to rooms and buildings ineradicably stained with the memory of gruesome events, material structures in which the past literally weighs like a nightmare on the brain of the living."[9] Nevertheless, he adds, during our postmodern era, sustained by finance capitalism and flexible accumulation, the combined impact of gentrification, new urban renewal projects (e.g., infilling vacant real estate near new light rail lines with new condos and apartments), and the rise of exurban gated residential communities, corporate campuses, and research parks have sanitized "the ancient corridors and bedrooms to which alone a ghost might cling." Thus, he urges us to consider how "a new kind of 'hauntology'" materializes in both urban architectures and contemporary economies of cultural expression. It is a hauntology now characterized by "the barely perceptible agitations in the air of a past abolished socially and collectively, yet still attempting to be reborn." It is a hauntology in *Less than Zero*, where "perceptible agitations in the air" conjure up "apparitions of the Wild West." These repressed ghosts of history saturate the living present, underscoring Clay's sense that time is out of joint: here are reports of haunted past Others haunting the living present, their performative acts with tomahawks threatening domestic interior spaces. And in the emergent postmodernist version of hauntology, Jameson further notes how instead of "ancient corridors" and Gothic bedrooms and basements, in contemporary ghost stories such architectural features as extreme isometric spaces and exterior and interior glass skin volumes predominate.

Extreme isometric spaces: such as the cellular iterations and replications in *Less than Zero* of bedrooms and living rooms and office reception areas and booths in clubs or restaurants. Spaces whose functions and modular frames or window partitions are free to transform into other functional modules, even as the spatial isometry itself does not change but rather expands or contracts in algorithmic proportions.

Exterior and interior glass skin volumes: Such space is evident both in the examples of Clay's (or the character Rip's) bedroom and especially in the office space in a high-rise building that Clay and his friend Julian enter: "a totally spare, totally white room, complete with floor-to-ceiling windows and mirrors on the ceiling."[10] While in this office's white room, Clay notices a feeling of vertigo washing over him—dizziness that soon gets accompanied by an unsettling paranoid feeling. For he realizes here—thanks to this white room's exterior and interior glass curtain walls—that he can see his father's penthouse apartment in a nearby high-rise building, an uncanny sighting which leads him to wonder whether, in turn, his father is gazing back from his window at his son in this fraught moment.

As Clay repeatedly gazes either out windows or at glass reflecting surfaces, the emergent paranoiac space produced in *Less than Zero* troubles modernity's "myth of transparency." Clay's aleatory perceptions, his stated irritations and affectations, his obsessive, rapid scanning of his everyday world through the clear glass windows of cars and bedrooms and office spaces, much less his repetitive gazes at mirrors in closets and bathrooms and at video screens—all these features, taken together, disclose not only what we might want to call the perceptual breaks and gaps, the mindless compulsions of an obsessional neurosis. They also expose the "local 'intensities,' accidents in the continuum of postcontemporary life."[11] It is a gaze at an increasingly illegible urban metropolis, which it cannot master, and that, as Julian Murphet has observed about James Ellroy's Los Angeles neo-noir novels, additionally "charts the dislocation of white individuality in a saturated consumer space."[12] It is a haunted gaze that markedly contrasts, on the one hand, with Phillip Marlowe's desire—as he looks out a window at the distant Los Angeles skyline in Raymond Chandler's detective novel *The Long Goodbye* (1953)—for some deeper truth to be found in the "angry city." And, on the other hand, it is a paranoid gaze whose focus uncannily anticipates the Seattle psychometropolis depicted in Sherman Alexie's *Indian Killer* (1996).

[Boredom; Exposure; Freeways; Motel noir; Noir motel; Television; Windows; Zombieland]

Queues for the gallows, sing the praises of the hallowed

EXTRACTS

> Three times a day the clanging of bells. Endless lines. The smell of liver drifting out across the black barrack roofs. The smell of catfish. From time to time the smell of horse meat. On meatless days, the smell of beans. Inside the mess hall, the clatter of forks and spoons and knives. No chopsticks. An endless sea of bobbing black heads. Hundreds of mouths chewing. Slurping. Sucking. Swallowing.
>
> —Julie Otsuka, *When the Emperor Was Divine* (2002)

> The store was full. The lines were long and slow. A Mexican family was walking up the aisles speaking Spanish. The lady with the dull voice began announcing specials over the intercom again. The girl walked down a few aisles before she set the basket down in front of the bathroom. Hiding herself in a stall she opened the bottle and took a drink.
>
> —Willy Vlautin, *Northline* (2008)

> Mouths open to the sky, they sleep. Boys, girls: lips chapped, cheeks cracked, for the wind whips day and night. They occupy the entire space there, stiff but warm, lined up like new corpses along the metal roof of the train gondola. From behind the rim of his blue cap, the man in charge counts them—six children; seven minus one. The train advances slowly along tracks parallel to an iron wall. Beyond, on both sides of the wall, the desert stretches out, identical. Above, the swart night is still.
>
> —Valeria Luiselli, *Lost Children Archive* (2019)

1. "*We cannot claim a triumph.*" Here is a representative image from *Dreamland: The Way Out of Juárez*, the 2010 collaboration between writer Charles Bowden

and artist Alice Leora Briggs. On the facing page of text, Bowden's prose supplies the context for this image's provocative scenography: "Lines of people" had been forming at the Juárez morgue in the wake of the news that twelve corpses had been unearthed from the back patio of what had turned out to be an ordinary condominium duplex located in one of the city's middle-class neighborhoods. Whether such people queued up for one day or up to six days, their hope was that one of these newly discovered victims of *sicario* violence would be identified by authorities as one of their family members and resolve the abiding mystery of their disappearance.[1] Moreover, in the aftermath of the authorities' discovery and investigation of these twelve murder victims, another discovery emerged: some Juárez city and Mexican state police officers were found guilty of aiding and abetting drug cartel operations. Nevertheless, as one of Bowden's female informants comments, "'We cannot claim a triumph. The abducted and disappeared never show up alive.'"[2] For this woman "whose brother-in-law, a Mexican state policeman, vanished about ten years ago, and . . . who eventually became a powerhouse in the matter of missing people in Juárez," the fate of the 914 abducted and disappeared persons in Juárez and its environs remains unknown—this calculation neither accounting for those undocumented migrants who disappeared while crossing the border nor for these twelve cartel victims whose bodies, along with the death house itself, form the ground zero of the visual images and verbal narratives comprising the text of *Dreamland*.

This full-page image, appearing approximately two-thirds of the way through *Dreamland*, displays the signature features of Briggs's aesthetic: the sgraffito technique; the grafting of an older art history image into a contemporary Juárez news story connected with drug cartel violence and the femicide epidemic; and a compositionality in which the picture plane is flattened or foreshortened to intensify the affective force of the entwined evidence of both the sacred and the profane. All told, what emerges here is no soft lullaby lulling us into dreamland, but rather an image whose haptic visuality sentences us, for the duration of the viewing experience, to exist—as is the case with the mourners who line up before the doors of the Juárez morgue—in that precarious, spatiotemporal moment between departure and arrival and between certainty and doubt. Take the Mary figure in the right foreground: her upraised right arm and her anguished face, with its imploring gaze off into

FIG. 9. Alice Leora Briggs, *Pietà*, 2007. Sgraffito drawing on clay panel, 24 in. x 36 in. Courtesy of the artist and Evoke Contemporary, Santa Fe NM. Collection of Tom Ford. © All rights reserved.

the distance, draw our own gaze into this image's visual field. On the one hand, then, Mary constitutes our surrogate agent of the gaze and, simultaneously, exists as an object of the viewer's gaze as well as that gaze of the media crowd we see clustered behind the massive foreground presence of the two figures composing this Pietà. On the other hand, this maternal figure's performative physical gesture and gaze display both empathic unsettlement and, I suggest, the nascent corporeal pose and face of an inquisitor. For rather than resolving enigmas and achieving closure, this image's temporality is positioned in the immediate aftermath of a monumental traumatic event and before its prophesied conclusion will become clarified, much less confirmed. Thus, in this transitional moment between a past life and the potential of a resurrected new life, questions regarding both the sight and site of death reign. What exactly is happening here and now? What are the paradoxes associated with the sight of death? How is it we see, and how is seeing itself a form of blindness? When, as in at what point, might our performance of looking— our desire to know more about death's advent—itself uncannily constitute a predatory act?

2. "*Drawn like a black veil across the earth.*" A dramatic contrast in lines and monochromatic shadings further underscores Briggs's spatial juxtaposition of the Pietà duo and this assemblage of media. There are the sinuous folds of Mary's clothing and the stark whiteness of the prone Jesus's exposed flesh, which is partially covered by a textured white shroud. In contrast to the relative breadth of the passages of whiteness, there is the more cluttered and claustrophobic space occupied by all these journalists and technicians holding their various cameras and microphones and notepads while they stand or kneel in front of the morgue's wall. Such description of what attracts my attention as I scan this image is rather straightforward, I suppose. Still, a second look at Briggs's spatial juxtaposition of these two different human assemblages literally and figuratively complicates the picture. At first glance, for example, the collective gaze of the media crowd appears to be angled toward the Pietà. Interestingly, at and on the edge where these two different embodied groups are in contact, it becomes rather clear that an approximately forty-five-degree diagonal line of demarcation traverses the image from its bottom left corner to its top right corner. And just like that, looking at the length of this diagonal rift within the image's compositionality exposes to view still another potential aporia or dead end (in addition to that embodied by Jesus's corpse). For it turns out that the collective gaze of the humans who form the leading edge of the media phalanx is actually directed toward some thing or things or persons hidden from view, obscured by the monumental architectonics of the Pietà group in the foreground. There is an elemental opacity here amid all the visual evidence of transparency. Whatever it is that has caused this swerve in the media assemblage's attention from the Pietà, it is missing in action—just like all those abducted and disappeared bodies described by Bowden and depicted by Briggs throughout the book.

This apparent rift both in knowledge and understanding occasioned by death's presence in the body of the Christ figure (as well as its presence as a theme and trope in the textual body of Bowden's prose) is doubled by still another rift in everyday life exposed by Juárez's contagious violence. The cognitive and corporeal trauma devolving from the everyday reality of abducted and disappeared family members gets repressed here and displaced into what we might call the crypt concealed behind and below the dead Jesus and his grieving mother. This crypt we can imagine as receiving the spectral undead (dead to life but alive in memory's blinding afterimage), those twelve once missing but now found persons whose demise at the Juárez death house haunts all who are waiting in vain here and elsewhere in Juárez, eclipsed by the lengthening shadow of their queue at the morgue, this shadow visible in the passage between Mary's hand and head, "drawn like a black veil across the earth," this veil revealing, even as it also obscures, the "endless graveyard of humanity."[3]

3. "*Profane negation.*" Lines that segment, that register a rift or trench—at the bottom of which, below a ledge, is a crypt. But there are lines that also connect, that compose a gathering on this spatial and temporal threshold where the living and the dead, the storied past and the wounded present commingle. Consider once again Mary's right arm and hand, straightened and upraised, as if in supplication, this affective gesture reaching toward the image's geometrical center, the clotted space occupied by the media crowd. And by following the imaginary line produced by her corporeal gesture's trajectory across the plane of the image, we arrive at still another instance of the "double" motif. For in the upper left rear quadrant of the image a cameraperson materializes before our eyes, his upraised arms and hands cradling a video camera replete with a microphone attached via an extended pole, as if his pose and technological apparatus are engaging, across the divides of time and space, in a call-and-response mode. What I want to recognizes as Briggs's analogical vision of relationality—both between and within the image's spatial and temporal registers—centers on the degree to which we, like the maternal figure who cradles the dead Jesus before our eyes, are called to bear witness not so much to the aporia embodied by the dualism of a binary opposition, but rather to a recognition of the dialectical entanglement of the sacred and profane—to how the sacred depends upon and has at its very center the "deep wound" of the profane.[4]

The potential affective force or resonance of this antithetical unity of the sacred and profane becomes further apparent, when we turn to consider the historical artwork informing Briggs's rendering here of the Pietà motif: Anthony van Dyck's *The Lamentation over the Dead Christ* (1635). Strictly speaking, with regard to the iconographical traditions depicting the crucifixion and death of Christ, van Dyck's painting, as its title suggests, represents a

FIG. 10. Anthony van Dyck, *The Lamentation over the Dead Christ*, ca. 1635. Oil on canvas, 115.5 cm x 208 cm (45.2 in. x 81.8 in.). Inventory no. 404. Cedric Verhalst, Collection KMSKA–Flemish Community (CCO).

lamentation. The distinction between the lamentation and the Pietà traditions centers on the presence of additional mourners grouped around the Christ figure's corpse and lamenting his death. Van Dyck positions two angels and one saint around Jesus and Mary, whereas Briggs of course substitutes a secular human group in the form of the media queue. One result of Briggs's revision of van Dyck's lamentation scene is to foreground a vision of the predatory nature inherent in the voyeuristic gaze that seeks to capitalize, literally and figuratively, on spectacles of traumatic loss, absence, and death. Her focus on the Pietà iconography underscores the abiding deep wound existing at the center of the sacred represented by the stigmata piercing Jesus's hand and feet. It also focuses attention on the framing field of whiteness created by her piercing a prepared black surface with a knife, this field signifying the emptiness of blank or void space—a profane negation of presence, let us say, rather than, for instance, an offering of a promissory note that the artist will apply pigment to fill the white blankness of a stretched and primed canvas. Lacking the presence of van Dyck's angels to elaborate grief and mourning as a shared collective experience, Briggs's Pietà image forwards the melancholy prospect that all involved here in looking at the face of death are, well, alone as well as lonely.[5]

Is it any wonder, then, that the grief-stricken mother of Jesus—in a manner we can imagine as replicating the posture of all those anxious mothers with their families queuing up outside the Juárez morgue—seeks for some sign, some form of solace as a result of this harrowing embrace with death? Death itself, whose horizon forever constitutes the ultimate disappearing act for all those ever fated to live. Here, then, is both the face of death and the facing of death. Here is the waiting of the living for and the weighting of the living by both the named and nameless dead, all the disappeared—all los desaparecidos.

4. "*Death as still life or Nature morte.*" Reflecting on Nicolas Poussin's painting *Landscape with a Man Killed by a Snake* (1648), T. J. Clark wonders "if the ultimate horror surrounding the dead body . . . has to do with our sensing that all the identities and faces we are obliged to give the corpse—faces of fear and otherness, faces of haunting proximity, even the face of a terrible Force rising up from inside it and claiming it at last—are no more than reaction formations. They try to shield us from the great fact, the ultimate uncanny: that Death, in the corpse, disappoints us—looks away from us, and no longer has a face of any kind."[6] As Clark's deployment of the passive voice in the phrase "we are obliged to give" suggests, the mental disarray caused by our proximity to dead bodies ultimately "disappoints us," primarily because both our sense of agency is suspended and the corpse "looks away from us," or fails to reciprocate our gaze. This disappointment, Clark further speculates, is linked to "the deep (and productive) confusion of mind" that any human experiences when looking at corpses.[7] Consider the potential category confusion one can experience when in the presence of a companion in a prone position with their eyes closed: Is this person merely sleeping or am I looking at the face of death? Moreover, our "confusion of mind" is deep, Clark argues, because intact (rather than ruined) dead bodies are, or at least still resemble, living people whom we can still recognize and call their name, still be available both for us to regard and for us to be regarded. As if it were possible to stop time and live with the newly dead in a present moment of mutual seeing, which of course constitutes, strictly speaking, an impossibility.

Yet the deep confusion spawned by our being in the presence of an intact corpse who still bears the imprint of a recognizable subjectivity, Clark adds, should also be considered a "productive" confusion. This possibility arises because our sight of death typically produces in the living a compelling, indeed somewhat paradoxical, desire: on the one hand, to draw nearer to the corpse whose residual subjectivity we can yet regard in the hope that our gaze will be reciprocated; on the other hand, to recoil from the intact corpse's presence because it is already falling prey to that silent, "terrible Force" of biological decomposition. Our inherently ambivalent response to the sight of death is why, as Julia Kristeva claims, "that compelling, raw, insolent thing in the morgue's full sunlight . . . that thing that no longer matches and therefore no longer signifies anything" represents the utmost of abjection.[8]

There is still another possible reason, Clark argues, that "death in the corpse" ultimately "disappoints" us: "the fact that any corpse, however domestic its passing, is seen by the unconscious mind as *prey*," which is to say as "the victim of successful predation."[9] In the overall poetics of exposure that propels the verbal and pictorial narratives throughout *Dreamland*, we certainly are exposed to the hard fact that human bodies are preyed upon. But additionally, as we see through Briggs's revisionist staging of the iconographic Pietà and lamentation traditions, this leitmotif emerges: looking as a hunting or seeking; hunting or seeking as looking, memorably exemplified here (and in Van Dyck's painting) by Mary's imploring gaze at the heavens. Like the ambivalence attached to our unconscious desire both to draw near and to recoil from the corpse's presence, the trajectory of Mary's gaze necessarily wavers between looking at, as Peter Schwenger describes, "an image that is essentially empty," that is, at a corpse which no longer has a face or reciprocates the gaze of the living, and looking at an image that is full, as if her searching gaze miraculously could resuscitate the dead.[10] With this predatory-type looking for and failing to find any evidence of a residual subjectivity in the corpse, our sight of death can be regarded as a compensatory reaction formation to the sight of death's mystery, its utter opacity. So it is that such performative looking is fated never to complete the visual transit between the exemplary (the materiality both of the image itself and of the corpse being imaged within it) and the abstract or transcendent realm of the explanatory (what the event means, if anything at all), in this moment endured in sight of the morgue's entrance.

In concert here with a leitmotif of upraised hands, it is as if the performative nature of the desiring look sentences us to cradle both the fugitive past and the indeterminate future in an expanded present moment abruptly experienced as an abyss. In this visualized space of waiting, what I earlier termed "living in the purgatorial meantime," living persons gather as claimants. But both their pleas and their bodies are held in abeyance. Death and terror, danger and risk, desire and suffering—it is as if all the anguished turmoil of human history becomes embalmed here in this image. Thus: death as still life or *nature morte*.[11] Briggs's nature morte motif here and elsewhere throughout the pages of *Dreamland* reminds me also of a contemporary real-life profane or secular double of Christ's stigmata: the *corte de florero*, or flowerpot cut, the name given by drug cartel sicarios and narcostate paramilitaries to describe a mutilation in which targeted victims' are decapitated and their thoraxes stuffed with their dismembered limbs, so the beheaded corpse weirdly echoes the look of flowers arranged in a vase.[12]

5. "*Your eyes.*" As if in explanation of this book's title and subtitle, Bowden observes that, yes, "there is a way out of here [Juárez], and it is called *levantón*, the lift or pickup. You are going about your business and suddenly men with guns come and you go with them. Sometimes you return as a corpse and this, of course, is a blessing, since then your family knows your fate and can visit your grave. But usually you never come back in any form and so you become, not even a ghost, but a question mark."[13] Both the relentless seriality of Bowden's prose and the periodic repetitions of Briggs's images (for example, the portrait of the grieving Mary's face from Rogier Van Der Weyden's *The Descent from the Cross* [ca. 1435]) press home not only the question mark, this sign of the eternal interrogative attached to death, but also this ontological question: How do we the living live with the dead who surround us?

My phrasing of this question is generally indebted to John Berger's observation, in his essay "Twelve Theses on the Economy of the Dead," that once upon a time "all the living awaited the experience of the dead," for it was their ultimate future, our shared fate. Now, however, capitalism has spawned "a uniquely modern form of egoism," one that annuls our once fundamental recognition of the interdependence of the living and the dead.[14] This particular development in modernity, Berger further speculates, has been "disastrous," especially for the living, who have come to regard the community of the dead somewhat cavalierly "as the *eliminated*," as in "those who once lived."[15]

Certainly in the *Dreamland* context, this word *eliminated* connotes "those who once lived." But like the vernacular usage attached to the Spanish verb form *levantón, eliminated* also can connote an expulsion or abandonment. Whether thought about as a process (to eliminate) or the product of such actions (the eliminated persons), the noun and verb forms of *eliminate* should be regarded as encompassing all those persons who have been expelled from sight or removed from consideration. But still not yet vanished from remembrance, such as the unidentified for whom all the families stand in line at the Juárez morgue, waiting like the Virgin Mary in Briggs's image for a revelation—a sign. Such as all those still missing persons whose disposability—at least from the point of view of those who have lifted them out of this life—conjures up one of the early etymological meanings of *eliminate*: the body's expulsion of waste matter.

This trope of the corporeal expulsion of waste matter routinely has been deployed whenever the integrity of the body under siege is that of a collective (the family, the community, the nation, the planet). This matter of waste elimination, in brief, thus connects with the mattering of certain lives and the expulsion of other lives regarded as not mattering. Necropolitics is Achille Mbembe's term to describe how "the ultimate expression of sovereignty" exercised by contemporary state and non-state powers (legal or criminal multinational corporate entities such as drug cartels) "resides to a large degree, in the power and the capacity to dictate who may live and who must die." In a necropolitical regime, "weapons are deployed in the interest of maximum destruction of persons and the creation of *death-worlds*" in which endless states of terror are justified in the name of security as well as profitability.[16] A death-world in *Dreamland*, where a metaphysical sadness reigns, its population stranded, as we have seen in that indeterminate ocean of white space between the shores of the exemplary and the explanatory, between waking and dreaming—that hypnogogic state where "the wide-awake people seem like living death to your eyes."[17] A death-world in which such an expression as "your eyes" connotes not only the facing of death both in the corpse and in the walking dead. On one level it connotes the chronic affective unsettlement felt by one and all human subjects (*your* as both singular and plural pronoun) for all those human subjects who have disappeared without a trace. But on another level, it connotes a chronic unsettlement, both for oneself, whose subjectivity has been sundered as a result of living through and with serial traumatic losses, and even for the loss of subjectivity itself as a viable concept in a death-world environment organized to deprive some lives, considered to be valueless, of life itself.[18]

As modeled for us in Briggs's Pietà and Bowden's words about the humans queued up at the morgue, this affective melancholia effectively gathers together all of us sentenced to live in death-worlds, just like this solitary figure of Mary who waits here in this spatiotemporal threshold populated by the already dead and the waking dead. You feel it and "your eyes" witness how the cognitive and affective disorientation accruing from one's proximity to the dead, in this instance, is mimicked here by this other pose: that of the journalists eager to publish breaking news—their predatory pose ghosting that of the families assembled in front of the morgue awaiting to identify one of the twelve corpses recovered from the cartel death house as their own. These anonymous dead whose abject manner of death—their sudden disappearance; their digging of their own graves while noting the nearby sacks of lime that will garnish their bodies; their secret execution—essentially recapitulates and anticipates the fate of all those people abducted and disappeared by other state and non-state powers during the seemingly endless global wars against drugs and against terrorist organizations.

[**Alphabet/Abecedario**; **Cryptography**; **Diapers**; **Kotex**; **Lipstick**; **Television**; **X-ray**]

Rivers, all my tears like water flown

EXTRACTS

Sleeping in dry washes or rolled up in cardboard under mesquite trees above the river, they would be ready when he called. It was simple arithmetic. The punks would have been in diapers the first time Rambo had gone to 'Nam.... Let them take whatever they needed, because the only legacy the U.S. had given them was as worthless as the string of dingy foster homes they had endured. Only a great and terrible war could explain how so many could find themselves sleeping in the street.
—Leslie Marmon Silko, *Almanac of the Dead* (1992)

Small bodies in secret cemeteries, piled on top of each other in pits. By a bend in the river. Under the ruins of a church turned to ash. In the muddy soil of an abandoned cornfield. Could their bones be lighter than soil? If the bones of the children floated to the top, people might know what Longoria did. Who could know? Who were the witnesses? The children knew, but they were only sand now, sand children.
—Héctor Tobar, *The Tattooed Soldier* (1998)

In a tent (later a shack) not far south of our ranch house, in post oak scrub near the West Fork of the Trinity River, lived a woman who had (reportedly) been traded for a whole winter's catch of skunk hides, the exchange occurring when she was about thirteen.... I rode to town with the old woman—once worth more than fifty skunk hides—many times but I never heard her speak a single word.
—Larry McMurtry, *Walter Benjamin at the Dairy Queen* (2001)

1. *"By a bend in the river."* In "John Wayne: A Love Story," an essay in her collection *Slouching Towards Bethlehem* (1968), Joan Didion describes a dinner party she and her husband attended with John Wayne and his wife Pilar, "in an expensive restaurant in Chapultepec Park," on one night during the last week of the filming of *The Sons of Katie Elder* in Mexico City in 1965. Didion frames this event by concisely summarizing the "number of ways" she had thought about Wayne's film persona since first seeing him in *War of the Wildcats* as an eight-year-old girl in the summer of 1943. Twenty-two years later, she recollects how, after a few drinks over dinner, she had "lost the sense that the face across the table was in certain ways more familiar than my husband's." But then "something happened": "suddenly the room seemed suffused with the dream, and I could not think why." This abrupt, unexpected transformation of "a nice evening, an evening anywhere" into a dreamscape from her childhood past occurs as three men playing guitars appear at their table. At this interruption Wayne raises his glass "imperceptibly" toward Pilar and then orders more wine for the table and "some red Bordeaux for the Duke." As the ensuing communion with wine proceeds at their table, the musicians play on and eventually, Didion comments, "I realized what they were playing, what they had been playing all along: 'The Red River Valley' and the theme from *The High and the Mighty*. They did not quite get the beat right, but even now, I can hear them, in another country and a long time later, even as I tell you this."[1]

At this essay's outset Didion claims that the John Wayne film persona "determined forever the shape of certain of our dreams," dreams whose utopian shape existed in stark contrast to the real-world shape of the turbulent 1960s, "characterized by venality and doubt and paralyzing ambiguities." His was a *reel* world "which may or may not have existed ever but in any case existed no more." His body was the "perfect mold" into which film directors could pour "the inarticulate longings of a nation wondering at just what pass the trail had been lost." Didion grounds this sense of a lost Edenic pastoral enclave of domestic harmony through three examples: by highlighting a line of dialogue the Duke utters (a house built by hand "at the bend in the river where the cottonwoods grow"); by quoting lines from "Out Where the West Begins," a 1911 cowboy poem set to music; and by contrasting the Durango, Mexico, location of the current film production's exterior scenes with Mexico City.

As is the case with Bel Air, Beverly Hills, and Acapulco—other urban locales referenced in this essay—Mexico City signifies domestic consumerism and the social scene of the film principals' wives, whereas Durango constitutes "Man's Country. Out where the West begins." Nevertheless, in the Churubusco Studios' sound stage in Mexico City, this "world peculiar to men who like to make Westerns"—this dream of a "man's country [that] was receding fast"—seemingly was preserved but "for just so long as the picture lasted." As it was also preserved, this dream, in the aftermath of the film's production: for the magical resurgence of "this dream of a man's country" experienced during a farewell dinner in the secluded inner sanctum of a Mexican restaurant gets reiterated in the enclave space of Didion's study, this room located literally and figuratively "in another country." That is, through its compression of time and space and its equation of architectural and psychological spaces, Didion's written remembrance of this special night celebrating the end of the filming of *The Sons of Katie Elder* transforms the terrain of her study into an analogue of the movie theater, the sound stage, and—at the last—the restaurant where the masculine code of the West resurfaces before her eyes as the music plays and "the Duke" orders red wine for the table.[2]

2. "*This dream of a man's country [that] was receding fast.*" Nested within this retrospective—and ultimately conflicted—longing for "the dream" emblematized by the Duke's monumental screen presence and his promise to build a home "at the bend in the river where the cottonwoods grow" exists the cowboy lament titled "The Red River Valley." As if in counterpoint to the dream of constancy and security realized by the outdoor spaces in "Out Where the West Begins," the lyric speaker in "The Red River Valley" desires to stay the moment of a loved one's departure to another country ("do not hasten to bid me adieu"). And yet, even within both the present tense of the song and the presence of the lyric's intended auditor, this speaker proceeds to imagine the pending farewell as a loss akin to that of death. For the river valley topography is not the only thing going to be left behind. The soon-to-be departed cowboy's "bright eyes and smile" are imagined as "taking the sunshine" with him, this nomadism configured as a theft that will enshroud both the valley and the lyric speaker's psyche in darkness. With the physical separation of the lovers paralleled by the speaker's abiding uncertainty as to

whether memories will be able to mitigate a bleak future defined by temporal and spatial distance, it is as if this song—like the overall tenor of the essays in *Slouching Towards Bethlehem*—composes a dark, haunted space of mourning in advance of its actual cause.

Didion initially confesses she "could not think why" the restaurant suddenly "seemed suffused with the dream." Although she eventually realizes the song being played in the room was "The Red River Valley," that she doesn't reproduce or comment on its lyrics presents this allusion as an unsettling parallel to the "obscure anxiety" that plagues her being and necessitates her trip to Mexico in the first place after she hears the news about Wayne's lung cancer diagnosis. As will be the case with the literature of new urban Wests in the wake of 1968, throughout Didion's essays there appears a certain corporeal and cognitive dissonance, as well as a certain pose of suspended agency. This dissonance is embodied by guitar players not quite getting the beat right; by the cancer that inhabits Wayne's body; and by the news about the discovery of decomposed and decomposing corpses in the Mojave Desert. And it is a dissonance embodied by the built environment one encounters in "the underside of Hollywood, south of Sunset Boulevard": where the architecture of middle-class slums—"'model studios' and warehouses and two-family bungalows"—bears little if any resemblance to Reyner Banham's precious "dingbat" apartment complexes, whose presence, he argued, exemplified the continuing legacy of the entrepreneurial frontier spirit and the American Dream.[3]

An emergent sense of suspended agency is embodied here by this proclamation: "California is a place in which a boom mentality and a sense of Chekhovian loss meet in uneasy suspension; in which the mind is troubled by some buried but ineradicable suspicion that things had better work here, because here, beneath that immense bleached sky, is where we run out of continent."[4] So via an imagined projection of a lesser future ("The Red River Valley") and by a retrospective memory that proceeds via fragmented, at times elliptical moments, in Didion's essays (and novels) what surfaces is a somber, denaturized nostalgia, grounded by an affective sense of dread. Any moment of plenitude that possibly could be conjured up from the distant or immediate past through one's work of recollection; any faith that the present, much less the future, will mushroom up into a moment of plenitude—this moment never materializes.

3. *"Its center was not holding."* Helpfully defining an emergent urban New West both historically and in terms of cultural production, Krista Comer claims "the signature text announcing the arrival of 1968 and the New West is Joan Didion's first collection of essays *Slouching Towards Bethlehem*." For Comer, the essay collection as a whole, and especially its title essay, dramatize "the postwar American Dream in total disarray," how its "center was not holding" because of the internal pressure exerted on it by heroes gone mad (like John Wayne in the classic film *The Searchers*), by powerful women (like Didion), and by its own rebelling suburban youth (middle-class, disillusioned hippies). And its "center was not holding" because of external pressure applied at its borders by those non-native Others whom it "excluded, displaced, and othered."[5] Moreover, for Comer the new, more critical regionalism that emerged after 1968 "is born out of, and responds to, the emerging culture of postmodernism." So from this perspective, Didion's motifs of corporeal and cognitive dissonance, as well as her speaker's pose of suspended agency, anticipate Fredric Jameson's call for producing new cognitive maps to aid our navigation of an emergent postmodern urbanism and architectural aesthetic.[6] To be sure, as historian Richard White observes, at the time of the 1970 census it was already apparent that "two different, but intertwined Wests had emerged: one mostly rural and largely powerless, and the other metropolitan and increasingly powerful."[7] Nevertheless, as suggested by Didion's triangulation in *Slouching Towards Bethlehem* of various California urban locales with Las Vegas, New York, Hawaii, and Mexico (Mexico City, Durango, Acapulco, Guaymas), literary and cultural production in the urban New West "is born out of, and responds to" a globalizing world system's restructuring of its economic, political, and social landscape into post-Fordist industrial metropolises or "world cities," such as Los Angeles, these embedded in "multiple networks of economic, social, demographic, and information flows."[8]

Whether one focuses on earlier or more recent case studies of "new" urban, western American literature, as Neil Campbell argues, any "new spatial cultural geohistory of the American West gathers the 'traces,' the artifacts, and the fragments in order to articulate, not a unified and totalizing story, but one in which many voices speak, many, often contradictory, histories are told, and many ideologies cross, coexist, and collide."[9] For example, here in

"John Wayne A Love Story," such fragments as a song or photograph or movie dialogue. Elsewhere in the literature of the new urban West: a postcard, a painted mural, a church's stained-glass windows, cemetery grave markers, a box of artifacts in a university anthropology building, animal taxidermy, a purported snuff movie. Campbell's contrast between a "unified and totalizing story" and one "in which many voices speak" foregrounds a narrative and spatial tension between concentration and dispersal that characterizes the literature of newer urban Wests. And though contradictory histories with many different ideologies emerge in such new stories, taken together, their representation of new urban Wests can be seen to share an investment in spectrality both as a theme (haunting absences in the present and being haunted by the past; the speculative flows of capital) and as image or trope (specters).[10]

This narrative tension and thematic investment often result first in image clusters of interior and exterior dark spaces (restaurant banquet rooms; basements; bathrooms; hotel and motel corridors; back alleys) that signify literal and metaphorical homelessness; and second in both plot structures and built environments that elaborate uncanny architectures of vagabondage and abandonment. A dialectic of mobility/immobility organizes such narrative and spatial architectures, so that various characters' nomadism through and across unhomely urban and suburban thresholds functions both to magnify and to critique urban systems that are, at bottom, "socially and spatially polarized between high value-making groups and functions on the one hand and devalued social groups and downgraded spaces on the other."[11] And what for Didion represents a declension away from "the unified and totalizing story" of the American Dream that was realized by the Duke's body and voice and imaged as "a house at the bend in the river where the cottonwoods grow" mutates, in Sherman Alexie's version of a John Wayne love story, "Dear John Wayne" (2000), into a retirement home on the Navajo reservation where a white anthropologist tapes an interview with a displaced 108-year old Spokane Indian woman who narrates her love affair with the Duke when she served as a youthful extra during the filming of *The Searchers*.[12]

[**D**iapers; **F**reeways; **H**otel life; **I**dyll; **U**rbicide; **V**agabondage; **Z**ombieland]

Scene of the crime

EXTRACTS

Traffic had slackened; in the distance I could see the Hollywoodland sign missing its last two letters.... As I approached the park area that bordered Mount Lee, I saw that all the excitement was contained behind ropes guarded by a cordon of bluesuits; double-parking, I glimpsed Harry Sears walking over, badge pinned to his coat front.

His breath was now rife with liquor, the stutter gone. "Jesus Christ, what a piece of luck. This foot hack was assigned to clear out the vagrants before they started the demolitions. He stumbled onto the shack and came down and got me. It looks like the tramps have been in and out since '47, but maybe you could still forensic it."

—James Ellroy, *The Black Dahlia* (1987)

I could see the blond boy's bloody body lying half across his machine, blood all over the floor, all over the shapes; blood on my hands; his face all cut to pieces, one eye hanging out and wrinkled like an empty grape skin. I came to the copper shop, kept on around to the back. For a moment at the back door I stopped and steadied myself. I took the knife out and opened it and got it in a stabbing grip. Then I saw a piece of wood on the ground. I picked it up and held it in my left hand, the knife in my right.

—Chester Himes, *If He Hollers Let Him Go* (1945)

There is an order to things. At the crime scene, yellow tape defines the killing ground. Little plastic kiosks dance on the pavement to mark the locations of cartridges and other evidence. Forensic experts make notations on their clipboards.

> All this information funnels into a system and never again sees the light of day. There is a precise inventory of the caliber of weapons that slaughtered someone, but the guns are never found. There is a precise count of the number of spent brass left at the scene, but the people pulling the triggers move like phantoms through the city. The dead merit an exact description of their clothing, height, and skin color, but their killers remain some vague term like "armed commandos," or, more often, are reduced to nothing but a notation of color and make of their getaway cars.
>
> —Charles Bowden, *Dreamland* (2010)

1. *"Maybe you could still forensic it."* In the contemporary homeless literature of the U.S. West, the architectural motif of the transit shed predominates, those structures whose function is defined by the continuous flows of bodies, images, and commodities through its interstitial spaces rather than by storage within them. Hotel and motels and boarding houses. Abandoned warehouses and shuttered factories. Commercial spaces and residential homes in foreclosure. Parking lots and public parks. Dive bars and diners and interstate highway truck stops. Bus and train stations, airports. Laundromats and morgues. This transit shed motif and its stress on kinetic movement across various spatial and temporal thresholds exists in dialectical relation with another motif, one where episodic narratives of transit and transient figures and objects come to ground in nested, recessed, or receptacle-like spaces of containment. Basements in abandoned fortune cookie factories; in a university department of anthropology; in a biomaterials lab specializing in harvesting human organs from the homeless; in a criminal fixer's office in a downtown office building; in a restaurant manager's office next to a wine cellar. Caves formed by utility tunnels, sewer pipes, and the underpasses of viaducts and freeways, the narrow alleys between buildings. Graveyards and garbage dumps, open air pits created by scraping the earth, or the sump pits below the rusting platforms supporting derelict oil derricks or pump jacks.

Regardless of their different prose contexts, such spaces of representation are invariably sepulchral, typically housing artefactual or forensic evidence whose excavation and exposure function in the manner of the uncanny: as a haunting return in the present moment of repressed or erased traumatic past histories. Consider the recessed, corrugated tin "copper shop" at the end of a shipyard dock within which Chester Himes's character Bob Jones fantasizes the bloody corpse of a white worker he has murdered will be draped across a machine. Or consider how, as he stands on the so-called last skyscraper under construction in Seattle, John Smith contemplates cutting the throat of a character named Wilson and dropping his body in a cement mixer, because he "knew that every building in Seattle contained the bones of fallen workers. Every building was a tomb."[1] In Leslie Marmon Silko's *Almanac of the Dead*, the character La Escapìa, as part of her raising of revolutionary consciousness, reads Karl Marx and arrives, in a fashion similar to John Smith and Bob Jones, at an insight that links labor exploitation and death to cryptlike spaces of containment, these fashioned at the outset of industrial modernity: "Marx backed every assertion with evidence; coroner's reports with gruesome stories about giant spinning machines that consumed the limbs and lives of the small children in the factories. On and on Marx went, describing the tiny corpses of children who had been worked to death—their deformed bodies shaped to fit inside factory machinery and other cramped spaces."[2]

From this perspective, construction sites and production lines of industrial factories represent scenes of crimes: their cramped spaces and niches containing the deformed bodies of the living; their dumpsters containing waste and sometimes the corpses of marginalized populations deemed surplus to requirements. Furthermore, this scene's focus on the fate of children worked to death also challenges the very integrity and security normally associated with the dominant culture's ideological fantasies of domestic family life. Consider the crime scene in James Ellroy's *The Black Dahlia*, for example, which turns out to be an abandoned cabin or house in the hills and canyons of the failed Hollywoodland housing development, where film westerns were made once upon a time. Acting on an anonymous tip, the police began to clear the area of homeless squatters on the very day the Hollywoodland sign's last four letters were being removed, these squatters serving as convenient murder suspects during the homicide investigation's early stages.

Such a crime scene in Ellroy's novel—located miles away from the actual discovery of the murder victim's body (and body parts)—relays how the unfettered spread of contagious violence metonymically indexes the overall sickness of the social and public as well as the private or individual body. In doing so, it exemplifies what D. A. Miller has diagnosed as the crime genre's "contradictory enterprises." On the one hand, as the Charles Bowden quote in the above extracts suggests, policing the crime scene via the maintenance of yellow tape boundaries and the application of forensic science protocols exemplifies the aim of all such disciplinary techniques deployed by the dominant culture's production of space: to maintain the illusion that a firm, blue (as well as yellow) line can be drawn between the police and an "unpoliced, unpolicing Other."[3] The crime scene for Bowden thus represents both the location of a criminal act and the "the unspoken world" of order where everything "works"—at least "for the moment." On the other hand, as revealed here by his phrase "for the moment," the crime scene boundary created by yellow tape represents a convenient fiction. As I noted above with regard to Ellroy's novel about the infamous Black Dahlia murders, what has already taken place inside the demarcated crime scene is inherently linked with what has happened before, and continues to happen, outside its artificially imposed boundaries. For at any future moment this "unspoken world" of order just might turn out to be, once the crime scene yellow tape and paraphernalia are removed and the blood stains fade away, the selfsame ground where the next killing will occur. Furthermore, conventional literary and visual representations of crime scenes also introduce an inherent epistemological uncertainty about knowledge production. Sometimes it happens, for example, that the crime scene is not the actual scene of the crime, just the site where the corpse has been discovered; and sometimes the actual scene of the crime, much less the identity of the victim, cannot even be established.

The crime scene thus provides both an alibi for the police to assert their power in everyday life and an alibi for the fact that, as Bowden observes, "everything works here, just not the way everyone pretends things work."[4] So the presence of the police and the sight of their work of policing—this informed by an ideology of science and rationality—does not so much redeem the existence of either the "free society" or the "free subject" that exists outside the boundaries of the crime scene's yellow tape and its orange kiosks decorating the pavement. Instead, especially through such leitmotifs as that of home invasion and the potential threat to order posed by the urban homeless population, such forensic work fundamentally highlights, albeit in displaced fashion, how our cherished "free" and sovereign subjectivity is in point of fact a "free-floating subjection."[5]

2. "*Move like phantoms through the city.*" The challenge, then, becomes how to represent at least two stories of subjection that the crime scene and the corpse manifest. There is the history of the violence enacted, as Escapia's reading of Marx recognizes, by the economic production of industrial space and the coercive fashioning of laboring bodies, such as women and underage children, to fit its machines' needs. And there is the related history of opposition, at times violent resistance, to that very subjection, this other history encrypted into the city's architectures, its transit sheds, and its layered, interstitial, and at times subterranean commercial, residential, and natural world spaces. Take the harrowing sequence in Sherman Alexie's *Indian Killer* when the anonymous Indian killer stabs one of his random victims under the cover of darkness and carries the corpse into a nearby suburban neighborhood. There, he deposits it on the living room floor of an empty house for sale and proceeds to scalp the dead white man and then stuff this bloody hairpiece into one of his own pockets as a souvenir. He then tears this corpse's still-open eyes out of their sockets and swallows them. This two-fold theft of the victim's sight (the murder itself and then this mutilation of the body) then leads to another signature action by this particular serial killer: the placement of two white owl feathers on the corpse's chest, at which point they turn a dark red color due to the blood already staining the victim's clothes and his exposed body.[6]

Prior to this killing and disposal of the victim's corpse, Alexie's narrator describes the Indian killer's stalking of his victim on an urban Seattle trail created out of an abandoned railway corridor. As this sequence proceeds, the narrator descriptively foregrounds this natural setting's tall evergreen trees and the shimmering light of a waxing moon. This description effectively transforms the nascent crime scene into that of an outdoor stage or stadium where a tragic performance will unfold under the light of the moon and an installed arc light. The uncanny effect created by this description's shimmer is matched by the cinematic description of the Indian killer's phantasmagoric performance: we witness his coiled stance, signifying his state of alertness;

then his sudden, apparitional appearance, like a phantom, before this random male victim; and then the killer performs a facial shape-shifting performance to camouflage his actual exterior appearance. In this sequence, then, the crime occurs at two different sites, thus effectively blurring any meaningful distinction between the domestic suburban home and the outdoor park—just as the frenzied, repetitious stabbing of the victim's chest and the removal of his eyes produce not only a mutilated body, but a kind of grotesque parody of the laboring and labored body, whose bloody corpse "mirrors not the outward appearance of the subject but its own, now transparent biological interior."[7]

It is as if this scene's overall choreography exemplifies Slavoj Žižek's claim that the most foundational phantasmatic scene for the human subject "is not that of a fascinating scene to be looked at, but the notion that 'there is someone out there looking at us'; it is not a dream, but the notion that 'we are the objects in someone else's dream.'"[8] With this suggestive claim before us, we might first observe how this emblematic crime scene repeats the novel's opening scene, in which John Smith remembers his childhood adoption as a nightmarish dream of being in thrall to the legal and technological machinations of power, this epitomized by the whir of cameras and the sounds and lights of helicopters hovering overhead. But in light of Žižek's speculation, perhaps the crime scene evidence of the mutilation and cannibalism prosecuted by the Indian killer dramatizes, somewhat counterintuitively, how the killer's morbid anxiety is intensified by "the prospect of *not* being exposed to the Other's gaze all the time."[9] By preserving the physical metonym of the Other's gaze (the victim's eyes) in the simultaneously literal and figurative interior crypt of his own corporeality, the killer's actions in this empty suburban house, as well as the massive publicity that follows on his exploits, surely interrupt the predominant discursive representation of the urban Indian homeless community in Seattle as the invisible, as the already dead who continuously move, like phantoms, through the city.

But on another level, I hasten to add that this particular crime scene—its scenography and forensic methodology on display—raises the stakes associated with this serial killer's urgent need for the phantasmic Other's gaze to guarantee his being and his genealogy. This spectral Indian killer's harvesting and cannibalistic ingesting of his white victim's eyes exemplifies the reproduction of his own body and being as another sepulchral space—as an externalization of a deep-seated psychic wound into an embodied corporeal cryptography. It also, performatively speaking, constitutes a ritual act of violence that arguably functions as a mimetic double of the "capitalist fascination for a particular cannibal fantasy," which is to say that "crude but effective method of producing capital gain through legalized murder, plunder, and/or inheritance, and compounding the gains by eating the dead."[10] Such ritual murder appropriates and inverts the settler-colonial culture myth of regeneration through violence, in the process magically and somewhat gruesomely exposing both an entire history of contagious colonial violence since Columbus. Furthermore, such ritual murder indexes, in our contemporary moment, the spread of a "visceral occult economy" founded on and sustained by the capitalistic violence of extraction and abstraction, "in which the majority are kept poor by the mystical machinations of the few . . . and in which profit depends on compressing space and time, on cannibalizing bodies, and turning labor into the spectral province of people in the night."[11]

[Alphabet/Abecedario; Cryptography; Psychometropolis; Television; Urbicide; Zombieland]

Television, the slow parade of fears

EXTRACTS

According to the show's host, the woman finds missing persons. The TV camera comes in for a close-up of a newspaper clipping: "Mass Murder Site Located." The old woman's face fills the screen. She is smiling but her eyes are not friendly. Her eyes know many things never meant to be seen.... Seese could feel the weight rising up in her chest, but the old woman's eyes continued: in villages in Mexico and Guatemala they lay out little children and babies every day. Their little white dresses and gowns are trimmed in blue satin ribbon. Seese was crying, but like the television, she seemed to make no sound. The maid ignored her, intent on the television show.
—Leslie Marmon Silko, *Almanac of the Dead* (1992)

Color was not what Grandmother saw. She removed her specs and wiped them with the corner of her apron and then returned them to the bridge of her nose because everyone and everything on television was limited to one common color and strained her eyes. The washing machines, the contestants on the game shows, the soap commercials, the panning camera of the Vietnam jungles. They all shared the color green. She stared at close-ups of the green Birmingham dogs unleashed and mauling flesh, their incisors as glistening as war planes on the nightly news.
—Helena María Viramontes, *Their Dogs Came with Them* (2007)

He opened the refrigerator and took out a carton of milk and opened it and smelled it and drank. He stood there holding the carton in one hand and looking out the window. He drank again and then he put the carton back in the refrigerator and shut the door.

> He went into the livingroom and sat on the sofa. There was a perfectly good twenty-one inch television on the table. He looked at himself in the dead gray screen.
> —Cormac McCarthy, *No Country for Old Men* (2005)

1. "*Like the television, she seemed to make no sound.*" At one moment in part 4 of Roberto Bolaño's novel *2666*, titled "The Part About the Crimes," the narrator summarizes everyday life along the U.S.-Mexico border in September 1996. There were the usual fights, drug deals, and arrests; the usual parties and long hot nights; the usual conversations and laughter. And there were the usual *narcocorridos* composing the soundtrack of everyday life under the sway of the drug cartels. And, too, there were the usual trucks loaded with cocaine crisscrossing the Chihuahuan desert and the "Cessna planes flying over the desert like the spirits of Catholic Indians ready to slit everyone's throats." Remarkably, during this particular September "there were almost no killings of women."[1] "Almost," but not quite a full reprieve from the femicide epidemic, for on the very last day of this particular month in this particular year of our Lord, two female corpses are found near Pueblo Azul. Law enforcement authorities eventually identify these victims as American sisters living outside of Tucson, women with prior arrests for drug trafficking charges. Perhaps, officials surmise, they were murdered in Arizona by competing *narcotraficantes*, their bodies then driven across the border by their killers and dumped in the Chihuahuan desert. Or perhaps they were abducted in Arizona and driven across the border into Mexico and killed by their competitors. Regardless, this haunting fact remains: even though September 1996 was noteworthy because of an apparent decline in the number of female abductions and murders, these two victims and the mystery of their manner and location of death represent but two of the nearly three hundred femicides that occurred in the environs of the U.S.-Mexican border city of Santa Teresa, Bolaño's fictional representation of Mexico's Cuidad Juárez in the years between 1993 and 1997.

In early 1997, the Santa Teresa police arrest a German-American male and charge him with murdering four of the women whose bodies are discovered as "The Part About the Crimes" section develops. This prime suspect had established an export company to distribute computer parts produced in a Santa Teresa *maquiladora,* and he was known to have close ties with the Santa Teresa drug cartels centrally involved in the femicides as well as the global traffic in illegal drugs. With this prime suspect in jail awaiting to be charged and then tried on multiple counts of murder, the mayor of Santa Teresa publicly declares "this is the end of the psychopaths" and that from now on whatever violent crimes happen in the city would fall "under the category of ordinary crime, what you'd naturally find in a city in a constant state of growth and development."[2] Nevertheless, the femicides continue unabated throughout 1997. "We've gotten used to death," one Santa Teresa citizen observes, this claim verified especially by the number of unidentified female victims who "ended up in a common grave at the cemetery because no one claimed their bodies."[3]

That the repetitive print and television news stories about the belated discoveries of the identified and unidentified dead in Santa Teresa could become accepted as the new normal of everyday life prompts still another character to observe that "no one pays attention to these killings, but the secret of the world is hidden in them."[4] By means of a prose assemblage that gathers together walking dead imagery, the cultural afterlife of the film western, the contemporary historical ravages spawned by the drug trade, and the epidemic of femicides in Santa Teresa, Bolaño represents how these ordinary crimes of violence index the rather uncanny repetition and return to this "city of growth and development" of a past history of contagious violence. In *2666*, it is a history whose temporal and spatial scales range from the Mexican-American War of the mid-nineteenth century through World War II and the Holocaust to the present moment of the Santa Teresa femicides. Whether or not the femicides result from the activities of psychopaths or of narcotraficantes or of unemployed men jealous of the women who labor in the maquiladoras, it is precisely because the contemporary violence against women can be regarded as, figuratively speaking, new wine in the old bottles produced throughout the history of the U.S.-Mexico borderlands that it indeed seems entirely plausible to suggest that "the secret of the world" is encrypted in this criminal epidemic.

On the sentence level, Bolaño's rendering of the serial Santa Teresa femicides in "The Part About the Crimes" invariably begins like this: "the next dead woman turned up on [date]"; or "the next dead woman was found"; or "in [name of month] the body of another woman was found in [name of place]." This introductory litany of discovery is then succeeded by an extended, usually highly graphic description, first, of the victim's body in situ, and then a straightforward accounting of what the forensic examiners later discover through their autopsy procedures and related lab work. Characterized by its deadpan tone and its grinding repetition of diction, syntax, and content (analogous to the assembly line-like production of corpses and commodities in the reigning maquila economy), Bolaño's aesthetic effectively immerses us in a temporality where the present moment both of the said (here there be dead bodies) and the saying of this fact (the repetitive discursive enunciation) resemble the impact of a legal plea in abeyance. That is, there is an admission of systemic guilt—that indeed something wrong has been happening and continues to happen here. And yet any act of sentencing, let alone reparations, for violent wrongdoings gets deferred. So in the meantime, the crimes continue unabated, and the authorities and citizens involved continue to imagine—but nevertheless cannot prosecute—a viable alternative future.[5]

At key moments in "The Part About the Crimes," however, Bolaño's predominant clinical or graphic realism shifts rhetorical registers to explore the ebb and flow of affective intensities that pass within and between all those individuals fated to bear witness to the corpses discovered at the various Santa Teresa crime scenes. One such person is homicide detective Juan de Dios Martínez, whose ongoing criminal investigations center on a particularly gruesome case in which a thirteen-year-old girl had been kidnapped, tortured, and raped before finally being killed by her assailants. In the wake of that horrific crime, Martínez is unable to find respite in the banality of his everyday life habits:

> For many days Juan de Dios Martínez thought about the four heart attacks Herminia Noriega had suffered before she died. Sometimes he thought about it while he was eating or while he was urinating in the men's room at the coffee shop or one of the inspector's regular lunch spots, or before he went to sleep, just at the moment he turned off the light, or maybe seconds before he turned off the light, and when that happened he simply *couldn't* turn off the light and then he got out of the bed and went over to

the window and looked out at the street, an ordinary, ugly, silent, dimly lit street, and then he went into the kitchen and put water on to boil and made himself coffee, and sometimes, as he drank the hot coffee with no sugar, shitty coffee, he turned on the TV and watched late-night shows broadcast across the desert from the four cardinal points, at that late hour he could get Mexican channels and American channels, channels with crippled madmen who galloped under the stars and uttered unintelligible greetings, in Spanish or English or Spanglish, every last fucking word unintelligible, and then Juan de Dios Martínez set his coffee cup on the table and covered his face with his hands and a faint and precise sob escaped his lips, as if he were weeping or trying to weep, but when finally he removed his hands, all that appeared, lit by the TV screen, was his old face, his old skin, stripped and dry, and not the slightest trace of a tear.[6]

2. "*Every last fucking word unintelligible.*" For the most part, I note above, Bolaño represents the femicide epidemic in the manner as if were a straightforward forensic report: its overall descriptive mode shorn of adjectives, adverbs, and figurative language, free from any intrusive interpretive asides or summary judgments. The tonality of its narrator's voice is entirely clinical or deadpan. But this particular passage attends to the psychic toll on an investigating detective in the aftermath of a crime, his being haunted by a seemingly endless replaying of this girl's particular manner of suffering and death. Bolaño focalizes this scene—its pacing oscillating between breathless narration and descriptive pauses—through Martińez's mobile gaze of surveillance. We oversee him initially scanning the lifeworld of an external street scene that he glimpses though his room's window, and then we watch as his gaze shifts to inventory his room's contents, in the process pausing at one moment to focus on his television (another type of window on the world), which delivers cinematic images and soundscapes from stations on both sides of the U.S.-Mexico border. Through his scanning gaze we are solicited to attend to the matter of materiality itself, as this becomes entwined with both epistemological and ethical registers. There is the matter of hearts, hands, skin, and faces. A coffeepot and mug and a kitchen table and chair. A bedside table and lamp and single bed. There is the highly problematic matter of how

to apprehend, much less comprehend, this world that is not only, so we are told, an "ugly" one but also one that is entirely "unintelligible," beyond all reckoning. And there is the ethical issue of what matters here, which is to say what is at stake ethically for a fictional homicide detective whose investigative work has hit a dead end and whose grief work is represented by the iterative mode (that is, his grief has occurred "for many days," but this hard fact is enunciated but once).

The vagabondage of Martínez's gaze as he scans both his apartment's interior space and the view of the "ugly, ordinary street" outside his window appears to be prompted by a specific, catalyzing desire that is itself underwritten by a faint hope. Consider how Bolaño's temporal dilation of the visual choreography produced by Martínez's visual inventory of the furniture and the furnishings of his domestic interior proceeds in the hope that repetitive encounters, with their substantial materiality, just might provide him with some compensatory solace amid all the bleakness of the "sometimes" that overdetermines his professional and often-baffled life as a homicide detective in the U.S.-Mexico borderlands. Sometimes he can eat, urinate, make coffee, watch television, look out his apartment window with interest, and even sleep. But when that sometimes is defined by intrusive thoughts about the girl's death, he sometimes cannot make things happen: when he reaches to turn off his bedside light, for example, he suffers catatonia to the degree that "he simply couldn't turn off the light." And there is that remarkable moment when the narrator's focalization of this scene through the inspector's gaze abruptly pivots, zooms out like a motion picture camera so that the visual field offers an external full shot of Martínez's body slumped over a table in the early morning darkness, only then for this external gaze at the grief-stricken detective to reverse direction and zoom back to focus on a close-up inspection of his aging face "lit by the TV screen." What we can call a metonymic logic based on sheer contiguity focuses our gaze on the "old skin" of this detective's face. Like the drought-ridden, wrinkled contours of the Chihuahuan desert depository of desiccated dead bodies, the folds of his old skin appear entirely bereft of moisture, entirely "stripped and dry," without "the slightest trace of a tear."

As this scene ends, no external visual signifier—for instance, a tear flowing down his face's old skin—appears that would validate the narrator's speculation that the faint sound made by the detective, in this moment, is that of a sob. Like the television programs being aired during this moment of abjection, this desiccated face, this barely uttered sound, and this slumped corporeal pose withdraw from the narrator's and reader's understanding and remain as "unintelligible" as the televised images of "crippled madmen" galloping under the stars and uttering greetings to each other in different languages. The tap water the detective uses to brew the shitty coffee he consumes does get efficiently rendered by his body as urine. Yet his face does not or cannot yet produce a tear, the presence of which just might signify this detective's cathartic release from his serial encounters with such horrific violence. Hence the rightness of the narrator's concluding shift to the more speculative subjunctive mode: "as if he were weeping or trying to weep." Hence too the rightness of the narrator's final phrase ("and not the slightest trace of a tear"), the falling cadences of its triad of dactyls paralleling the nascent fissures within the inspector's being and between his being and the encompassing world of darkness that looms outside his apartment window.

3. *"Looked at himself in the dead gray screen."* At one point in Cormac McCarthy's *No Country for Old Men*, the death-dealing character Anton Chigurh enters Llewellyn Moss's mobile home in a trailer park in West Texas and conducts a fruitless search for a briefcase full of money that Moss has accidentally come across in the aftermath of an abortive drug deal. Unable to locate the briefcase, he sits down on a couch and "look[s] at himself in the dead gray screen" of a twenty-one-inch television set. Keyed by the reflexive pronoun "himself," McCarthy's grammar here establishes a closed circle, as if distantly echoing the myth of Narcissus through the imagery of mirror reflection: the reflected image of "himself" in the television screen emerges as an actual double, not just an image of a man who bears an uncanny resemblance to the hitman. Since McCarthy's narrator does not provide us with any of Chigurh's internal reflections, "himself" also emerges as the object of a gaze, inert and spectral in and before the "dead gray screen." It is as if Chigurh, in looking at his proxy, glimpses a sight of his own future death even as he, emphatically, still lives. As Freud theorizes in his 1919 essay "The Uncanny," the sort of repetition compulsion displayed by Chigurh—when he looks either at himself in the reflections formed in dead TV screens or into

his various victims' dying eyes—manifests a desire to strip death of its auratic power, its affective hold over his psychic life. In one direction, this desire is projected outward, in the form of predatory violence directed at various scapegoat figures whose deaths at his hand offer, for the time being at least, a cathartic resolution of his intolerable self-loathing about "himself" being held hostage, as all humans are, by the sentence of mortality.

In another direction, this reactive desire to the felt trauma and morbid anxiety associated with one's proximity to death can manifest itself, as I believe we witness in the case of inspector Juan de Dios Martínez, as an internalized non-cathartic condition: an affective numbness or shock state occasioned by having reached a fundamental impasse. It is an impasse rendered by corporeal imagery: this detective's temporary catatonia; his inability to produce either a tear or a legible sound in his grief-stricken state. And with this additional context supplied by Freud's theorization of the uncanny, an earlier scene in "The Part About the Crimes" bears further consideration. I am thinking here of that moment when the director of a local psychiatric hospital asks Martínez which of two phobias—pantophobia or phobophobia—he would choose if he were forced to suffer from one of them. Martínez's answer: phobophobia, that condition of "being afraid of my own fears." After all, he reasons aloud to the psychiatric hospital's female director, if he suffered from pantophobia, the condition of "being scared of everything," then he couldn't very well do his job as a policeman, could he? Still, the director responds, if you suffer from phobophobia "you're forced to live in constant contemplation of [your fears], and if they materialize, what you have is a system that feeds on itself, a vicious cycle."[7] In the psycho-social theatrical space in which insomnia and suspended agency reign in Martínez's life, then, his pose of abjection and his desiccated face arguably exemplify that "vicious cycle" inherent in a system parasitically feeding on itself. In *2666*, such systematic self-cannibalization materializes as the working detective's train of inductive and deductive thinking. His is a coursing train of thought that inherently moves at a tangent to the substantial material evidence he compiles during the course of the murder investigation, just as the faint sounds from his mouth and the barely perceptible shudder of his body move at a tangent to any exact determination of their meaning by any external observer.

4. *"Stripped and dry as a corpse."* That affective state known as melancholia, theorizes Giorgio Agamben, fundamentally displays the desire to regard a lost object or person of desire as "neither appropriated nor lost, but both possessed and lost at the same time." For the melancholic subject, this state of ambivalence creates a "fundamental impasse," one that can be explained in either or both of two ways: 1) the lost object of desire constitutes an "impossible possession," in the sense that, owing to certain intractable realities, it was never going to be possessed in the first place (and hence was never truly lost); or 2) this lost object of desire was indeed at one point possessed before it disappeared or passed away, so its loss eventually gets regarded as only "a contingent or local loss or malfunction." This latter rationalization enables the melancholic human subject to move forward and resolve the fundamental impasse occasioned by traumatic loss through a reconciliation with "the governing reality principle." It is this moment of radical acceptance, then, that transforms the abjection of melancholia into the successful work of mourning.[8]

Agamben further defines the melancholic subject's "fundamental impasse" as accruing from not only individual traumatic loss, absence, and death but also as the result of "an antagonism tearing at the social substance." In "The Part About the Crimes," senseless, inexplicable violent crimes against children and adolescents and women produce lost objects of desire that simultaneously haunt the psychic lives of families, communities, and homicide detectives like Martínez and that also expose deep-seated "antagonisms tearing at the social substance" of any "city of growth and development," such as Juárez. The architecture of crime scenes and the autopsy tables in morgues and the unidentified dead hastily buried in makeshift cemeteries—these architectures encrypt this stage of global capitalism's inherent contradictions, its uneven economic development and its territorial and gendered divisions of labor which inherently produce excess waste and wasted bodies. As Dean MacCannell has suggested, such architectures and contradictions exemplify "the capitalist fascination for a particular cannibal fantasy with its own distinctive mythic contours. It is not Montaigne's cannibal with an unbreakable resolve to maintain honor. Rather, it is cannibalism as a crude but effective method of producing capital gain through legalized murder, plunder, and/or inheritance, and compounding the gains by eating the dead."[9]

In the conventional examples of the police or forensic procedural genre, such "antagonisms" tearing at the social substance are indeed typically rationalized as merely contingent or local losses—or the unnatural acts of psychotic killers. As I mentioned at the outset of this essay, at one point in *2666* the mayor of Santa Teresa announces that the police have arrested a psychotic suspect and that the "governing reality principle" has been restored. Yet once again the killings and the belated discoveries of dead female victims continue unabated. Expelling his breath, lowering his hands to grip a kitchen table, as if to ward off the sudden onset of positional vertigo, Juan de Dios Martínez's abject posture and internalized recognition of his suspended agency evocatively relay his obsession with facing either the haunting face of death displayed by Herminia Noriega's corpse or his own future death, anticipated here by the narrator's description of his facial skin as "stripped and dry" as a corpse. Still, is it not also the case that what perhaps magically surfaces here is the sight of the cringe of melancholy attaching itself to loss, refusing any argument cynically grounded by the desire of a "system that feeds upon itself for expediency"? Such a system, in short, would consign such death throes as endured by thirteen-year-old Herminia Noriega to "a local accident or contingent malfunction," the new normal, so to speak, so as to move on or get on with everyday life in the transnational maquila economy.

[**A**lphabet/Abecedario; **C**ryptography; **E**xposure; **Q**ueues; **S**cene of the crime; **Z**ombieland]

Urbicide, what the master plan was

EXTRACTS

He remembered years ago. Neighborhood meeting at the old recreation center. City bureaucrats come over to explain how they were gonna widen the freeway. Move some houses over, appropriate streets, buy out the people in the way. Some woman just like grandma stood up and wanted to know what the master plan was. How'd she know it wasn't gonna be more than just widen the freeway? . . . Who was gonna guarantee she was gonna have a place to live under the master plan?

—Karen Tei Yamashita, *Tropic of Orange* (1997)

The streets Mama remembered had once connected to other arteries of the city, rolling up and down hills, and in and out of neighborhoods where neighbors of different nationalities intersected with one another. To the west, La Pelota Panadería on Soto Street crossed Canter's Kosher Deli on Brooklyn Avenue, which crossed Pol's Chinese Kitchen on Pacific Boulevard to the east. But now the freeways amputated the streets into stumped dead ends, and the lives of the neighbors itched like phantom limbs in Mama's memory.

—Helena María Viramontes, *Their Dogs Came with Them* (2007)

South-Central Los Angeles looked a lot like Longoria's neighborhood, though there were fewer people on the streets. Entire blocks were empty of pedestrians. On other blocks all but a handful of the stores were shut down. Here and there he saw buildings that were only empty shells: four walls and no ceiling, painted announcements on the front almost erased by time. A few buildings seemed to have been burned out many, many years ago: scorched brick walls left standing alone, like part of

a movie set, broken iron bars, twisted and rusting. Longoria looked at those buildings and thought a war must have been fought here, though he had no idea when.
—Héctor Tobar, *The Tattooed Soldier* (1998)

War is architecture. Architecture is war.
—Lebbeus Woods, *War and Architecture* (2002)

1. "*The freeways amputated the streets into stumped dead ends.*" At one point in Sherman Alexie's novel *Indian Killer* (1996), its major character, John Smith, feels, while working on the construction of "the last skyscraper in Seattle," that he is beginning to understand "the myths and lies of its construction, the myths and lies of its architect."[1] What Smith means by "myths and lies" eventually becomes clarified in the novel's chapter titled "Cousins," which centers on one of his journeys from the Seattle suburb where his white adoptive parents live to this city's downtown area. As he walks the city's streets and highways, going through its parks and across its bridges and under its viaducts, the symptoms of what appears to be his depersonalized-derealization mental disorder manifest themselves. During this day's particular journey, he begins to understand the historical settler-colonial conquest of the U.S. frontier and West through a hallucinatory vision of "white flames and white lights" building dams to produce electricity that would lead, in turn, to residential and commercial development and the overall transformation of the American West into great "cities of lamps."[2]

As this vision of the coloniality of power develops during his vagabondage, its leitmotif of white light (candles, flames, lamps) abruptly concludes with a neo-Gothic vision of white people as transforming from white "animals with neon eyes" back into "white flames" that were "everywhere" in Seattle.[3] Indeed, when he reaches the Alaskan Way Viaduct, where the homeless Indian population tends to congregate, he sees three "large white flames" threatening a "tiny, old Indian woman" with physical harm. Smith rescues her from danger, and in the dialogue exchange that follows, he is tutored by this Indian woman about the "myths" and the continuing "lies" embedded in and camouflaged by Seattle's sleek, ahistorical skyline. Though she is literally houseless, this tribal woman informs him: "I ain't homeless. I'm Duwamish

Indian, and all this, the city, the water, the mountains, it's all Duwamish land. Has been for thousands of years. I belong here, cousin. I'm the landlady. And all these white people, even the rich ones living up in those penthouses, they're the homeless ones."[4]

In Alexie's staging of both John Smith's vagabondage in the Seattle area and his encounter with the elderly Duwamish woman in the Alaskan Way Viaduct, what we witness is not merely a psychotic vision of a de-realized or de-anthropomorphized white radiance that emanates from modernity's architectural developments. Rather, what *Indian Killer* underscores here and elsewhere in the novel is how the uncanny and unsettling presence of crime, waste, injustice, and the working poor and the homeless in the very center of the capitalist production of urban disciplinary space does not underscore an either/or ontology. Rather, Alexie's staging also allegorizes how at the very center of "white light"—this chromatic radiance supposedly exemplifying the sacred triumph of the forces of light over darkness—there exists a profane wound or scar, the materiality of which exposes how a repetitious history of past traumatic events continues into the tensed present. Both the original theft and the more recent clearing of so-called empty land in order to fill urban void spaces with the steel skeletons of skyscrapers in *Indian Killer* thus emerge as uncanny doubles of the dark, psychopathological crawlspaces and crevices of alleys, the tunnels and viaducts, and the abandoned commercial and blighted residential spaces occupied by a homeless cohort.

As a result, the novel intervenes in the official production of "the beauty of myths and the power of lies" in Seattle's history by presenting a spatial archaeology across a range of spatial scales: there is the macrocosmic level constituted by Seattle's architectural skyline, as noted above, the foundations of which are constructed above a hidden necropolis and aligned with a history of theft and exploitation; there is the microcosmic level constituted, for example, by the material presence of audiotapes of a Native woman's voice hidden in boxes in a university building's labyrinthine basement. It is a spatial archaeology whose excavation of this city "reveals various layers of past and present inhabitants of the city, of regulations that restricted access to certain areas, and of the [unequal] distribution of resources and development of infrastructures in those neighborhoods."[5] So the novel's spatial archaeology exposes to view various architectures of abandonment—the visible ruins of built environments; the trauma associated with the relinquishing of parental rights. And as we see throughout this novel, as well as in this scene from the "Cousins" chapter, there is the additional connotation of abandonment as an organized forgetting: as in memory loss; as in the outright suppression of the plural histories associated with any place of habitation where urbicide happens. "Every building was a tomb," John Smith realizes, as he contemplates burying the body of his own double figure—the putative mixed-blood Indian author Jack Wilson—into the "last" skyscraper in Seattle's concrete foundation.[6]

2. "*A war must have been fought here, though he had no idea when.*" Put most simply, *urbicide* connotes the murder of a city or greater urban area. More specifically, as Martin Coward has argued, the concept of urbicide alludes to three distinct forms of violence: "peacetime patterns of urban development characteristic of modernity that are perceived in some sense to deprive the city of part of its essential urbanity; the effects upon the city of the perceived relocation of war into its environs; the manner in which destruction of the built environment underpins a politics of exclusion." In times of war, such as the 1992–95 conflict in Bosnia that followed on the breakup of the former Yugoslavia, urbicide primarily connoted cities under siege; cities divided by walls and zones of demarcation; and cities in ruins as a result of the relocation of war into urban areas, the effects of which included—as we have seen in the cases of Sarajevo, Tripoli, Beirut, and now the Ukraine—the targeting of civilian populations. Whereas in peacetime, urbicide as a concept centers on emergent and extensive urban renewal and development initiatives (e.g., freeway construction; gentrification) designed to renovate not only a city's familiar downtown architectural sites (government centers; transportation corridors; museums and libraries; places of worship; monuments) but also to transform, and sometimes totally erase, historic neighborhoods that for decades served as visible material reminders of a city's historical plurality of various communities and their cultural traditions. So it is that in peacetime as well as in times of war, urbicide ultimately represents for Coward a series of "chronic disasters" that have been "inflicted not on explicitly defined enemies, but on a city and its citizenry."[7]

Take Hurricane Katrina's devastation of New Orleans, which exposed to view, as Andrew Herscher has commented, "a paradigmatically American variety of Urbicide, a form of urban destruction that occurs through the confluence of racial segregation, structural impoverishment, urban disinvestment, and natural hazard."[8] I quote Herscher at this juncture because his judgment stresses how urbicide as a distinct form of violence directed against a city and its citizenry results not only from a "natural hazard," such as a hurricane or earthquake or tornado. His judgment also includes, to borrow Coward's phrasing, the "chronic disasters" created by the segregation, regulation, and surveillance of marginalized urban spaces and peoples by those in economic and political power invested in a politics of exclusion. So it is that the American form of urbicide that Herscher describes represents a primary rationale to argue how, as illustrated by the Duhamish woman's comments to John Smith in *Indian Killer*, acts of urbicide and genocide cannot and should not in certain contexts be distinguished.

In any event, the crucial additional point to make about the "chronic disasters" represented by the varieties of urbicide is how, taken together, their implementation represents an assault not only on architectures and the production of space but also on urbanity itself. In this context, *urbanity* refers to the development of public spaces: civic buildings and public schools; museums and historical cultural sites and religious institutions; parks and cemeteries; commercial spaces and the so-called street life. Theoretically speaking, such spaces and architectural structures are available to all—hence the crucial adjectival term *public*. Because urbanity represents the potential for sharing such public spaces and architectures with both strangers and intimates, urbanity thus primarily connotes an existential and phenomenological street-level encounter with plurality and heterogeneity. "In this sense," Coward suggests, "it seems valid to describe the plurality constituted by the built environment as urbanity, and the destruction of buildings as urbicide."[9]

Take the Viramontes passage quoted above, for example, where the character named Mama registers the transformation of her Los Angeles neighborhood by means of the rhetorical figure of personification. Regarded here as an embodied network of the human body's arteries and limbs, the relentless amputation of the neighborhood's commercial enterprises and their residential blocks by new freeway construction exemplifies urbicide as a motivated attack on the very potential, much less the actual existence, of this neighborhood's heterogeneous urban fabric. Urbicide, then, constitutes the deliberate destruction of the architectural features of the urban built environment so as to erase the strata of alternative histories and cultures of a place. This erasure of plurality and difference reveals how urbicide indeed entails both urbanity and genocide. And as we see in the above extract from *Their Dogs Came with Them*, the character Mama's cognitive and affective disorientation as a result of the destruction of her neighborhood by new freeway construction is likened to the need to itch a phantom limb, this corporeal action symptomizing how the amputation of a certain material history and culture nevertheless leaves memory traces haunting this character's historical present.

3. "*War is architecture. Architecture is war.*" Published originally in the same year as his novel *Indian Killer*, Sherman Alexie's long poem "Inside Dachau," raises, in its third section, the following questions about his visit to the site of this abandoned concentration camp: "Why are we here? What have we come to see?" In the poem's final section, titled "below freezing," a recognition scene presented by a pair of tercets begin to answer such questions:

> Each building sat at right angles to the rest.
> Around each corner, I expected ghosts.
> Dachau was so cold I could see my breath.
>
> Everything was clean, history compressed
> into shoes, photographs, private notes.
> I have nothing new to say about death.[10]

Just as the museum itself is characterized earlier in the poem as being "simple," so too we learn that in advance of his visit to Dachau the poem's speaker anticipates experiencing "simple" emotions, such as the ones that go by the names of "hate, anger, sorrow."[11] But, unsurprisingly, once this speaker ventures inside Dachau's walls and fences and carefully restored buildings, he realizes "there were no easy answers inside the camp."[12] And as we witness in the two stanzas above, Alexie's persona focuses his specular gaze on this concentration camp's spatial archaeology: how the framing walls of the various buildings are precisely positioned at exact right angles to each other. In another direction, his gaze focuses on one building's display of material artifacts, these simply rendered here by a serial list: "shoes, photographs, private notes."[13] A horrific history thus "compressed" into clean architectural lines and interiors cleaned of human corpses by the museum's creators and their sponsors.

Through the discipline required by either the villanelle or sestina poetic formats it adopts, this long poem's aesthetic economy—its own orderly surface texture of regular metrics and rhymes—formally mirrors this concentration camp museum's territorialization and disciplining of space. Here then, both architectural and poetic lines together establish a seme/seam of composition. But this ambition to tell a historical narrative with a logical plot and a legible, contained meaning becomes unsettled throughout this poem and, as we witness in these two exemplary stanzas, by the swirling, spectral lines of decomposition interjected by the reference to the speaker's exhaled breath. A diverting sign of departure, a literal and figurative vanishing into thin air, this visible but ephemeral exhalation that foreshadows the lyric speaker's various, entwined temporal and spatial lines of flight away from the poem's presiding lyric present. One line of flight focuses on the genocidal violence the U.S. Army directed against tribal peoples during the nineteenth century at such sites as Sand Creek and Wounded Knee; another line of flight centers on this lyric speaker's melancholy shift from the memorializing architecture of abandonment at Dachau to introduce the glaring lack of historical reparations and the absence of any American Indian genocidal memorial museum in the United States.

Indeed, it turns out that the sight of the Holocaust victims' shoes heaped together in a building at Dachau prompts the lyric speaker's recall of still other abandoned shoes, all the "shoes of our dead" buried in the mass graves occupied by the tribal peoples massacred by the U.S. Army at such places as Sand Creek and Wounded Knee during the late nineteenth-century Indian wars in the United States. Such places that surely exemplify, as Alexie's German host Mikael suggests, but two of "all the Dachaus in the United States":

> We too could stack the shoes of our dead and fill a city
> To its thirteenth floor. What did you expect us to become?
> What do we indigenous people want from our country?
> We are waiting for the construction of our museum.[14]

And so, amid this camp's renovated architecture of abandonment and ruin, the fragile, somber truce between the poem's form and content—between its mutual investment in composition and decomposition—begins to fray and unravel. For as the poem proceeds inexorably toward its end, an initial repeated word such as *hosts* gets substituted for in the stanzas deploying the word *ghosts*. There is the presence of the "ghosts of unrepentant Nazis" who either presided over the death camp or escaped to South America.[15] And in the poem's final "below freezing" section, there are the "ghosts" that his haunted imagination conjures up as lurking behind any one of the death camp's buildings with their rational geometry of right-angled corners. These include the Nazis for sure but also, of course, the ghosts of the Jewish dead haunting Dachau, this former the site of flames and smoke and ashes located a mere ten miles from Munich.

The implied and explicit presence of such ghosts functions as a silent critique of the Dachau memorial site's compression of its history into displays of heaped-up and cleaned-up material artifacts, such items designed to provide a type of suture that would serve to mend a deep, festering wound in the skin of history, to turn an abiding melancholia into a successful stage for completed mourning. But such artifacts' material presence conjures up for Alexie's speaker the contrary impulse to defetishize the shoes, the photographs, and the personal notes—these harrowing material remainders and reminders of once whole bodies—and attend instead to the actual furnaces and to the fires and the ash clouds and to all the shallow graves whose visible disturbance of the earth leaves a scar on its surface as well one that sears the consciousness of the living. In the poem's final section, the contrapuntal parallelism supplied by Alexie's slant rhyming of the words "guest" and "ghost" echoes the similitude of homely and unhomely in the architectural uncanny's funereal cryptography of receptacle-like, recessed spaces of containment. Such as the concentration camp's fenced enclosure and the architecture of a poem's stanzas. Such as the shallow graves that once held and hid the decomposing dead, their absent presence now outlined by the crepuscular winter light at Dachau and Sand Creek and Wounded Knee. Such as shoes, the insoles of which encrypt the foot. Such as the crypt formed by the psychic receptacle of the unconscious produced by the repression of historical traumas in the serial chronic disasters prosecuted by urbicide and genocide.

4. *"I have nothing new to say about death."* This line concludes four of the seven stanzas in the poem's final "below freezing" section and also serves as the poem's final line. The uncanny repetition of this line performatively responds to the speaker's opening query: "What could I say about Dachau?" And so the line repeats itself at the end, in the process underscoring the poem's overarching theme about the aporia of meaning production, which accrues as a result of the inherently unspeakable and ungraspable nature of human mortality, especially as this fate is rendered by industrial scale repetition of labor and scientific management. And so the line repeats, this declaration annulling itself in the very act of its enunciation ("I have nothing new to say"), its insistent metrical rhythm and its regular return at the end of various stanzas underscoring the bass line of the poem's soundscape around which the solo riffs, the lyric speaker's improvisation and provocations grounded by a spectral materialism—the shoes and the letters that remain to remind us of the host of the dead and gone—these literal and figurative dead things and letters that nevertheless speak to us from beyond the grave. And so the line repeats itself, the phrase "nothing new" underscoring the poem's overall investment in exploring not only spatial but also temporal registers.

Such memento mori surely reconfigure external and internal spaces as a haunted cryptography, as I noted above. Their spooky presence also transforms this lyric speaker's phenomenological experience of everyday life into a liminal, betwixt-and-between spatiality and temporality. On the one hand, his felt stuckness in the temporal mode of the meantime: caught out in the present between that which is no longer (the dead and gone past) and that which has not yet happened (the future to come). In this meantime mode, the "no longer" remains uncannily alive, haunting the here and now. On the other hand, the "not yet" effectively saturates his historical present as well, to the degree that an anticipatory anxiety emerges, overdetermining this lyric speaker's mode of being in the world. "I have nothing new to say about death": the numbing beauty realized by the regular disappearance and return of this line to the poem's textured, granular surface embodies both the poem's motivation (to force the ghosts of traumatic, violent genocidal and urbicidal histories into the open) and, in the process, its accomplishment (to expose a spatial archaeology and a liminal temporality in which scabs and scars, not mending sutures, predominate). So as is the case with the visionary "injection architecture" proposed by Lebbeus Woods for the radical reconstruction of buildings destroyed by urbicide and genocide in such places as Sarajevo, San Francisco, and Havana, the historical scars parachuted or injected into the poem's present moment by Alexie's lyric speaker effectively produce "a stretched, extended, and crumpled space, a space of conjunction and disjunction, where the potentials of multiplicities and pluralities"—that is, the very heterogeneity that defines urbanity—just might spawn a transformative future amid the precariousness that defines how all this living is always just a hard way to go.[16]

Moreover, whether our critical focus centers on representations of urbicide or genocide, Alexie's creative work further exposes the complexity not only of the grieving process itself but also the difficult work of remembrance. As if exemplifying what Karen Barad has theorized about memory, such works as *Indian Killer* and "Inside Dachau" expose how remembering is not simply a cognitive reproduction of what was, which is to say not a simple matter of assembling and ordering past events as one might fit pieces of a jigsaw puzzle together. Instead, Alexie's creative works disclose how remembering and working through any traumatic event ought to be regarded as transpiring in a cognitive and affective field of dynamic, unruly longing within which guests as ghosts and ghosts as guests become entangled and yet differentiated in this world of shadows and hidden corners, where breath is aligned also with death in our own private Alaskan Way Viaduct or interior Dachau. As a process of discovery whose yearning enmeshes disparate spatial and temporal registers and statuses—Wounded Knee and Dachau; being a Spokane and being a Jew—*without* effacing the heterogeneity of the other.

And yet, an open question remains evident in "Inside Dachau," both the architecture of the place and that of the poem: What if the arrival of the anticipated future to come, this fabled "not yet," reveals, instead of this utopian hope, the rather uncanny compulsion—on the part of the people to come—to repeat the historical traumas that have been set in motion by those who no longer exist? For as he waits in the pause afforded by the meantime mode and in the below freezing weather of Dachau, Alexie's pensive lyric persona wonders "which people will light fires next and which people will soon be turned to smoke."[17] And with this prospect in mind, which is to say the uncanny repetition in the future of historical past genocides and urbicides, then surely the lyric speaker is absolutely right in his ritual sounding of the line "I have nothing new to say about death."

[**A**lphabet/Abecedario; **C**ryptography; **E**xposure; **G**raves; **P**sychometropolis; **R**ivers; **S**cene of the Crime]

Vagabondage, all this venturing in the slipstream

EXTRACTS

> Ah, that *via dolorosa* of the destitute, that *chemin de la croix* of the homeless. Ah, the mile after mile of granite pavement that *must* be, *must* be traversed. Walk they must. Move, they must; onward, forward, whither they cannot tell; why they do not know.
>
> —Frank Norris, *The Octopus* (1901)

> Where the train tracks intersected the road we followed the tracks, which led to the lake and the railroad bridge. The hoboes built on the shore in the bridge's very shadows. Our grandmother, to instill caution in us, had told us that a child who came too near a train was liable to be scalded to death where she stood by a sudden blast of steam, and that hoboes made a practice of whisking children under their coats and carrying them off.
>
> —Marilynne Robinson, *Housekeeping* (1981)

> For, as we know, vagabondage has had a double face in the modern period: a social and legal construction of bourgeois society that endows a "person without estate, without domicile" with the attributions of criminality, it is also—and for this very reason—a preferred role of the bohemian, the outcast artist, the rebellious poet. . . . Thus to have a "vagabond imagination" was the desired state of the poet.
>
> —Anthony Vidler, *The Architectural Uncanny* (1992)

> Understanding a sentence is much more like understanding a theme in music than one might think.
>
> —Ludwig Wittgenstein, as quoted in Stanley Cavell, *Here and There* (2022)

1. *Vagabond architecture*: "A new type of urban space and manner of habitation, in which nomadic, heterogeneous spaces of becoming intersect with the more established, demarcated and regulated space of urban realms."[1] Such as, for example, the intersection of a road with train tracks that cross a lake, on the shores of which "hoboes" camp in the railroad bridge's shadow. Such as part-time and seasonal "workampers" or "rubber tramps" who live in RVs, travel trailers, vans, cars, and pickup campers parked at KOA campgrounds or in Walmart parking lots and who work in distribution centers, warehouses, and vegetable and fruit fields.[2] In novelist and singer-songwriter Willy Vlautin's musical compositions and lyrics (recorded and performed with his band Richmond Fontaine), emphasis is placed on various characters' haunted vagabondages through a western landscape "where suburb, strip, and urban center have merged indistinguishably into a series of states of mind and which is marked by no systematic map that might be carried in the memory."[3] In "I Fell into Painting Houses in Phoenix, Arizona" (*Thirteen Cities*), the lyric speaker declares, "The suburbs in that town are a sprawl/ We never knew where we were at all." Literally and metaphorically, Vlautin's nomads are "Lost in This World," to cite the title of another track on this album, an epistemological and ontological predicament condensed for us in the song "Western Skyline" (*Winnemucca*) by repetitious images of blindness, inclement weather, and by a predominance of the interrogative mode: "The sky was cloudy, it was near dark/and you said, 'I can't see. Can you tell me where are we?'"

Through the journeys of their vagrant imaginations and bodies, Vlautin's characters, like Poe's nightwalker in "The Man of the Crowd," endure the essential unhomeliness of experience. In his music there are repetitive images of bleeding and scars and broken glass; of traumatized bodies reeling from beatings and seeking haven by being on the move—only then to arrive in a basement room or in a "foreign room with foreign noise,/ in a foreign bed, in a foreign town" ("Don't Look and It Won't Hurt"). The catalog of motel names that comprises the bulk of the lyrics to "Westward Ho" (*Thirteen Cities*) concludes with the lines, "Motel life ain't much of a life, and a motel ain't much of a home/But I found out years ago that a house ain't either."

In Vlautin's lyrical and sonic landscape, the settings and imagery of human vagabondage either across architectural thresholds (hallways; doors and windows) or their pausing temporarily to inhabit transit sheds (motels; restaurants; casinos; bars and clubs; parking lots and garages; warehouses; boarding houses and rental rooms) operate as physical and psychical metaphors for the overall contemporary erosion of bourgeois psychical, bodily, and social well-being.⁴ Such examples as this attest to the accuracy of Neil Campbell's comment about the overall atmosphere of precarity evident in Vlautin's production of both novels and songs: "*Dislocation* takes us away from the expectations of location—the myth of the West and its people as good life 'go-getters'—and plunges us into a different, murkier world of disappointment and loss, where characters are running *away* from something rather than *toward* its possibilities."⁵ Vagabondage, in short, being on the road or simply roughing it outside can connote, on the one hand, highest happiness—a life beyond the tedium of "stability and security"; and vagabondage also can connote insecurity, a life without guarantees—"life as 'emptiness,' life as the loneliness of the vagabond."⁶

2. "*Vagabond imagination was the desired state of the poet.*" This recurrent Vlautin theme gets underlined musically by the discordant chord progressions that mirror the lyric speakers' "continuous vertiginous sliding between affective states of terror, amusement, and sheer banality."⁷ This "vertiginous sliding" between affective states in Richmond Fontaine's lyrical and musical soundtracks of vagabondage is attached to the nomadism of bodies and minds. Yet it is also forwarded by Vlautin's signature montage construction, whose features function to trouble the lyric speakers' ability to make sense of their experiences, whether in the present moment or as conjured up by memory work: illusory optical effects; abrupt shifts in thought as well as spatial or temporal registers; the uncanny agency of vivid part objects, such as scarred white legs and bloodshot blue eyes, the blue glare of a TV screen across a face, a worn-out sock on a corpse found in an abandoned mining camp. Like the commodity form's fusion of concrete materiality and spectral exchange value, a casino's neon lights blaze into the night, but this optical illumination gets introjected by Vlautin's cast of pedestrian vagabonds as a felt darkness ("Casino Lights"). Conversely, the ghostlike, flickering apparition created by the glare of streetlamps on a white curtain of snow on a city street weirdly transforms "the night time into light," in the process illuminating an emergent paranoiac space in which a young couple seek asylum, occupying the claustrophobic confines of a public telephone booth when they flee from the sight of a car wreck in the near distance ("Somewhere Near").

The illusory and seemingly unnatural exchange of properties between night and day in these examples suggests how the phantasmagoria spawned by Vlautin's montage of various exposures—to the elements; to the opacity of the Other; to the structural dislocations of late capital—relays the haunting return of the repressed traumas produced by personal, regional, and transnational histories of loss and suffering. As the speaker in "I Got Off the Bus" (*You Can't Go Back*) belatedly recognizes: "I know what you abandon dies/ What you leave leaves you too/I know you can't go back/If there's nothing to go back to." This speaker's shift from a narrative mode (the various stops on his ultimately failed journey home) to this final summary judgment crucially deploys diction (such as the *what* and *nothing* here) that hovers in a liminal or interstitial space between ordinary everyday speech and lyric expression, achieving neither the concreteness of the denotative (what is the *what* and *nothing* here) nor the figurative level of lyric expression as it exhausts itself in the overall tonal uncertainty signaled by the subjunctive mode inaugurated by the *if*. It is as if here and elsewhere in Vlautin's lyrics the desire is to convey how "the state of homeless drifting" being described is conveyed by the straying of language. Indeed, Vlautin's lyric speakers' characteristic rhetorical compression, misnaming, and use of mixed metaphors represent a calculated deployment of the rhetorical figure of catachresis: where "language moves from word to word in a perpetual drifting," its unsettling obfuscation or gnomic abstraction underscoring Vlautin's post-urban sensibility "of the fragmentary, the chance, and the marginal."[8]

3. "*That* via dolorosa *of the destitute.*" The lyric narrative in "5 Degrees Below Zero" (*Winnemucca*) focuses on a man sitting in the claustrophobic interior of a Greyhound bus, on his way to his uncle's house in Las Vegas, having lost his money at gambling and having pawned all his stuff—including his music collection. Vlautin focalizes the narrative through this character, who has taken note of a guy sitting behind him, probably high on speed; an obese woman sitting next to him with metal braces on her legs; and, in front of him, two guys drinking a bottle, while across from his seat a girl gives herself an

ink pen tattoo while ignoring her crying child. He tries to ignore his interior surroundings and look out the bus window to glimpse the Great Basin Desert, but "snow covers everything" on the ground and, moreover, clouds make the "sea of stars unseen." His gaze into the distance thwarted, he cannot avoid seeing his own reflection in the window, an optical effect that triggers his increasingly morbid self-reflection about his recent history of loss and disappointment.

In this optical network of glances and reflections, shaped by the psychological dynamic of projection and introjection, the motif of the "double" emerges: his own reflection in the window's glass; the doubling of the present moment with his retrospective reflections. Due to the bus window, now a reflecting mirror rather than a transparent glass opening onto an external world, the affective field created by his anxiety is simultaneously an unhomely internal and external space: on the one hand, the snow-covered desert blankness outside the window mirrors his own feeling of emptiness; on the other hand, his anticipatory anxiety over some repressed desire he presumably has already known and perhaps will not be able to resist in this moment, when he begins to feel its seductive pull. "Swimming in a sea of rage," he demands the bus driver drop him off, who obliges his request. And so he gets off the bus and begins traipsing through the snow-covered desert plain, leaving his coat and his few other personal belongings on the bus. Spying city lights in one direction, he walks in the opposite direction for hours, so it seems, and eventually gets lost, unable to find the snow-covered highway, and is fully exposed to the elements out there in the open in the five-degrees-below-zero weather.

In this song of homeless wandering, the uncanny effect created by its repetition of "the double" motif through the optics of reflection accrues precisely because the double motif does not really double a visual presence at all. Rather, this motif underscores this song's depiction of reality as fundamentally fissured by difference, distance, and separation—by alien gaps or abysses. The promise of similitude or likeness inherent in mirror reflections and in spatial doublings and, to take another example, in the reverberating sound of echoes—this promise cannot and will never be realized. In this harrowing optical network of observer and observed, then, all of us are trapped in a voyeuristic space of glances and reflections, this space initially provoking an unsettling, affective dread, and then this persona's abrupt vagabondage into a void constituted by the blankness of white space. An errant wandering in this song foreshadows the vagabondage envisioned by the lyric speaker out and away in the southwestern desert depicted in "A Ghost I Became" (*Thirteen Cities*). And as this latter song's highly compressed, self-reflexive narrative unfolds, we witness how its speaker's projection of himself as becoming a dematerialized specter (ghost) is linked with another desire: for the self to become reduced not only to a corporeal mirage but also to one defined by sheer velocity.

So he is portrayed as "heading farther, heading farther now/ I'm heading farther out and away" across the blank page of the desert toward the vanishing point of the horizon. But implicit in this song's lyric, as well as by the narrative of "5 Degrees Below Zero," is that such vagabondage is not directed toward any definable goal in any mapped territorial space, and certainly not toward philosophical closure or abstract thinking. This and other journeys by those seeking solace in Vlautin's music inclines rather toward an external space whose abiding silence and apparent blankness, whether imaged as the desert or snow-covered earth, does not constitute the end of language (nor that of the sound of music), but rather "the directionless and unforeseeable transformation of abstraction into meaning, from referent into figure, from biographical contingency into linguistic expression" inexorably linked to concrete, corporeal human existence and the matter and mattering of things.[9]

[**B**oredom; **E**xposure; **F**reeways; **I**dyll; **M**otel noir; **N**oir motel; **O**il rich; **R**ivers; **W**indows]

Windows

EXTRACTS

He found himself in the window of a pawnshop, full of fur coats, diamond rings, watches, shotguns, fishing tackle, mandolins. All these things were the paraphernalia of suffering. A tortured high light twisted on the blade of a gilt knife, a battered horn grunted with pain.
—Nathanael West, *Miss Lonelyhearts* (1933)

Brandon pressed his nose against the glass and looked downward, spotting a line of shelters between the train tracks and the river, teetering house-tents of oil-stained plywood, sun-bleached blue tarpaulin, frayed nylon rope, and aluminum foil. They looked like ground-hugging tree houses, improvised assemblages built by children and taken over by tubercular adults. A few humans sat on chairs in between their creations in this village as it followed the curve in the tracks, their roofs a quilt of tarpaulin and wood forming a long crescent dotted with the occasional column of smoke. . . . The train rolled slowly toward the man, and for a few seconds Brandon was directly above him. He bore a long scar on his cheek oozing red and black liquids. A battle wound? Brandon wondered.
—Héctor Tobar, *The Barbarian Nurseries* (2011)

She looked out at the country mushrooming on the other side of the glass. She knew what it contained, its colors, the penury and the opulence, hazy memories of a less cynical time, villages emptied of men. But on contemplating the tense stillness of the night, the darkness dotted here and there with sparks, on sensing that insidious silence, she wondered, vaguely, what the hell might be festering out there: what grows and what rots when you're looking the other way. What's going to appear? She whispered to herself, pretending that as soon as they passed that lamppost, or that one, or that one, she'd see what it was that had been going on in the shadows.

—Yuri Herrera, *Signs Preceding the End of the World* (2015)

1. "*What's going to appear*?" In the literature of contemporary unhomely urban Wests, the psychological and geocultural cognitive mapping of social relations by narrators and characters focuses on the phenomenology associated with threshold zones or precincts of transition and passage. The segmentation of space provided by windows and doors and glass curtain walls; the transitional passageways of hallways and corridors and elevators or escalators—such threshold zones or precincts mark both corporeal and optical commerce between or across different spatial and even temporal registers, a development that often transforms a given narrative's descriptive tableau into a transgressive singular event disclosing cognitive and psychological dissonance or unease. Consider, for starters, the examples provided by the extracts from Héctor Tobar's *The Barbarian Nurseries* and Nathanael West's *Miss Lonelyhearts*. In Tobar's novel, the familiar and somewhat monotonous repetitive temporality of one character's daily commute to work gets abruptly interrupted as his scanning gaze of surveillance out of a passenger train's window sights a homeless encampment sprawling below the railway's elevated tracks. This brief moment in the train's journey gets dilated in narrative time, as the spectator on the moving train initially takes a visual inventory of this homeless encampment, noting how its spread and sprawl constituted an architectural disfigurement of the cityscape, before attending to how this unhomely, temporary built environment has its visual equivalent in the homeless human bodies inhabiting it: he sees the collective gaggle of "tubercular adults"; he has a close-up view of one homeless man displaying a wounded face.[1] In the extract from Nathanael West's novel *Miss Lonelyhearts*, the narrator describes an abject character's street-level view of disparate items displayed behind a pawnshop window. This optical positioning in space and this character's scanning gaze combine here to articulate—that is, both to express and to connect—these disparate items on display comprising, this character judges, the "paraphernalia of suffering."[2]

Like human skin—simultaneously an impermeable and permeable surface membrane—clear plate glass windows constitute architectural components of transitional or threshold space, their presence mediating the encounter between a projective human gaze of desire and an exterior world mushrooming into shape beyond the window in the morning or evening light. Along with modern architecture's investment in open floor plans that allow for the greater circulation of air, light, and physical movement, such technological developments as plate glass windows materialize what Anthony Vidler labels as modernity's investment in the "myth of transparency": the transparency of the self both to itself and to the natural world that encompasses it; the transparency of the self to other selves; and the transparency of all selves to the larger social formation. Transparency thus connotes the utopian dream of legibility, of coherence, and of a mutual co-presencing achieved by a projective gaze's apprehension of that which heretofore has been hidden or unknown and hence not yet comprehended. Nevertheless, as we witness in all of the above textual excerpts, this utopian dream of transparency can morph in uncanny fashion into one or more of a trio of nightmarish doubles or antithetical opposites of transparency. Instead, "what's going to appear" is material and corporeal evidence of everyday life's elemental opacity; the diffused light of translucence; and the distorting and disorienting effects of reflectivity or mirroring.[3] Tobar's character is left wondering whether or not the one homeless man's face reveals a "battle wound." West's character displaces his suspended agency and suffering onto the material objects arrayed behind the glass of the pawnshop window: the blade of a gilt knife "tortures" the artificial light shed by an overhead electrical fixture; a "battered" musical instrument "grunts" in pain instead of sounding melodic notes.

With this context in mind, let us consider briefly the above extract from Yuri Herrera's novel *Signs Preceding the End of the World*, which focuses on a young female protagonist who has been sent on a mysterious and fateful journey north to El Norte. In this early moment of her trip she is described as looking out a bus window and contemplating the swart night—its "darkness dotted here and there with sparks"; its "insidious silence." In the daylight hours she knows with some certainty the country outside the window she passes through, the familiar signs of its "penury and opulence," of its villages empty of men, either already dead or forced to seek work in El Norte. But now, as darkness surrounds the bus and she approaches the border of unfamiliar country, she begins to wonder with some trepidation "what the hell might be festering out there: what grows and what rots when you're looking the other way." Without a map to guide her, and with her anticipatory anxiety underscored as the bus passes by lamppost after lamppost, she keeps her faint future hope for a legible world to appear eventually by pretending that one of the highway's lampposts suddenly would shine a light on "what it was that had been going on in the shadows."[4] Such scenography as this effectively binds together both ontological and epistemological speculation (the contemplation of or inchoate thoughts about the future); the specular, as in the motifs of the gaze and of reflected and refracted images; and spectrality, as exemplified either by the haunting presence in the narrative's continuous present of undead, restless specters or the phantasmagoric, dreamlike state in which real and apparitional elements blur together, effectively transforming a familiar domestic space into an uncanny paranoid or even panic space. Even as Joan Didion claims, in her essay "Notes from a Native Daughter," that the truths about any particular place are "elusive and must be tracked with caution," the point to make in this context is how this dialectical interplay between transparent and enigmatic opaque spaces, bodies, utterances, and material objects in all of these textual extracts represents one of the truths repetitively unveiled by literary and cultural histories of settler colonialism both in the North American West and Greater Mexico.[5] In brief, one answer to the question "What's going to appear?" in all of these textual encounters of transit and transience that are structured by a leitmotif of visual surveillance is how an unsettling spectacle of primitive violence saturates everyday life.

2. "*A battle wound*?" In his mapping of the new social relations of the urban West as depicted in Raymond Chandler's crime novels published between the Great Depression and the 1950s, Fredric Jameson elaborates how Chandler's architectural modeling of his thematic content inevitably centers on an expanded sense of "the office." Business offices. Bedrooms with chaise lounges and kitchen nooks and studies with couches and books. Secluded guest houses. Front porches with furniture. Public and private libraries. Hotel lobbies. Private booths in restaurants and clubs and bars. In Jameson's view, all these spaces populating Chandler's crime fiction essentially represent isometric transformations of the office, whose original form is that of private detective Philip Marlowe's office in a downtown Los Angeles business building. What happens in this office doesn't stay there. Rather, it migrates to an analogue such as Marlowe's rented, private residence in the Los Angeles hills near Laurel Canyon Boulevard. Structurally speaking, such interior and exterior spaces duplicate or replicate each other: they function similarly as spaces for meetings and exchanges of information; their spatiality represents the conflation of private and public affairs. In Chandler's prose, their architectures provide descriptive pauses in which to assay a phenomenology of waiting and watching.[6]

Toward the end of Raymond Chandler's 1953 novel *The Long Goodbye*, private detective Philip Marlowe drives to his rented house in the hills above Los Angeles after being grilled by police detectives investigating his client Roger Wade's death. After arriving home, he mixes himself a drink and then sips it while he gazes out a picture window at the vast array of the city's lights illuminating the darkness, all the while hearing the continuous sound of traffic streaming on the nearby Laurel Canyon Boulevard. The banshee wail of police cars and fire trucks he hears in the distance illustrates how a soundscape outside the home saturates both its interior space and prompts in Marlowe a stream of critical reflections:

> Twenty-four hours a day somebody is running, somebody else is trying to catch him. Out there in the night of a thousand crimes people were dying, being maimed, cut by flying glass, crushed against steering wheels or under heavy tires. People were being beaten, robbed, strangled, raped, and murdered. People were hungry, sick, bored, desperate with loneliness or remorse or fear, angry, cruel, feverish, shaken by sobs. A city no worse than others, a city rich and vigorous and full of pride, a city lost and beaten and full of emptiness.
>
> It all depends on where you sit and what your own private score is. I didn't have one.
>
> I didn't care. I finished the drink and went to bed.[7]

We oversee Marlowe as he gazes out his window and, for starters, speculates about the two major chronotopes or narrative time-space configurations predominant in the literary and cultural representation of Los Angeles: cars on the highway and death.[8] The affective force relayed by Marlowe's rendering of such familiar chronotopes flows from the combined pressure of its grammatical and linguistic patterning. As his projective gaze strives in this moment to articulate the noir reality of this urban landscape and soundscape's continuous noise and motion ("twenty-four hours a day"), Marlowe's enunciation introduces each grammatical unit of meaning via anaphora, or the repetition of initial words or phrases: "somebody is running"/"somebody else is trying"; "People were dying"/"People were being beaten"/"People were hungry"; "A city no worse"/"a city rich"/"a city lost." The effect of this cadenced, aural repetition is to gather this passage's separate clauses and phrases into a spatial synchrony, a type of refrain instead of a mere heaping together of disparate things.

And yet, functioning as a counterweight to such relatively regular pacing and aural repetitions is the sprawl and spread promoted by this passage's serial grammar and syntax. Take Marlowe's itemized inventory of types of car accidents and of violent crimes. And then consider the strings of brief clauses and phrases Chandler deploys to register Marlowe's understanding of the mental and physical effects of human abjection: "People were hungry, sick; bored, desperate with loneliness or remorse or fear, angry, cruel, feverish, shaken by sobs." From referencing human death or disfigurement by broken windows or windshields to human bodies being crushed either by steering wheels or by the weight of heavy tires; from name-checking various violent crimes against persons to noting the corporeal privation (hunger) and illness of marginalized citizens who live bare lives; from listing such affective states as existential boredom or the ugly feeling of rage to assaying different interpretations of this city's ultimate truth—this passage's propulsive movement oscillates between plain talk (the concrete examples) and heavy judgment (the register of the explanatory), variously changing its pace before its spread and sprawl across the page exhausts itself via a single sentence paragraph describing his retreat to his bedroom, in the wake of which he declares his indifference to any particular interpretive evaluation of the city's true meaning.

That Marlowe's pensive reflection on the city's truth pivots between assertion and self-doubt and then concludes with his proclamation of indifference is not all that unexpected, I suppose, since his existential ennui in the wake of his interrogation by the police is compared to the spatial distance he notices between the stars illuminating the Los Angeles night sky, this rhetorical figure flowing seamlessly into his personification of the Hollywood Hills as having its "shoulder" slashed by Laurel Canyon Boulevard as it knifes through the canyon. The rhetoric of this passage reveals how Marlowe's projective gaze of surveillance out of a window with a panoramic view discovers external objective correlatives for his interior world's cognitive and affective unsettlement. Consider his observation that a temporal and spatial rift exists between the world of human history and the geological and ecological history of the earth. The visible rift in the topography and geology of the foothills created by the boulevard's construction (and the arterial network of streets branching from it) then provides him with a metaphor to describe his hard-won belief about a complementary rift that defines human social relations. So he considers the anonymous individuals accidentally dead or maimed, lying in the privacy of their own vehicles or under the heavy tires of other vehicles driven by complete strangers. So he considers, while looking through his car's windshield after crossing a saddle in the hills and entering Idle Valley, the postwar transformation of this rural location into an exclusive suburban community. And as his gaze settles on the vast watery expanse of the Pacific Ocean in the near distance from Idle Valley, his thoughts focus on its endless tidal motion and the continuous prevailing winds that cut through rifts in the coastal range of hills, an ecology, Marlowe speculates, that explains not only Idle Valley's climate but also the atmospheric torpor of its inhabitants—their existential drift and overall languor.

With the modernist thematic of anomie and alienation materializing through an entwined imagery of spatial and social rifts, we arrive at what I shall call the emergent problem of abstraction prominent throughout the length of *The Long Goodbye*. With the exception of his topological allusion to Laurel Canyon Boulevard, the content of Marlowe's cascading reflections proceeds via rhythmic repetitions of indefinite pronouns and common nouns. On one level, the cadenced repetition and return of the same words at regular intervals in this passage provides both a measure of acoustic coherence and a degree of affective comfort or relief as Marlowe's melancholy appraisals course from the passage's beginning to its weary end. On another level, however, the relative abstraction forwarded by Marlowe's diction and his sententious pronouncements dislocates his imagined scenarios regarding the evidence of human alienation and abjection from the immediate Los Angeles socioeconomic and cultural context. I am thinking here of an earlier scene in the novel when Marlowe interviews the financial tycoon Harlan Potter and listens to his lengthy disquisition on the evils of the money form, the problem with organized labor, and the corruption of politics and the police. By contrast, Marlowe's cognitive and affective mapping of the "angry city" arrayed outside and below his view from the window sublimates or elides local issues and local historical factors that haunt his investigative casework: the systemic class and racial hierarchies spatialized in the segregated Los Angeles built environment; the local histories of continuous human migration to the area spawned by uneven economic development; the boom and bust cycles associated with finance-capitalism's speculative endeavors. Instead of sociology or social history, Marlowe offers up an epitomizing moral judgment: that no matter the accumulating record of vehicular and human mayhem the "people" endure in their everyday lives, Marlowe concludes—in a moment of radical acceptance that also constitutes a relinquishment of his caring—that Los Angeles represents "a city no worse than others."

Nevertheless, as we can see by the string of two parallel, balanced phrase fragments that follow this abstraction of Los Angeles as a city equivalent to all other cities in the emergent Cold War era, Marlowe immediately refines this summary judgment. This "city no worse than others" apparently, like any city, also can be judged either as "rich and vigorous and full of pride," "lost and beaten and full of emptiness," or perhaps both. Each interpretive perspective is possible, he suggests. And any of these perspectives can be justified, for in the end, "It all depends on where you sit and what your own private score is." In what constitutes a revelatory act of bad faith on his part, Marlowe claims he neither possesses an opinion on the validity of these dueling interpretive perspectives on the city's "truth" nor has any "private score" to settle. And so he finishes his drink, leaves his glass window on the world, and turns to go to his bedroom, leaving this "night of a thousand crimes" to proceed as it always has, as it is now in this moment, and as it will always proceed into the foreseeable future regardless of his presence or absence. Grounded by his voice's continuous present tense and his logic of abstraction ("people"; "a city"), Marlowe's withdrawal here to lick his wounds underscores not only his mental and bodily exhaustion. It also represents his having achieved, for the time being at least, the exalted cognitive, affective, and corporeal pose of cynical indifference. Such a classic noir move!

3. "*I don't care.*" Exploring the distinction between the "ugly feelings" of disgust and indifference, Sianne Ngai notes how the latter term connotes the kind of contempt ultimately associated with complacency. Rather than, say, an active distaste for the object of contempt, indifferent persons never truly doubt their superiority or rank. Indifference thus can be related both to pity and that milder form of disgust known as disdain. And in order to achieve that exalted feeling state of indifference, my relationship to an object or person within my purview must be deemed unworthy of my affective investment. They or it can and should be dismissed or ignored—or at best (barely) tolerated.[9] To be sure, Marlowe's achieved pose of indifference perhaps results from a deep-seated arrogance, rather than flowing from his pity or disdain. Nevertheless, I want to suggest that his pose of indifference is more brittle, less assured than this passage's overall brusque tonality would have us believe. His indifference more closely resembles a defensive reaction, one triggered by his increasingly troubled, inchoate recognition of his ineffectuality in managing, and hence mastering, the intricate plots emerging during his investigation. Take the initial moment of Marlowe's gaze out the window when he characterizes the city's nighttime illumination as casting an "electric glare." This declaration seems rather straightforward, but *glare* can function grammatically here either as a noun or verb. Considered as a noun, *glare* signifies the degree of visible illumination produced by electricity or, say, the look of an agitated, threatening, or unfriendly face. Considered as a verb, *glare* connotes the city's illuminated lights as themselves looking—as agential subjects reciprocating Marlowe's gaze rather than solely existing as passive objects under his sway.

Such a recognition of the city's potential sentience as a quasi-object/quasi-subject solicits us also to recognize Marlowe's abjection in the wake of his earlier interrogation by the police. At the end of the police interrogation sequence immediately preceding the scene where Marlowe contemplates the view of Los Angeles from his rented home's window, Captain Hernandez says to him: "No hard feelings, I hope." Marlowe's response: "No feelings at all, Captain. No feelings at all." Validating the police captain's hope while at the same time correcting this man's operating assumption that "hard feelings" might be in play, Marlowe judges, on his drive home, that his ambiguous response to the captain's question was "exactly right." His response both indicates that the captain and the police interrogation itself are not worthy of his affective investment, and simultaneously, through his repetition of the "no feelings" phrase, he affirms the paradoxical truth of the matter. He says he does not harbor "hard" feelings "at all," much less toward the police captain. But what he does feel is a numbed blankness or void—a nothingness "as hollow and empty as the spaces between the stars."[10] This intriguing, Chandleresque astral simile asserts that an affinity exists between his interior affective state and the vast, external and dark emptiness of the cosmos. Furthermore, his projection that the stars of the night sky metaphorically constitute an external "double" for his interior world gets torqued even further, for his next observation returns to earth, his scanning gaze shifting to consider a technological double of the distant stars—the city's electric lights. This speculative labor, which confirms his alienation, can be seen to complement Marlowe's corresponding social isolation, spatialized here by his detached prospect view above the cityscape's glaring lights and its discordant noises and nonstop mayhem.

Such rhetorical figures provide a stark contrast to the more recognizable and codifiable feelings he attributes to all the people who live below his window with its view overlooking this "angry city" on this and any other "night of a thousand crimes" in Los Angeles: boredom; the desperation associated "with loneliness or remorse or fear"; anxiety; and hysteria ("shaken by sobs"). What, then, is at stake with regard to Marlowe's achieved pose of affective indifference? One could say of course that his pose of indifference recapitulates a cynical noir perspective that things are as they are, have been, and seemingly always will be. And with perspective in mind, the indifference he feels and voices to himself through a series of abstractions and totalizing summary judgments would seem to endorse, by default, the existing institutional structures and hierarchical power relations as *eternal* entities and verities. Still, could it not also be the case that his achieved pose of indifference discloses—via its final ironizing of the pious bromides which would have us believe this city is "no worse than any other"—his drive to resist any interpretive much less legal closure? Put differently, in this moment it is as if we oversee him mentally and physically withdrawing both from "the project of representing and transmitting easily recognizable sentiments" and of closing down on interpretive options.[11] And given the impersonal second-person pronoun "you" that Marlowe introduces as this textual moment draws to an end, should we not also consider here that Chandler represents his major character's achieved indifference precisely to unsettle our identification with and attachments to the status quo of cultural and genre expectations?

At the level of literary form as well as theme, then, we witness in Marlowe's abjection here a refusal of modernity's myth/dream of transparency, legibility, and continuous progress. Marlowe's translation of local historicity into the abstraction of a universal subject ("people"), his pose of indifference, and his nascent recognition of his suspended agency in the matter of Terry Lennox's disappearance and Roger Wade's murder—these very features embedded in his effort at cognitively mapping Los Angeles while he gazes out one of his house's windows eerily anticipate both the waning of affect and the breakdown in coherence that, along with the nostalgia mode, will be regarded as the key features of an emergent postmodern aesthetic that Jameson will claim, approximately three decades after the publication of *The Long Goodbye*, to be the cultural logic of multinational corporate capitalism or so-called late capitalism. All that is missing here in this prospect view from a window is the paranoiac tonality that will come to the foreground in Brett Easton Ellis's *Less Than Zero*, published in the same year (1985) as Jameson's groundbreaking essay.

[**B**oredom; **F**reeways; **M**otel Noir; **N**oir Motel; **P**sychometropolis; **S**cene of the Crime; **T**elevision]

X-ray, let us talk crossly now

EXTRACTS

From letters by A. P. Ousdal, Doctor of Osteopathy in Santa Barbara, to J. P. Harrington. On December 9, 1930, Ousdal was issued US Pat. No. 1,784,382, for an apparatus for utilizing solar radiations for therapeutic purposes.

    1. I took it upon myself to take care of this Indian as he has been very sorely neglected. I found him sick with gangrene of the leg. I immediately began to photograph and X-ray him in order to get some records for comparative studies before he should die. . . . I am trying to make several sets of X-rays, not neglecting any bone whatever. . . . When I get the sets completed, I will certainly cooperate with the Smithsonian Institution, making an interesting exhibition and a small booklet of my study.
    —Deborah A. Miranda, *Bad Indians: A Tribal Memoir* (2013)

All day long the heavy hearselike Cadillacs of Care Ambulance back up just to the left of emergency parking. All day long, just outside my window, their gurneys sail past to cobalt, radiation therapy. The ambulances are gray, the drivers wear gray, the blankets are gray, the patients are yellow-gray except where the doctors have marked their skulls or throats with a dazzling red Magic Marker X.
    —Lucia Berlin, *A Manual for Cleaning Women* (2015)

The boy's father tries to chime in, mediating. He tells the boy about Man Ray's "rayographs," and the strange method with which Ray composed them, without a camera, placing little objects like scissors, thumbtacks, screws, or compasses directly on top of photosensitive paper and then exposing them to light.

FIG. 11. Man Ray, *Untitled Rayograph (Gun with Alphabet Stencils)*, 1924. Gelatin silver print, 29.5 cm x 23.5 cm (11 ⅝ in. x 9¼ in.). © Man Ray Trust ARS-ADAGP. Courtesy of the J. Paul Getty Museum.

> He tells him how the images Ray created with this method were always like the ghostly traces of objects no longer there, like visual echoes, or like footprints left in the mud by someone who'd passed by long ago.
>
> —Valeria Luiselli, *Lost Children Archive* (2019)

1. *X as signifying an intersection or crossing.* In a vignette appearing toward the end of *Dreamland: The Way Out of Juárez*, Charles Bowden introduces an extended framing narrative. This narrative opens by drawing our attention to the reciprocal interplay that exists in the Chihuahuan desert ecosystem between its higher-elevation grasslands and mesas, its valley floors, and its seasonal cycles of heat and monsoonal rains. Whereas the grasses flow "golden in the heat," the arrival of monsoonal rains triggers their somewhat magical transformation into a green "sheet of life" that brings into sharper relief the contours of both the mesa tops and the valley floor.[1] Bowden then suggests that the very agency embodied by this vegetation's seasonal germination and its spread of vibrant color across the high desert lands signifies the inextinguishable, surging presence of desire itself: this green sheet of life represents for him an ancient "sea of yearning." This rhetorical swerve from depicting the greened-up grasslands of spring and summer as a sheet of life to portraying them as a labile, flowing sea also underscores how this personified desert ecosystem's yearning constitutes a transgressive desire. After all, its flow trespasses both private property boundaries and the geopolitical survey line demarcating the U.S.-Mexico border. And just as the desert ecosystem yearns, so too do human subjects. Border cities such as Juárez have emerged in this desert ecosystem and have increased in size due to the serial migration of people from both the isolated ranchos adorning the Chihuahuan high desert grasslands and mesas and the jacales dispersed across the desert valley floor below, the latter of which are more primitive dwellings, barely shaded from the desert heat by stands of forlorn-looking mesquite trees. And as he further observes, as a consequence of more recent international trade agreements (such as NAFTA) and the rise of the maquiladora economy, the drug cartels with their *sicarios* and their secret death houses and the people who are tortured and murdered in them also define this desert ecosystem's intersection with human ecologies.

For Bowden, the crucial point is that all this ceaseless human and nonhuman migration and all this enmeshment of human ecology with that of the Chihuahuan desert ecology has fostered a deadly and ultimately debilitating kind of category confusion of appearance and reality. "Just as the homes of slaughter look like every other home on the block," Bowden writes, "so too does the land surrounding the city look normal and good for the soul." So

Bowden, by stages, arrives at a crucial point: that the seasonal emergence of the desert as a green, grassy sheet of life functions more like a trance state or beautiful mirage, distracting us from the harsh reality that the grinding machinery of global trade has transformed Juárez into a flourishing necropolis. The result is a chiasmus, or crossing, of appearance, dream, and reality: "There is no line between the grasslands or the deserts and the grave with a dose of lime, it all flows together and it comes from what we are and what the land is and what we have become." "It all flows together": in the dialectical entanglement of human and natural history transpiring in this regional borderland, a singular part object (a grave with a dose of lime) represents the whole of "it," just as—in the manner of the rhetorical figure known as synecdoche—the whole of "it" simultaneously gets condensed into this part object. In the macrocosmic "there" of the surrounding high desert grasslands and valley floors of the Chihuahuan desert, bodies layered with a dose of lime are decomposing in secret graves, just as is the case in the microcosmic "here" represented by the backyard and patio of a cartel death house in Juárez, under which lie corpses similarly layered with a dose of lime.

In this opening vignette describing the intersection of ecologies and topographies and overlapping zones of morbidity, Bowden's quasi-allegorical vision portrays "a sense of life bereft of any secure reference to transcendence, of life utterly exposed to the implacable rhythms of emergence and decay, of erosion and entropy."[2] In one direction, "what commentators and politicians call problems" devolving from this regression to creaturely life, Bowden asserts, "are no more than how these facts manifest themselves."[3] These "implacable rhythms" of natural history are paralleled by the rhythms of capitalist economic and cultural development, such as the facts of a human population's appetite for illegal drugs; the unceasing demand for cheap and docile labor; the economic and political policies that promote both deracination and increased inequalities in standards of living; and the violence against women perpetrated both on the immigrant trails in the Chihuahuan desert and in the streets of Juárez. And because no one along this geopolitical and ecological borderland desires to face "the implications of our appetites and policies," the cartel death house on Calle Parsioneros that resides at the center of the text of *Dreamland* arguably represents this city's "truth center." As a result of the "slaughter" that happened there as a result of sicario labor, the cartel death house emblematizes the hemispheric drug crisis, Bowden claims, precisely because its very existence—this unassuming, normal-looking, two-story beige townhouse—beggars both our understanding and imagination, as well as challenges the capacity of our verbal and visual discourse to represent its horror. And because the existence of the cartel death house exposes the systemic bad faith and false consciousness evident in the prevailing bureaucratic and political language, and because neither forensic science nor the legal apparatus seems able to "catch the music of a new world being born," Bowden further argues "we need a decent X-ray machine, one that can go beyond staring through flesh and seeing bone, one that can unravel more than DNA, one that can capture what we cannot even remember, a ray that sees where we came from and what we have become."[4]

2. X *as an unknown quantity, variable, or identity*. In traditional two-dimensional or plain X-ray radiography, where high-energy, invisible wave lengths pass through a patient or object and strike a plate of undeveloped film, the resulting exposure to electromagnetic radiation allows us, as a result of the developed photographic image or plate, to stare through flesh and see bone. Furthermore, like the desert grasslands' ephemeral green sheet of life and the death house's familiar beige stucco front, traditional X-ray radiography exposes an elemental rift between the visible realm of appearances, the way things look, and the substantial reality of an observed thing or event. For the technical fact about traditional X-ray imaging is this: the static X-ray image we view on a photographic plate or glass screen is not and cannot really be the material thing in and of itself.[5] What we really see when looking at the result of an X-ray imaging process are reflections of the object being exposed to view. That is, what the photographic record—this also filtered so as to reduce scatter—of a selected material object reveals is its transmission of isotopes of itself in response to the applied kinetic energy of invisible light waves that are shorter than ultraviolet rays and typically longer than gamma rays.

Given this inherent temporal lag in X-ray radiography, then, what the resulting X-ray image reveals is actually the record, in the present moment of our viewing, of an object's immediate past existence. Any X-rayed image constitutes a spectral arrivant bearing visual evidence of what we were, what we have become, and where we are headed—which may well be toward a future beyond all reckoning (if the X-ray scan reveals a terminal disease in progress). It is as if we are sentenced always to look at "the ghostly traces of objects no longer there, like visual echoes, or like footprints in the mud by someone who'd passed long ago," to draw from the description of Man Ray's "rayographs" (or photograms) in the above extract from Valeria Luiselli's novel *The Lost Children Archive*.

To be sure, Bowden's critique of traditional X-ray radiography is not that such diagnostic medical technology fails to expose a body's hidden trauma. Rather, his implied critique of traditional X-ray radiography centers on how it serves to petrify or freeze history and thus, in the end, only provide partial diagnostic data. After all, traditional radiological snapshots can neither provide 3D information nor examine the inspected body part or object in real time (as, say, a CAT scan can do). Moreover, since bones absorb the electromagnetic radiation during the procedure, X-rays do not necessarily provide significant medical data with regard to the health of organs or soft tissue masses. Bowden's claim that we need a "decent X-ray machine" represents his desire to "go beyond" any mimetic or realistic representation of flesh and bone, any quantification of human life as a DNA strand, so as to bring all "the curious and the ignorant and the idle" closer to comprehending the full dimension of the "new kind of reality" shaping the illusory, yet seductive "lullaby of consumption and ease" that composes the official soundtrack of "planet murder."[6]

The above lines, in any event, represent how I understand why Bowden's critique of traditional X-ray radiography centers on its inability to provide the real (rather than the official) truths about "where we came from and what we have become" that are exposed by the plague of contagious violence in Greater Mexico. Gazing at photographic slides of a human hand rising out of the Chihuahuan Desert sand or looking at the decomposing dead bodies exhumed from the cartel death house crime scene in Juárez, Bowden confesses to feeling that any interpretations are destined to lag behind full apprehension and, hence, comprehension: "I can't decide if I'm hearing the cries of a hard birth, or something more like a death rattle."[7] In our current state of emergency in the borderlands, we are sentenced to inhabit a state of suspended agency and a degree of ignorance: "The future is here, even though I can't even catch a trace of the rotting bodies with their gaping toothy mouths."[8] The confident declaration ("the future is here") is immediately put under erasure ("even though I can't even catch a trace"). To borrow Walter Benjamin's phrasing, it is as if everything about the natural and unnatural history of this borderland place "from the very beginning, has been untimely, sorrowful, unsuccessful . . . expressed in a face—or rather in a skull."⁹

3. *X as a transit, an exchange of properties*. So what would a decent X-ray look like? Bowden supplies one answer to this question, for immediately after he critiques traditional X-ray radiography, he presents a surreal prose version of a Dadaist photomontage or, perhaps better yet, given this X-ray context, a prose version of a Man Ray "rayograph" visual collage:

> A giant Gulliver is strapped to the table, and the Lilliputians lower the lens of the machine and suddenly we see a Clovis spear point tearing into the hide of a woolly mammoth, we see a child smiling at the table as his mother serves him eggs, beans, and a tortilla, and outside the door, that rose blooms and a waft comes off the giant Gulliver and we smell the girls walking by in their summer clothes, the scent of gun oil coming off the barrel, hear the crack of automatic rifle fire, have a huge, four-door pickup with tinted windows streak toward our eyes, notice the kilos piled up neatly, feel the heft of a bag of lime, stop still as we hear the tear of duct tape, the soft moaning of a man suffocating, and a fiesta dances through the body on the table, a narcocorrido roars out of the liver, the prayers of a priest rise up as an undulating voice over a row of corpses in a church, the scrape of the shovel as a new hole is dug in the patio, and birds migrate and come out of Gulliver's mouth, the stars twinkle in his intestines, Venus and Mars are in the same house, the band strikes up and the dance begins, and the grass flows across all lines, the storms roll through, the beasts migrate, buffalo, mammoths, antelope, hummingbirds, killer bees, everything moving and it is all visible, right there on the X-ray plate, frozen in time, but then it shifts and we see more and more and we suddenly realize that the house of death is our little house on the prairie and our little house on Elm Street and that it is the entryway and the exit for all our dreams and dreads and limits.¹⁰

And breathe. What to make of this discursive chaff—this riot of lines that inventory diverse spatial and temporal (dis)orders and perform disorienting leaps and swerves, as if each line itself were being generated by some image or word or sensory sensation from a prior line, as if Bowden is channeling Beat poetry or modal jazz?

Our own X-ray of this lengthy passage's anatomical structure might focus, for starters, on how its profligate presentation of fragmented visual perceptions and haptic responses is organized from start to finish via serial independent clauses, these grammatical units either chained together by the periodic, rhythmic repetitions of the conjunction *and*—or by their being simply spliced together by commas. Such a heaping up of content and such periodic elisions of conjunctions create a rich, dense metric texture, one whose variations in tempo and rhythmic repetitions (of the adjective *all* in the final lines; of the liquid consonance of *l* sounds throughout) drive home the sheer fact and force, the operatic pleasure, of flow and transit. Everything here passes in front of the gaze of the rhetorical collective nominated by the *we* and *our*, everything named in Bowden's inventory flows together in and across various permeable topographies of transition: the transparent glass windows and the glass camera lens itself; the skins of humans and animals (these adorned with perforations and scars, incisions and bruising); the human body's orifices of ear, mouth, and nose. So categories or concepts of same/difference, inside/outside, here/there, and now/then flow together, creating a kind of 3D photomontage as this "decent" X-ray camera lens moves across and even inside Gulliver's body, in the process suturing together the various orders—social, economic, geological, biological, astronomical, and political—comprised by the object world of late capitalism.

And then, as the passage begins its movement toward an epitomizing summary statement, there appears that vertiginous moment when the scanning gaze of the rhetorical *we* shifts from the sheer fact of the techno-prosthetic process itself (the X-ray camera lens' movement across Gulliver's body and the itemized visual and aural and olfactory assemblages) to the sudden motion of the X-ray plate itself, enabling us to see "more and more" than that which is "frozen in time" and to recognize a phantasmagoric assemblage—not of "Venus and Mars in the house" this time around—but rather of two fictional (one literary and one cinematic) houses that are articulated with our contemporary Juárez cartel house of death. It is of course as if Bowden's primary ambition here is not to represent experience in any ordinary mimetic sense. His ambition seems rather to convey, with some affective intensity, two things: the immediacy and the ephemerality of an accelerating, layered conjunctural presentness; and the necessity for an analogical imagination to enable us to begin to see what we are, what the land is, and what, crucially, we have become. So we witness here how amid all the churning of the clauses in this singular compound sentence a typological similitude emerges at the end of the sentence that is simultaneously a paragraph. Three different architectural houses that function as threshold passageways for human subjects with dreams and desires and that are located in three different dwelling places and times are linked together: a fictional little house on the prairie, a cinematic house on Elm Street, and the actual cartel death house on Juárez's Calle Parsioneros. Thus, as a result of this extended prose simulation of a "decent X-ray machine," a photographic plate is said to emerge, enabling us to recognize the synchronicity of such architectural structures. So the heaping together of disparate things and sights in this passage becomes an intertextual loop bearing an affective charge that inchoately gestures toward some totalizing structure of feeling—toward some complete, meaningful utterance or epitomizing statement that would make everything cohere, such as the claim that the cartel death house represents "the entryway and the exit for all our dreams and dreads and limits."

I say "gestures toward" here because it remains for the reader to recognize what is also implied by Bowden's grafting together the two fictive (one literary and one cinematic) popular culture houses with the all-too-real Juárez death house. That is, in addition to speculating that the cartel death house is the contemporary example of an architecture that symbolizes our collective "dreams and dreads and limits," the temporal scope of his other named dwelling places suggests a symbolic genealogical succession ranging from the violent transit of life and death from the era of settler-colonial occupation on the western frontier (the *Little House* book series) through the so-called crabgrass frontier of suburban development in the mid-twentieth century (the film *Nightmare on Elm Street*) and onward into our own globalizing world system shaped by the illegal face of transnational capitalism (the cartel death house in Juárez).

"We come from green ground teeming with insects," Bowden writes, thus supplying one answer to his desire for a decent X-ray, whose developed image would show us where we come from, this very earth which "hums now as the summer rains wash the dust from our eyes and we briefly say life before we return to death." Whatever endows any life story with any degree of intelligible truth about what we are and will become, Bowden explicitly and implicitly argues, should simultaneously be regarded as a death story.[11] That mysterious story existing on either side of any life's beginning and end. That mysterious story about and embodied by the dead who surround the living who remember them. That mysterious story whose fated ending calls out to and at times determines the very plot of a life story in progress, even as the summer rains arrive to wash the dust from our eyes, this very dust that we all are fated to become. For just as the life sentence of mortality declares that it is the very nature of human and of natural history to constitute, at bottom, elusive objects of knowledge, so too are Bowden's sentences equally elusive here. His prose scuttles from part object to part object and from affective response to affective response, ceaselessly searching to realize the utopian promise informing the technological prosthesis of a traditional X-ray machine: that if we can just see and rightly name some thing or event happening out there in the world, then perhaps we can know and better comprehend it—and, as a result, presumably better discipline and master its unruly mobilities, its errant trajectories.

Instead of mastery, however, what we discover through this passage's unabashed courting of chaos is that things themselves are agents: they perform, they make things happen, they flow and migrate across various borderlines and time lines, including that border existing between the X-ray camera's viewing plane and the viewing plane of the observer who gazes at Gulliver's body on the table, which is described at one point as emitting a "waft." This sensory and sensual body that feels and hears the passing of a speeding pickup truck. That listens as a narcocorrido "roars" out of his liver and as the prayers "rise up" and the shovels "scrape." This body that sees stars "twinkle" in the night sky and watches the grass as it "flows," its blades parting to allow the migration of a menagerie of animals and insects and birds. Like both the crossed lines configuring the letter *X* itself and Bowden's kinetic grammar and syntax, the events of our perceiving Gulliver's body through this decent

X-ray camera expose to view a transcorporeal topography of reciprocal exchange. Human subjects both observe and are subjected to the agential force of objects; material objects and other bodies constitute that which is observed as well as that which makes stuff happen. As a result, the key point here about the "theater of dust and blood being staged in the cartel death house" is this: both cognitive perception and sensory apprehension emerge as transitive events deconstructing the so-called objectivity and detachment of the clinical-anatomical gaze of technological surveillance.[12] As Elizabeth Grosz has noted in another context, we thus bear witness here to how art, literary art in this example, is valuable because it "addresses not matter's regular features as science does, but its expressive qualities, its 'aesthetic' resources," in order to see beyond DNA.[13]

4. *X as signifying multiplication*. So Bowden's alternative vision of a ray that would expose "where we come from and what we have become" invests heavily in accounting for the visual expressiveness of and the contrapuntal soundscapes attached to disparate quasi-objects/quasi-subjects. Such as, to itemize some of the material things referenced in the above quoted passage: body parts (human livers, intestines, and mouths); beans and eggs and tortillas; blooming roses and scented female bodies; gun oil, automatic rifles, and speeding pickup trucks; and a church. Such incommensurate material things are rendered as fragments or part objects—disarticulated from any image of a whole body or social totality—and then juxtaposed to each other, their presence in independent clauses brought into parallel spatial relationality simply through some kinetic logic of surrogacy and substitution. It is as if Bowden's aesthetic reimagines such organic and inorganic forms of embodiment as being simultaneously "unthinkable as wholes and unthinkable apart from each other."[14] Bowden's analogical imagination reconsiders part-part or part-whole relationality not by simply presenting one image after another in serial succession (in accord with, say, simple mathematical addition or counting). Rather, the seriality of his prose progresses as "one image *plus* another," the italicized *plus* here underscoring how the logic informing a combinatory assemblage is more aligned with, say, chemical addition (for example, Na + Cl = Sodium Chloride).[15] Such is the case, for example, when Bowden's vision of a "decent X-ray machine" stages a visual and aural congruence between the kilos of drugs stacked in rows inside a cartel death house and the lined rows of corpses being prayed over by a priest inside a church. As is evident in this symmetrical pairing of a cartel death house and a house of worship containing the dead, the equation of sacred and profane lifeworlds intensifies the passage's potential to unsettle, if not shock, the rhetorical *we* addressed here, to wake us up from the daydreams that go "on and on because that it is how we avoid this hard reality."[16]

Even though this particular death house on Juárez's Calle Parsioneros is closed and now resembles an archaeological dig as forensic investigators continue to process its crime scene for evidence, the "hard reality" that Bowden alludes to here remains: that "there are other houses in the city just like it. And in other cities. And these houses seem to be multiplying."[17] These replicant houses where, presumably, there would also exist—as we see with regard both to the uncanny death house composed by Gulliver's body and the corpses buried in the cartel death house—a transcorporeal transit among human and nonhuman and celestial bodies: "the stars twinkle in [Gulliver's] intestines, Venus and Mars are in the same house."[18] Thus, the uncanny body as a house: the dark interior cavities (liver; intestines) of a human body are said to house twinkling planets and constellations, these contained within the dark crypt formed by the vault of night sky that encompasses "planet murder," this celestial body that houses Juárez, this border city that houses the cartel death house on its Calle Parsioneros. Thus, the house as an uncanny body: this cartel death house as a literal and figurative "black hole in the body politic," the dark holes beneath its backyard and patio housing the mutilated and violated bodies of both the named and the nameless dead.[19] Like this supine faux-Gulliver body, whose interior organs are said to mediate a crossing between the heavens and earth, and just like the center nodal point of the letter *X* marks a convergence and divergence, an arrival and a departure, so too this borderland transit hub—both this city and this death house—comprises the "the entryway and the exit for all our dreams and dreads and limits" as we journey toward that darkness awaiting us on either side of life.[20]

Just as the Lilliputians manipulation of the X-ray camera's transit produces Gulliver's anatomy as a collision of spatial and temporal registers, so too does Bowden's prose version of a "decent X-ray machine" reproduce the uncanny anatomy of this faux-Gulliver both as a body where different spatial and temporal orders are layered together, and a body that is simultaneously physiological and social, private and public, subject and object.[21] We can venture a similar observation about Bowden's prose: that its predominant serial grammar and paratactic syntax not only desires to imitate the spread and sprawl of this passage's porous descriptive content but also to form and perform a parallel linguistic morphology, one that indexes social and cultural codifications or ideologies. It is not just that Bowden's cluttered and clattering style offers us a refracted vision of a fragmented social, political, and economic order. His X-ray aesthetic of rendering wholes into fragments and then recomposing them in new assemblages also exposes how violent housekeeping labor at the cartel death house constitutes an uncanny double both of the exploitation of bodies and resources on the maquiladora assembly lines and in the escapist pleasures afforded by the entertainment outlets of an intensified consumer capitalism. In the process, this aesthetic's seemingly indiscriminate and discontinuous heaping together of material things and human and nonhuman bodies targets both "official ideas about reality and dreams" and punctures any corollary faith in representational mimesis or documentary realism.

[**A**lphabet/**A**becedario; **D**iapers; **E**xposure; **L**ipstick; **Q**ueues; **S**cene of the crime; **Z**ombieland]

Yellow ribbons, yellow light

EXTRACTS

They had done the neck-breaking and had then loaded the corpse, with his motorcycle, and driven them to a little grove of paloverde trees growing by the Speedway Exit ramp of I-10. Max had rather liked that it was March and the paloverdes had been thick with bright yellow blossoms when they had hung the "motorcyclist" upside down in a paloverde and left the bike appropriately skidded and smashed lying at the bottom of the exit ramp. Max had liked the newspaper report that a woman on her way to work had sighted "strange fruit" in the flowering desert tree at six-o'clock in the morning.

—Leslie Marmon Silko, *Almanac of the Dead* (1991)

I tossed the beer bottles into the garbage disposal, then I turned on the record player without looking to see what record was on it. With a glance at the door behind which the child was sleeping, Claire turned down the volume a little. The record was called *She Wore a Yellow Ribbon* and consisted of some tunes from John Ford's movies played on the jew's-harp. "In Providence I heard a regimental band playing those things," I exclaimed, and repeated the sentence very softly, as though Claire couldn't have understood it when I said it in a loud voice.

—Peter Handke, *Short Letter, Long Farewell* (1974)

Tie a yellow ribbon around these.
Tie a yellow ribbon around strong young men
the future of a nation
dancing death postures
as they burn in their tanks.
Tie a yellow ribbon around ragged white flags,

blasted to bits, truth retreating as Sand Creek's ghosts
sit on the memory of black bayonets.

—Wendy Rose, "Yellow Ribbons," *Bone Dance* (1991)

And with that reference to yellow in his famous book on color, Goethe noted in 1810 that gold in its perfectly unmixed state gives us what he called a new and high idea of yellowness. It is an agreeable and gladdening color, which in its utmost power is serene and noble. Yet yellow, he goes on to say, is extremely liable to contamination, and he singles out sulfur as an example for having something unpleasant about it—this same sulfur, or "pale sulfure," that van Gogh said he used to create an atmosphere of the devil's furnace in his painting *Night Café*.

—Michael Taussig, *My Cocaine Museum* (2004)

1. "*Strange fruit*." Published in 1972, translated into English in 1974, and then reprinted by New York Review Books in 2009, Peter Handke's episodic novel *Short Letter, Long Farewell* centers on a meandering journey across the United States made by an unnamed protagonist and first-person narrator from Austria. *Short Letter, Long Farewell* has been variously described by critics as a road novel, a bildungsroman, and a postmodern play on the conventions of traditional detective fiction. The textual surface of this novel is rather painterly, distinguished by its descriptive vignettes of finely grained visual impressions, these shifting between the protagonist's present journey across the continent from the East to the West and his often-unsettling remembrances of things past triggered by events along the way. As his travel across the continent from Providence, Rhode Island, to California unfolds, the narrator-protagonist is portrayed as both searching for and being stalked by his ex-wife, a woman named Judith, whose occasional surprise appearances and threatening messages act as catalytic events during his journey that prompt changes in his itinerary and hence the trajectory of the novel's plot. Indeed, the novel begins in Providence, with his receipt of the first of such short letters or notes from her, which explains the use of the novel's title "Short Letter" for its first section, while the "farewell" in the novel's title both

refers toward the title of its second and final section and represents an intertextual reference to such Raymond Chandler hard-boiled detective novels as *Farewell, My Lovely* or *The Long Goodbye*.[1]

On the novel's last page, when the film director John Ford asks the narrator and Judith to tell him their story, her response is not directly given but rather succinctly summarized by the narrator-protagonist in one complete sentence: "And Judith told him how we had come to America, how she had followed me, how she had robbed me and wanted to kill me, and how at last we were ready to part in peace."[2] Now this narrator's deadpan rendering of his ex-wife's version of their story chains together four kernel events, tells us broadly what happened and then proclaims, via a summary judgment, that a transformative closure had been obtained ("at last we were ready to part in peace"). By novel's end, however, the reader should be skeptical of the narrator's ventriloquism of his antagonist's story. For the narrative texture and ambition of *Short Letter, Long Farewell* strives to graft together a rather nonlinear, random, and episodic adventure narrative with a plurality of intertextual allusions and references so as to foreground what happens rather than what happened, confirming Handke's phenomenological investment in the subversion of any desire for the pleasure of familiar narrative traditions—especially the pleasure associated with an ending that resolves all enigmas. After all, throughout the length of the novel, he has been haunted by Judith, who stalks him with short letters and phone messages and, as she does mention to John Ford, employs total strangers to prosecute her various schemes to harm him during his trip across the continent.

At the novel's outset, this introspective first-person narrator discloses his quest for a redemptive self-transformation, this idea crucially shaped by his immersion in American popular culture. To fulfill this desire, for example, he wants to jettison his inherent "predisposition to fear and panic" and acquire instead the "warmth, attentiveness, serenity, and happiness" he unironically associates with F. Scott Fitzgerald's literary character Jay Gatsby. At the same time, he expresses a "physical need" for an external verification, amid the slurry of his conscious thoughts, that his transformed feelings would become incarnate, publicly visible by means of his bodily gestures and his ordinary language spoken out loud. So the question becomes not only whether or not he is "capable of being different" but also whether there exists an external environment and audience that would validate his inner sense of personal transformation. So an anxious sense of a doubled world emerges in *Short Letter, Long Farewell*, one founded on a felt belief in a difference between who I am and the true self I want to become, between appearance and reality, between originals and copies or simulations, and between the past and the present. Handke's prose thus moves both inward and outward, between spatial scales and temporal registers, and foregrounds an image pattern centered on copies or simulacra, on mirrors and echoes. In the novel's second section, for example, the narrator recollects "how as a child I had longed for a double, someone exactly like myself; and I took it as a good sign that since then the whole idea of a double, of someone just like me, had come to horrify and disgust me."[3] At other points in the novel this self-loathing will center on his chronic stuckness: how his "impressions were repetitions of impressions already known to me"; how certain "longings that I thought I'd forgotten have been cropping up again." Indeed, the uncanny return of repressed longings to his conscious mind is unsettling precisely because he traces their origin back to a primal childhood recognition scene: a traumatic moment when he worries "that the world around me might suddenly burst and turn into something different, a monster's maw, for instance."[4]

This fraught sense of a doubled world; this evidence of paranoia or, at a minimum, of generalized anxiety disorder; this leitmotif of unsettling disclosures of heretofore hidden past trauma—such aspects of the uncanny deployed throughout Handke's novel are underwritten by the narrator's pronounced fear of his own and of other people's death. His chronic morbidity also surfaces through the narration's repetitive intertextual references to Gottfried Keller's memoir *Green Heinrich*. On one occasion when reading this text during his second journey to the United States, he judges that his own vision of the world is both inauthentic—that it essentially represents an outright copy of Keller's vision—and twisted because reading it reminds him of a debilitating period in his life when he was "more interested in ruins than houses" and addicted to visiting graveyards in order to count "the suicide's graves along the walls."[5]

Now the repetition and return to the novel's surface texture of these features of the uncanny provide some coherence to the narrator's episodic plot and the peregrinations of his vagrant imagination, and they contribute to the novel's overall neo-Gothic atmosphere. Also providing some degree of coherence to the spread and sprawl of the narrator's narrative quest for self-transformation are the iterative allusions to yellow—the light itself and the color of certain material things, such as a tequila bottle's label picturing a Mexican desert's yellow sand. Such as yellow ribbons, which are referenced in the song and mise-en-scène of director John Ford's cavalry western film *She Wore a Yellow Ribbon*. And there is the Yellow Ribbon restaurant, "in front of which there was a luminous statue of a pioneer woman with a yellow neckerchief."[6] As we shall see as this essay develops, a crucial question that emerges in relation to the novel's frequent allusions to the color yellow centers on the ontological and epistemological gap existing between, on the one hand, the harsh realities of everyday life and, on the other hand, that sense of everyday life (what it is and can be) afforded us by ordinary language and by literary or visual artforms. Will this inherent gap foreclose this narrator's quest to become different and better, an original person who is less prone to paranoia and more able to see things as they really are in a society overwhelmed by images? It is a crucial question, for as Handke's narrator-protagonist comments about his prior trip to the United States, "I was only interested in images: gas stations, yellow taxis, drive-in movies, advertising posters, highways, a Greyhound bus, a bus-stop sign on the highway, the Santa Fe Railway, the desert. There were no people in my consciousness and I felt good about it. Now I'm sick of all these images."[7]

The rhetoric of the text here wallows in serial description and the tedium of this narrator's recourse to the sheer heaping up of disparate items anticipates his eventual recognition—in the two closing sentences above that present a completed narrative in condensed form—that once upon a time he felt healthy, but now he is sick. One could further observe how even that brief time of feeling "good about it" constitutes a curse as well as a blessing for this narrator. For one thing, while this cataloging of the images he sees during his trip seems to improve his mental health (his consciousness becomes free from intrusive thoughts about or by Others), this result is achieved at the cost of making him an isolate ("there were no people in my consciousness"). And for another thing his becoming ill at the sight of such images populating everyday life is due to their ubiquity: the materials he itemizes are things discovered, over and over, in plain sight. So the familiar or homely—brand names and visual images of American life that he has consumed via popular media—becomes regarded as the unhomely, this transformation puncturing this narrator's carapace of egotism and nakedly exposing his vulnerability to the world as a result of his inauthentic life. Whether referencing the fictional Jay Gatsby or characters in John Ford films such as *Young Mr. Lincoln* and *She Wore a Yellow Ribbon*, Handke's unnamed narrator—essentially an outsider attempting on his second trip to America to understand his own tormented history through American culture (and vice versa)—resembles, in Nathaniel Lewis's words, "a postmodern neurasthenic, turning to regional simulations for his West cure."[8] Whether the cure he desires actually occurs or instead emerges as a phantasmagoria in the course of his journey and what role the leitmotif of yellow and the cascade of "regional simulations" play in foreclosing on a potential cure for his condition—these are the chief concerns I want to consider as this essay develops.

2. "*Everything shimmers yellow from within.*" In the sequence that opens the "The Long Farewell," the second section of the novel, our narrator-protagonist stands in a garden outside a St. Louis-area home as night falls, sipping wine and watching as his friend and traveling companion Claire Madison puts her daughter to bed in the home of one of her friends, this guest bedroom opening onto a backyard and garden.[9] He stands in this garden with the homeowner, a man who paints movie posters and "episodes in the settlement of the West, landscapes with covered wagons and riverboats."[10] The same types of episodes are foreshadowed during the narrator's journey west by a Pennsylvania hotel room's window curtain that reproduces a print of Lewis and Clark "shooting Blackfoot Indians (one of the Indians, on a hill far in the distance, was still holding his arm half-upraised in the direction of the rifle barrel)."[11] As this sequence unfolds, the narrator, the painter—and eventually the painter's wife—all become transfixed while they stand in this home's backyard garden and gaze at the play of the setting sun's light on the canvas provided by another bedroom's interior white wall. So rapt is their attention to the bare white wall's framing of the yellow light of sunset that it magically seems to them as if "there was only the bare wall, which, as the darkness deepened round about, shone more and more brightly, with an even, deep-yellow light, which the wall seemed to generate rather than reflect."[12]

"You'll only find that kind of yellow light in the Western paintings of the last century," said the painter. "That light doesn't come from somewhere else, the sky for instance, it's given off by the ground itself. In Catlin's or Remington's paintings the sky is always pale, smoky, and colorless, you never see the sun, but a strangely deep yellow shines from the ground and lights up the faces from below. In all those pictures yellow is the dominant color: wagon wheels, powder smoke rising from rifles, the teeth of dying horses, railroad tracks—everything shimmers yellow from within; it makes every single object stand out as in a coat of arms. Nowadays you see imitations of that yellow wherever you go: the signs on parking lots, the markings on highways, the arches of the McDonald's restaurants, traffic lights, U.S.A. T-shirts." "The yellow arrow of the Holiday Inn," I said.[13]

In this moment we witness an image of the homely and familiar, the daily event of sunset, becoming unhomely and unfamiliar. Not just because of the sheer ephemerality of this "strangely, deep-yellow light," but because the source of this light is mysterious. It appears to be produced by either the ground or perhaps even by one of the nearby bedroom's walls.[14] The movie poster painter strives to make sense of this optical phenomenon by alluding to the deep-yellow color found in nineteenth-century western paintings by such artists as George Catlin and Frederic Remington. He further suggests that both the "strangely deep yellow" evident in certain Catlin and Remington artworks and the "even, deep-yellow light" shining on the bedroom's white wall are far more authentic than all the "pale imitations" of this yellow color he finds in certain cultural artifacts and commodities of everyday commercial life. For unlike the commodification of yellow exemplified by, say, McDonald's arches or yellow taxicabs, both the "strangely deep-yellow" color shimmering in the paintings of Catlin and Remington and the "even, deep yellow light" emanating from a bedroom's bare white wall represent "a color that makes you remember.... And the longer you look at it, the further back you remember, till you reach a point where you can't go any further. At that point you can only stand there and dream." And as if completing her husband's developing thought, his wife suddenly blurts out one example of the memory work spawned by this particular color: a nostalgic vision of their shared youth that she labels the "years of gold."[15]

Along with the characteristic bildungsroman focus on the narrator-protagonist's quest for self-transformation, then, one of this novel's major themes centers precisely on the fluid interplay between representations of historical reality and the recollections shaped by dreams and memories.[16] As this sequence in *Short Letter, Long Farewell* begins to wind down after the sun fully sets in the west, the group will play a word association game provoked by a comment made by the painter's wife that the color the group beholds reminds her of the 1960s, which she labels the "years of gold." At one point during their game, the movie poster painter confidently announces that personal recollections of music from that era will enable the retrieval of the historical past's reality and hence a fuller understanding of its enduring truths. Knowledge, then, is not so much the province of mimesis as it is of *aletheia*, a process of discovery or a form of reflection that reveals something new before the eye of the mind. Now what is of interest here is the contradictory nature of this movie poster painter's overall vision of aesthetics and of historiography. Let us consider, for instance, how at another point in this textual sequence, the narrator comments that this movie poster painter was one of those artists "unable . . . to conceive of sketching anything that did not exist: his landscapes had to be exact imitations of real landscapes, the people in them had to have really lived, and they had to have done what they were doing in the pictures." Thus he doesn't like to paint the Battle of the Little Bighorn, because the "Indians didn't leave a single American survivor, and there were no eye-witness accounts."[17] So from this perspective it would seem that if his movie posters and historical paintings of western settler-colonial history have any pedagogical value, it will be because such visual representations offer a version of what we might call documentary realism. His ultimate ambition, then, would appear to be to embalm history: "to fix or represent figures without movement or words, mute or immobile figures where the colors don't change or vary with the lighting."[18] Or, as the narrator's friend Claire remarks to the dramaturge of a traveling German theater group after their St. Louis performance of *Don Carlos*, "We're used to seeing historical figures in stationary tableaux. Instead of letting them play their parts, we pose them, and always with their officially known gestures. . . . We remember them as they appear in monuments and postage stamps."[19]

Yet regardless of his apparent faith in the capacity of certain artistic representations to fix historical truth, and regardless of his interpretive logic's opposition of so-called authentic originals and their latter-day popular culture's more blatantly commercial imitations, the movie poster painter's desire to obtain authenticity nevertheless kneads together what we might call an objective knowledge of the real external world (real landscapes lived in by real people) with suppositions about subjectively imagined perceptual worlds: the historical participants themselves as eyewitnesses; a later audience's reconstruction of the past through memory work. Both of these are labors of projection shaped by conscious and unconscious desires, fears, and anxieties—and by ideological biases. Furthermore, let us recall how this painter's observations about the play of color during the sunset in the garden scene progresses through a precisely graduated, incremental play of perceptual substitutions: from the sun's light to its apparent reflection on an interior bedroom wall's white canvas; from this white wall's production or perhaps reproduction of an "even, deep yellow" light to its analogue in western paintings produced by Catlin and Remington; from these artistic productions to examples of the economic and industrial commodification of yellow; from such contemporary material artifacts to the more personal zone of remembrance; from an individual's selective recollection of the past to, finally, the intangible stuff out of which dreams themselves are made. And as these serial perceptions pivot from the external world of nature through various artistic and commercial reproductions of yellow to the internal world of human cognition and imagination, the emerging lesson appears to be this: the empirical fact of yellow light shimmering in the garden and provoking one's subjective remembrances of an irrevocably lost historical past will reach a limit.

At this limit or horizon where our gaze dwells as if in an "indefinite prolongation of the visible itself," the true value accruing from our patient beholding of the uncanny mystery or ordinary sublime of everyday life emerges. It is as if Handke's nuanced rendering of this scene of beholding anticipates his own thoughts on the "real presence" he feels when standing before Cézanne's paintings and beholding what the artist had described as his *réalisations*, achieved by color and shape rather than by line or figure per se. Handke likens these secular painterly realizations to "a transformation and sheltering of things endangered—not in a religious ceremony, but in the form of faith that was the painter's secret."[20] So as the serial perceptions of the movie poster painter swerve from the external world of nature through cultural constructions to the internal world of cognition and imagination, the empirical fact of yellow color in the novel's garden scene, as Nathaniel Lewis concludes, "seems to evoke a primary moment at the dawn of history, a moment in which memory fades into dream, but it's unclear whether he [the painter] is talking about personal history, American history, or some deeper sense of a mythical past."[21]

In contradistinction to the movie poster painter, who seems unaware of the logical contradictions in his defense of what I've called a version of documentary realism, we should attend to how Handke's narrator focuses our attention on the phenomenological event of seeing and knowing rather than on an already fixed and embalmed fact or entity posed in monumental form. Ironically, then, this entire sequence seems to recover a version of the settler-colonial past—only then to displace it into what we might call an aestheticized moment of presence created by the enchanted play of an "even, deep yellow light." This yellow light that, in the moment of beholding, seems paradoxically immune from time and history. This yellow light that offers us a compensatory respite from considering the role power plays in determining what counts as history, as well as from our having to confront, in this ephemeral moment, our own future disappearance below the horizon.

3. "*Nothing is made up.*" This unnamed European narrator's journey of western discovery near the end of the twentieth century seems to me different only by degree, rather than kind, from the analogous "West cure" sought at the beginning of the twentieth century by such modern neurasthenics as, to name a short list, Frederic Remington, Theodore Roosevelt, Owen Wister, and Frank Hamilton Cushing. But for Handke's first-person narrator, the movies of director John Ford constitute the primary "regional simulations" that shape his therapeutic journey of discovery during his second trip to the United States. The several allusions throughout the novel to yellow ribbons conjure up Ford's 1949 cavalry film *She Wore a Yellow Ribbon*, starring John Wayne and Maureen O'Hara. And just prior to the sunset scene in St. Louis, this narrator describes his viewing of Ford's 1939 film *Young Mr. Lincoln*, starring Henry Fonda. So moved is he by this film that he declares his intention to visit the director when he eventually reaches California on his westward

journey: "I'm going to tell him that I learned about America from that picture, that it taught me to understand history by seeing people in nature, and that it made me happy. I'm going to ask him to tell me what he used to be like and how America has changed since he stopped making pictures."[22]

In the novel's final sequence, the narrator and his ex-wife Judith do end up meeting with director John Ford at his colonial-style house in the Los Angeles area. He does tell Ford what he learned from watching his films, and he does ask him for his thoughts about the relationship between art, history, and natural history, as well as the changes Ford has observed in America over the course of his long career. At one point in this sequence, Handke stages another scene in which a small group of human subjects behold the yellow light of a setting sun, its thematic content and its imagery uncannily doubling the earlier scene in St. Louis with the movie poster painter and his wife. Looking down into the valley on the hilltop behind Ford's house as the last rays of sunlight shine through the leaves of orange trees, the now-retired movie director remarks, "When I see the leaves moving like that and the sun shining through, I have a feeling that they've been moving that way since the world began. . . . It gives me a feeling of eternity, and I forget that there's such a thing as history. You people call it a medieval feeling. It's as if the whole world were still in a state of nature."[23] Ford then adds that when he is moved by this play of sunlight with the orange tree's leaves, it makes him want to "forget myself and my existence. Then I wish that nothing would ever change, that the leaves would go on moving forever, that the oranges would never be picked and everything would stay just the way it is."[24]

The elderly Ford's wistfulness betrays his plangent desire literally and figuratively to escape time's nick just in the nick of time. This nostalgic desire is structured by an opposition between history, regarded as the realm of change and transformations, and eternity, the realm of timelessness and stasis. And this desire is tethered to a ritual and aesthetic of relinquishment—of the ego and even of the memory of one's existence—in order to achieve a primal atonement with an original state of nature bound only to the cyclical repetition of the seasons. It is as if Handke's fictive version of John Ford here uncannily channels Owen Wister's main character in his cowboy novel *The Virginian* (1902), who confides "dreamily" to his new bride Molly during their honeymoon camp in a Wyoming mountain range that he has desired "to become the ground, become the water, become the trees, mix with the whole thing. Not know himself from it—never unmix again."[25] But the crucial difference between the Virginian's pastoral desire during the era of industrial modernization and Handke's fictive version of John Ford in postmodernity is that the latter's vision centers on a redemptive return to a state of nature in which "everything would stay just the way it is." The tree leaves would always be in motion due to a slight breeze, the oranges would never be picked, and the sun, with its desaturated, pale yellow light, presumably will always be at the same position in the sky. Not a vision of nature as shaped by the solar and lunar cycles and by the cyclical round of the seasons, then, but rather nature as a simulacrum, a framed topographical enclave viewed from a prospect, preserved as if it were a work of taxidermy—still life as a stilled life, or nature morte.

Prior to this moment, during the group's climb up the hill overlooking the orange trees and the cypress trees in the valley below, the narrator notes how Ford continuously "talked about his pictures and kept insisting that the stories were true. 'Nothing is made up,' he said, 'It all really happened.'"[26] Judith, too, in the novel's final words, echoes Ford's sentiment: when he asks if the story she relates about her American trip is "true" rather than "made up," she replies "it all happened."[27] So it seems, then, that one can only know and perhaps even eventually "understand history" through simulations and simulacra—in this case through a print and visual cultural archive whose serial projection of images on screen or in storied words are to be taken as potentially revealing the "real" thing, what "really happened." And so in this final scene of instruction, the lesson forwarded by *Short Letter, Long Farewell* uncannily recapitulates and, in the end, extends even further the concluding wisdom uttered in the final spoken words of Ford's film *The Man Who Shot Liberty Valence* (1962): "When the legend becomes fact, print the legend." With this imperative direction in mind, then, it is not a lie for Ford to say that "nothing is made up" in his films because, well, everything is made up, the result of a performative (re)production.

4. "*Dreams and poses*." In that earlier scene in St. Louis, the play of light at sunset produces an "even, deep-yellow" hue on a bedroom's bare white wall that, as the movie poster painter exclaims, "makes you remember." In

the novel's penultimate scene, lightning strikes the hills across the valley and rain begins to fall on the orange trees standing below the assembled group—the film director, our narrator, and his ex-wife Judith—that has left the terrace of Ford's house and climbed a nearby hill. The sight of rain in the near distance prompts Ford to recall a recent moment when he was driving through the Arizona desert and had to use the car's windshield wipers to remove the morning dew. Upon hearing the phrase "down in Arizona," our narrator reports that "at those words I began to remember." Then, as he leans forward in anticipation of hearing another Ford story, he explains, "I realized that I was imitating the gesture of a character in one of his pictures who without shifting positions cranes his long neck over a dying man to see if he's still alive."[28] On one level, this epiphany fosters Handke's postmodernist sense that a hyperreality of images and copies mediates, if not entirely replaces, how we experience the realities of everyday life. "There are postures that make you feel like yourself," Ford announces, and so "'Yes,' you think, 'this is really me.'"[29] You think, in short, that your authentic inner self has become fully realized and communicated via your visible performance of certain corporeal gestures. "Unfortunately," Ford continues, "you're usually alone when that happens. Then you try it with people around and you're not yourself anymore, you fall into a pose. That's no good."[30]

Ordinary everyday life can be so disappointing! Just when you feel you truly are your true self, the people around you cannot or perhaps do not care enough to recognize the corporeal signs of your transformation. So instead of experiencing a transformative ascent, your emergent authentic self communicated by your posture, your bearing in the world, inevitably falls into an inauthentic pose. But Ford does not notice how our narrator, in response to the phrase "down in Arizona," adopts a pose he has learned from a character in one of the director's movies, suggesting that the distinction between performing a posture and assuming a pose (which in this context could be likened to playing a role in a movie), is a precious one—ultimately neither clear-cut nor convincing. For is it not also the case that one could perform a pose or play a role in such a manner that any distinction one might draw between the performer and performance dissolves? Is it entirely possible that the supposed truth of oneself is not what one already knows (and thinks about oneself) but rather what unfolds through the performance of a role (in the narrator's case, trying to imitate the visible postures of a fictional Jay Gatsby or a character in a John Ford film)? Take the analogous example provided by the world of cosmetics, where the application of, say, mascara or lipstick to one's face is sometimes colloquially described as one's taking leave "to go make my face." Is one's true face supplied by nature, or is it the case that one's true face is the one that emerges before the mirror as a result of a particular application of supplements to original nature that disguise rather than advertise their presence through artifice?

The answers to such a question are not all that important here, for surely one could argue on behalf of either position. Rather, my perhaps too obvious point is that any argument about the difference between a posture and a pose, or the look of a face with or without makeup, will involve aesthetic tastes—and hence will be shaped by an ideological position about what constitutes the beautiful or, to take our earlier example, a state of nature (and by extension what constitutes the natural and hence the unnatural). Once again, let us consider that earlier scene of beholding the yellow light of a St. Louis sunset. This time around, though, let us focus on how the painter's wife uses the word *nature* in advancing an interpretation about the relationship between stories, actual landscapes, and the production of historical meaning or truth. Unlike Ford in the novel's concluding scene, this woman is more transparent about the fact that stories "made up" to represent what "really happened" in the past also possess pedagogical, which is to say ideological, designs on their audiences: "Everything we've seen since we were children had stories connected with it, and all those stories were heroic. So what we see in the landscape isn't nature, but the deeds of men who took possession of America, and at the same time a call to be worthy of such deeds. We were brought up to look at nature with a moral awe."[31]

Now when Handke's narrator catches himself imitating a posture he has learned from a John Ford movie, and when the seventy-six-year-old John Ford produces what I've called his still life as nature morte vision of an eternal state of nature immune to historical change, the novel clearly underscores how simulations and simulacra reign in the everyday life of postmodernity. At the same time, such scenes also dramatize something else: how these and other characters cannot resist forging some continuity between their aesthetic encounters with books and movies and the fragmented and unstable narratives that make up their personal histories. Handke's novel thus foregrounds how judgments made in narrative time about either the status of one's subjectivity or of what constitutes historical truth are primarily the result of affective investments or subjective identifications. But the crucial point that the movie poster painter's wife adds to conversation is this: such affective investments are shaped by evolving social, cultural, and political contexts. The comment by the narrator's friend Claire, about her childhood having been saturated with historical stories shaped by "the deeds of men who took possession of America" and an imperative "call to be worthy of such deeds," adds to the same discussion. By means of the dominant myth-ideology of Manifest Destiny, alternative narratives about the course of settler-colonial dispossession of peoples from their homelands are effectively foreclosed or relegated to the margins of historical discourse.

In the end, what remains problematic fifty years after the original publication of *Short Letter, Long Farewell* is the novel's ambiguous investment in historical contexts. On the one hand, the novel's rhetoric and its patterned texture of uncanny repetitions disclose an intense investment in personal history, primarily, of course, the narrator's past relationship with his now ex-wife Judith and his autobiographical reflections on the impact of reading and film viewing on his identity formation. On the other hand, the novel does allude to the larger course of American settler-colonial history as its characters discuss historiographical issues raised by visual and verbal narratives purporting to document what "really happened" in the individual or collective past. But with the exception of the movie poster painter's wife and the narrator's ex-wife Judith (who only appears in person toward the end of the novel), this novel's introspective narrator never really questions or critiques the proclamations being made by other characters about American history, let alone his idol John Ford's nostalgic desire to escape from history into some fantasized original state of nature. And from this perspective, it is as if *Short Letter, Long Farewell*, on one level, foreshadows what would become, approximately two decades after publication, the controversial travel reports and public gestures that Handke produced about Yugoslavia during the Serbian-Bosnian war, such as his attendance at the war criminal Slobodan Miloševic's funeral.[32]

And yet it is not as if there is no evidence in this novel's final sequence of a Barthian punctum that would provide a counter-memory or potential critique of the flow of discourse by both the narrator and the fictive John Ford. I am thinking here of the two instances in the novel when the contradictions inherent in the various characters' approach to and flight from history so as to experience "real people living in nature" are foregrounded. As we see in the statement made by the movie poster painter's wife quoted above, there is her opening clause: "What we see in the landscape isn't nature, but the deeds of men who took possession of America." And in the novel's final sequence, there is this telling response made by the narrator's ex-wife Judith to John Ford's comment that witnessing the yellow sunlight playing through the leaves of a grove of orange trees makes him think of eternity and as a result to "forget that there's such a thing as history." Her response is both direct and succinct: "'But those orange trees were planted,' said Judith. 'They're not nature.'"[33] Which is to say, we as readers must supply the larger context implied by her remark: that orange trees exist as a materiality in history; and that orange trees themselves embody a continuous history of being planted and tended, of their fruit being harvested by laborers and commodified by the market, of being possessed by and dispossessed from the land—and of their being represented in verbal and visual discourse.

[**B**oredom; **M**otel noir; **N**oir motel; **P**sychometropolis; **S**cene of the crime; **V**agabondage]

Zombieland

EXTRACTS

I'd wander for days in the fog, scared I'd never see another thing, then there'd be that door, opening to show me the mattress padding on the other side to stop out the sounds, the men standing in line like zombies among shiny copper wires and tubes pulsing light, and the bright scrape of arcing electricity.

—Ken Kesey, *One Flew Over the Cuckoo's Nest* (1963)

The two tiers below Nut Run were reserved for cons who had committed minor infractions and were on lockdown for a short period, from a day to a week. It wasn't as dark as the dungeon, nor did it reek, like places that hadn't had fresh air or sunshine in a long time. Nut Run was quiet, except when the zombies occasionally freaked. Intermittent shrieks crackled throughout the night, trailing off into the throbbing silence. My first night there I tossed and turned and couldn't sleep.

—Jimmy Santiago Baca, *A Place to Stand* (2001)

We have looked at many different ways in which the zombie can be conceptualized: we see the zombie as *animal laborans*, the reified laborer of capitalist production, and the zombie as threatening body, the zombie as brain-dead, the zombie as brain eater, the zombie blindly following its own primal urges; the zombie that is pure necessity, the zombie that is anti-productive, the zombie that is female, the zombie that is avid consumer; we have looked at the zombie as cyborg, the zombie as postcyborg, the zombie as posthuman, the zombie as slave, and as slave rebellion.

—Sarah Juliet Lauro and Karen Embry, "A Zombie Manifesto" (2008)

1. "*The cowboys were zombie hunters.*" Proceeding as a series of vignettes ranging in length from one paragraph to several pages in Roberto Bolaño's novel *2666*, "The Part About the Crimes" splices together stories about various police investigators, political figures, journalists, business people, and an imprisoned German American suspect, with the graphic descriptions of the tortured, sexually assaulted, and mutilated bodies of 108 female murder victims found in the Sonoran desert and the environs of the U.S.-Mexican border city of Santa Teresa, Bolaño's fictional representation of Cuidad Juárez. The belated discoveries of these female victims by various citizens and police officers transformed this city's familiar topographies—its legal and illegal garbage dumps; its colonias' vacant houses and empty lots; its network of drainage pipes and sewage ditches and irrigation canals; its highway viaducts and its sprawling industrial parks, factories, and warehouses—into crime scenes, the existence of which is enmeshed with another transformation fueled by a globalizing economic and political system. I am referring here of course to the then-booming maquila economy that epitomized, in the words of a Black U.S. journalist covering a boxing match in Santa Teresa during the 1990s femicide epidemic, "the industrial landscape in the third world."[1]

You could say—as Bolaño's diverse cast of characters certainly do throughout the novel—that this border city's femicide epidemic represents a consequence of the Mexican drug cartels competing for dominance in the various vice trades. Or you could believe that perhaps these violent crimes signify a localized, predatory male backlash against the teenage girls and adult women who fill the vast majority of the low-paying jobs on the maquiladora assembly lines, producing such commodities as electronic devices and household appliances and clothing. And you might even agree with the rumors that the femicides are linked by the intersection of human trafficking and the sex trade with the region's low-budget film industry. For in "The Part About the Crimes," we learn that by the end of 1996 the Mexican media had declared Santa Teresa to be the snuff film capital of the world. In one sequence in "The Part About the Crimes," Bolaño's narrator swerves from the serial, repetitive representation of the discovery of and forensic reports on the murder victims' corpses to focus on an Argentinian journalist who visits Santa Teresa in order to research and write about the ongoing femicides. While there, it turns out that as a result of secret arrangements made by a friend of a friend of a friend, he watches a supposed snuff film in one of the Santa Teresa's northernmost colonias. And to his great surprise, this journalist learns that the term "snuff film" apparently was coined by an American couple who travelled to his home country of Argentina in order to make such a film at a remote ranch in the Pampas, about a four-day car trip from Buenos Aires. This was in 1972, a time "when there was still talk in Argentina about revolution," whether Peronist, socialist, or even a mystical one.[2]

Bolaño elaborates on the story about this American couple, named Mike and Clarissa Epstein, and their Argentinian adventure. We learn that during the making of the film at the Pampas cattle ranch, Mike Epstein confesses to his wife "that all of this, and in explanation he spread his arms wide, was like the West, the American West, but better than the American West, because in the West, when you thought about it, all the cowboys did was herd cattle, and here, on the pampa, as he had come to see more closely, the cowboys were zombie hunters."[3] It turns out the couple complete their hybrid western zombie film by using the blood, flesh, and organs of a slaughtered calf instead of human body parts and blood. But later, in the post-production phase of editing and marketing of this low-budget, faux snuff film back in Buenos Aires, Epstein intentionally spreads a rumor that an actress had died during the filming of a zombie massacre scene. Given the global mediascape's circulation of images and news about the entertainment industry, this tidbit of gossip soon reaches "some cinephile circles in the United States." Through such word-of-mouth publicity, the Epsteins' film, titled *Snuff*, eventually opens both in New York and in Los Angeles. The few critics who saw the film judged it "a total flop, dubbed as it was into English, chaotic, with a weak script and pitiful performances." For her part, Clarissa Epstein remained in Buenos Aires and moved in with an Argentinian movie producer, a Peronist, it turns out, who "later became an active member of a death squad that began by killing Trotskyites and guerrillas and ended up orchestrating the disappearance of children and housewives."[4]

Such developments emerging during the film's production and initial reception exemplify the transgression of both the boundaries of film genres and of geopolitical scales. For one thing, Mike Epstein's revisioning of cowboys as zombie hunters rather than as cattle herders exemplifies how a kind of screen memory of U.S. history and the western film genre gets transferred onto the Pampas landscape. There are also the hypermobile travels of both print journalists and filmmakers through a logistical and technological transportation network that triangulates the rural and urban U.S. West, Mexico, and the hemispheric South. Along with such economic and technological developments, furthermore, there is the parallel globalized media network circulating cultural products (movies; tabloid gossip; industry news and reviews) beyond the southern hemisphere's geopolitical and linguistic borders. And on still another level, as this sequence's closing description of Clarissa Epstein consorting with a Peronist death-squad member reveals, there is abundant evidence testifying to the globalizing world system's jumping of temporal as well as spatial scales. The Santa Teresa femicides and missing persons cases in the 1990s are of a piece with the "disappearance of children and housewives" alluded to in 1970s Argentina. Furthermore, Bolaño's inclusion of the signifier Perón in this sequence semiotically entangles the various abductions and disappearances of women and children and Trotskyites and guerillas and journalists to the trauma of World War II and the Holocaust, both these historical events referenced in *2666* by the presence of both German Nazis and emigrant Jews in Argentina after the war, and by the migration of German refugee and femicide suspect Klaus Reiter to Santa Teresa, where he eventually is arrested and jailed.

2. *"As if an atomic bomb had dropped nearby and no one had noticed."* In still another moment in "The Part About the Crimes," we learn that a former FBI agent and serial killer investigator Albert Kessler has been invited both to speak at the university in Santa Teresa and to consult with the local police investigating the femicides. On one particular day of his visit, Kessler asks to be driven to the El Chile dump, the largest private dump in Santa Teresa, a place "where waste was disposed of not only by the maquiladora trucks but also by garbage trucks contracted by the city and some private garbage trucks and pickups, subcontracted or working in services that public services didn't cover."[5] Kessler's interest in this dump is triggered by the fact that it has served as a disposal site for the raped, mutilated, and decomposing bodies of female murder victims, their corpses eventually discovered by the trash pickers and the truck drivers as they labor in the wasteland. As his journey by car nears the dump, Kessler observes his driver steering the car off the city's paved roads and then making its final approach to the dump via a wide, unpaved, and deeply rutted dirt track. At this point, when Kessler looks out the car's windows, he notices:

> How even the brush was covered with a thick layer of dust as if an atomic bomb had dropped nearby and no one had noticed, except the victims, thought Kessler, but they didn't count because they'd lost their minds or were dead, even though they still walked and stared, their eyes and stares straight out of a Western, the stares of Indians or bad guys, of course, the stares in other words of lunatics, people living in another dimension, their gazes no longer able to touch us, we're aware of them but they don't touch us, they don't adhere to our skin, they shoot straight through us, thought Kessler as he moved to roll down the window. No, don't open it, said one of the inspectors. Why not? The smell, it smells like death. It stinks.[6]

Kessler's gaze of surveillance from inside the slow-moving vehicle organizes this scene and itself is mediated by the protective shield formed by the car's glass windows and its metal and chrome and plastic body. As this textual passage concludes, the initial spatial opposition of inside/outside the moving car gets underscored by the police inspector's admonition to Kessler not to roll down a car window and allow the external odor of decomposing garbage to pollute the car's interior as well as its passenger's sense of smell. As the car progresses toward the dump, Kessler's gaze notes, in serial fashion, both pedestrians walking along the side of the dirt road and the rising and falling dust plumes that literally blanket everything in sight. The initial inside/outside binary metastasizes into additional imagistic contrasts: health/contamination (the danger of toxic exposure); life/death (the smell of death). In addition, embedded similes or analogies ("as if an atom bomb had dropped") and rhetorical markers ("thought Kessler") periodically interrupt the surface procession of Kessler's mostly notational gaze of surveillance, thus providing a layered, archaeological feel as the prose pulses across the page.

While his scanning gaze registers the sheer fact of dust and the bare, physiological act of anonymous humans walking in slow motion along the dirt road to the dump, we also witness how it periodically zooms in to focus on the human faces, especially these pedestrians' eyes. Such close-up views then trigger Kessler's interpretation of the manner and the meaning of their stares. He likens the "stares" of the human "victims" before him, for example, to "the stares of Indians or bad guys" in a classic western film. This abrupt swerve from the passage's predominant descriptive mode into an interpretive judgment grounded by a cinematic allusion then immediately splinters into his explanation of the rationale for this allusion. For Kessler, it turns out, the blank stares of this abject human collective shrouded by the landfill's dust resembles the "stares in other words of lunatics, people living in another dimension." So as Kessler attempts to comprehend what he sees outside the window of his moving car, he makes a judgment, merging speculation with an optics of spectrality, of these apparitional "people living in another dimension" as having already "lost their minds or were dead." Regarded as being neither mortal nor conscious, neither subject nor object, neither exactly alive nor dead, such emergent zombie-like figures looming before Kessler's sight are unsettling precisely because they reside in that liminal space "somewhere between the ontic [lost their minds] and the hauntic [dead]."[7] In his configuration of the environs and inhabitants of the El Chile dump as a necropolis haunted by the walking dead, then, Kessler's cognitive and affective act of exhumation braids together the novel's present moment of the femicides with the specters of colonial violence and genocide (the nineteenth-century Indian Wars and settler culture dominance indexed by the traditional film western's "Indians or bad guys"); World War II (the Holocaust); and the Cold War (the atom bomb).

3. "*The men standing in line like zombies.*" What appears to be at stake here as Kessler's speculative cultural archaeology surfaces during his visit to the El Chile dump and its resident revenants? There is, of course, the crucial matter here of his dawning recognition that present-day traumas, such as the femicide epidemic and *narcotraficante* violence, disclose the uncanny repetition and return of past historical violence. From Kessler's perspective, the El Chile dump—this sepulchral site that contains both secreted waste matter and the wasted bodies spawned by the sanctioned and unsanctioned activities of the transnational maquila economy—constitutes both an inactive and active crime scene. Both the vivid details Kessler's gaze records about the walking dead and his driver's morbid anxiety about contamination illustrate how this wasteland scenography allegorizes not only "the scandal of the present," but also "the

present itself *as* scandal."⁸ Along with the assortment of vampires, ghosts, and phantoms introduced throughout the novel's length, the zombie horde on the move both toward and inside the confines of the El Chile dump here embodies a variety of contemporary fears and anxieties: the loss of human subjectivity and place-based or local knowledges as a result of deracination; the seemingly unstoppable global spread of contagious violence, especially directed against women; and the stark fact of our being held captive to an intensified, hegemonic consumer capitalism, this fate materialized by the dump's waste by-products, which are monetized for profit.

The phantasmagoric specter of the walking dead and the corpses of the abducted and disappeared women in *2666* embody various ruptures associated with the transformed nature of labor and property in the accelerated space-time compression of a globalizing world system, with its uneven economic development and new territorial divisions of labor. There is the rupture between the value granted to labor on the production line and the lack of value afforded to reproductive or affective labor; the rupture between human subjects relentlessly hailed as individual consumers and their sense of being in a collective; and the rupture both between the present and the past that it devours, as well as between the present and the future.⁹ As Deleuze and Guattari claim, multinational capitalist production inherently represents a zombiefication, what they call a "work myth" rather than a "war myth." As in zombies regarded as nonstandard workers, the phantom proletariat populating a low-wage, often nocturnal, service economy (temporary clerical help, nannies, maids, janitors, repairmen, sex workers, line cooks and waitstaff positions). As in zombies who comprise the relatively invisible and disempowered daytime "ghost workers" who serve as living/dead appendages to repetitive assembly line machine production. As in zombies held hostage to the commodity form, which is to say the dead/undead magically resurrected or reanimated at the point of consumption through the mechanistic projection of fetishistic desire.¹⁰ As Hannah Arendt explains the matter, the commodity form, epitomizing the "waste economy" of an emergent global capitalism, "must be almost as quickly devoured and discarded as they have appeared in the world, if the process itself is not to come to a sudden catastrophic end."¹¹ These dead/undead figures "living in another dimension" and portrayed walking by the side of a road as collateral victims of a nuclear holocaust exemplify "the way power works, and the history of man's subjugation and oppression of its 'Others'" deemed unworthy of sovereign life during times of social, political, and economic crises. Others such as the undocumented worker or political refugee, those held hostage in sex-trafficking rings or by slave labor, the abjected homeless individuals and families living on the street.[12] In Jeffrey Jerome Cohen's words, "The zombie figures the return of the injustices we quietly practice against people we prefer to keep dim in a twilight that marks a willed blindness."[13]

4. *"It is a becoming that is the end of becomings."* As Lauro and Embry suggest in their "Zombie Manifesto," the *animal laborans*—the laboring human reduced to a dehumanized object or slave of capitalist production and consumption—epitomizes the fabled "bad" zombie. To the degree that global capitalism and its troika of privatization, deregulation, and entrepreneurialism depends on an ideology of possessive individualism, then, any cultivation of a collective consciousness and potential for democratic change necessarily will be forestalled. But let us also recognize, they insist, that there exists in certain cultural productions, as well as in folklore and legend the opposed figure of the "good" zombie. This positive manifestation of the zombie figure is fabled precisely because of its resistance both to the continuous quantification and embalming of all life through the processes of rationalization and reification and—with regard to the zombie horde motif—resistance to the siren call of consumerism. As a spectral, live/dead being whose individual consciousness has been exchanged for membership in a collective hive mind, what this "good" zombie figure's resistance to the status quo exposes is the human condition as an "endgame: it is a becoming that is the end of becomings."[14]

Lauro and Embry's play here with the singular and plural form of the word *becoming* produces a rather gnomic saying, one whose flirtation with tautology itself risks another kind of "endgame": that of the incommunicability of meaning. But in the overall context of Lauro and Embry's manifesto, *becomings* serves as shorthand for how our intensified culture of consumption relentlessly pushes us to regard human subjectivity as a continuous developmental or improvement project. The "endgame" of the human condition, defined as the "becoming" of the "good" zombie, then, would represent the terminus of zombie capitalism in its current phase, which emphasizes the serial becomings of the real you or the all that you can be, so that—as the marketing of plastic surgery or cosmetics puts the matter—you will become, well, more becoming. "As if an atomic bomb had dropped nearby and no one had noticed": with the homicide detective Kessler's imaging of an apocalyptic "endgame" in conjunction with the appearance of the walking dead who seemingly are conjured up from the depths of a garbage dump and now afoot in the land, is it perhaps the case that the phantasmagoric scene he surveys through the car window's glass can be read as a harbinger of the endgame to the human condition represented by the good zombie? That these spectral walking dead/undead figures who "live in another dimension" and whose stares "shoot straight through us" uncannily embody an alternative and collective kind of historical unconscious, anticipate the apocalyptic future after the endgame of global finance capitalism? Or is it just my imagination running away with me?

[**A**lphabet/Abecedario; **D**iapers; **K**otex; **L**ipstick; **S**cene of the Crime; **U**rbicide; **T**elevision]

Notes

About this book
Extracts: Bloch, "The Philosophy of the Detective Novel," 262; Belcourt, *A History of My Brief Body*, 12; Sebald, *On the Natural History*, 33.

1. See Bhabha, *The Location of Culture*, 141.
2. Soja, *Postmodern Geographies*, 190.
3. Harper, "The Philosopher as Detective," *Philosophy Now* (online), accessed June 17, 2022. https://philosophynow.org/issues/5/The_Philosopher_as_Detective.
4. Urrea, *By the Lake of Sleeping Children*, 45–46.
5. "Transcendental homelessness": Lukács, *The Theory of the Novel*, 61–62.
6. Davis, *Dead Cities*, 8.
7. Vidler, *The Architectural Uncanny*, 167–68.
8. Tatum, "Spectrality and the Postregional Interface," 10–11; Soja, *Postmodern Geographies*, 157–89.
9. Tobar, *The Tattooed Soldier*, 63.
10. Ghosh, *The Nutmeg's Curse*, 222.
11. Nixon, *Slow Violence*, 62. The two quoted phrases within this quote represent Nixon's citation of the British cultural studies theorist Raymond Williams.
12. Sebald, *On the Natural History of Destruction*, 31; 41.
13. Bowden and Briggs, *Dreamland*, 6. Emphasis added.
14. Roland Barthes, *Roland Barthes*, 148.
15. Here my phrasing references the title of Maryam Jafri's article, "Through, Around, and Against the Document," 29.
16. "A different sensibility": Gordon, *The Hawthorn Archives*, xi.
17. My brief remarks on coherence are shaped by Sianne Ngai's discussion of Gertrude Stein's prose, the coherence of which centers on the way things adhere as "a mushy mass." See Ngai, *Ugly Feelings*, 289.
18. "One image *plus* another": Cameron, *The Bond of the Furthest Apart*, 14.
19. Belcourt, *A History of My Brief Body*, 12; "waiting in the meantime": Cazdyn, *The Already Dead*, 6–7; "the sadness of life": Kundera, *The Art of the Novel*, 25: "There would seem to be nothing more obvious, more tangible and palpable than the present moment. And yet it eludes us completely. All the sadness of life lies in that fact." Thanks to Stephen Ruffus for this Kundera reference.
20. With regard to "spectrality," see my "Spectral Beauty and Forensic Aesthetics in the West" (2006) as well as "Spectrality and the Postregional Interface" (2007). Also valuable in this context is Campbell's *Post-Westerns*, especially the introduction, "Big Hats, Horses, and Dust: The Visible and Invisible West," 1–17. As Campbell writes, his

book's "starting point is to think about the 'phantom architecture' of the West imagined through its cinematic representation (its 'ghost Westerns') and to begin to understand how in the post-West there might live on the haunting presence of the past within the present and future and that *together* these multiple stories provide some fuller and better understanding of the contemporary West itself" (2). For an important early essay contrasting so-called classic American novels in which the plots focus on "leaving" home with Native American novels with plots focusing on "homing in," see Bevis, "Native American Novels."

21. Jameson, *The Cultural Turn*, 187.
22. Jameson, *The Cultural Turn*, 187.
23. "The specific settings of human history": Santner, *On Creaturely Life*, 57: "spectral materialism" connotes one's capacity "to register the persistence of past suffering that in some sense has been absorbed into the substance of lived space, into the 'setting' of human history."
24. Fisher, "Hauntology Now," n.p.
25. 2Bears, "My Post-Indian Technological Autobiography," 27.
26. 2Bears, "My Post-Indian Technological Autobiography," 28.

Alphabet/Abecedario

Extracts: Baca, *A Place to Stand*, 183; Viramontes, *Their Dogs Came with Them*, 236; Luiselli, *Lost Children Archive*, 270.

1. Though the collaboration between Cardona and Briggs on this topic began in late 2012, when writer Charles Bowden introduced them to each other at a meeting in Las Cruces, New Mexico, their earlier writing, photographs, and artworks already had focused, albeit separately, on the violence and border politics in Juárez. Some of the images from Cardona's 1995 photo exhibit *Nada se Ver* (Nothing to See) had appeared in Bowden's 1998 book *Juárez: Laboratory of Our Future*. Starting in 2008, Calderon's longform journalistic work, which centered on his interviews with and photographs of various citizens of Juárez engaged in legal as well as illegal activities, led him to begin collecting the new slang words and phrases that would eventually appear in the *Abecedario*. As for Briggs, she had spent time living in Juárez in 2008, and over the next two years she began collecting the *narco* and gang-related street slang that would inform her art installation *Abecedario de Juárez, 2010*. This installation included thirty-two sgraffito illustrations, several of which also appeared in her collaboration with Bowden for the 2010 book *Dreamland: The Way Out of Juárez*.
2. See Briggs, "Abecedario de Juárez."
3. Cardona and Briggs, *Abecedario*, vii.
4. Briggs explains her sgraffito technique as a process that begins by treating a wood panel with rabbit skin glue and kaolin clay before she sprays its entire surface with black India ink. Then she cuts the resulting black surface primarily with X-Acto knives, creating the image via cuts, scratches, and etching (which may also involve using steel wool, sandpaper, and fiberglass brushes). See *Abecedario*, 214–15.
5. As quoted in Cabrera and Rice, "The Grim ABCs of Life and Death in Juárez."

6. Barthes, *Roland Barthes*, 148.
7. Sekula, "Photography Between Capitol and Labor," 193–94.
8. Abigail De Kosnick: "What I call 'rogue archives' are defined by constant 24/7 availability; zero barriers to entry for all who can connect to the internet; content that can be streamed or downloaded in full, with no required payment, and no regard for copyright restrictions; and content that has never been and would likely never be contained in traditional memory institutions." See her *Rogue Archives*, 2. The *Abecedario de Juárez* is obviously not an internet site (though one could imagine one being created to update and expand the lexicon), but it does fulfill certain aims of internet rogue archives: the possibility of preserving cultural content of emerging or degraded genres; the possibility for subcultural and marginalized groups to have archives of their own; the possibility of a certain style of memory work based on embodied modes of performance.
9. Sekula "Photography Between Labor and Capital," 193–94.
10. "territory of images" is a phrase drawn from Sekula, "Photography Between Labor and Capital," 194.
11. Cardona and Briggs, *Abecedario*, vii.
12. Cardona and Briggs, *Abecedario*, 113.
13. Cardona and Briggs, *Abecedario*, 119.
14. Hans Holbein the Younger (1497–1543) produced the woodcuts for his *Dance of Death* between 1522 and 1526, but it wasn't until 1538 that the book itself was published in Lyon, France, with forty-one woodcuts. In 1547 "The Soldier" woodcut, along with twelve other additions to the original edition of *Dance of Death,* appeared. Hollar's representation of Holbein's "The Soldier" figure was retitled "The Knight and Death," and his version adheres closely to the earlier artist Arnold Birckmann's revision of the Holbein's original: the skeletal figure of Death attacks the soldier with an arrow or lance instead of a bone; Death carries no shield and is grabbing the knight around his right collarbone. And unlike in the Holbein version of "The Soldier," a memento mori in the form of an hourglass appears here on the chest of one of the dead soldiers lying just to the right of the femur bone of this allegorical figure of Death.
15. See "*The Writing on the Wall*: Alice Leora Briggs and Julián Cardona."
16. The phrase "uncanny economy of revenance" appears in Castricano, "Cryptomimesis," 6.
17. Baudrillard, *Symbolic Exchange and Death*, 147. For grammatical purposes I have rearranged the order of the quoted phrases in the original text.
18. Baudrillard, *Passages*, 17.
19. Some key resources with regard to Posada's life and career include Tyler, ed., *Posada's Mexico*; Wollen's "Introduction" to *Posada*; and Jim Nikas, "Day of the Dead (Dia de Muertos) Calavera Images and José Gaudelupe Posada."
20. As quoted in Hyde, *A Primer for Forgetting*, 163.

Boredoms

Extracts: Debord, "The Bad Old Days Will End," 36; Didion, *Slouching Towards Bethlehem*, 133–34; Berlin, *A Manual for Cleaning Women*, 246; Coupland, *Generation X*, 143.

1. Patricia Spacks argues that "In its nature... boredom opposes desire... it [boredom] constitutes desire's antithesis, assuring its victim of the utter impossibility of wishing for anything at all." See her *Boredom*, 259.
2. Compare Isis Leslie's definition: "Boredom is defined as a sense of emptiness, that is accompanied by mad pursuit of and/or passive waiting for the trivial, insubstantial stimulations and distractions that are ultimately unfulfilling." See her "From Idleness to Boredom," 35.
3. Spacks, *Boredom*, 252.
4. Spacks, *Boredom*, 254.
5. See Lukács, *Theory of the Novel*, especially chapter 2, "The Problem of the History of Forms," 61–62: "For crime and madness are objectivations of transcendental homelessness—the homelessness of an action in the human order of social relations, the homelessness of a soul in the ideal order of a supra-personal system of values."
6. Lukács, *Theory of the Novel*, 41.
7. Debord, *Society of the Spectacle*, 30. For more on the boredom caused by satiety, see Svendsen, *A Philosophy of Boredom*, 41–42.
8. Coupland, *Generation X*, 11.
9. Phillips, *On Kissing, Tickling*, 77.
10. Hebdige, *Hiding in the Light*, 197.
11. Phillips, *On Kissing, Tickling*, 78.
12. Baudrillard, as quoted in Svendsen, *Philosophy*, 48.
13. Coupland, *Generation X*, 4.
14. Coupland, *Generation X*, 7.
15. Coupland, *Generation X*, 8.
16. Coupland, *Generation X*, 8, 14.
17. Coupland, *Generation X*, 30.
18. Coupland, *Generation X*, 31.
19. Svendsen, *Philosophy*, 44.
20. Coupland, *Generation X*, 91.
21. Coupland, *Generation X*, 73.
22. In order, Coupland, *Generation X*, 31, 10, 11, 113.
23. In order, Coupland, *Generation X*, 7, 31, 36.
24. Dinerstein, *The Origins of Cool in Postwar America*, 33.
25. Coupland, *Generation X*, 16.
26. Liu, *The Laws of Cool*, 294.
27. Liu, *The Laws of Cool*, 296.
28. Benjamin, "The Storyteller," in *Illuminations*, 91: "If sleep is the apogee of physical relaxation, boredom is the apogee of mental relaxation. Boredom is the dream bird that hatches the egg of experience. A rustling in the leaves drives him away."
29. Coupland, *Generation X*, 58.
30. Coupland, *Generation X*, 3–4.
31. Coupland, *Generation X*, 116.
32. Coupland, *Generation X*, 175–76.

33. In order, Coupland, *Generation X*, 176, 179.
34. In order, Stewart, "Regionality," 283, 278.
35. Coupland, *Generation X*, 178; Stewart, "Regionality," 275.
36. The quoted material in this sentence is, in order, from Stewart, "Regionality," 278; Coupland, *Generation X*, 14, 179.
37. Coupland, *Generation X*, 178.
38. Coupland, *Generation X*, 59.
39. Coupland, *Generation X*, 91.
40. Coupland, *Generation X*, 95.
41. Coupland, *Generation X*, 173.
42. Žižek, *Welcome to the Desert of the Real*, 6–7.
43. Žižek, *Welcome*, 10.
44. Žižek, *Welcome*, 176–77.
45. Žižek, *Welcome*, 177.
46. Žižek, *Welcome*, 10.

Cryptography

Extracts: McCarthy, *All the Pretty Horses*, 300–301; Alexie, *Indian Killer*, 139; Herrera, *Signs Preceding*, 11–12; Castricano, "Cryptomimesis," 19.

1. Héctor Tobar, *The Tattooed Soldier*, 44.
2. Abraham and Torok, *The Shell and the Kernel*, 130, 159.
3. See Gabriele Schwab, "Writing against Memory and Forgetting," 107; emphasis added. As Schwab explores Abraham and Torok's theorizing of individual, familial, communal, and national crypts, she defines *cryptonymy* as a form of "haunted language [that] refers to what is unspeakable through ellipsis, indirection, and detour, or fragmentation and deformation."
4. Tobar, *The Tattooed Soldier*, 7.
5. Tobar, *The Tattooed Soldier*, 17.
6. Tobar, *The Tattooed Soldier*, 20.
7. Tobar, *The Tattooed Soldier*, 81.
8. Castricano, "Cryptomimesis," 4.
9. Tobar, *The Tattooed Soldier*, 157.
10. Tobar, *The Tattooed Soldier*, 81.
11. Hebdige, *Hiding in the Light*, 197.
12. Tobar, *The Tattooed Soldier*, 185.
13. Tobar, *The Tattooed Soldier*, 183.
14. Tobar, *The Tattooed Soldier*, 186.
15. Castricano, "Cryptomimesis," 18n2, 16. The phrase quote within her words is drawn from Abraham and Torok's essay "The Lost Object—Me."
16. Tobar, *The Tattooed Soldier*, 181.
17. Tobar, *The Tattooed Soldier*, 187.
18. Tobar, *The Tattooed Soldier*, 187.
19. Tobar, *The Tattooed Soldier*, 307.

20. Tobar, *The Tattooed Soldier*, 304.
21. Tobar, *The Tattooed Soldier*, 305.
22. Tobar, *The Tattooed Soldier*, 306.
23. Tobar, *The Tattooed Soldier*, 306.
24. Vidler, *The Architectural Uncanny*, 53. In discussing Surrealist artists and theorists such as Todorov and Dalí, Vidler notes how they psychoanalytically theorized an "architecture of hysteria, of digestion, or of the uncanny, intrauterine cave" (137).
25. Boym, *The Future of Nostalgia*, 13: "The object of romantic nostalgia must be beyond the present space of experience, somewhere in the twilight of the past or on an island of utopia where time has happily stopped, as on an antique clock."
26. Schwenger, *The Tears of Things*, 157.
27. Tobar, *The Tattooed Soldier*, 308, 309.
28. Tobar, *The Tattooed Soldier*, 310.
29. Tobar, *The Tattooed Soldier*, 311.
30. Antonio learns about Guevara's notion of "revolutionary love" from his wife Elena, and he references this concept several times during his Los Angeles sojourn, especially this summary statement, which appears on the novel's penultimate page: "The revolutionary is guided in all of his actions by great feelings of love." See Tobar, *The Tattooed Soldier*, 311.
31. Tobar, *The Tattooed Soldier*, 312.
32. Campbell, *Post-Westerns*, 348.

Diapers and loading docks

Extracts: Yamashita, *Tropic of Orange*, 215; Proulx, *That Old Ace in the Hole*, 6; Viramontes, *Their Dogs Came with Them*, 176–77; Cardona and Briggs, *Abecedario de Juárez*, 54.

1. Philip Webb, *Homeless Lives in American Cities*, 80.
2. In addition to chapter 3 of DePastino's *Citizen Hobo*, see Allen, *Homelessness in American Literature*, and Barber, "The Tramp," 356: "The great theme, or tension, of the literature about homelessness is the conflict between the romantic appeal of the road and the brutal realities of the vagabond life."
3. See Wald, "'Refusing to Halt,'" for an extended critical analysis of the motif of freeway construction and the erasure of neighborhoods in novels by Viramontes and Yamashita.
4. Vidler, *The Architectural Uncanny*, 186.
5. Bowden and Briggs, *Dreamland*, 25.
6. Quotes in this paragraph are from Bowden and Briggs, *Dreamland*, 16, 18.
7. Bowden and Briggs, *Dreamland*, 16.
8. Bennet, *Vibrant Matter*, 32.
9. "A force that has the power" is a concept in Weil, *War and "The Iliad,"* 3–6.
10. See Cameron, "Animal Sentience," 6.
11. See Cameron's reading of director Robert Bresson's cinematography and editing techniques in her "Animal Sentience" essay, especially pages 1–4.
12. Bowden and Briggs, *Dreamland*, 43.
13. Jameson, *Archaeologies of the Future*, 75.

14. Bowden and Briggs, *Dreamland*, 18.
15. Bowden and Briggs, *Dreamland*, 25.
16. Bowden and Briggs, *Dreamland*, 40.
17. Comer, "Thinking Otherwise," 8.
18. These questions are shaped by Ben Lerner's essay "The Storyteller," which reflects on the works of W. G. Sebald in a review of a recent biography of this late writer.
19. Jameson, *The Geopolitical Aesthetic*, 5.
20. Žižek, *Welcome to the Desert of the Real*, 149.
21. For a critique of Bowden on this question with regard to his *Juárez: The Laboratory of Our Future*, see Alice Driver's excellent, *More or Less Dead*, 72–76.

Exposure

Extracts: Silko, *Almanac of the Dead*, 159; Alexie, *Indian Killer*, 8; Tobar, *The Tattooed Soldier*, 180; Viramontes, *Their Dogs Came with Them*, 295.

1. For Barthes, see *Camera Lucida*, part 2. On the concept of a "poetics of exposure" that connotes "the specific nature of openness to a world under the dual impact of historical violence and the structural dislocations generated by capitalist modernity," see Santner, *On Creaturely Life*, 49.
2. Cameron, *The Bond of the Furthest Apart*, 11.
3. Luiselli, *Lost Children Archive*, 55.
4. McCarthy, *The Crossing*, 411.
5. See Iverson, *Beyond Pleasure*, 133–45.
6. Iverson, *Beyond Pleasure*, 125.
7. Tobar, *The Tattooed Soldier*, 180.
8. Castricano, "Cryptomimesis," 10–11.
9. See also Tatum, "Spectral Beauty and Forensic Aesthetics in the West" and "Spectrality and the Postregional Interface."
10. Mbembe's concept of necropolitics draws upon and extends Michel Foucault's theory of biopower, where "to exercise sovereignty is to exercise control over mortality and to define life as the deployment and manifestation of power." See Mbembe, "Necropolitics," 11–12.
11. Silko, *Almanac of the Dead*, 228.
12. Beck, *Dirty Wars*, 264.
13. Beck, *Dirty Wars*, 267.
14. Goodman, *A Planetary Lens*, 192.

Freeways and highways

Extracts: Walter Benjamin, as quoted in Hanson, *Walter Benjamin and the Arcades Project*, 98; Kristeva, *The Kristeva Reader*, 37.

1. Influential in the development of this essay's format has been David Shields's *Reality Hunger: A Manifesto*. As Anna Gibbs also suggests in her "Fictocriticism, Affect, Mimesis" essay, fictocritical modes "borrow from certain Situationist practices," such as the derive (or digression) and detournement (the turning around or turning in on

itself), and—as this fictocritical "Freeways and highways" essay illustrates—it adapts "broadly modernist strategies, especially the collage, montage and the cut up" (n.p.).

Graves and gravestones

Extracts: Welch, *Winter in the Blood*, 143; Silko, *Almanac of the Dead*, 587–88; Fuller, *The Legend of Colton H. Bryant*, 168; De Leon, *The Land of Open Graves*, 46; Jones, *Ledfeather*, 107.

1. McCarthy, *All the Pretty Horses*, 301.
2. McCarthy, *All the Pretty Horses*, 239.
3. McCarthy, *All the Pretty Horses*, 135.
4. McCarthy, *All the Pretty Horses*, 301, 299.
5. McCarthy, *All the Pretty Horses*, 252.
6. McCarthy, *All the Pretty Horses* 287.
7. McCarthy, *All the Pretty Horses*, 300–301.
8. McCarthy, *All the Pretty Horses*, 7.
9. McCarthy, *All the Pretty Horses*, 5.
10. McCarthy, *All the Pretty Horses*, 300.
11. Santner, *On Creaturely Life*, 52.
12. Abel, "Skin, Flesh, and the Affective Wrinkles of Civil Rights Photography." Abel focuses on how, in terms of affect, we move from the legibility of faces to "the tactile sensations of skin, where intensities are registered and transmitted at the body's interface with other bodies." Thus, affect on one level is "what overflows the face."
13. Stewart, *On Longing*, 151.
14. Harrison, *The Dominion of the Dead*, 15.
15. Harrison, *Dominion*, 20.
16. Harrison, *Dominion*, 148.
17. McCarthy, *The Crossing*, 413.

Hotel life

Extracts: Kracauer, "The Hotel Lobby," 55–56; Didion, *The White Album*, 13; Fante, *Ask the Dust*, 46–47.

1. Kracauer, "The Hotel Lobby," 54.
2. Jameson, "Postmodernism; or, the Cultural Logic of Late Capitalism," 85.
3. Yamashita, *I Hotel*, 424.
4. Jameson, *Postmodernism*, 127–28.
5. Jameson, *Postmodernism*, 128.
6. Murphet, "Postmodernism and Space," 123–24.
7. Davis, *City of Quartz*, 227.
8. Campbell, *Affective Regionality*, 187.
9. Yamashita, *I Hotel*, 590–91.
10. Yamashita, *I Hotel*, 579–80.
11. Yamashita, *I Hotel*, 599.
12. MacCannell, "Homeless," 294.

13. "Counter-memory" is from Foucault, "Nietzsche, Genealogy, History," 139–64.
14. Yamashita, *I Hotel*, 605.
15. Comer, "Place and Worlding," 154.

Idyll of the idle

Extracts: McWilliams, *Southern California*, 294; Davis, *City of Quartz*, 227; Soja, *Thirdspace*, 297.

1. Tobar, *The Tattooed Soldier*, 5.
2. For helpful historical and sociological views and cultural studies perspectives, see Kusmer, *Down and Out*; Webb, *Homeless Lives in American Cities*; De Pastino, *Citizen Hobo*; Goodman, *Lost Homelands*; Watson and Austerberry's feminist perspective in *Housing and Homelessness*.
3. Bhabha, "DissemiNation," 141.
4. Tobar, *The Tattooed Soldier*, 73.
5. Castells, "The Informational City," 349.
6. Murphet, "Postmodernism and Space," 130, 126.
7. Tobar, *The Tattooed Soldier*, 53.
8. Tobar, *The Tattooed Soldier*, 13, 15, 43, 46.
9. Simmel, "The Ruin," in "Two Essays," 385.
10. Turner, "Social Forces in American History," 317.
11. For "the wageworker's frontier," see DePastino, *Citizen Hobo*, 4, 61.
12. Davis, *Planet of Slums*, 9–10.
13. Sobchack, "Lounge Time," 129–70.

Junkspaces

1. Urrea, *Into the Beautiful North*, 267.
2. Vidler, *The Architectural Uncanny*, 177.
3. Baudrillard, *America*, 133.
4. Soja, *Postmetropolis*, 190.
5. LeMenager, "The Aesthetics of Petroleum, after *Oil*!" 64.
6. Soja, *Postmetropolis*, 179.
7. Tatum, "Spectrality and the Postregional Interface," 13.
8. Foster, "Designing a Second Modernity?" 106.
9. Here, I am importing David Spurr's conception of the contemporary literary fragment in his *Architecture and Modern Literature*, 30–31.
10. Coleman, *Jazz and Twelve O'Clock Tales*, 55.
11. Banham, *Los Angeles*, 143, 159.
12. Vidler, *The Architectural Uncanny*, 183.
13. Gordon, *The Hawthorn Archive*, 234.
14. For "disjunctive inclusion," see Žižek, "The Architectural Parallax," 286.
15. Coupland, *Generation X*, 30.
16. Coupland, *Generation X*, 71.
17. For "junkspace," see Koolhaas, *"Junkspace,"* 175.

18. As Spurr summarizes in *Architecture and Modern Literature*, 222–23.
19. Spurr, *Architecture and Modern Literature*, 222–23.
20. Coupland, *Generation X*, 63.
21. Coupland, *Generation X*, 70.
22. Coupland, *Generation X*, 71.
23. Charles Bowden and Briggs, *Dreamland*, 90.
24. Bowden and Briggs, *Dreamland*, 60.
25. Bowden and Briggs, *Dreamland*, 81.
26. Ross, "Keeping House," in *Fast Cars, Clean Bodies*, 111: "So too do the newly modernized French interiors and techniques, the electricity and indoor plumbing, appear in a distorted, nightmarish guise in their narrative reflection across the sea [in Algeria]."
27. Bowden and Briggs, *Dreamland*, 146; 140.
28. Bowden and Briggs, *Dreamland*, 138.
29. Vidler, *The Architectural Uncanny*, 167; Pollack, "The Image in Psychoanalysis," 11.

Kotex, Keds, ketchup
Extracts: Yamashita, *Tropic of Orange*, 193–94; Erdrich, *The Antelope Wife*, 118; Urrea, *Across the Wire*, 12.

1. Leong, "Ulterior Spaces," *Harvard Guide to Shopping*, 767.
2. Leong, "Ulterior," 769.
3. Leong, "Ulterior," 767.
4. Zuboff, *The Age of Surveillance Capitalism*, 11–12.
5. Harvey, *The Condition of Postmodernity*, 286.
6. MacCannell, "Homeless," 288–89.
7. Bauman, *Wasted Lives*, 96–97.
8. Urrea, *By the Lake of Sleeping Children*, 44.
9. Urrea, *By the Lake*, 44.
10. Taussig, *My Cocaine Museum*, 177.
11. Urrea, *By the Lake*, 45.
12. Urrea, *By the Lake*, 45.
13. Iversen, "The World Without a Self," 20.
14. Bauman, *Wasted Lives*, 22.
15. Urrea, *By the Lake*, 45–46.
16. "Process geography" and "cross-cutting map" are drawn from Appadurai, "Grassroots Globalization," 5, 7.
17. Urrea, *By the Lake*, 45–46.

Lipstick traces
Extracts: De Leon, *The Land of Open Graves*, 191–92; Bolaño, *2666*, 355; Herrera, *Signs Preceding*, 34–35.

1. Bowden and Briggs, *Dreamland*, 38. The other quotations in this paragraph are also from this page.
2. Bowden and Briggs, *Dreamland*, 40.

3. Bowden and Briggs, *Dreamland*, 40.
4. Bowden and Briggs, *Dreamland*, 40.
5. Bowden and Briggs, *Dreamland*, 132.
6. Bowden and Briggs, *Dreamland*, 63.
7. Bowden and Briggs, *Dreamland*, 63.
8. These definitions and etymologies are drawn from separate entries for these words in Dictionary.com, accessed July 7, 2021.
9. Taussig, *Walter Benjamin's Grave*, viii.
10. Bowden and Briggs, *Dreamland*, 38.
11. For an excellent discussion of things as "stuff," see Boscaglia, *Stuff Theory*, especially the chapter "Garbage in Theory: Waste Aesthetics."
12. Bowden and Briggs, *Dreamland*, 105.
13. Bowden and Briggs, *Dreamland*, 105.
14. See Julian Yates, "Orange," 86. As Yates explains, color is a "multispecies sensory process or network that generates biosemiotic-material effects that then take on a metaphorical life of their own as they are translated to different registers." This understanding of color and history is exemplified by the women who sold oranges in Restoration-era theaters being called "orange-women."
15. Taussig, *What Color Is the Sacred?*, 198.
16. A key trait of Bowden's narrative persona is its stuckness. As we see in this textual moment from *Dreamland*, even in the act of enunciating a judgment ("So it all hangs together"), this passage swerves to a description whose metonymic logic, I argue, draws a transhistorical, biosemiotic, and gendered equivalence between red blood, red cheeks, and red lips. One might well want to honor, as I do, the Bowden persona's confessional honesty about not being able fully to apprehend and comprehend the meaning of the cartel death house event—even as he speaks otherwise to the logic of global capitalism. Still, the inherent challenge attached to Bowden's prismatic archive of the colors white and red in *Dreamland* is that the narrative persona neither questions the stereotypical virgin/whore binary opposition disseminated by his Spanish sources nor fully recognizes how such abstractions as "a woman" dilute the force of critique of the local history of exploitation. For a critique along these lines in relation to what she calls the "Border-Brothel → Maquiladora Paradigm," see Carroll, "'Accidental Allegories.'"
17. For "dual formation" and "transhistorical fatalism," see Lerner, "The Storyteller." My discussion here of Bowden's historiography as a "dual formation" advancing a "transhistorical fatalism" raises the question as to the ethical risks Bowden's body of work takes due to its erasure, in certain textual moments, of historical specificity. In an endnote to his "Introduction" to the *Abecedario de Juárez* book collaboration by Julián Cardona and Alice Leora Briggs, Howard Campbell briefly summarizes critiques of Bowden's work, some of them written by "more literal, empirically obsessed or politically minded academics" who single out his writing as "chauvinistic orientalism or as imperialistic or as sexist misogyny of the very worst kind." Still, "despite the harshness of many of these critiques," he judges that Bowden and Briggs, "far more than any journalist, writer, or social scientist, made the outside world aware of the catastrophe unfolding in Juárez:

the serial killings of women, mass casualties of the Mexican drug war, and the extreme social deprivation and suffering aggravated by the neoliberal economic development model and the 'twin plant' maquiladora industry, as well as by cruel U.S. immigration policies." See Campbell, "Introduction," 214.

18. Bowden and Briggs, *Dreamland*, 19–20.
19. Bowden and Briggs, *Dreamland*, 159.
20. Jameson, *Valences of the Dialectic*, 153.
21. In his *What Color Is the Sacred?*, Taussig refers to Roland Barthes's observation about how the chemical production of synthetic colors in the nineteenth century indexed a history of colonial endeavors through such labels for color as "Indian yellow" or "Persian red" (44–45).
22. Ellen Meloy traces the trade in cochineal dye between Mexico and Europe that was monopolized for over two centuries by the conquering Spaniards—until a French naturalist smuggled cactus pads out of Mexico to Haiti. What ultimately interests her is what happens in the late-nineteenth century, when cochineal-dyed blankets of red flannel appeared in trading posts in the American Southwest. Navajo weavers would trade for these blankets and unravel their red threads, then weave the used red yarn into their own rugs or blankets. See her *The Anthropology of Turquoise*, 241–42.
23. Bowden and Briggs, *Dreamland*, 138.
24. To supplement this *Dreamland* theme about the lengthy history of exploitation and violence against Indigenous women, let us also note how the intersection of the stuff of clothing with the color red also materializes in the contemporary Red Shawl Solidarity Project, created to honor all Native people who have survived domestic and sexual violence.

Motel noir

Extracts: McMurtry, *The Last Picture Show*, 147; Silko, *Almanac of the Dead*, 63–64; Coupland, *Generation X*, 115.

1. See Levin, *Edward Hopper*, 510–11.
2. Nochlin, "Edward Hopper," 136.
3. See O'Doherty, "Hopper's Look," 80. O'Doherty notes the central paradox in Hopper's paintings in which "Everything seems massively stable, but, if you look closer, transient or in transit."
4. Wallace Jackson explores how this key motif of "waiting" in Hopper's artwork is coupled with a "double act of looking," which happens when we "look at those who are looking at something else and our act is duplicated in the act represented on the canvas." See Jackson, "*To Look*," 135–36.
5. Strand, *Hopper*, 25.
6. In his assessment of "Western Motel," Richard Lacayo suggests that the woman directly looking toward the space of the artist and the viewer is "a spiritual and psychological stand-in" for Hopper himself, and her steady gaze "a reminder of the power of the artist's vision—to fix in place the passage of time." See his *Lost Light*, 271.
7. Strand, *Hopper*, 44.

8. My gloss of Strand's concluding remarks on Hopper's "Western Motel" is influenced by Michael Fried's conceptualization of "presentness" in his canonical 1968 essay in art criticism, "Art and Objecthood." See Fried, *Art and Objecthood*, 45–46
9. McMurtry, *The Last Picture Show*, 147.
10. Rilke, *Duino Elegies*, 3.
11. Campbell, *Affective Critical Regionality*, 10.
12. Žizek, *Enjoy Your Symptom!*, 153.
13. Žizek, *Enjoy*, 153.
14. Žizek, *Enjoy*, 154.
15. Jackson, "*To Look*," 145.
16. My reading of this figure's face as exemplifying a mask of "pure exteriority" is shaped by Parveen Adams's revisionist psychoanalytic observations on the issue of what happens between the spectator and the art object. See her *The Emptiness of the Image*, especially 127–31.
17. Joan Copjec, "The Orthopsychic Subject," 69.
18. Jackson, "*To Look*," 137. Compare Margaret Iversen's definition of "the blind field" in Hopper's artworks: "the space implied by the composition, but not shown, which incites an anxious reverie in the spectator." See Iversen, *Beyond Pleasure*, 14.
19. Jackson, "*To Look*," 143.
20. See Benjamin, "On Some Motifs in Baudelaire," in *Illuminations*, 141. For an extended discussion of Benjamin's concept of the "optical unconscious" in cinema, see Hansen, "Benjamin, Cinema, and Experience," 212–17.

Noir motel

Extracts: Yamashita, *Tropic of Orange*, 18–19; Vlautin, *The Motel Life*, 1; Luiselli, *Lost Children Archive*, 121.

1. Smith, *In Lonely Places*, 152. As Smith notes, in *Touch of Evil* "Susie is always near windows: the hotel window that has no shade, the plate-glass window through which she gestures uncomprehendingly at a messenger; the doors and windows through which the Night Man at the Mirador Motel keeps popping in and out while she tries to talk to him" (155).
2. See Ngai, *Ugly Feelings*, 210: "Yet while intimately aligned with the concept of Futurity, and the temporal dynamics of deferral and anticipation in particular, anxiety has a spatial dimension as well."
3. Vidler, *The Architectural Uncanny*, 224–25.
4. Vidler, *The Architectural Uncanny*, 225.
5. Jameson, *Postmodernism*, 25.
6. See Campbell, *Post-Westerns*, 252.
7. "Actions and events come to be interpreted in relation to the self" is from Guilmette, "The Age of Paranoia," 94. Like my developing argument, Guilmette's overall point here is that paranoia also needs to be regarded as "a sociohistorical framing of experience" that is "heightened and elicited in a late-capitalist service economy."
8. Jameson, *The Political Unconscious*, 287.

9. Murphet, "Film Noir," 26. As Lee Clark Mitchell also suggests, "film noir is the only other genre [other than the western] to locate Mexico as a utopian site." Among the titles he lists in this regard is Orson Welles's *Touch of Evil*. See his *Late-Westerns*, 274n9.
10. Harris, "Film Noir Fascination," 4.
11. Murphet, "Film Noir," 29.
12. Murphet, "Film Noir," 31.
13. Murphet, "Film Noir," 26.
14. Ngai, *Ugly Feelings*, 298–99.
15. See Becker, et al., "Lesbians and Film," in Doty and Creekmur, *Out in Culture*, 26.
16. Butler, *Precarious Life*, 28–29.
17. Butler, *Precarious Life*, 27, 29.
18. Butler, *Precarious Life*, 32.
19. Butler, *Precarious Life*, 30.

Oil rich

Extracts: "Oil" and "Petroleum," *Online Etymological Dictionary*, n.p.; "Ledger," *Webster's Unabridged Dictionary of the English Language*, 1097; Proulx, *Fine Just the Way It Is*, 180; McCarthy, *All the Pretty Horses*, 36–37, 226; Jones, *The Only Good Indians*, 3; McMurtry, *Duane's Depressed*, 17; McMurtry, *The Last Picture Show*, 56; Watkins, *Gold Fame Citrus*, 338; Knausgard, "Petrol," 29; Strand, "The Continuous Life," 21–22.

1. See Revelation 9:6, The Holy Bible, King James Version: "And in those days shall men seek death, and shall not find it; and shall desire to die, and death shall flee from them."
2. In her groundbreaking 2014 book *Living Oil*, Stephanie LeMenager quotes author Michael Watts, who observes that because of oil's "liquid mobility" and "subterranean" origin, its presence can be believed to nourish "all manner of extraordinary magic events," including the "power to tarnish and turn everything into shit." The term "devil's excrement" emerged in 1975 in a comment made by the then-president of Venezuela. See *Living Oil*, 92.
3. This equation of freeways and driveways comes from Reyner Banham's *Los Angeles*, a study in which one of his four "ecologies" of this city is named "Autopia." As Stephanie LeMenager notes by way of critique, the Autopia produced by "ubiquitous freeways" promoted a "distinctly European exoticization of American frontierism" that served to repress how such rampant freeway construction "produces space to restlessly destroy and reorganize it in the service of capital." See Banham, *Los Angeles*, 193, 204; LeMenager, *Living Oil*, 75.
4. Adapted from Benjamin, "The Storyteller," in *Illuminations*, 91.
5. See "Litigation Release No. 9344/April 21, 1981," *SEC Docket* 22, no. 10 (May 1981): 900.
6. In April 1997 Badger also would plead guilty to criminal indictments issued by the U.S. District Court for the Southern District of New York in connection with a scheme, enacted in both Salt Lake City and Manhattan, both to manipulate prices of selected small company stocks and bribe registered broker-dealers to recommend their clients to purchase shares in these companies.

7. Adapted and revised from Stewart, *Ordinary Affects*, 106: "One thing leads to another. An expectation is dashed or fulfilled. An ordinary floating state of things goes sour or takes off into something amazing and good. Either way, things turn out to be not what you thought they were."
8. Fuller, *The Legend of Colton H. Bryant*, 84–85.
9. Bass, *Oil Notes*, 165.
10. Rilke, *Duino Elegies*, 7.

Psychometropolis

Extracts: Alexie, *Indian Killer*, 362–63; Viramontes, *Their Dogs Came with Them*, 119–20; Orange, *There There*, 224.

1. Ellis, *Less than Zero*, 73.
2. Ellis, *Less than Zero*, 63.
3. "Impossible experience" is from Phillips, *On Kissing, Tickling*, 77.
4. Ellis, *Less than Zero*, 115.
5. Ellis, *Less than Zero*, 114–15.
6. Ellis, *Less than Zero*, 63.
7. Ellis, *Less than Zero*, 114.
8. Ellis, *Less than Zero*, 206.
9. Jameson, *The Cultural Turn*, 187.
10. Ellis, *Less than Zero*, 168.
11. Jameson, *The Cultural Turn*, 112.
12. Murphet, *Literature and Race*, 58–59.

Queues for the gallows

Extracts: Otsuka, *When the Emperor Was Divine*, 50; Vlautin, *Northline*, 15; Luiselli, *Lost Children Archive*, 142.

1. Bowden and Briggs, *Dreamland*, 100.
2. Bowden and Briggs, *Dreamland*, 75, 100.
3. See Sebald, *The Rings of Saturn*, 79.
4. "Deep wound" is from Taussig, *What Color Is the Sacred?*, 157.
5. My thanks to Audrey Goodman for this insight.
6. Clark, *The Sight of Death*, 227.
7. Clark, *The Sight of Death*, 227–28.
8. Kristeva, *The Powers of Horror*, 4.
9. Clark, *The Sight of Death*, 228.
10. Schwenger, *The Tears of Things*, 169.
11. My remarks here about *nature morte* are shaped by the "Still Life" and "Last Things" chapter of Schwenger's *The Tears of Things*, especially his concluding remarks in the "Still Life" chapter about novelist Georges Perec's *Life: A User's Manual* (1973).
12. See Taussig, *My Cocaine Museum*, 278.
13. Bowden and Briggs, *Dreamland*, 2.

14. Berger, "Twelve Theses," 4–5. This theme about the capitalist modernity's severing a once vital interdependence of the living and the dead permeates other essays in this book, especially "Oil Rich."
15. Berger, "Twelve Theses," 5.
16. Mbembe, "Necropolitics," 11.
17. Clark, *The Sight of Death*, 124.
18. Schwenger, *The Tears of Things*, 2.

Rivers

Extracts: Silko, *Almanac of the Dead*, 394; Tobar, *The Tattooed Soldier*, 66; McMurtry, *Walter Benjamin at the Dairy Queen*, 19.

1. Didion, "John Wayne: A Love Story," in *Slouching Towards Bethlehem*, 40–41.
2. Didion, "John Wayne," 30–31, 35–36, 40–41.
3. Banham, *Los Angeles*, 159.
4. Didion, *Slouching Towards Bethlehem*, 66, 172, 177.
5. Comer, "New West," 250.
6. Jameson's initial comments on how architect John Portman's Hotel Bonaventure provides a signature example of postmodern urban architecture appear in his 1984 article "Postmodernism, or the Cultural Logic of Late Capitalism," 80–84.
7. See Comer, *Landscapes*, 2; White, *"It's Your Misfortune,"* 541.
8. Smith and Timberlake, "Hierarchies of Dominance," 118.
9. Campbell, *The Cultures of the American New West*, 20.
10. See Tatum, "Spectrality and the Postregional Interface," 3–29.
11. Castells, "The Informational City," 27.
12. Alexie, "Dear John Wayne," 208.

Scene of the crime

Extracts: Ellroy, *The Black Dahlia*, 285; Himes, *If He Hollers Let Him Go*, 35; Bowden and Briggs, *Dreamland*, 29.

1. Alexie, *Indian Killer*, 405.
2. Silko, *Almanac of the Dead*, 312.
3. Miller, "Alibis of the Police," 47.
4. Bowden and Briggs, *Dreamland*, 29.
5. Miller, "Alibis," 47.
6. Alexie, *Indian Killer*, 54.
7. Vidler, *The Architectural Uncanny*. 225.
8. Žižek, *Enjoy Your Symptom!*, 229.
9. Žižek, *Enjoy Your Symptom!* 230.
10. The trope of cannibalism is anticipated in Silko's 1991 *Almanac of the Dead*, where Marx and vampiric capitalism feature. See its Book Two, "Reign of Fire-Eye Macaw." For the quotation regarding capitalism as a cannibalistic fantasy of "producing capital gain through legalized murder, plunder, and/or inheritance, and compounding the gains by eating the dead," see MacCannell, *Empty Meeting Grounds*, 53.
11. See Comaroff and Comaroff, "Alien-Nation," 293.

Television

Extracts: Silko, *Almanac of the Dead*, 46–47; Viramontes, *Their Dogs Came with Them*, 143–44; McCarthy, *No Country for Old Men*, 80.

1. Bolaño, *2666*, 519.
2. Bolaño, *2666*, 539.
3. Bolaño, *2666*, 265. 258.
4. Bolaño, *2666*, 348.
5. "In the meantime" and "chronic abyss" are from Cazdyn, *The Already Dead*, 6–7.
6. Bolaño, *2666*, 534.
7. Bolaño, *2666*, 383.
8. The phrases in this paragraph drawn from Agamben's work are as quoted in Santner, *On Creaturely Life*, 89–91.
9. MacCannell, *Empty Meeting Grounds*, 53.

Urbicide

Extracts: Yamashita, *Tropic of Orange*, 82; Viramontes, *Their Dogs Came with Them*, 32–33; Tobar, *The Tattooed Soldier*, 192; Woods, *War and Architecture*, 1.

1. Alexie, *Indian Killer*, 24, 132.
2. Alexie, *Indian Killer*, 250.
3. Alexie, *Indian Killer*, 250.
4. Alexie, *Indian Killer*, 250–51.
5. "Reveals various layers of past and present inhabitants" is from Mermann-Joziak, "Yamashita's Post-National Spaces," 2.
6. Alexie, *Indian Killer*, 134, 252–53, 405.
7. Coward, "'Urbicide' Reconsidered."
8. Herscher, "American Urbicide," 18.
9. See Coward, "'Urbicide' Reconsidered."
10. Alexie, "Inside Dachau," 16.
11. Alexie, "Inside Dachau," 12.
12. Alexie, "Inside Dachau," 12.
13. Alexie, "Inside Dachau," 16.
14. Alexie, "Inside Dachau," 14, 13.
15. Alexie, "Inside Dachau," 13.
16. Menser, "We Still Do Not Know," 161.
17. Alexie, "Inside Dachau," 16.

Vagabondage

Extracts: Norris, *The Octopus*, 1052; Robinson, *Housekeeping*, 95–96; Anthony Vidler, *The Architectural Uncanny*, 209; Ludwig Wittgenstein, as quoted in Cavell, *Here and Now*, 278.

1. Vidler, *The Architectural Uncanny*, 214.
2. Also of interest in this context is Bruder, *Nomadland*.
3. Vidler, *The Architectural Uncanny*, 184–85.

4. Vidler, *The Architectural Uncanny*, 167.
5. Campbell, "Introduction" to *Under the Western Sky*, 25–26.
6. Hamilton and Baer, *The Rilke Alphabet*, 182.
7. Vidler, *The Architectural Uncanny*, 186.
8. Vidler, *The Architectural Uncanny*, 185.
9. My concluding remarks here are shaped by the entry on "Vagabondage" in Hamilton and Baer's *The Rilke Alphabet*, 184–85.

Windows

Extracts: West, *Miss Lonelyhearts*, 30; Tobar, *The Barbarian Nurseries*, 313; Herrera, *Signs Preceding*, 33.

1. Tobar, *The Barbarian Nurseries*, 313.
2. West, *Miss Lonelyhearts*, 30.
3. Vidler, *The Architectural Uncanny*, 216.
4. Herrera, *Signs Preceding*, 33.
5. Didion, *Slouching Towards Bethlehem*, 178.
6. Jameson, "The Synoptic Chandler," 44.
7. Chandler, *The Long Goodbye*, 273–74.
8. Murphet, *Literature and Race*, 27–29.
9. Ngai, *Ugly Feelings*, 336–39.
10. Chandler, *The Long Goodbye*, 273.
11. Smith, *In Lonely Places*, 18.

X-ray

Extracts: Miranda, *Bad Indians*, 102; Berlin, *A Manual for Cleaning Women*, 88; Luiselli, *Lost Children Archive*, 56.

1. The vignette that is the focus of this critical essay is from Charles Bowden and Alice Leora Briggs, *Dreamland*, 135–36. Unless otherwise noted, direct quotes in this and the following paragraphs will be drawn from these pages. Although this essay focuses on Bowden's prose, not on Briggs's illustrations, the following citations include both authors' surnames as is the case elsewhere in this book.
2. Santner, *On Creaturely Life*, 18.
3. Bowden and Briggs, *Dreamland*, 138.
4. Bowden and Briggs, *Dreamland*, 14.
5. This discussion of X-rays and the inherent rift between appearances and reality is indebted to Timothy Morton's "X-Ray," especially 314–20.
6. Bowden and Briggs, *Dreamland*, 1, 51.
7. Bowden and Briggs, *Dreamland*, 40.
8. Bowden and Briggs, *Dreamland*, 46.
9. The Walter Benjamin quote is from his *The Origin of German Tragic Drama*, as quoted in Santner, *On Creaturely Life*, 18.
10. Bowden and Briggs, *Dreamland*, 135–36.

11. My thinking here on the mystery of the death story is generally indebted to an observation made by Adam Phillips in his book *Darwin's Worms*, 79: "In Freud's mysterious Ur-creation myth, it is indeed as though life is resistant to itself; oblivion is the subject and object of desire. For Freud the original life story was a death story, a how-to-die story."
12. Bowden and Briggs, *Dreamland*, 149.
13. Grosz, *Chaos, Territory, Art*, 61.
14. "Unthinkable as wholes" is from Cameron, *The Bond of the Furthest Apart*, 18.
15. "One image *plus* another" is from Cameron, *The Bond*, 14.
16. Bowden and Briggs, *Dreamland*, 159.
17. Bowden and Briggs, *Dreamland*, 152.
18. Bowden and Briggs, *Dreamland*, 135–36.
19. Bowden and Briggs, *Dreamland*, 41.
20. Bowden and Briggs, *Dreamland*, 136.
21. See Lewis and Tatum, *Morta Las Vegas*, 211: "With their incisions and perforations, their scars and tattoos, such dead bodies create, to use Elizabeth Grosz's phrasing, 'not a map of the body but the body precisely as a map, one whose differentially valued regions of skin expose not only intensities of pain (and pleasure) but also 'forms of social codification.'"

Yellow ribbons, yellow light
Extracts: Silko, *Almanac of the Dead*, 355; Handke, *Short Letter*, 58; Rose, "Yellow Ribbons," 89; Taussig, *My Cocaine Museum*, 5.
1. As Christoff Parry has written, "the plot is little more than a structural scaffold," while the novel on the whole "abounds in openly marked intertextual references." See his *Peter Handke's Landscapes of Discourse*, 74.
2. Handke, *Short Letter*, 167.
3. Handke, *Short Letter*, 139.
4. Handke, *Short Letter*, 61, 80.
5. Handke, *Short Letter*, 53.
6. Handke, *Short Letter*, 65.
7. Handke, *Short Letter*, 67.
8. Lewis, *Unsettling the Literary West*, 232.
9. Handke, *Short Letter*, 118.
10. Handke, *Short Letter*, 84.
11. Handke, *Short Letter*, 118.
12. Handke, *Short Letter*, 118.
13. Handke, *Short Letter*, 118.
14. My exploration here of the uncanny nature of this textual moment is influenced by philosopher Stanley Cavell's *In Quest of the Ordinary*, especially the essay "The Uncanniness of the Ordinary," 153–78. An excellent guide about Cavell's theorizing of the uncanny is Niklas Forsberg's "Carver, Cavell, and the Uncanniness of the Ordinary."

15. Handke, *Short Letter*, 118–19.
16. Parry, *Peter Handke's Landscapes*, 67. Parry also links Handke's fictional representations of the liminal zone between waking and sleeping to the influence of painter Paul Cézanne. Translated into English, Handke's 1980 book on Cézanne is titled *The Lesson of Mont Sainte-Victoire*.
17. Handke, *Short Letter*, 100.
18. Schefer, *The Enigmatic Body*, 107.
19. Handke, *Short Letter*, 125.
20. As quoted in Parry, *Peter Handke's Landscapes*, 169.
21. Lewis, *Unsettling the Literary West*, 233.
22. Handke, *Short Letter*, 116.
23. Handke, *Short Letter*, 162.
24. Handke, *Short Letter*, 162–63
25. Wister, *The Virginian*, 384–85.
26. Handke, *Short Letter*, 165.
27. Handke, *Short Letter*, 167.
28. Handke, *Short Letter*, 167.
29. Handke, *Short Letter*, 163–64.
30. Handke, *Short Letter*, 164.
31. Handke, *Short Letter*, 101.
32. For a nuanced, extended discussion of this controversy, see Parry's "Landscape in Conflict" chapter, especially 207–22, from *Peter Handke's Landscapes*.
33. Handke, *Short Letter*, 162.

Zombieland

Extracts: Kesey, *One Flew Over*, 117; Baca, *A Place to Stand*, 210; Lauro and Embry, "A Zombie Manifesto," 105–6.

1. Bolaño, *2666*, 294.
2. Bolaño, *2666*, 541.
3. Bolaño, *2666*, 541–42.
4. Bolaño, *2666*, 545.
5. Bolaño, *2666*, 602.
6. Bolaño, *2666*, 602–3.
7. Lauro and Embry, "A Zombie Manifesto," 86.
8. Ross, "Parisian Noir," 108.
9. See Comaroff and Comaroff, "Alien Nation," 795–98.
10. "Above all, the State apparatus makes the mutilation, and even death, come first. It needs them preaccomplished, for people to be born that way, crippled and zombie-like. The myth of the zombie, of the living dead, is a work myth and not a war myth." From Deleuze and Guattari, *A Thousand Plateaus*, 425.
11. Arendt, *The Human Condition*, 106, 99.
12. Lauro and Embry, "A Zombie Manifesto," 86–87.
13. Cohen, "Grey," 280.
14. Lauro and Embry, "A Zombie Manifesto," 106.

Bibliography

Abel, Elizabeth. "Skin, Flesh, and the Affective Wrinkles of Civil Rights Photography." *Qui Parle: Critical Humanities and Social Sciences* 20, no. 2 (Spring–Summer 2012): 35–69.
Adams, Parveen. *The Emptiness of the Image: Psychoanalysis and Sexual Differences*. New York: Routledge, 1996.
Alexie, Sherman. "Dear John Wayne." In *The Toughest Indian in the World*, 189–208. New York: Grove, 2000.
———. *Indian Killer*. New York: Grove, 1996.
———. "Inside Dachau." *Beloit Poetry Journal* 46, no. 4 (1996): 12–16.
Allen, John. *Homelessness in American Literature: Romanticism, Realism, and Testimony*. New York: Routledge, 2002.
Appadurai, Arjun. "Grassroots Globalization and the Research Imagination." *Public Culture* 12, no. 1 (2000): 1–19.
Arendt, Hannah. *The Human Condition*. Chicago: University of Chicago Press, 1998.
Baca, Jimmy Santiago. *A Place to Stand*. New York: Grove, 2002.
Banham, Reyner. *Los Angeles: The Architecture of Four Ecologies*. Selected by Mary Banham. Berkeley: University of California Press, 2009.
Barber, Charles. "The Tramp." In *Encyclopedia of Homelessness, Vol. 1*, edited by David Levinson, 357–60. Newbury Park CA: Sage, 2004.
Barad, Karen. "Transmaterialities: Trans*/Matter/Realities and Queer Political Imaginings." GLQ: *A Journal of Gay and Lesbian Studies* 21, nos. 2–3 (2015): 387–422.
Barthes, Roland. *Roland Barthes*. Translated by Richard Howard (1977). New York: Farrar, Straus and Giroux, 2010.
Bass, Rick. *Oil Notes*. New York: Houghton Mifflin, 1989.
Baudrillard, Jean. *America*. Translated by Chris Turner. New York: Verso, 2010.
———. *Passwords*. Translated by Chris Turner. New York: London, 2003.
———. *Symbolic Exchange and Death*. Translated by Iain Hamilton Grant. Los Angeles: Sage, 2017.
Bauman, Zygmunt. *Wasted Lives: Modernity and Its Outcasts*. Malden MA: Polity, 2004.
Beck, John. *Dirty Wars: Landscape, Power, and Waste in Western American Literature*. Lincoln: University of Nebraska Press, 2009.
Becker, Edith, Michelle Citron, Julia Lesage, and B. Ruby Rich. "Lesbians and Film." In *Out in Culture: Gay, Lesbian, and Queer Essays on Popular Culture*, edited by Corey K. Creekmur and Alexander Doty, 25–43. Durham NC: Duke University Press, 1995.
Belcourt, Billy-Ray. *A History of My Brief Body*. Columbus OH: Two Dollar Radio, 2020.

Benjamin, Walter. "The Storyteller: Reflections on the Works of Nikolai Leskov." In *Illuminations*, edited by Hannah Arendt, translated by Harry Zohn, 83–110. New York: Schocken, 1969.

———. "Theses on the Philosophy of History." In *Illuminations*, edited by Hannah Arendt, translated by Harry Zohn, 253–54. New York: Schocken, 1969.

Bennett, Jane. *Vibrant Matter: A Political Ecology of Things*. Durham NC: Duke University Press, 2010.

Berger, John. "Twelve Theses on the Economy of the Dead." In *Hold Everything Dear: Dispatches on Survival and Resistance*, 3–6. New York: Vintage International, 2008.

Berlin, Lucia. *A Manual for Cleaning Women*. New York: Picador, 2015.

Bevis, William. "Native American Novels: Homing In." In *Recovering the Word: Essays on Native American Literature*, edited by Brian Swann and Arnold Krupat, 580–620. Berkeley: University of California Press, 1987.

Bhabha, Homi. "DissemiNation: Time, Narrative, and the Margins of the Modern Nation." In *Nation and Narration*, edited by Homi K. Bhabha, 291–322. London: Routledge, 1990.

———. *The Location of Culture*. New York: Routledge, 2004.

Bloch, Ernst. "A Philosophical View of the Detective Novel." In *The Utopian Function of Art and Literature*, edited and translated by Jack Zipes and Frank Mecklenburg, 245–64. Cambridge MA: MIT Press, 1988.

Bolaño, Roberto. *2666*. Translated by Natasha Wimmer. London: Picador, 2009.

Boscagli, Maurizia. *Stuff Theory: Everyday Objects, Radical Materialism*. New York: Bloomsbury Academic, 2014.

Bowden, Charles, and Alice Leora Briggs. *Dreamland: The Way Out of Juárez*. Austin: University of Texas Press, 2010.

———. *Juárez: The Laboratory of Our Future*. Reading PA: Aperture, 1998.

———. *Murder City: Cuidad Juárez and the Global Economy of the Killing Fields*. New York: Nation, 2010.

Boyle, T. Coraghessan. *The Tortilla Curtain*. New York: Viking, 1995.

Boym, Svetlana. *The Future of Nostalgia*. New York: Basic, 2002.

Briggs, Alice Leora. "Abecedario de Juárez." Passagevision.com, accessed April 2022. http://passagevision.com/briggs.html.

Bruder, Jessica. *Nomadland: Surviving America in the Twenty-First Century*. New York: Norton, 2017.

Butler, Judith. *Precarious Life: The Powers of Mourning and Violence*. London: Verso, 2006.

———, and Gayatri Chakravorty Spivak. *Who Sings the Nation-State?* London: Seagull, 2010.

Butler, Octavia. *Parable of the Sower*. 1993. New York: Grand Central, 2019.

Cabrera, Kristin, and Laura Rice. "The Grim ABCs of Life and Death in Juárez." Texasstandard.org, accessed February 24, 2022. https://www.texasstandard.org/stories/the-grim-abcs-of-life-and-death-in-juarez/.

Cameron, Sharon. "Animal Sentience: Robert Bresson's *Au Hasard Balthazar*." *Representations* 114 (Spring 2011): 1–35.

———. *The Bond of the Furthest Apart: Essays on Tolstoy, Dostoevsky, Bresson, and Kafka*. Chicago: University of Chicago Press, 2017.

Campbell, Howard. Introduction to Julián Cardona and Alice Leora Briggs, *Abecedario de Juárez: An Illustrated Lexicon*, translated by Alice L. Driver, 1–4. Austin: University of Texas Press, 2022.

Campbell, Neil. *Affective Critical Regionality*. London: Rowman and Littlefield, 2016.

——. *The Cultures of the American New West*. Chicago: Fitzroy Dearborn, 2000.

——. "Introduction." In *Under the Western Sky*, edited by Neil Campbell, 3–37. Reno: University of Nevada Press, 2018.

——. *Post-Westerns: Cinema, Region, West*. Lincoln: University of Nebraska Press, 2013.

Cardona, Julián, and Alice Leora Briggs. *Abecedario de Juárez: An Illustrated Lexicon*. Translated by Alice L. Driver. Austin: University of Texas Press, 2022.

Carroll, Amy Sara. "'Accidental Allegories' Meet 'The Performative Documentary': *Boystown*, *Señorita Extraviada*, and the Border-Brothel → Maquiladora Paradigm." *Signs: Journal of Women in Culture and Society* 31, no. 2 (2006): 357–96.

Castells, Manuel. "The Informational City Is a Dual City: Can It Be Reversed?" In *High Technology and Low-Income Communities*, edited by D. Schon, B. Sanyal, and W. Mitchell, 25–41. Cambridge MA: MIT Press, 1999.

Castricano, Jodey. "Cryptomimesis: The Gothic and Jacques Derrida's Ghost Writing." *Gothic Studies* 2, no. 1 (2000): 8–22.

Cavell, Stanley. *Here and There: Sites of Philosophy*. Edited by Nancy Bauer, Alice Crary, and Sandra Laugier. Cambridge MA: Harvard University Press, 2022.

——. *In Quest of the Ordinary: Lines of Skepticism and Romanticism*. Chicago: University of Chicago Press, 1988.

Cazdyn, Eric. *The Already Dead: The New Time of Politics, Culture, and Illness*. Durham NC: Duke University Press, 2012.

Chandler, Raymond. *The Long Goodbye*. 1953. New York: Vintage Crime/Black Lizard, 1988.

Cohen, Jeffrey Jerome. "Grey." In *Prismatic Ecology: Ecotheory Beyond Green*, edited by Jeffrey Jerome Cohen, 270–89. Minneapolis: University of Minnesota Press, 2013.

Coleman, Wanda. *Jazz and Twelve O'Clock Tales: New Stories*. Jaffrey NH: Black Sparrow, 2008.

Comaroff, Jean, and John L. Comaroff. "Alien-Nation: Zombies, Immigrants, and Millennial Capitalism." *South Atlantic Quarterly* 101, no. 4 (2002): 779–805.

——. "Occult Economies and the Violence of Abstraction: Notes from the South African Postcolony." *American Ethnologist* 26, no. 2 (1999): 279–303.

Comer, Krista. *Landscapes of the New West: Gender and Geography in Contemporary Women's Writing*. Chapel Hill: University of North Carolina Press, 1999.

——. "New West, Urban and Suburban Spaces, Postwest." In *A Companion to the Literature and Culture of the American West*, edited by Nicolas S. Witschi, 244–60. Malden MA: Wiley-Blackwell, 2011.

——. "Place and Worlding: Feminist States of Critical Regionalism." In *Transcontinental Reflections on the American West: Words, Images, Sounds Beyond Borders*, edited by Angel Chapparro Sainz and Amaia Ibarraran Begalondo, 153–71. Valencia: Portal, 2015.

——. "Thinking Otherwise Across Global Wests: Issues of Mobility and Feminist Critical Regionalism." *Occasion: Interdisciplinary Studies in the Humanities* 10 (2018): 1–18.

Copjec, Joan. "The Orthopsychic Subject: Film Theory and the Reception of Lacan." *October* 49 (Summer 1989): 53–71.

Coupland, Douglas. *Generation X*. New York: St. Martin's, 1991.

———. *Polaroids from the Dead*. New York: Harper Perennial, 1997.

———. *Shampoo Planet*. New York: Washington Square, 1992.

Coward, Martin. "'Urbicide' Reconsidered." *Theory and Event* 10, no. 2 (2007): n.p. DOI:10.1353/tae.2007.0056.

Davis, Mike. *Dead Cities: And Other Tales*. New York: New Press, 2002.

———. *City of Quartz*. New York: Vintage, 1992.

———. *Planet of Slums*. New York: Verso, 2006.

Debord, Guy. "The Bad Old Days Will End." In *Leaving the 20th Century: The Incomplete Work of the Situationist International*, 33–37. 1963. London: Rebel, 1998.

———. *Society of the Spectacle*. 1967. Detroit: Black & Red, 2002.

De Kosnik, Abigail. *Rogue Archives: Digital Cultural Memory and Media Fandom*. Cambridge MA: MIT Press, 2016.

De León, Jason, with Michael Wells. *The Land of Open Graves: Living and Dying on the Migrant Trail*. Berkeley: University of California Press, 2015.

Deleuze, Gilles, and Felix Guattari. *A Thousand Plateaus: Capitalism and Schizophrenia*. New York: Continuum, 2002.

DePastino, Todd. *Citizen Hobo: How a Century of Homelessness Shaped America*. Chicago: University of Chicago Press, 2003.

Derrida, Jacques. *Spectres of Marx*. Translated by Peggy Kamuf. New York: Routledge, 1994.

Didion, Joan. *Play It as It Lays*. New York: Farrar, Straus and Giroux, 1970.

———. *Slouching Towards Bethlehem*. New York: Farrar, Straus and Giroux, 2008 [1968].

———. *We Tell Ourselves Stories in Order to Live: Collected Nonfiction*. New York: Everyman's Library, 2006.

———. *The White Album*. New York: Farrar, Straus and Giroux, 1990 [1970].

———. *The Year of Magical Thinking*. New York: Vintage, 2005.

Dinerstein, Joel. *The Origins of Cool in Postwar America*. Chicago: University of Chicago Press, 2017.

Dos Passos, John. *USA*. New York: Library of America, 1996.

Driver, Alice. *More or Less Dead: Feminicide, Haunting, and the Ethics of Representation in Mexico*. Tucson: University of Arizona Press, 2015

Ellis, Brett Easton. *Imperial Bedrooms*. New York: Vintage, 2011.

———. *Less Than Zero*. New York: Simon and Schuster, 1985.

Ellroy, James. *The Black Dahlia*. New York: Grand Central, 2006.

Erdrich, Louise. *The Antelope Wife*. New York: HarperCollins, 2016.

———. *The Round House*. New York: HarperCollins, 2012.

Fante, John. *Ask the Dust*. 1939. New York: HarperCollins, 2006.

Fisher, Mark. "Hauntology Now." Accessed January 17, 2006. http://k-punk.abstractdynamics.org/archives/007230.html

Ford, Richard. *Rock Springs*. New York: Grove, 2009.

Foster, Hal. "Designing a Second Modernity?" In *The Political Unconscious of Architecture, Re-opening Jameson's Narrative*, edited by Nadir Lahiji, 97–106. Burlington VT: Ashgate, 2011.

Forsberg, Niklas. "Carver, Cavell, and the Uncanniness of the Ordinary." *New Literary History* 49, no. 1 (Winter 2018): 1–22.

Foucault, Michel. "Nietzsche, Genealogy, History." In *Language, Counter-Memory, Practice: Selected Essays and Interviews*, edited by Donald F. Bouchard, translated by Donald F. Bouchard and Sherry Simon, 139–64. Ithaca NY: Cornell University Press, 1977.

———. "The Panopticon." In *Rethinking Architecture: A Reader in Cultural Theory*, edited by Neil Leach, 336–57. New York: Routledge, 1997.

Franklin, Ruth. "Rings of Smoke." In *The Emergence of Memory: Conversations with W. G. Sebald*, edited by Lynne Sharon Schwartz, 119–44. New York: Seven Stories, 2007.

Freud, Sigmund. "The Uncanny." In *The Standard Edition of the Complete Works of Sigmund Freud, Vol. 17*, edited and translated by James Strachey, 219–56. London: Hogarth, 1994.

Fried, Michael. *Art and Objecthood: Essays and Reviews*. Chicago: University of Chicago Press, 1998.

Fuller, Alexandra. *The Legend of Colton H. Bryant*. New York: Penguin, 2008.

Gage, John. *Color and Culture: Practice and Meaning from Antiquity to Abstraction*. Berkeley: University of California Press, 1993.

Gibbs, Anna. "Fictocriticism, Affect, Mimesis: Engendering Difference." TEXT: *Journal of Australian Association of Writing Programs* 9, no. 1 (April 2005): n.p.

Goodman, Audrey. *A Planetary Lens: The Photo-Poetics of Western Women's Writing*. Lincoln: University of Nebraska Press, 2021.

———. *Lost Homelands*. Tucson: University of Arizona Press, 2010.

———. "Visuality." *Western American Literature* 53, no. 1 (Spring 2018): 91–96.

Goonewardena, Kanishka, and Stefan Kipfer. "Postcolonial Urbicide: New Imperialism, Global Cities and the Damned of the Earth." *New Formations* 59 (Autumn 2006): 23–33.

Ghosh, Amitov. *The Nutmeg's Curse: Parables for a Planet in Crisis*. Chicago: University of Chicago Press, 2021.

Gordon, Avery F. *The Hawthorn Archive: Letters from the Utopian Margins*. New York: Fordham University Press, 2018.

Grosz, Elizabeth. *Volatile Bodies: Toward a Corporeal Feminism*. Bloomington: Indiana University Press, 1994.

———. *Chaos, Territory, Art: Deleuze and the Framing of the Earth*. New York: Columbia University Press, 2020.

Guilmette, Lauren. "The Age of Paranoia: Teresa Brennan's Posthumous Insights for the Present." DIFFERENCES: *A Journal of Feminist Studies* 30, no. 2 (2019): 93–114.

Hamilton, Andrew, and Ulrich Baer. *The Rilke Alphabet*. New York: Fordham University Press, 2014.

Handke, Peter. *Short Letter, Long Farewell*. Translated by Ralph Manheim. New York: New York Review of Books, 2009.

Hansen, Miriam. "Benjamin, Cinema and Experience: 'The Blue Flower' in the Land of Technology." *New German Critique* 40 (Winter 1987): 179–224.

Hanssen, Beatrice. *Walter Benjamin and the Arcades Project*. New York: Continuum, 2006.

Haraway, Donna J. "A Cyborg Manifesto." In *Simians, Cyborgs and Women*, 149–82. New York: Routledge, 1991.

Harper, Colin. "The Philosopher as Detective." *Philosophy Now* 5 (1993). https://philosophynow.org/issues/5/The_Philosopher_as_Detective.

Harris, Oliver. "Film Noir Fascination: Outside History, But Historically So." *Cinema Journal* 43, no. 1 (Fall 2003): 3–24.

Harvey, David. *The Condition of Postmodernity*. New York: Blackwell, 1990.

Herrera, Yuri. *Signs Preceding the End of the World*. Translated by Lisa Dillman. London: And Other Stories, 2015.

Herscher, Andrew. "American Urbicide." *Journal of Architectural Education* 60, no. 1 (September 2006): 18–20.

Himes, Chester. *If He Hollers Let Him Go*. 1945. New York: Thunder's Mouth, 2002.

Hyde, Lewis. *A Primer for Forgetting: Getting Past the Past*. New York: Farrar, Straus and Giroux, 2019.

Iversen, Margaret. *Beyond Pleasure: Freud, Lacan, Barthes*. University Park: Penn State University Press, 2007.

———. "The World without a Self: Edward Hopper and Chantal Akerman." *Art History* 41, no. 4 (2018): 3–20.

Jackson, Wallace. "*To Look*: The Scene of the Seen in Edward Hopper." *South Atlantic Quarterly* 103, no. 1 (Winter 2004): 133–48.

Jafri, Maryam. "Through, Around, and Against the Document: Maryam Jafri in Conversation with Patricia Reed." *Art Papers Magazine* (February 2009): 29–33. www.maryamjafri.net/Press/Art%20PAPERS_Jafri.pdf.

Jameson, Fredric. *The Cultural Turn: Selected Writings on the Postmodern, 1983–1998*. London: Verso, 1998.

———. *The Geopolitical Aesthetic: Cinema and Space in the World System*. Bloomington: Indiana University Press, 1995.

———. "Postmodernism; or, the Cultural Logic of Late Capitalism." *New Left Review* 1, no. 146 (July-August 1984): 59–92.

———. *Postmodernism, or the Cultural Logic of Late Capitalism*. Durham NC: Duke University Press, 1991.

———. "The Synoptic Chandler." In *Shades of Noir*, edited by Joan Copjec, 33–56. London: Verso, 1993.

———. *Valences of the Dialectic*. London: Verso, 2010.

Jones, Stephen Graham. *Ledfeather*. Tuscaloosa: University of Alabama Press, 2008.

———. *The Only Good Indians*. New York: Saga, 2020.

Kelley, Tanya. "Yellow." Britannica.com, Encyclopedia Britannica, accessed November 22, 2021. https://www.britannica.com/science/yellow-color.

Kesey, Ken. *One Flew Over the Cuckoo's Nest*. New York: Penguin, 1976.

Koolhaas, Rem. "Junkspace." *October* 100 (Spring 2002): 175–90.

Knausgaard, Karl Ove. "Petrol." In *Autumn*, 29–31. New York: Penguin, 2017.

Kracauer, Siegfried. "The Hotel Lobby." In *Rethinking Architecture: A Reader in Cultural Theory*, edited by Neil Leach, 53–59. New York: Routledge, 1997.
Kristeva, Julia. *Powers of Horror: An Essay on Abjection*. New York: Columbia University Press, 1982.
———. *The Kristeva Reader*. Edited by Toril Moi. New York: Columbia University Press, 1986.
Kundera, Milan. *The Art of the Novel*. Translated by Linda Asher. New York: Perennial Classics, 2003.
Kusmer, Kenneth L. *Down and Out, On the Road: The Homeless in American History*. New York: Oxford University Press, 2002.
Lacayo. Richard. *Lost Light: How Six Great Artists Made Old Age a Time of Triumph*. New York: Simon & Schuster, 2022.
Lauro, Sarah Juliet, and Karen Embry. "A Zombie Manifesto: The Nonhuman Condition in the Era of Advanced Capitalism." *boundary 2* 35, no. 1 (2008): 85–108.
"Ledger." *Webster's Unabridged Dictionary of the English Language*. New York: Random House, 2001.
LeMenager, Stephanie. "The Aesthetics of Petroleum, after *Oil*!" *American Literary History* 24, no. 1 (Spring 2012): 59–86.
———. *Living Oil: Petroleum Culture in the American Century*. New York: Oxford University Press, 2014.
Leone, Sze Tsung. "Ulterior Spaces." In *Harvard Design School Guide to Shopping*, edited by Judy Chung Chuihua, Jeffrey Inaba, Rem Koolhaas, and Sze Tsung Leong, 764–95. Köln: Taschen, 2001.
Lerner, Ben. "The Storyteller." *New York Review*, October 21, 2021. https://www.nybooks.com/articles/2021/10/21/wg-sebaldstoryteller/?lp_txn_id=1286261.
Leslie, Isis. "From Idleness to Boredom: On the Historical Development of Modern Boredom." In *Essays on Boredom and Modernity*, edited by Barbara Dalle Pezze and Carlo Salzani, 35–59. Amsterdam: Rodopi, 2009.
Levin, Gail. *Edward Hopper: An Intimate Biography*. New York: Rizzoli, 2007.
Lewis, Nathaniel, and Stephen Tatum. *Morta Las Vegas: "CSI" and the Problem of the West*. Lincoln: University of Nebraska Press, 2017.
Liu, Alan. *The Laws of Cool: Knowledge Work and the Culture of Information*. Chicago: University of Chicago Press, 2004.
Locke, Attica. *The Cutting Season*. New York: Harper Perennial, 2013.
Luiselli, Valeria. *Lost Children Archive*. London: Fourth Estate, 2019.
Lukács, Georg. *Theory of the Novel*. 1920. Cambridge MA: MIT Press, 1974.
Lyotard, Jean-François. "Domus and Megapolis." In *Rethinking Architecture: A Reader in Cultural Theory*, edited by Neil Leach, 271–85. New York: Routledge, 1997.
MacCannell, Dean. "Democracy's Turn: On Homeless Noir." In *Shades of Noir*, edited by Joan Copjec, 279–97. New York: Verso, 1993.
———. *Empty Meeting Grounds: The Tourist Papers*. New York: Routledge, 1992.
Machado, Carmen Maria. *In the Dream House*. Minneapolis: Graywolf, 2020.
Mbembe, Achille. "Necropolitics." Translated by Libby Meintjes. *Public Culture* 15, no. 1 (2003): 11–40.

McCarthy, Cormac. *All the Pretty Horses*. New York: Vintage, 1992.

——. *The Border Trilogy: All the Pretty Horses, The Crossing, Cities of the Plain*. New York: Everyman's Library, 1999.

——. *No Country for Old Men*. New York: Vintage, 2005.

——. *The Crossing*. New York: Vintage, 1994.

McMurtry, Larry. *Duane's Depressed*. New York: Simon & Schuster, 1999.

——. *The Last Picture Show*. 1966. New York: Liveright, 2018.

——. *Walter Benjamin at the Dairy Queen*. New York: Simon & Schuster, 1999.

McWilliams, Carey. *Southern California*. 1946. Layton UT: Peregrine Smith, 1980.

Meloy, Ellen. *The Anthropology of Turquoise*. New York: Pantheon, 2002.

——. *The Last Cheater's Waltz: Beauty and Violence in the Desert Southwest*. New York: Henry Holt, 1999.

Menser, Michael. "We Still Do Not Know What a Building Can Do." In *Radical Reconstruction*, edited by Lebbeus Woods, 156–67. New York: Princeton Architectural Press, 1997.

Miller, D. A. "Alibis of the Police." *L'Esprit Créateur* 26, no. 2 (Summer 1986): 37–47.

Miranda, Deborah A. *Bad Indians: A Tribal Memoir*. Berkeley CA: Heyday, 2013.

Mitchell, Lee Clark. *Late Westerns: The Persistence of a Genre*. Lincoln: University of Nebraska Press, 2018.

Morton, Timothy. "X-Ray." In *Prismatic Ecology*, edited by Jeffrey Jerome Cohen, 311–27. Minneapolis: University of Minnesota Press, 2013.

Mosley, Walter. *Devil in a Blue Dress*. New York: Washington Square, 1990.

Murphet, Julian. *Literature and Race in Los Angeles*. Cambridge: Cambridge University Press, 200l.

——. "Postmodernism and Space." In *The Cambridge Companion to Postmodernism*, edited by Steven Conner, 116–35. Cambridge: Cambridge University Press, 2004.

——. "Film Noir and the Racial Unconscious." *Screen* 39, no. 1 (Spring 1998): 22–35.

Nabokov, Vladimir. *Lolita*. New York: Vintage, 1989.

Nikas, Jim. "Day of the Dead (Dia de Muertos) Calavera Images and José Gaudelupe Posada." Posada Art Foundation, accessed May 5, 2022. https://www.posada-art-foundation.com/posada-s-day-of-the-dead.

Nguyen, Viet Thanh. *Nothing Ever Dies: Vietnam and the Memory of War*. Cambridge MA: Harvard University Press, 2016.

Nixon, Rob. *Slow Violence and the Environmentalism of the Poor*. Cambridge MA: Harvard University Press, 2011.

Nochlin, Linda. "Edward Hopper and the Imagery of Alienation." *Art Journal* 41, no. 2 (1981): 136–41.

Norris, Frank. *The Octopus: A Story of California*. In *Norris: Novels and Essays*, 573–1097. New York: Library of America, 1985.

O'Doherty, Brian. "Hopper's Look." In *Edward Hopper*, edited by Sheena Wagstaff and David Anfam, 87–88. London: Tate, 2004.

"Oil." Online Etymological Dictionary, accessed July 1, 2022. https://www.etymonline.com/search?q=oil.

Orange, Tommy. *There There*. New York: Vintage, 2019.

Otsuka, Julie. *The Buddha in the Attic*. New York: Vintage, 2011.
―――. *When the Emperor Was Divine*. New York: Vintage, 2002.
Palahniuk, Chuck. *Fight Club*. 1996. New York: Norton, 2005.
Parry, Christoph. *Peter Handke's Landscapes of Discourse: An Exploration of Narrative and Cultural Space*. Riverside CA: Ariadne, 2003.
Pattison, Dale. "'Born in the USA': Breeding Political Violence in Héctor Tobar's *The Tattooed Soldier*." *Studies in American Fiction* 44, no. 1 (Spring 2017): 113–37.
"Petroleum." Online Etymological Dictionary, accessed July 1, 2022. https://www.etymonline.com/search?q=petroleum.
Phillips, Adam. *Darwin's Worms: On Life Stories and Death Stories*. New York: Basic, 2000.
―――. *On Kissing, Tickling, and Being Bored: Psychoanalytic Essays on the Unexamined Life*. Cambridge MA: Harvard University Press, 1993.
Pirsig, Robert. *Zen and the Art of Motorcycle Maintenance*. New York: William Morrow, 1979.
Pizzolatto, Nic. *Galveston*. New York: Simon & Schuster, 2011.
Pollack, Griselda. "The Image in Psychoanalysis and the Archaeological Metaphor." In *Psychoanalysis and the Image: Transdisciplinary Perspectives*, edited by Griselda Pollack, 1–29. Malden MA: Blackwell, 2006.
Proulx, Annie. *Fine Just the Way It Is: Wyoming Stories 3*. New York: Scribner, 2008.
―――. *That Old Ace in the Hole*. New York: Scribner, 2002.
Pynchon, Thomas. *The Crying of Lot 49*. New York: Harper Perennial, 2006.
―――. *Gravity's Rainbow*. 1973. New York: Penguin, 2000.
―――. *Inherent Vice*. New York: Penguin, 2010.
Rilke, Rainer Maria. *Duino Elegies and The Sonnets to Orpheus*. Translated by Stephen Mitchell. New York: Vintage, 2009.
Robinson, Marilynne. *Housekeeping*. New York: Picador, 2020.
Rose, Wendy. "Yellow Ribbons." In *Bone Dance: New and Selected Poems, 1965–1993*, 88–89. Tucson: University of Arizona Press, 1994.
Ross, Kristin. "Keeping House." In *Fast Cars, Clean Bodies: Decolonization and the Reordering of French Culture*, 105–22. Cambridge MA: MIT Press, 1996.
―――. "Parisian Noir." *New Literary History* 41, no. 1 (Winter 2010): 95–109.
Santner, Eric L. *On Creaturely Life*. Chicago: University of Chicago Press, 2006.
Schefer, Jean Louis. *The Enigmatic Body: Essays on the Arts by Jean Louis Schefer*. Edited and translated by Paul Smith. Cambridge: Cambridge University Press, 1995.
Schwab, Gabrielle. "Writing against Memory and Forgetting." *Literature and Medicine* 25, no. 1 (Spring 2006): 95–121.
Schwenger, Peter. *The Tears of Things: Melancholy and Physical Objects*. Minneapolis: University of Minnesota Press, 2013.
Sebald, W. G. *On the Natural History of Destruction*. Translated by Anthea Bell. New York: Random House, 2003.
―――. *The Rings of Saturn*. Translated by Michael Hulse. New York: New Directions, 1999.
Sekula, Allan. "Photography Between Labour and Capital." In *Mining Photographs and Other Pictures, 1948–1968*, edited by Benjamin H. D. Buchloh and Robert Wilkie,

193–268. Halifax: Nova Scotia College of Art and Design/University College of Cape Breton Press, 1983.
Shields, David. *Reality Hunger: A Manifesto*. New York: Knopf, 2010.
Silko, Leslie. *Almanac of the Dead*. New York: Simon and Schuster, 1991.
Simmel, Georg. "Two Essays: The Handle, and The Ruin." *Hudson Review* 11, no. 3 (Autumn 1958): 379–85.
Smith, David, and Michael Timberlake. "Hierarchies of Dominance Among World Cities: A Network Approach." In *Global Networks, Linked Cities*, edited by Saskia Sassen, 117–42. New York: Routledge, 2002.
Smith, Imogen Sara. *In Lonely Places: Film Noir Beyond the City*. Jefferson NC: McFarland, 2011.
Sobchack, Vivian. "Lounge Time: Postwar Crises and the Chronotope of Film Noir." In *Refiguring American Film Genres: History and Theory*, edited by Nick Browne, 129–70. Berkeley: University of California Press, 1998.
Soja, Edward W. *Postmetropolis: Critical Studies of Cities and Regions*. Malden MA: Blackwell, 2000.
———. *Postmodern Geographies: The Reassertion of Space in Critical Social Theory*. New York: Verso, 2011.
———. *Thirdspace: Journeys to Los Angeles and Other Real-and-Imagined Places*. Malden MA: Blackwell, 1996.
Solnit, Rebecca. *A Field Guide to Getting Lost*. New York: Viking, 2005.
Spacks, Patricia Meyer. *Boredom: The Literary History of a State of Mind*. Chicago: University of Chicago Press, 1995.
Spurr, David. *Architecture and Modern Literature*. Ann Arbor: University of Michigan Press, 2012.
Stewart, Kathleen. *Ordinary Affects*. Durham NC: Duke University Press, 2007.
———. "Regionality." *Geographical Review* 103, no. 2 (April 2013): 275–84.
Stewart, Susan. *On Longing: Narratives of the Miniature, the Gigantic, the Souvenir, the Collection*. Durham NC: Duke University Press, 1993.
Strand, Mark. "The Continuous Life." In *The Continuous Life: Poems*. New York: Knopf, 1991.
———. *Hopper*. Hopewell NJ: Ecco, 1994.
Svendsen, Lars. *A Philosophy of Boredom*. Translated by John Irons. London: Reaktion, 2005.
Swigart, Rob. *Little America*. New York: Houghton Mifflin, 1977.
Tatum, Stephen. "Spectral Beauty and Forensic Aesthetics in the West." *Western American Literature* 41, no. 2 (2006): 123–45.
———. "Spectrality and the Postregional Interface." In *Postwestern Cultures: Literature, Theory, Space*, edited by Susan Kollin, 3–29. Lincoln: University of Nebraska Press, 2007.
———. "Unhomely Wests: Meditations in Critical Archaeology." *Western American Literature* 53, no. 1 (Spring 2018): 31–44.
Taussig, Michael. *My Cocaine Museum*. Chicago: University of Chicago Press, 2004.
———. *Walter Benjamin's Grave*. Chicago: University of Chicago Press, 2006.
———. *What Color Is the Sacred?* Chicago: University of Chicago Press, 2006.

Tobar, Héctor. *The Barbarian Nurseries*. New York: Picador, 2011.

———. *The Tattooed Soldier*. New York: Picador, 1998.

Turner, Frederick Jackson. *The Frontier in American History*. New York: Henry Holt, 1920.

2Bears, Jackson. "My Post-Indian Technological Autobiography." In *Coded Territories: Tracing Indigenous Pathways in New Media Art*, edited by Steven Loft and Kerry Swanson, 3–31. Calgary: University of Calgary Press, 2014.

Tyler, Ron, ed. *Posada's Mexico*. Washington DC: Library of Congress/Amon Carter Museum of Western Art, 1979.

Urrea, Luis Alberto. *By the Lake of Sleeping Children*. New York: Anchor, 1996.

———. *Into the Beautiful North*. New York: Little, Brown, 2009.

———. *The Water Museum: Stories*. New York: Little, Brown, 2015.

U.S. Securities and Exchange Commission. *SEC Docket* 24, no. 3 (1981): 299.

Van Houten, Christina. "bell hooks, Critical Regionalism, and the Politics of Ecological Returns." *Politics and Culture*, March 9, 2014. https://politicsandculture.org/2014/03/09/bell-hookscritical regionalism-and-the-politics-of-ecological-returns-by-christina-van-houten.

Vidler, Anthony. *The Architectural Uncanny: Essays in the Modern Unhomely*. Cambridge MA: MIT Press, 1992.

Viramontes, Helena María. *Their Dogs Came with Them*. New York: Washington Square, 2007.

———. *Under the Feet of Jesus*. New York: Penguin, 1996.

Vlautin, Willy. *The Free*. New York: Harper Perennial, 2014.

———. *The Motel Life*. New York: Harper Perennial, 2014.

———. *Northline*. New York: Harper Perennial, 2008.

Wald, Sarah D. "'Refusing to Halt': Mobility and the Quest for Spatial Justice in Helena María Viramontes's *Their Dogs Came with Them* and Karen Tei Yamashita's *Tropic of Orange*." *Western American Literature* 48, nos. 1 & 2 (Spring-Summer 2013): 70–89.

Watkins, Claire Vaye. *Gold Fame Citrus: A Novel*. New York: Riverhead, 2015.

Watson, Sophie, and Helen Austerberry. *Housing and Homelessness: A Feminist Perspective*. London: Routledge and Kegan Paul, 1986.

Webb, Philip. *Homeless Lives in American Cities: Interrogating Myth and Locating Community*. London: Palgrave Macmillan, 2014.

Weil, Simone, and Rachel Bespaloff. *War and the Iliad*. Translated by Mary McCarthy. New York: New York Review of Books, 2005.

West, Nathanael. *Miss Lonelyhearts & The Day of the Locust*. New York: New Directions, 2009.

White, Richard. *"It's Your Misfortune and None of My Own": A History of the American West*. Norman: University of Oklahoma Press, 1991.

Wister, Owen. *The Virginian: A Horseman of the Plains*. New York: Penguin, 1988.

Wollen, Peter. "Introduction." In *Posada: Messenger of Mortality*, edited by Julian Rothenstein, 14–23. London: Redstone, 1989.

Woods, Lebbeus. *War and Architecture (Pamphlet Architecture 15)*. New York: Princeton Architectural Press, 1996.

"*The Writing on the Wall*: Alice Leora Briggs and Julián Cardona." TiA collection, accessed April 2, 2022. https://tiacollectioncatalogues.org/exhibitions/the-writing-on-the-wall-alice-briggs/.

Yamashita, Karen Tei. *I Hotel*. Minneapolis: Coffee House, 2010.

———. *Tropic of Orange*. Minneapolis: Coffee House, 1997.

Yates, Julian. "Orange." In *Prismatic Ecology: Ecotheory beyond Green*, edited by Jeffrey Jerome Cohen, 83–105. Minneapolis: University of Minnesota Press, 2013.

Žižek, Slavoj. "The Architectural Parallax." In *The Political Unconscious of Architecture: Re-opening Jameson's Narrative*, edited by Nadir Lahiji. Burlington VT: Ashgate, 2011.

———. *Enjoy Your Symptom!: Jacques Lacan in Hollywood and Out*. New York: Routledge, 2001.

———. *Welcome to the Desert of the Real: Five Essays on September 11 and Related Dates*. London: Verso, 2002.

Zuboff, Shoshana. *The Age of Surveillance Capitalism: The Fight for a Human Future at the New Frontier of Power*. New York: Public Affairs, 2019.

Index

Page numbers in italics indicate illustrations.

abecedario, 1–19, 48–49
Abel, Elizabeth, 306n12
Abraham, Nicolas, 36–37
Adams, Parveen, 311n16
Agamben, Giorgio, 230
aletheia, 6, 280
Alexie, Sherman: "Dear John Wayne," 214; *Indian Killer*, 34, 58, 59, 61, 98, 190, 197, 219–20, 233–34; "Inside Dachau," 237–42
Allen, John, 304n2
alphabet, 1–19
anamorphosis, 62–63
archaeology: spatial, 112, 234, 237, 240; of signs, 103–6, 294
architectonics of the crypt, 34–47
architectural uncanny, xxi–xxii, 153, 214, 239, 243, 304n24
architecture: injection, 241; junkspace, 110; myths of, 233–34; of ruins, 121, 127, 133; vagabond, 244–45; war as, 233, 237–39
Arendt, Hannah, 295
Aztecs, 16, 132, 136

Baca, Jimmy Santiago, 1, 289
Badger, George, 177, 179–82, 312n6
Banham, Reyner, 111–13, 212
Barad, Karen, 241
Barthes, Roland, 1, 5, 12, 287–88, 305n1, 310n21
Bass, Rick, 182
Baudrillard, Jean, 16, 24, 108–10
Bauman, Zygmunt, 121
Beat poetry, 267

Beck, John, 65
Belcourt, Billy-Ray, xv, xxix
Benjamin, Walter, 67, 145, 266; on artwork's aura, 147–48; on boredom, 302n28; on "optical unconscious," 311n20
Berger, John, 206
Berlin, Lucia, 20, 260
Bhabha, Homi, xv–xvi, xxii–xxiii
Bingham Silver Lead Company, 177, 179–81
Birckmann, Arnold, 8, 301n14
Black Panthers, 99
Bloch, Ernst, xv–xviii
Bolaño, Roberto, xxix, 126, 223–231, 290–293
boredom, 20–33, 193–94; Benjamin on, 302n28; Debord on, 20; Leslie on, 302n2; Spacks on, 302n1
Bowden, Charles, xxviii, 208, 217, 309n17; *Dreamland*, xxiv, 53, 115–18, 127–36, 198–99, 215–16, 262–72, 309n16
Briggs, Alice Leora, xxvi; *Abecedario de Juárez*, 2–19, 48–49, 300n1, 301n8, 309n17; *Dreamland*, 127–30, 135, 199, 262; *Música*, 12–15, *13*, 17–18; *Narcoinsurgencia*, 6–9, *8*; *Pietà*, 199–208, *200*; sgraffitos of, *3*, *8*, *13*, *200*, 300n4
Bush, George H. W., 178
Butler, Judith, 159

calaveras, 9, 11–19
Calderón, Felipe, 2, 5, 8, 13, 300n1
Cameron, Sharon, 60
Campbell, Howard, 309n17

Campbell, Neil, 46–47, 213, 245, 299n20
cannibalism, 195, 220–21, 230, 314n10. *See also* zombies
Cardona, Julián, 2–19, 48–49, 300n1, 301n8, 309n17; images of, 12–15, *13*, 18–19; *The Writing on the Wall*, 9–11
carne asada, 2–4
cartography, 81. *See also* maps
Castells, Manuel, 103, 106
Castricano, Jodey, 35, 39, 64
catachresis, xxvii, 246
Catlin, George, 279, 281
Cavell, Stanley, 317n14
cemeteries, 68, 74–75, 81, 85, 234. *See also* graves
Cézanne, Paul, 281–82, 318n16
Chad, 176
Chandler, Raymond, 197, 252–59, 275
Chekhov, Anton, 212
Clark, T. J., 204–5
cochineal dye, 136, 310n22
Cohen, Jeffrey Jerome, 296
Cohen, Leonard, xx
Coleman, Wanda, 111–13
colonialism. *See* settler colonialism
Comer, Krista, 99, 213
control space, 120–21, 125
corte de florero (beheading), 206
Cortés, Hernán, 132, 134
cosmetics. *See* makeup
Coupland, Douglas, 20–21, 113–15, 137
Coward, Martin, 235, 236
crime novels. *See* detective fiction
crime scene, 215–21, 271. *See also* forensics
critical regionalism, 56, 99, 213
crypt: architectonics of, 34–47; of a camera, 59; definitions of, 35–36, 41–42; etymology of, 35
cryptocurrencies, 35
cryptography, 34–47, 221
cryptomimesis, 35, 39
cryptonymy (haunted language), 37, 303n3
cubist style, 152

Cushing, Frank Hamilton, 282
cyborgs, 289

Dachau concentration camp, 237–42
Dadaism, 266
Dalí, Salvador, 304n24
dance of death, 8–12, *10*, 16, 301n14
Davis, Mike, xxi, 96, 100
death house. *See* "house of death" (Juárez)
Debord, Guy, 20
deindustrialization, 106
De Kosnick, Abigail, 301n8
De León, Jason, 126
Deleuze, Gilles, 295, 318n10
depression. *See* melancholia
Derrida, Jacques, xxxi; on crypts, 41–42; on "ghost writing," 39, 64
detective fiction, 215–21; Bloch on, xv, xvii–xviii; Chandler's, 197, 252–59, 275. *See also* film noir
diapers, 48–57, 119, 121–24
Díaz del Castillo, Bernal, 132
Didion, Joan, 72; "Notes from a Native Daughter," 252; *Slouching Towards Bethlehem*, 20, 210–13; *The White Album*, 93, 95
dislocation, 245
Disney Corporation, 171
Don Quixote calaveras, *14*, *15*, *17*
doppelganger, xviii, 11–12, 39, 115, 247, 251
Durán, Diego, 132

Ellis, Brett Easton, xxix, 191–97, 259
Ellroy, James, 197; *The Black Dahlia*, 215, 217–18
Embry, Karen, 289, 296–97
Erdrich, Louise, 119
exposure, poetics of, 58–66, 205, 305n1

Fante, John, 94
fatalism, 134
femicides, 49, 199, 230–31; Bolaño on, 223–26, 290–92, 295

film noir, 7, 106, 149, 157–58. *See also* detective fiction; noir motel
Fisher, Mark, xxxi
Fitzgerald, F. Scott, 275, 285
Fonda, Henry, 282
Ford, John, 275, 283–88; *The Man Who Shot Liberty Valence*, 284; *She Wore a Yellow Ribbon*, 277, 278, 282; *Young Mr. Lincoln*, 278, 282–83
forensics, 6–7, 60–61, 218–19, 225–26, 231, 264, 271, 290.
Fouquet, Betty Lansdown, 93
freeways, 68–69; accidents on, 71–72; design of, 64; embankments of, 69–70; lanes of, 73; maps of, 74, 79; overpasses of, 68, 75–76, 78; signs along, 70, 77–79, 82; sounds of, 67, 77; traffic jams on, 72, 76
Freud, Sigmund: on thanatos, 317n11; on uncanny, xv–xvii, 37, 194, 228–29
Fried, Michael, 142, 311n8
Fuller, Alexandra, 86, 181–82

garbage dumps, 50, 125, 216, 290, 297. *See also* landfills
gaze, 53, 62–63, 94, 112, *151*, 194, 220, 251; in Bolaño's *2666*, 226–28, 292–93; in Briggs's *Pietà*, 199–201, 203–5; in Chandler's *The Long Goodbye*, 197, 253–59; in Ellis's *Less Than Zero*, 257; in Hopper's *Western Motel*, 140–42, 146–48; unconscious optics of, 150; Žižek on, 220. *See also* surveillance
Gehry, Frank, 95–96
genocide, xviii, 224, 236–42, 292, 294. *See also* urbicide
gentrification, xxi, 96, 196
Geronimo, 65
ghosts, 71, 82, 86; "ancestral," 156, 160; stories about, xxx–xxxi, 195–96; ungraspable, 98. *See also* revenants; spectrality
"ghost Westerns," 299–300n20

"ghost workers," 295
"ghost writing," 39, 64
Gibbs, Anna, 305n1
globalization, 50, 57, 104–6, 108, 213. *See also* multinational corporations
Goethe, Johann Wolfgang von, 274
Goodman, Audrey, 66
Gordon, Avery, 112
Gothic fiction, 64
graves, 85–92, 162. *See also* cemeteries
Great Depression, 101, 173
grief, 90, 104, 160, 184, 186–87, 204, 227. *See also* melancholia
Grosz, Elizabeth, 270, 317n21
Guattari, Félix, 295, 318n10
Guevara, Ernesto "Che," 46, 47, 304n30

Handke, Peter: on Cézanne, 281–82, 318n16; *Short Letter, Long Farewell*, 273–88
Harper, Colin, xviii, xix
Harris, Oliver, 157
Harrison, Robert Pogue, 91
haunted language (cryptonymy), 37, 303n3
hauntology, xxx–xxxi, 196
Herrera, Yuri, 34–35, 126, 251–52
Herscher, Andrew, 235–36
Heston, Charlton, 150, 156–57
Himes, Chester, 215, 217
hoboes. *See* tramps
Holbein, Hans, the Younger, 8–9, *10*, 16, 301n14
Hollar, Wenceslaus, 8–9, *10*, 13, 301n14
Holocaust, xviii, 224, 236–42, 292, 294
homelessness, xv, xx, 106–7; Alexie on, 98, 233–34; Allen on, 304n2; Jameson on, 96; Tobar on, xxiii, 36, 100–102; tramps versus, 50; transcendental, 22, 94, 302n5; Yamashita on, 98
homesickness, xviii–xix, 31, 45. *See also* nostalgia
homesteading, xv, 101–2; urban, 111, 112
Hopper, Edward: *Gas*, 138; *Hotel Lobby*, 141; *House by the Railroad*, 124;

INDEX 333

Hopper, Edward (*continued*)
   Nighthawks, 141; *Western Motel*, xxvi, 138–47, *139*, 150, 151
Hopper, Jo, 138, 141, 145
hotel life, 93–99, 116, 158, 171, 191, 214, 244–45. *See also* noir motel
"house of death" (Juárez), 117–18, 130, 199, 202, 262–71
Hughes, Howard, 171
human sacrifice, 160, 290, 296
human trafficking, 160, 290, 296
Hurricane Katrina (2005), 235–36

"idyll of the idle," 100–107
imagination, 67, 132–34, 156, 264; afterlife of, 91; analogical, 268, 270; cognition and, 281–82; haunted, 239; memory and, 187; vagrant, 133–34, 243–46, 276
intertextuality, 4, 7, 12, 67
intratextuality, 4, 194
investigative edification, xv, xxvii
Israel, 175
Ivanoff, Assen, 181
Iversen, Margaret, 62, 124, 311n18

Jackson, Wallace, 141, 310n4
Jameson, Fredric, 94–95, 98, 195–96, 259; on "bag people," 96; on Chandler, 252–53; on cognitive maps, 213; on ghost stories, xxx, 195–96
jazz music, 267
Jones, Stephen Graham, 86, 172
junkspaces, 95, 108–18.

Keller, Gottfried, 276
Kennedy, Robert, 93
Kesey, Ken, 289
Knausgaard, Karl Ove, 182–83
Koolhaas, Rem, 95, 114, 116
Kracauer, Siegfried, 93, 94
Kristeva, Julia, 67, 205
Kundera, Milan, 299n19

labor: affective or reproductive, 50, 56, 295; assembly line, 50, 225, 272, 290, 295; changing patterns of, 96, 105, 117; "deregulation and depeasantization of," 105; laboring bodies, 44, 50, 55; territorial divisions of, 101, 121, 195, 230; as violent housekeeping, 263, 272
Lacan, Jacques, 62–63
Lacayo, Richard, 310n6
landfills, 46, 98, 119, 121–24
Lange, Dorothea, 50
Lauro, Sarah Juliet, 289, 296–97
ledgers, 161, 162, 187
Leigh, Janet, 150–160, *151*
LeMenager, Stephanie, 109, 312nn2–3
Leong, Sze Tsung, 119–21
Lerner, Ben, 134
lesbianism, 154, 158
Leslie, Isis, 302n2
Lewis, Nathaniel, xvi, 278, 282, 317n21
Lewis, Sinclair, 177
Liddy, Gordon, 178
limpieza social, 7–8
lipstick traces, 126–36. *See also* makeup
literary montage, xxvii, 67
Little Bighorn, Battle of (1876), 280
Luiselli, Valeria, 1–2, 149, 198, 260–61, 264
Lukács, George, 22, 302n5

MacCannell, Dean, 230
magical realism, 149, 156
Magruder, Jeb Stuart, 178
makeup, 130, 131, 134–35, 137, 285, 297
manifest destiny, 287. *See also* settler colonialism
Man Ray (Emmanuel Rudnitsky), 260–61, *261*, 266–67
maps, 68, 74, 79, 252, 317n21; cognitive, 213; digital technologies and, 120; yuppies and, 81
maquiladoras (border assembly plants), 55, 57, 117, 130, 224, 225; economy of, 231, 262, 290, 294, 309–10n17

Marcuse, Herbert, 74
Marx, Karl, 217, 314n10
Mayans, 39, 44, 99, 102–3
Mbembe, Achille, 64, 207, 305n10
McCambridge, Mercedes, 154
McCarthy, Cormac, xxix; *All the Pretty Horses*, 34, 87–92, 165, 167; *The Crossing*, 64, 91–92; *No Country for Old Men*, 222–23, 228–29
McMurtry, Larry: *Duane's Depressed*, 174; *The Last Picture Show*, 126, 143–46, 177; *Walter Benjamin at the Dairy Queen*, 209
McWilliams, Carey, 100
meantime (temporal mode), xxix, 23, 141–42, 148, 150, 192, 206, 240–41
melancholia, 19, 31, 208, 230, 239, 255. *See also* grief
Meloy, Ellen, 310n22
memento mori, *10*, 41, 89, 91, 240, 301n14
Mexican-American War, 224
miasmatic process, 123
Middle Passage, 93
Miller, D. A., 218
Milošević, Slobodan, 287
mimesis, 35, 39, 280
Minella, Manuel, 15
Miracle Mile (Tucson), 137
Miranda, Deborah A., 260
Mitchell, Lee Clark, 312n9
modernity, 197; Bauman on, 121; Soja on, 109
montage, xxvii, 98, 117, 123–24, 305–6n1; Bowden's use of, 133–35; literary, xxvii, 67; Man Ray's use of, 260–61, *261*, 266; Vlautin's use of, 245–46
Montaigne, 230
motel life, 93–99, 116, 149, 244–45. *See also* hotel life
motel noir, 137–48; noir motel and, 149–60
multinational corporations, xxii, 94, 292; maquiladora economy of, 231, 262, 290, 294, 309–10n17. *See also* globalization

Murphet, Julian, 157–58, 197
My Lai Massacre (1968), 93

narcocorridos, 223, 266, 269
narcoeconomy, 4
Narcoinsurgencia (Briggs), 6–9, *8*
narcotraficantes, 8, 135, 223–34
necropolis, 74–75, 234. *See also* cemeteries
necropolitics, 64, 207, 305n10
neoliberalism, 105–6, 213. *See also* multinational corporations
Ngai, Sianne, 257, 299n17
Nightmare on Elm Street (film), 268
9/11 attacks, 159
Nixon, Richard M., 175
Nixon, Rob, xxiv, 299n11
Nochlin, Linda, 138
noir motel, 149–60; motel noir and, 137–48. *See also* film noir; hotel life
Norris, Frank, 97, 243
North American Free Trade Agreement (NAFTA), 50, 56, 125, 262
nostalgia, 31, 45, 110; etymology of, xviii–xix; of future, 47; Gordon on, 112; romantic, 304n25; Vidler on, 44–45

O'Doherty, Brian, 310n3
O'Hara, Maureen, 282
oil, 161–88. *See also* petroleum
"oil rich," 174
Olney IL, 165–67, 172–74
Orange, Tommy, 190–91
Organization of Petroleum Exporting Countries (OPEC), 175, 178
Orozco, José Clemente, 15
Otsuka, Julie, 198

parataxis, xxvii, 46, 133, 272
Parker, Fess, 171
Parry, Christoff, 317n1
Perec, Georges, 313n11
Pérez, Carlos Andrés, 312n2
Perón, Juan, 292

INDEX 335

petroculture, 64
petroleum, 121, 164–65, 170, 174–76; etymology of, 161; Fuller on, 181–82; Knausgaard on, 182–83; OPEC embargo on, 175, 178. *See also* oil
petrotopia, 76–77, 109
"phantom proletariat," 50
Phillips, Adam, 23, 317n11
photomontage, 266–67
Poe, Edgar Allan, 244
poetics: of exposure, 58–66, 205, 305n1; of movement, 17–18
police jargon, 2, 6
Populist Party, 105
Popul Vuh, 39, 44
pornography, 195, 214, 290–91
Portman, John, 94–95, 314n6
Posada, José Guadalupe, 15–17
postmetropolis, 109–10
postmodernism, 21, 98; Baudrillard on, 110; capitalism and, 64; Gehry on, 96; Handke on, 274, 278, 284–87; Jameson on, 94–95, 195–96, 213, 259, 314n6
Poussin, Nicolas, 204–5
prostitution. *See* sex workers
Proulx, Annie: *Fine Just the Way It Is*, 162; *That Old Ace in the Hole*, 48
psychometropolis, 190–97

queues, 198–208

radiography. *See* X-rays
Reagan, Ronald, 101
Red Lodge MT, 162–65
"Red River Valley" (song), 211–12
Red Shawl Solidarity Project, 310n24
relaxation, nirvana of, 93
Remington, Frederic, 279, 281, 282
"residual space," 98, 121, 124, 125
revenants, xxxi, 64, 294; uncanny economy of, 11–12, 39, 42, 64, 294, 301n16. *See also* ghosts; zombies

"revolutionary love" (Guevara coinage), 46, 47, 304n30
Richmond Fontaine (band), 244, 245
Rilke, Rainer Maria, 144, 186–87
Rivera, Diego, 15
rivers, 209–14
Robertson, Dale, 171
Robinson, Marilynne, 243
Roosevelt, Theodore, 282
Rose, Wendy, 273–74
Ross, Kristin, 308n26
ruins, 87, 95, 103, 108, 209; Alexie on, 234–35, 239; architecture of, 121, 127, 133; Keller on, 276; McMurtry on, 174

Salt Lake City UT, 177–82
Sand Creek Massacre (1864), 238, 239
Santner, Eric L., 300n23
Sarasota FL, 182–88
Schwab, Gabriele, 303n3
Schwenger, Peter, 45, 205, 313n11
Sebald, W. G., xv, 134, 305n18
Securities and Exchange Commission (SEC), 177, 179–80
settler colonialism, xv, 99, 133, 221, 233, 252, 268, 280–87
sex workers, 8, 50, 290, 295
sgraffito technique, 2–4, *3*, 6–7, *8*, *13*, 199–201, *200*, 300n4
Shields, David, 305n1
signs, 134; archaeology of, 103–6; freeway, 70, 77–79, 82
Silko, Leslie Marmon, 209; *Almanac of the Dead*, 58, 60, 63–66, 85, 137, 222, 273
Simmel, Georg, 94, 104
situationists, 305n1
Skelton, Red, 171
sleepwalking, xxii, 38, 77, 135, 191–95
Smith, Imogen Sara, 152, 311n1
Sobchack, Vivian, 106
Soja, Edward, 109–10
Spacks, Patricia, 302n1

spectrality, xxix–xxx, 214, 252, 294, 299n20. *See also* ghosts
spectral materialism, 92, 240, 300n23
Spurr, David, 114
Stein, Gertrude, 299n17
Stewart, Kathleen, 30, 313n7
still life, 117, 185, 204–6, 284, 286
Strand, Mark, 141, 142, 145–46, 184
streetlights, 6, 70, 245–46
suburbs, xxi, 81, 171. *See also* urbanism
surrealists, 304n24
surveillance, 112, 120, 236, 252, 270; in Bolaño, 226–27, 292–93; of cryptocurrency, 35; in Ellis, 191, 194; in Hopper's *Western Motel*, 145–47; in Leong, 120; in Silko, 64–65; in Soja, 100; in Tobar, 250; in Urrea, 111, 122–23; voyeuristic gazes of, 53, 94, 112, 143, 154, 194, 203; in Welles's *Touch of Evil*, 150–53, *151*, 160. *See also* gaze

tattoos, 36, 37, 317n21
Taussig, Michael, 123, 130; *My Cocaine Museum*, 274; *What Color Is the Sacred?*, 136, 310n21
television, 171, 193–95, 222–31
thresholds, 43, 102, 202, 208; architectural, 244–45, 268; spatial, 139–40, 194, 250–51; as a state of consciousness, 132
Tobar, Héctor, 36; *The Barbarian Nurseries*, 249, 250; *The Tattooed Soldier*, xxiii–xxiv, 37–38, 58–62, 100–107, 209, 232–33
Todorov, Tzvetan, 304n24
Toltecs, 16
Torok, Maria, 36–37
tramps, xx, 243–48; with campers, 244; "crisis" of, 104; homeless persons versus, 50; labeling of, 49; Turner on, 97
transnationalism. *See* multinational corporations

transparency myth, 197, 251, 259
Turner, Frederick Jackson, 97, 104–5, 111, 130–31
2Bears, Jackson, xxxi

the uncanny, 50, 216; Alexie on, 216, 234, 239–42; architectural, xxi–xxii, 153, 214, 239, 243, 304n24; aura of, 147–48; Bhabha on, xxii–xxiii; Bloch on, xv–xviii; Bolaño on, 224; Cavell on, 317n14; Clark on, 204; doppelganger as, xviii, 11–12, 39, 46, 115, 247, 251; Ellis on, 194–96; etymology of, xvii; Freud on, xv–xvii, 37, 194, 228–29; Handke on, 287; stylistic features of, 53–54, 135; Vidler on, xxi–xxii, 153, 243; Welles on, 150–53, *151*, 160
uncanny economy of revenance, 11–12, 39, 42, 64, 294, 301n16
undead, 36, 41, 89–91, 187, 201–2. *See also* zombies
unheimlich (unhomely), xxxi, xxv; etymology of, xvii. *See also* the uncanny
urbanism: geohistory of, 109; industrialization and, 105; postmodern, 213; regional, 110. *See also* suburbs
urbicide, xxi, 64, 224, 232–42; definitions of, 235, 237; New Orleans and, 235–36. *See also* junkspaces
Urrea, Luis Alberto: *Across the Wire*, 119; *By the Lake of Sleeping Children*, xx, 121–25; *Into the Beautiful North*, 108–11

vagabondage, 18–19, 214, 243–48. *See also* tramps
vagabond architecture, 244–45
vagrant imagination, 133–34, 243–46, 276
Van Der Weyden, Rogier, 206
van Dyck, Anthony, 202–3, *203*, 205
van Gogh, Vincent, 274
vertigo, xvii, 79, 88, 90, 151; Ellis on, 194, 196, 231

via dolorosa, 246–48
Vidler, Anthony, 251; on architectural uncanny, 243; on nostalgia, 44–45; on uncanny, xxi–xxii, 153
Vietnam, 74–75, 93
Viramontes, Helena María, 1, 48, 59, 63–64, 190, 222, 232, 236–37
Vlautin, Willy, 244; *The Motel Life*, 149, 244–45; *Northline*, 198; *Thirteen Cities*, 248; *Winnemucca*, 244, 246–48
voyeurism, 94. *See also* gaze

Watkins, Claire Vaye, 179
Wayne, John, 210–11, 213, 214, 282
Weaver, Dennis, 153
Welch, James, 85
Welles, Orson: *Citizen Kane*, 36; *The Lady from Shanghai*, 152; *Touch of Evil*, xxvi, 149–60, *151*
West, Nathanael, 249, 250
White, Richard, 213
Williams, Raymond, 299n11
Wister, Owen, 282–84

Wittgenstein, Ludwig, 243
Woods, Lebbeus, 233, 241
Wounded Knee Massacre (1890), 238, 239

X, crucial, 145
X, as erasure, 80–81
X-rays, 260–72, *261*

Yamashita, Karen Tei, xxix; *I Hotel*, 96–99; *Tropic of Orange*, 48, 119, 149, 232
Yates, Julian, 309n14
yellow ribbons, 273–88
Yom Kippur War (1973), 175
Yugoslavia, 235, 287
yuppie cartography, 81

zero-degree writing, 82
Žižek, Slavoj, 145, 147, 220
zombies, 224, 296–97, 318n10; as cyborgs, 289; undead and, 36, 41, 89–91, 187, 201–2. *See also* cannibalism; revenants
Zuboff, Shoshana, 120

IN THE POSTWESTERN HORIZONS SERIES

The Places of Modernity in Early Mexican American Literature, 1848–1948
José F. Aranda Jr.

Dirty Wars: Landscape, Power, and Waste in Western American Literature
John Beck

Post-Westerns: Cinema, Region, West
Neil Campbell

The Rhizomatic West: Representing the American West in a Transnational, Global, Media Age
Neil Campbell

The Comic Book Western: New Perspectives on a Global Genre
Edited by Christopher Conway and Antoinette Sol

Weird Westerns: Race, Gender, Genre
Edited by Kerry Fine, Michael K. Johnson, Rebecca M. Lush, and Sara L. Spurgeon

Positive Pollutions and Cultural Toxins: Waste and Contamination in Contemporary U.S. Ethnic Literatures
John Blair Gamber

A Planetary Lens: The Photo-Poetics of Western Women's Writing
Audrey Goodman

Dirty Words in Deadwood: *Literature and the Postwestern*
Edited by Melody Graulich and Nicolas Witschi

True West: Authenticity and the American West
Edited by William R. Handley and Nathaniel Lewis

Teaching Western American Literature
Edited by Brady Harrison and Randi Lynn Tanglen

Manifest Destiny 2.0: Genre Trouble in Game Worlds
Sara Humphreys

Speculative Wests: Popular Representations of a Region and Genre
Michael K. Johnson

We Who Work the West: Class, Labor, and Space in Western American Literature
Kiara Kharpertian
Edited by Carlo Rotella and Christopher P. Wilson

Captivating Westerns: The Middle East in the American West
Susan Kollin

Postwestern Cultures:
Literature, Theory, Space
Edited by Susan Kollin

Westerns: A Women's History
Victoria Lamont

Manifest and Other Destinies:
Territorial Fictions of the
Nineteenth-Century United States
Stephanie LeMenager

Unsettling the Literary West:
Authenticity and Authorship
Nathaniel Lewis

Morta Las Vegas: CSI *and*
the Problem of the West
Nathaniel Lewis and Stephen Tatum

Late Westerns: The
Persistence of a Genre
Lee Clark Mitchell

María Amparo Ruiz de Burton:
Critical and Pedagogical Perspectives
Edited by Amelia María de
la Luz Montes and Anne
Elizabeth Goldman

In the Mean Time: Temporal
Colonization and the Mexican
American Literary Tradition
Erin Murrah-Mandril

Unhomely Wests: Essays from A to Z
Stephen Tatum

To order or obtain more information on these or other University of Nebraska Press titles, visit nebraskapress.unl.edu.

www.ingramcontent.com/pod-product-compliance
Lightning Source LLC
Chambersburg PA
CBHW030603230426
43661CB00053B/1828